DEFENCES IN CONTRACT

This book is the third in a series of essay collections on defences in private law. It addresses defences to liability arising in contract. The essays range from those adopting a predominantly black-letter approach to others that examine the law from a more theoretical or historical perspective. Some essays focus on individual defences, while some are concerned with the links between defences, or with how defences relate to the structure of contract law generally. One goal of the book is to determine what light can be shed on contract law doctrines by analysing them through the lens of defences. Many scholars are unaccustomed to thinking of defences to contract law and so fresh light is shed on an old topic. The contributors—judges and academics—are all leading jurists. The essays are addressed to all of the major common law jurisdictions.

Volume 3 in the series Hart Studies in Private Law: Essays on Defences

Hart Studies in Private Law: Essays on Defences

The series offers a systematic treatment of defences in private law as a connected field. It addresses tort law, unjust enrichment, contract law and equity, in that order. Its aim is to contribute to this theoretically challenging and practically important, yet understudied, area of the law. The essays that constitute each of the collections in this series are written by some of the world's leading judges and scholars. They bring together insights from several jurisdictions, including civilian jurisdictions. The series is of value to academics and practitioners alike.

Defences in Contract

Edited by
Andrew Dyson
James Goudkamp
and
Frederick Wilmot-Smith

•HART•
OXFORD • LONDON • NEW YORK • NEW DELHI • SYDNEY

HART PUBLISHING
Bloomsbury Publishing Plc
Kemp House, Chawley Park, Cumnor Hill, Oxford, OX2 9PH, UK

HART PUBLISHING, the Hart/Stag logo, BLOOMSBURY and the Diana logo are trademarks of Bloomsbury Publishing Plc

First published in hardback, 2017
Paperback edition, 2019

A catalogue record for this book is available from the British Library.

Library of Congress Cataloging-in-Publication Data

Names: Dyson, Andrew, editor. | Goudkamp, James, 1980– editor. | Wilmot-Smith, Frederick, 1986– editor.

Title: Defences in contract / edited by Andrew Dyson, James Goudkamp, and Frederick Wilmot-Smith.

Description: Oxford [UK] ; Portland, Oregon : Hart Publishing, 2017. | Series: Hart studies in private law : essays on defences ; volume 3 | Includes bibliographical references and index.

Identifiers: LCCN 2016045789 (print) | LCCN 2016046052 (ebook) | ISBN 9781849467230 (hardback) | ISBN 9781509902149 (Epub)

Subjects: LCSH: Contracts. | Breach of contract. | Good faith (Law) | Estoppel.

Classification: LCC K840 .D44 2017 (print) | LCC K840 (ebook) | DDC 342.02/2—dc23

LC record available at https://lccn.loc.gov/2016045789

ISBN: HB: 978-1-84946-723-0
PB: 978-1-50993-008-1
ePDF: 978-1-50990-213-2
ePub: 978-1-50990-214-9

Typeset by Compuscript Ltd, Shannon

Foreword

This is the third in a series of books comprising essays on defences in private law. In contrast to the first two books on defences in tort and unjust enrichment, this title is somewhat startling. We do not conventionally think in terms of there being defences in contract other than, most obviously but relatively peripherally, where there is a claim for damages for breach of contract and, for example, limitation or contributory negligence (or, perhaps, exclusion or illegality) might be raised by the defendant. So, in contrast to books on unjust enrichment or tort, one does not find chapters in contract textbooks on defences. It is an intriguing question to ask: Why not? And that question leads on to many others, most centrally: What do we mean by a 'defence' in private law?

At one level, one might say that anything that a defendant can raise to defeat a claim for breach of contract might be regarded as a defence. On that wide view, a defendant's argument that there is no valid contract because the contract was induced by misrepresentation or undue influence, or that the contract has been automatically terminated for frustration, constitutes the raising of a defence. More conventionally, one can suggest that the reason one does not normally think in terms of defences in contract is because much of the law is focusing on whether there is a valid contract and that the question of defences cannot arise until one has a cause of action for breach of a valid contract. Even illegality might, on one view, be said to be going to the question of whether there is a valid contract rather than constituting a defence to a claim for the breach of a valid contract.

The importance of this book is not only that it requires us to think about these questions but also that it encourages us to look afresh—from the perspective of a defendant—at material that we are unlikely to have thought about in this way. Even if one concludes that there is no stable definition of a defence, or that the material in this book goes well beyond one's own preferred understanding of a defence, this title delivers a feast of stimulating reading for anyone interested in contract and private law generally. It is a further great feature of this series, not least in ensuring that the focus is on practical justice and providing workable answers to difficult questions, that judges as well as academics are involved.

As with the first two books in the series, drafts of the essays were presented at a workshop in All Souls College, Oxford. I had the privilege, for which I would like to thank the organisers, of attending that workshop as a (non-silent) observer. The excitement of that event, and the high standard of the debate, is reflected in the quality of this book. It is sometimes suggested that private law scholarship is on the way out and is no longer at the cutting edge of academic thinking. This collection can only serve to demonstrate that, on the contrary, it is very much alive and kicking, and continues to explore complex and fascinating issues that go to the very heart of law as a practical discipline.

Andrew Burrows

Preface

This book is the third volume in the series *Defences in Private Law*. It explores defences in contract. The previous two volumes concerned defences in the law of torts and unjust enrichment respectively.[1] As we suggested in our opening chapter to the first volume of the series,[2] we think that there is merit in considering defences in private law as a connected whole. To many, the concept of defences will seem less familiar in contract law than in other areas of private law. However, as we consider in our opening chapter, 'Thinking in Terms of Contract Defences', the concept of a defence may have a useful role to play in this field. Even if the reader is unpersuaded by this contention, they will find that the individual chapters in this collection shed significant light on the doctrines that they consider.

The chapters that comprise this volume are based on papers that were delivered at a workshop at All Souls College, Oxford, in January 2016. We are grateful, first and foremost, to All Souls College for hosting the event and subsidising its cost. This project was also funded by the John Fell Oxford University Press (OUP) Research Fund, the Oxford Law Faculty's Research Support Fund and a Keble College Small Research Grant. We have incurred many debts of gratitude. The workshop debate was enriched by the contributions of the following observers: The Rt Hon the Lord Hoffmann, Professor Andrew Burrows, Professor Mindy Chen-Wishart, Associate Professor Paul Davies, The Rt Hon the Lord Mance, Mr Frank McArdle, Dr Ewan McGaughey, Professor Donal Nolan, The Rt Hon Chief Justice Beverley McLachlin PC and Mr Nicholas McBride. We wish to thank the following individuals for assisting in the editorial process: Cynthia Ang, Ines Veloso and Zhicheng Wu. Finally, we wish to acknowledge Professor Burrows for generously agreeing to write the foreword to this volume and, indeed, for his support of the Defences in Private Law series generally.

Andrew Dyson
James Goudkamp
Fred Wilmot-Smith

31 August 2016

[1] A Dyson, J Goudkamp and F Wilmot-Smith (eds), *Defences in Tort* (Oxford, Hart Publishing, 2015); A Dyson, J Goudkamp and F Wilmot-Smith (eds), *Defences in Unjust Enrichment* (Oxford, Hart Publishing, 2016).

[2] A Dyson, J Goudkamp and F Wilmot-Smith, 'Central Issues in the Law of Tort Defences' in A Dyson, J Goudkamp and F Wilmot-Smith (eds), *Defences in Tort* (Oxford, Hart Publishing, 2015) 3–4.

Contents

List of Contributors

The Rt Hon Dame Mary Arden DBE PC is a Lady Justice of Appeal in the Court of Appeal of England and Wales.

Kit Barker is Professor of Law at TC Beirne School of Law at the University of Queensland.

Hugh Beale QC (Hon) FBA is a Professor of Law at the University of Warwick, Senior Research Fellow at Harris Manchester College, Oxford, and a Visiting Professor of Law at the University of Oxford.

Andrew Dyson is an Assistant Professor of Law at the London School of Economics and Political Science.

James Goudkamp is a Fellow of Keble College, Oxford, an Associate Professor of Law at the University of Oxford, an Associate Academic Fellow of the Honourable Society of the Inner Temple, a Senior Honorary Research Fellow at the Faculty of Law, University of Western Australia, a Professorial Fellow at the School of Law, University of Wollongong, and a barrister at 7 King's Bench Walk.

Daniel Markovits is Guido Calabresi Professor of Law at Yale Law School.

Ewan McKendrick QC (Hon) is a Fellow of Lady Margaret Hall, Oxford, Professor of English Private Law at the University of Oxford, and Registrar of the University of Oxford.

Gerard McMeel is Professor Commercial Law at the University of Manchester and a barrister at Guildhall Chambers and Quadrant Chambers.

Janet O'Sullivan is a Fellow of Selwyn College and University Senior Lecturer at the Faculty of Law, University of Cambridge.

Solène Rowan is an Associate Professor of Law at the London School of Economics and Political Science.

The Rt Hon Lord Toulson PC is a former Justice of the Supreme Court of the United Kingdom.

Robert Stevens is a Fellow of Lady Margaret Hall, Oxford, and Herbert Smith Freehills Professor of English Private Law at the University of Oxford.

Stephen Waddams is University Professor and Goodman/Schipper chair at the Faculty of Law, University of Toronto.

Niranjan Venkatesan is a barrister at One Essex Court chambers.

Frederick Wilmot-Smith is a Fellow of All Souls College, Oxford.

Table of Cases

Australia

Canada

European Court of Justice

France

New Zealand

Singapore

Uganda

United Kingdom

United States of America

Table of Legislation

Canada

European Union

United States of America

Table of Statutory Instruments and Rules

United Kingdom

Table of Restatements

Table of Conventions

1

Thinking in Terms of Contract Defences

ANDREW DYSON, JAMES GOUDKAMP
AND FREDERICK WILMOT-SMITH

I. INTRODUCTION

WHILE THE TERMINOLOGY of defences is commonplace in other fields of private law, contract lawyers seem relatively unaccustomed to thinking in terms of defences. For example, although the leading texts in other areas of private law reserve a prominent place for defences,[1] the latest edition of *Chitty on Contracts* does not.[2] Similarly, although Andrew Burrows dedicates Part 4 of his *Restatement of the English Law of Unjust Enrichment* to defences,[3] he includes no equivalent section in his *Restatement of the English Law of Contract*. Indeed, references to 'defences' in that work are few and far between.[4]

Although the word 'defence' is used periodically in writing on contract law,[5] contract law scholars tend not to employ the concept of a defence in structuring their analyses, and they do not seem to attach particular significance to the term. They may even struggle to identify rules that count as defences. In his chapter in this volume, Kit Barker sums up the situation as follows:[6]

> Ask most lawyers to name defences in the criminal law, law of torts, or the law of unjust enrichments and they will readily be able to reel off a list with some confidence. Request from them instead a list of contractual defences and they will probably pause longer for thought.

[1] eg, A Dugdale (ed), *Clerk & Lindsell on Torts*, 21st edn (London, Sweet & Maxwell, 2014) ch 3 ('General Defences'); C Mitchell, P Mitchell and S Watterson (eds), *Goff & Jones on Unjust Enrichment*, 8th edn (London, Sweet & Maxwell, 2011) Pt 6 ('Defences').

[2] H Beale (ed), *Chitty on Contracts*, 32nd edn (London, Sweet & Maxwell, 2015).

[3] A Burrows, *A Restatement of the English Law of Unjust Enrichment* (Oxford, Oxford University Press, 2012).

[4] A Burrows, *A Restatement of the English Law of Contract* (Oxford, Oxford University Press, 2016). The index does not even contain the term 'defence' as a main entry.

[5] See, eg, *Contributory Negligence as a Defence in Contract* (Law Com No 219, 1993); Law Commission, *The Illegality Defence* (Law Com No 320, 2010); Law Commission, *Privity of Contract: Contracts for the Benefit of Third Parties* (Law Com No 242, 1996) [10.2].

[6] See Chapter 2 of this volume, p 17.

The overarching aim of this chapter is to explore the reluctance of contract lawyers to think in terms of defences. The apparent opposition to terminology that is ubiquitous elsewhere in private law is, at least at first glance, a puzzling feature of contract law scholarship that merits attention. The analysis is in three parts. In Section II, we ask whether contract law has defences. We argue that, on three popular definitions of that term, there are defences to contract claims. This, combined with three further matters, which we canvass in Section III, explains what, specifically, is prima facie puzzling about the fact that contract lawyers do not think in terms of defences. Finally, in Section IV we address whether contract lawyers ought to speak in terms of defences. As a prelude to this analysis, we isolate a range of related questions that can be asked about defences. Considerable confusion, we believe, has flowed from a failure on the part of many theorists to be clear about the questions that they are asking. Having explained the question with which we are concerned, we offer reasons for and against using the language of defences in the contractual context.

II. ARE THERE DEFENCES IN CONTRACT?

One possible explanation for the dearth of references to defences in writings on contract law is simply that there *are* no defences to contract law claims. While this suggestion might seem surprising, it should not be dismissed out of hand. For example, in her chapter in an earlier volume in this series, Helen Scott ventures that the South African law of unjust enrichment may leave no room for defences because of the way in which the elements of the cause of action in unjust enrichment are defined.[7]

Whether contract law recognises defences depends on how the concept of a defence is understood.[8] In this section we argue that there are several examples of contract law doctrines that meet each of three popular definitions.[9] The upshot is that the failure of contract law scholars to employ the concept of defences cannot be explained on the ground that there are no defences in the law of contract.

A. Rules that are External to the Cause of Action

In his chapter in *Defences in Tort*, Graham Virgo wrote that '[a] denial negates an element of the [claim], whereas a defence is a rule that relieves the defendant

[7] H Scott, 'Defence, Denial or Cause of Action: "Enrichment Owed" and the Absence of a Legal Ground' in A Dyson, J Goudkamp and F Wilmot-Smith (eds), *Defences in Unjust Enrichment* (Oxford, Hart Publishing, 2016) 64.

[8] Without clarifying the definition of the concept, there is a risk of a 'merely verbal' dispute: see generally D Chalmers, 'Verbal Disputes' (2011) 120 *Philosophical Review* 515.

[9] We discuss the definition of defences at greater length in A Dyson, J Goudkamp and F Wilmot-Smith, 'Central Issues in the Law of Tort Defences' in Dyson, Goudkamp and Wilmot-Smith (eds), *Defences in Tort* (Oxford, Hart Publishing, 2015) 5–11; A Dyson, J Goudkamp and F Wilmot-Smith, 'Defences in Unjust Enrichment: Questions and Themes' in Dyson, Goudkamp and Wilmot-Smith (eds), *Defences in Unjust Enrichment* (Oxford, Hart Publishing, 2016) 2–7.

of liability where all the elements of the [claim] for which the claimant sues are present'.[10] This analysis, which Kit Barker describes as 'probably the most popular of modern academic conceptualisations of the idea of a "defence"', offers a contrast with the concept of a denial.[11] It explains defences in terms of a distinction between the 'elements of the claim' and those doctrines that are external to the claim, but which relieve the defendant, wholly or partly, of liability.[12] The latter group of doctrines are regarded as defences. They are rules to which the defendant can appeal to escape or limit her liability even if the elements of the claimant's claim are satisfied. In this chapter, we will assume an intuitive, pre-theoretical notion of the concept of 'elements of a claim' to develop our own analysis.

Many contract law doctrines seem to operate as denials. Barker writes:[13]

> If one understands a contractual cause of action as the set of facts both sufficient and necessary to meet the requirements of contractual inception doctrines (the 'elements' of a binding contract) then ... it is pretty clear that no argument concerning agreement, consideration, intention to create legal relations or uncertainty of terms is really a defence argument.

All of these arguments assert that the preconditions of contractual validity are absent, and without a contract, the elements of the action for breach of contract cannot be established.

Nevertheless, at least some contract law doctrines seem to amount to defences in the sense currently under consideration. Consider, for example, limitation.[14] It is not an element of the cause of action in breach of contract that no limitation bar applies. As Burrows observed in the context of tort defences, 'no one has ever suggested that limitation should instead be viewed as specifying an element of the cause of action'.[15] A plea that a limitation bar applies cannot, it follows, be a denial. Instead, a limitation bar prevents a claim from succeeding even if all of the elements of the cause of action for breach of contract are present. Scholars analysing other compartments of the law of obligations routinely refer to limitation as a 'defence';[16] there is no reason to distinguish contract law in this respect.

Limitation is certainly not the only example of a contractual defence in the relevant sense of the word. Many other doctrines, including rules that are typically

[10] G Virgo, 'Justifying Necessity as a Defence in Tort Law' in A Dyson, J Goudkamp and F Wilmot-Smith (eds), *Defences in Tort* (Oxford, Hart Publishing, 2015) 139.

[11] Barker, Chapter 2 of this volume, p 35. For an assessment of this conception of a defence, see L Duarte d'Almeida, 'Defining "Defences"' in A Dyson, J Goudkamp and F Wilmot-Smith, *Defences in Tort* (Oxford, Hart Publishing, 2015). Daniel Markovits uses this definition of the term defence in his contribution to this volume. He writes that 'a party that seeks to avoid enforcement of boilerplate does not offer a defence against contractual obligation so much as directly deny that the boilerplate belongs in the contract to begin with': Markovits, Chapter 3 of this volume, p 46 (Markovits).

[12] On some accounts, rules that only partially relieve the defendant of liability are not defences.

[13] Barker, Chapter 2 of this volume, p 35.

[14] Limitation Act 1980 (UK) ss 5–7. Compare Duarte d'Almeida (n 11) 51–52 (arguing that limitation is a procedural bar, not a defence).

[15] A Burrows, 'Some Recurring Issues in relation to Limitation of Actions' in A Dyson, J Goudkamp and F Wilmot-Smith (eds), *Defences in Tort* (Oxford, Hart Publishing, 2015) 310.

[16] See, eg, N McBride and R Bagshaw, *Tort Law*, 5th edn (Harlow, Pearson Education, 2015) (treating limitation within Ch 26, which is entitled 'Defences'); Mitchell, Mitchell and Watterson (n 1) (addressing limitation within a part of the book that is headed 'Defences').

thought of as being central to the law of contract, are arguably defences too, on the meaning of that term that is presently in issue. Consider the doctrine of undue influence, which is discussed by Stephen Waddams in his chapter. The absence of undue influence does not seem to be a part of the cause of action in breach of contract, yet the doctrine can be used to avoid a contract. If this is the proper analysis of the rule, it is a defence. Waddams writes: 'From one point of view the use of such a power may be regarded as a defence to contractual obligation'.[17] The doctrines of duress and misrepresentation might be similarly understood: the absence of duress and misrepresentation do not seem to be part of the cause of action in breach of contract; yet the doctrines can be raised to resist an action for breach. Substantially the same points can be made in relation to the illegality doctrine.[18] The absence of illegality is not usually cited as part of the cause of action in breach of contract. Accordingly, the doctrine appears to be a defence.

The law of contract provides for many rules that enable a defendant who is shown to have breached a contract to reduce the quantum of damages. Any such limiting doctrines can be thought of as defences, and arguably should be understood in this way.[19] The doctrine of remoteness of damage is, for example, such a limiting rule,[20] and in his chapter, Niranjan claims that 'remoteness ... is an answer or defence to what is in any case a complete cause of action'.[21] Much the same could be said about the contributory negligence doctrine.[22] That rule is a damages-limiting device and, as such, can be understood as a defence on the defence/denial framework. It is no part of the cause of action in breach of contract that the claimant took reasonable care of her own interests.[23]

[17] Waddams, Chapter 4 of this volume, p 66.

[18] The illegality doctrine is addressed by Lord Toulson in his chapter: see Chapter 13 of this volume.

[19] Some writers deny that rules that affect only the remedy are defences: see, eg, J Goudkamp, *Tort Law Defences*, revd edn (Oxford, Hart Publishing, 2016) 2. An intermediate position was adopted by the Law Commission in its report *Privity of Contract: Contracts for the Benefits of Third Parties*: Law Commission (n 5) [10.2]. The Commission wrote that: 'we do not include as defences matters which bar a particular remedy such as that specific performance is not available of a contract for personal service'.

[20] *Hadley v Baxendale* (1854) 9 Ex 341; 156 ER 145; *Transfield Shipping Inc v Mercator Shipping Inc ('The Achilleas')* [2008] UKHL 48; [2009] 1 AC 61.

[21] Niranjan, Chapter 10 of this volume, p 203.

[22] Law Reform (Contributory Negligence) Act 1945 (UK) s 1. Rightly or wrongly, the contributory negligence doctrine applies where (and only where) a defendant breaches a term that called for the exercise of reasonable care and she incurs liability concurrently in the tort of negligence: *Forsikringsaktieselskapet Vesta v Butcher* [1989] AC 852 (CA).

[23] It has periodically been suggested (or held) that the contributory negligence doctrine can reduce damages to nil: see, eg, *McMullen v National Coal Board* [1982] ICR 148 (QBD); *Jayes v IMI (Kynoch) Ltd* [1985] ICR 155, 159; *McEwan v Lothian Buses plc* 2006 CSOH 56; 2006 SCLR 592, [32]–[35]; *Byron Avenue* [2010] NZCA 65; [2010] 3 NZLR 445, [63]; cf *Wynbergen v Hoyts Corp Pty Ltd* (1997) 72 ALJR 65 (HCA); *Anderson v Newham College of Further Education* [2002] EWCA Civ 505; [2003] ICR 212; *Buyukardicli v Hammerson UK Properties plc* [2002] EWCA Civ 683, [7]. Where the doctrine has this consequence, it is difficult to see it other than as a defence: it completely eliminates the obligation to pay damages, but on no view does it suggest that there was no wrong.

B. Rules that are External to the Cause of Action that Must Be Pleaded by the Defendant

Robert Stevens claims that the first definition of a defence is subject to a rider. He writes: 'Anything that the defendant pleads which can resist the claimant's action, that does not merely constitute a denial of an element of the claim, is a defence'.[24] This yields a second way of understanding the concept of a defence. Applying this definition, Stevens argues that the doctrine of waiver is a defence.[25] Limitation is also a defence in this sense of the word. The rules governing limitation are external to those that specify the scope of the action in breach of contract, and the defendant carries the onus of pleading limitation (although once put in issue, it falls to the claimant to prove that the bar does not apply).[26] Another rule that is a defence on this definition is contributory negligence.[27] We have noted already that the contributory negligence doctrine is not part of the cause of action in breach of contract,[28] and it is well established that the defendant must plead it.[29] A final illustration is the mitigation doctrine. That doctrine is an external rule, and it is well established that the defendant bears the onus of pleading in respect of it.[30]

While all rules that are defences on the first definition of that term that we have canvassed are also defences on Stevens's definition, the converse is not true. Thus, illegality would seem to be a defence on the first definition,[31] but it cannot be on Stevens's meaning of that word as it is unnecessary for the defendant to plead it.[32] The court is permitted, perhaps required, to consider the illegality doctrine provided that it emerges on the evidence that the preconditions for its application are likely to be satisfied.[33]

C. Pleading and Proof

Other writers understand defences to be rules in respect of which the defendant carries the burdens of pleading and proof. This yields a third popular definition of the term 'defence'. This definition does not employ the distinction between a denial

[24] R Stevens, 'Should Contributory Fault be Analogue or Digital?' in A Dyson, J Goudkamp and F Wilmot-Smith (eds), *Defences in Tort* (Oxford, Hart Publishing, 2015) 246. See also Stevens's chapter in this volume: Chapter 7, text to fn 7 ('In private law, a defence is a reason that the defendant must assert in his pleadings that will defeat an otherwise good claim').

[25] 'Generally therefore, waiver operates as a defence to a claim that would otherwise succeed': Stevens, ch 7, p 127.

[26] See Burrows (n 15) 310.

[27] Expressly stated in Stevens (n 24) 244–48.

[28] See the text accompanying n 22.

[29] *Fookes v Slaytor* [1978] 1 WLR 1293 (CA).

[30] *Anselm v Buckle* [2014] EWCA Civ 311, [24] (Briggs LJ).

[31] See the text accompanying n 18.

[32] *Lipton v Powell* [1921] 2 KB 51 (Div Ct); *Ferguson v John Dawson & Partners (Contractors) Ltd* [1976] 1 WLR 1213 (CA) 1218; *Pickering v Deacon* [2003] EWCA Civ 554; *The Times*, 19 April 2003.

[33] As to these preconditions, see, now, *Patel v Mirza* [2016] UKSC 42; [2016] 3 WLR 399.

of the elements of the action in which the claimant sues and rules that are external to those elements.[34] It is hence quite separate from the definitions considered thus far (even though rules that are identified as defences on either or both of the preceding definitions may also constitute defences on this third definition). Tony Weir embraced this third definition of the term 'defence' when he asserted that the contributory negligence doctrine is 'unquestionably a defence ... [since] it is for the defendant to plead and prove it'.[35] There are many other contract law doctrines that are defences on this definition. Because the onuses of pleading and proof usually go hand in hand,[36] rules in respect of which the defendant carries an onus of pleading must usually also be proved by the defendant.[37] Accordingly, the rules identified in the previous section in respect of which the defendant carries the onus of pleading are defences on this third definition.

III. THE PUZZLE OF CONTRACT DEFENCES

There are doctrines in contract law which *could* be analysed as defences, regardless of how that word is understood. This, coupled with the fact that the language of defences is ubiquitous in other branches of private law, renders it curious that contract law scholars shun the term. In this section, we give three additional reasons why it is, at least at first glance, puzzling.

A. Similar Terminology for Similar Doctrines

It has been argued that we should discuss rules that share the same or a similar logical form in a unitary lexicon, regardless of the historical or jurisdictional pedigree of those rules. This proposition is particularly prominent in debates over the distinction between legal and equitable rules. For example, Andrew Burrows, a leading exponent of this way of thinking, argues that 'lawyers are not doing enough to eradicate the needless differences in terminology used, and the substantive inconsistences, between common law and equity'.[38] This deepens the puzzle with which we are concerned. As we have shown, contract law has various doctrines which *could* be called defences. (Some of these doctrines, like limitation, Burrows himself even calls defences when writing about other areas of the law.)[39] Nevertheless, scholars often seem to resist linguistic assimilation of these doctrines in their

[34] Compare Duarte d'Almeida (n 11), who explains the distinction between defences and denials in terms of probative burdens.

[35] T Weir, *Introduction to Tort Law*, 2nd edn (Oxford, Clarendon Press, 2006) 129. Weir seems to think that the burden of proof is important when it comes to ascertaining whether a rule is a defence. This view is not shared by Stevens, who focuses on the burden of pleading.

[36] *Semper necessitas probandi incumbit ei qui agit* (he who asserts must always prove).

[37] As Weir observes, the defendant carries the onus of proof in in relation to contributory negligence: *Wakelin v London & South Western Railway Co* (1886) 12 App Cas 41 (HL) 47 (Lord Watson); *SS Heranger (Owners) v SS Diamond (Owners)* [1939] AC 94 (HL) 104 (Lord Wright).

[38] A Burrows, 'We do This at Common Law but That in Equity' (2002) 22 *OJLS* 1, 1.

[39] See the sources mentioned in n 16.

writing on contract law.[40] In the absence of explanation, this resistance to invoking in the law of contract language that is used freely elsewhere in the law of obligations is puzzling.

B. Statutory Recognition of Defences

Another reason why it is surprising that lawyers do not think about contract doctrine via the concept of a defence is that certain features of the law *require* them to do so. For example, when a third-party beneficiary brings proceedings to enforce a contract, a promisor has a statutory entitlement to certain defences that she would have had against the promisee.[41] Section 3(3)(b) of the Contracts (Rights of Third Parties) Act 1999 (UK) provides that

> [t]he promisor shall also have available to him by way of defence or set-off any matter if … it would have been available to him by way of defence or set-off if the proceedings had been brought by the promisee.

This provision mandates the use of the terminology of defences, and requires the parameters of the term 'defence' to be identified. This statute is not the only piece of legislation concerned with contract law that utilises the concept of defences.[42]

C. Use of Concept of Defence in Theoretical Discussions

The final reason that contract law scholars' failure to invoke the language of defences is surprising is the fact that legal theorists use the concept in thinking about the law of contract.[43] In *Contract Theory*, Stephen Smith invokes the terminology of defences. He applies it to a variety of doctrines including duress, unconscionability, mistake, frustration and estoppel.[44] Further, HLA Hart's earliest published essay, which introduced legal philosophers to the concept of defeasibility, concerned defences in contract.[45] Borrowing from the law of real property, Hart illustrated the 'defeasible character of legal concepts' in the contractual context.[46] He explained:[47]

> When the student has learnt that in English law there are positive conditions required for the existence of a valid contract, *i.e.*, at least two *parties*, an *offer* by one, *acceptance* by

[40] See the text accompanying nn 3–4.

[41] Contracts (Rights of Third Parties) Act 1999 (UK) s 3.

[42] See, eg, Third Parties (Rights against Insurers) Act 2010 (UK) s 2(3)–(4).

[43] See, further, PS Atiyah, 'Contract and Fair Exchange' in his *Essays on Contract* (Oxford, Oxford University Press, 1986) 329.

[44] S Smith, *Contract Theory* (Oxford, Oxford University Press, 2004), esp ch 9.

[45] HLA Hart, 'The Ascription of Responsibility and Rights' (1949) 49 *Proceedings of the Aristotelian Society* 171, also in AGN Flew (ed), *Logic and Language* (first series, Oxford, Blackwell, 1951). Hart later disowned the paper: HLA Hart, *Punishment and Responsibility: Essays in the Philosophy of Law*, 2nd edn (Oxford, OUP, 2008) v.

[46] Hart (1949) (n 45) 181.

[47] ibid, 174–75 (emphasis in original).

> the other, ... [etc] his understanding of the legal concept of a contract is still incomplete ... For these conditions, although necessary, are not always sufficient and he has still to learn what can *defeat* a claim that there is a valid contract, even though all these conditions are satisfied.

These defeating factors are, Hart says, defences to claims in contract. He went on to list a number of defences in contract law, including duress, insanity, intoxication and frustration, which he classified into seven distinct categories.[48] The essay has spawned a vast philosophical literature on 'defeasibility'.[49]

The reluctance of the authors of leading treatises on the law of contract to organise and discuss contract law in terms of defences thus appears out-of-step with some theoretical literature on contract. This is not attributable simply to ignorance of this philosophical literature: both Hart's paper and Smith's book are well known and widely discussed. Not only does mainstream writing regarding contract law depart from the theoretical literature to which we have referred, the difference in approach is unexplained.

IV. SHOULD CONTRACT LAWYERS THINK IN TERMS OF DEFENCES?

We have suggested that the absence from doctrinal scholarship of the concept of defences in contract law is, at least at first glance, puzzling. In this section we ask, first, whether the asymmetry with other areas of the law of obligations is justifiable; we ask, next, what advantages might flow from thinking of contract law using the concept of a defence. Before we proceed, however, we attempt to clarify the precise question we are asking. It is important that we do so, for much of the literature regarding defences, in private law and beyond, fails to isolate the exact question that is being addressed.

A. Clarifying the Question

To create a contract, it is usually sufficient that there be offer and acceptance, consideration and an intention to create legal relations. If, however, there is a fundamental change in circumstances such as to render performance 'radically different from that which was undertaken by the contract', the contract will be frustrated.[50] Let us, for now, prescind from whether the doctrine of frustration is a 'defence'; we can, instead, call it an 'exception' to a more general rule. We should distinguish at least six questions that arise in relation to 'exceptions'; our question in this section is the sixth.

[48] ibid, 175–76.

[49] For an overview of some of the key debates, see JF Beltrán and GB Ratti (eds), *The Logic of Legal Requirements: Essays on Defeasibility* (Oxford, Oxford University Press, 2012). For a book building a theory of defeasibility and defences out of Hart's essay, see L Duarte d'Almeida, *Allowing for Exceptions: A Theory of Defences and Defeasibility in Law* (Oxford, Oxford University Press, 2015).

[50] *Davis Contractors v Fareham Urban District Council* [1956] AC 696 (HL) 728 (Lord Radcliffe).

One question that can be asked about a specific exception, like frustration, is what the law is on the subject. This requires an analysis of the relevant doctrinal materials. What does 'radically different' mean? Does frustration occur automatically?[51] And so on.

Second, we might ask whether the relevant law, whatever it may be, is justified. Is it right that the law excuses the parties from further performance when it would be 'radically different'? Or should the parties bear the risk of prejudice from these shifts?

Particular exceptions can be categorised within a broader class of doctrines. A third question that we can ask, then, is whether the exception in question is a token instance of some more abstract type. This is the sort of question which people address when they ask whether contract law has defences: a category of 'defences' is posited, and it is asked whether some particular doctrine (such as frustration) belongs within it. There are numerous (mutually consistent) possible classifications that can be discussed. Frustration might be (along with duress and undue influence, for example) within the more abstract category of 'doctrines which can cancel valid contracts' and (along with common mistake, for instance) within the category of 'doctrines which deal with circumstances being radically different from that expected'.

In proposing an answer to this third question, a more abstract category than the particular exception must be put forward. We can then ask, fourth, whether the law should recognise exceptions of the type gathered together by this category; most abstractly we can ask, as Richard Epstein does, 'why it is necessary to think of exceptions to the general proposition at all'.[52] Scholars sometimes ask what reasons there are to recognise *defences*.[53] This is another way of asking the fourth question. A danger of asking it in this way is that the term 'defence' is used in various ways by different authors.[54] However, if a clear answer is given to the third question, this will clarify the sense of 'defence' in question. The fourth question differs from the second: the second question is about a particular doctrine, and so might point to quite particular features of that doctrine; the fourth question is about a more abstract category, so answers must draw on more general features shared by all members of the set.

[51] As to which, see Ewan McKendrick's chapter: Chapter 8 of this volume.

[52] RA Epstein, 'Pleadings and Presumptions' (1973) 40 *University of Chicago Law Review* 556, 558.

[53] See, eg, ibid (arguing that defences can be used to structure legal argument and clarify difficult issues of law); RA Epstein, 'Nuisance Law: Corrective Justice and Its Utilitarian Constraints' (1979) 8 *Journal of Legal Studies* 49 (arguing that defences can be used to limit the scope of utilitarian arguments in law); B Chapman, 'Law, Incommensurability, and Conceptually Sequenced Argument' (1998) 146 *University of Pennsylvania Law Review* 1487 (arguing that defences enable the law to cope rationally with incommensurable values); B Chapman, 'Defeasible Rules and Interpersonal Accountability' in JF Beltrán and GB Ratti (eds), *The Logic of Legal Requirements: Essays on Defeasibility* (Oxford, Oxford University Press, 2012) 410 (arguing that defences ensure 'a process that knits the parties together in a self-confirming exchange of mutual respect'); J Goudkamp and C Mitchell, 'Denials and Defences in the Law of Unjust Enrichment' in C Mitchell and W Swadling (eds), *The Restatement Third, Restitution and Unjust Enrichment: Comparative and Critical Essays* (Oxford, Hart Publishing, 2013) (suggesting five possible reasons for recognising defences in the law of unjust enrichment and rejecting several others).

[54] We sketched three definitions above in Section II. That list is not exhaustive.

The fifth question that we can ask is what, if anything, we can learn from the fact that some doctrine is within a more general category. It might be thought, for instance, that the classification of some doctrine as a defence can have practical implications. For example, in his chapter Daniel Markovits writes that[55]

> the doctrinal distinction between a defence against and a direct denial of contract liability, although largely rhetorical when stated as a matter of general theory, can make a difference to outcomes when embedded in a particular sphere of commercial and legal practice.

Some have argued, more concretely, that quite general practical consequences can flow from the classification of some doctrine as a defence. A good illustration is found in Robert Stevens's work. He writes that '[t]he most important practical effect of characterising an issue as being a defence is that it will usually determine who has to prove what as a matter of evidence'.[56] These arguments do not seem to be concerned with whether some particular category of exceptions should exist, or how we should categorise those exceptions; they are concerned with what follows *from* that categorisation. Arguments of this type, while popular, are controversial. Although it is a short detour, we wish to say something about this controversy as these arguments have not been explored in detail in the literature. One reason why the suggestion is controversial is that it might be thought, instead, that all of the 'consequences' of characterising a doctrine as a defence are in fact constituents of the definition.[57] Furthermore, the success of such practical arguments may depend on whether the concept of a defence is internal to the law or merely an analytic device for thinking about the law. On one view, the concept of a defence is part of the positive law.[58] The idea here is that the law, rightly or wrongly, embraces the idea of a defence. For example, if defences are understood in contradistinction to denials,[59] the claim is that the law itself classifies rules as either denials or defences based on an organisational divide found within the law. This may be John Gardner's position. Of the distinction between offences and defences in criminal law, he asks 'what line is it that … legal systems … are trying to draw?'[60] It might be argued that the law should not be arranged in this way. Perhaps the divide between denial and defences is incoherent; and, even if it is not, perhaps the law does not draw the line in the right place. However, on this first view, this would be irrelevant to a description of the law: there is a line, and it is drawn by the law itself. Another view is that the concept of a defence is one that we use merely to think about the law. The law might be such that a claimant can establish liability only by proving a certain set of facts, and the defendant can resist that liability only by proving some other set of

[55] Markovits, Chapter 3 of this volume, p 62.
[56] Stevens (n 24) 250.
[57] For development of this analysis, see Dyson, Goudkamp and Wilmot-Smith (2016) (n 9) 5–6.
[58] Goudkamp (n 21) xvii. On the idea of law claiming, see J Gardner, *Law as a Leap of Faith: Essays on Law in General* (Oxford, Oxford University Press, 2012) ch 5.
[59] See Section II.A.
[60] J Gardner, *Offences and Defences: Selected Essays in the Philosophy of Criminal Law* (Oxford, Oxford University Press, 2007) 143–44. Whether Gardner is in this first camp depends on what he means by the concept of an offence.

facts. However, this view claims, once we know all the facts about when liability arises, how it might be defeated, who bears the burden of pleading and proof, and so on, we know *everything* salient that there is to know about the law. There is, in other words, no further question about whether some of these rules are classified as a defence by the law. Scholars and judges might refer to certain rules as defences but, on this alternative way of understanding things, such references are nothing more than an exegetical tool: perhaps the label 'defence' is shorthand for 'rules in respect of which the defendant bears the burden of proof', for example. For our purposes, the relevance of this distinction is this. If the classification of some doctrine as a defence is internal to the law, it may be that the law attaches consequences to that classification. If, however, the concept is merely an analytical device for thinking about the law, it is less clear that inferences can be drawn from the classification of a doctrine as a defence.[61]

It is possible to ask and answer all five questions without employing the language of defences; indeed, contract lawyers seem to do so already. The puzzle we have isolated does not, therefore, seem to concern any of these questions. Instead, it appears to relate to a sixth question: what value is there in thinking about some abstract category of exceptions using the *language* or *terminology* of 'defences'? This question is not about whether some particular exception, like frustration, or class of exceptions, such as those often designated with the label of 'defences', should be recognised (that is question four). The question, instead, concerns the way we talk about those rules and categories. As we have illustrated, we might discuss these areas of law using the language of 'exceptions'; we could discuss them, instead, using a foreign or formal language;[62] why, then, discuss the law using the language of 'defences'?

B. Is the Language of Defences Valuable?

The concepts we use are sometimes thought to be important if we are to describe reality correctly. For example, Theodore Sider writes that '[f]or a representation to be fully successful, truth is not enough; the representation must also use the right concepts, so that its conceptual structure matches reality's structure'.[63] Similarly, in the legal context, Ernest Weinrib writes that a theoretical account of the law should 'orient itself to the features salient in legal experience' and seek to 'understand those (and other) features as they are understood from within the law'.[64] These claims suggest that legal scholars who are concerned to describe the law should use the law's concepts.

[61] It is important to be quite precise here about what we mean. On this view, the classification of some doctrine as a defence is a conclusion we draw from various characteristics of legal doctrine—for example, from the rules of pleading and proof. We do not suggest that no further consequences should follow from the nature of legal rules on pleading and proof, only that the classification of those rules as a defence adds nothing to such an argument.

[62] We could, for example, discuss some rule as '*P*→*Q unless r*', where '*P*' is the set of circumstances defeasibly sufficient to yield a legal conclusion ('*Q*'), and '*r*' is the exception to that rule; we could then ask in virtue of what *r* is a member of some broader set of exceptions, C. And so on.

[63] T Sider, *Writing the Book of the World* (Oxford, Oxford University Press, 2012) vii.

[64] EJ Weinrib, *The Idea of Private Law* (Cambridge MA, Harvard University Press, 1995) 11.

Even if what Weinrib claims here is true, it would not follow that contract lawyers need to invoke the *terminology* of defences. It is entirely possible to grasp the *concept* of a defence (regardless of the definition that one embraces) without using the word 'defence'. The question here is: what would be wrong, for example, with an account of contract law, including defences, expressed in (say) a formalised language? One possible answer to this question is that, although nothing is intrinsically wrong with such an account, it may be harder for some people to understand than an account in natural language. A key concern for most people writing about the law is how best to articulate the claims about the law. For example, a textbook writer must be alive to her audience: construction lawyers might find it helpful to place certain rules front and centre which shipping lawyers can relegate to a footnote. In the context of the present volume, one might hypothesise, therefore, that contract lawyers are disinclined to use the language of defences because they consider that it does not help people understand the content of contract law.

This analysis pushes the question back one level: why do contract lawyers find the language of defences less useful than scholars of other areas of law? As we have shown, the language of defences could be applied to large swathes of contract law.[65] Why is it harder (if, indeed, it is) to describe contract law using the terminology of defences than, for example, criminal law, tort law and unjust enrichment law? One possible answer to this question is that contract law, unlike many other fields, does not make use of certain distinctions within the concept of a defence, such that that between justifications and excuses. These latter concepts are widely thought by criminal law scholars to be of profound significance for their subject.[66] Similarly, torts scholars have also suggested that the difference between the ideas of justification and excuse is important for their discipline.[67] Conversely, few contract scholars have made much of them when discussing contract law.[68] There are, it is true, innumerable references in the case law and literature to contracting parties being 'excused' from their obligations, for example subsequent to the contract becoming impossible to perform.[69] In these cases, however, the term 'excuse' is not being used in contrast

[65] See Section II.

[66] For instance, HLA Hart asserted that 'the distinction between [justification and excuse] is ... of great moral importance': Hart (n 45) 13. Kent Greenawalt believes that 'the basic distinction between justification and excuse is very important for moral and legal thought': K Greenawalt, 'The Perplexing Borders of Justification and Excuse' (1984) 84 *Columbia Law Review* 1897, 1927. George Fletcher writes that '[t]he distinction between justification and excuse is of fundamental theoretical and practical value': GP Fletcher, 'The Right and the Reasonable' (1985) 98 *Harvard Law Review* 949, 955.

[67] See, eg, JL Coleman, *Risks and Wrongs* (Oxford, Oxford University Press, 1992) ch 11; GP Fletcher, 'Fairness and Utility in Tort Theory' (1972) 85 *Harvard Law Review* 537, esp 556–64; JCP Goldberg, 'Inexcusable Wrongs' (2915) 103 *California Law Review* 467; JCP Goldberg, 'Tort Law's Missing Excuses' in A Dyson, J Goudkamp and F Wilmot-Smith (eds), *Defences in Tort* (Oxford, Hart Publishing, 2015); Goudkamp (n 21) 82–101.

[68] Compare, however, AJ Morris, 'Practical Reasoning and Contract as Promise—Extending Contract-Based Criteria to Decide Excuse Cases' (1997) 56 *CLJ* 147.

[69] See, eg, *Taylor v Caldwell* (1865) 3 B & S 826, 840; 122 ER 309, 315 (Lord Blackburn); *Poussard v Spiers and Pond* (1876) 1 QBD 410 (QBD) 414 (Blackburn J); *Howell v Coupland* (1876) 1 QBD 258 (CA) 262 (James LJ); *Robinson v Davison* (1871) LR 6 Ex 269 (Exch) 275 (Kelly CB).

with that of 'justification'; it is being used to denote the parties' *release* from their obligations. If the language of defences is useful as a tool for making this further distinction, and if contract law has no use for the distinction, that may go some way to explaining why contract lawyers have not used the term. Notably, however, unjust enrichment lawyers make use of the language of 'defences' and few have thought about those doctrines in terms of justifications and excuses.[70]

A second answer to the question 'why do contract lawyers find the language of defences less useful than scholars of other areas of law?' may rest on convention: because judges do not use the language of defences in deciding contractual claims, it may not be illuminating to introduce what is essentially a foreign term into the discourse.[71] This does not, of course, explain why judges do not employ the terminology of defences. But that is not to the point; the mere fact that, for whatever reason, judges eschew the language of defences in the contractual context may provide some warrant not to use the term 'defence' in expositions of contract law.

We have, so far, suggested possible reasons that contract lawyers might have to avoid the term 'defence'. Would there be any value in their using the language of defences? Two possibilities suggest themselves: first, to illuminate links with doctrines both within contract law and between contract law and other parts of private law; second, to express morally important features of the law. We have already considered the first reason.[72] The idea we addressed is that rules that share the same or a similar logical form should be treated in a unitary lexicon, regardless of their historical or jurisdictional pedigree. The language of defences might enable similar links to be drawn within contract law and between contract law and other areas of law.

This virtue, if it is a virtue, must be balanced against a possible disadvantage to employing the language of defences. While the language may make it easier for certain distinctions to be grasped, it might occlude others. To see what we have in mind, consider the doctrines of common mistake and frustration. Common mistake operates where the requirements of offer and acceptance are satisfied, but the parties have dealt with one another on the basis of a shared false assumption. If the mistake is sufficiently important, no contractual rights arise.[73] Frustration is distinguished from common mistake only by the moment in time when the assumption is falsified.[74] Frustration deals with cases where the event arises *after* the contract has been formed. The parties' contract is thereby cancelled.[75] Given that the only

[70] Compare D Klimchuk, 'What Kind of Defence is Change of Position?' in A Dyson, J Goudkamp and F Wilmot-Smith (eds), *Defences in Unjust Enrichment* (Oxford, Hart Publishing, 2016).

[71] Another hypothesis could be drawn from Barker, Chapter 2 of this volume p 40.

[72] See Section III.A.

[73] The leading case is *Bell v Lever Bros* [1932] AC 161 (HL). See, also, *Great Peace Shipping Ltd v Tsavliris Salvage (International) Ltd* [2002] EWCA Civ 1407; [2003] QB 679.

[74] This is most clearly illustrated by *Amalgamated Investment & Property Co Ltd v John Walker & Sons Ltd* [1977] 1 WLR 164 (CA), where it was unclear whether the event took place before or after frustration.

[75] *Hirji Mulji v Cheong Yue Steamship Co Ltd* [1926] AC 497 (PC) 505 (Lord Sumner); *Davis Contractors v Fareham Urban District Council* [1956] AC 696 (HL) 728 (Lord Radcliffe); *J Lauritzen AS v Wijsmuller BV ('The Super Servant Two')* [1990] 1 Lloyd's Rep 1 (CA) 8, 9, 14 (Bingham LJ).

distinction between these doctrines is the time when the frustrating event occurs, contract scholars arguably ought to treat these rules together.

However, it could be difficult to do so if the law is presented using the language of defences. Consider the denials/defences model of defences.[76] Common mistake prevents a contract from ever having existed, and as such might be more amenable to being analysed as a denial: if there is no contract, there can be no breach. This may explain why *Chitty* deals with common mistake in its section on 'Formation of the Contract'.[77] Conversely, the doctrine of frustration is easier to analyse as external to the elements of the action in breach of contract: it does not deny that there was a contract, but asserts that the contract has been cancelled. We are not, of course, suggesting that common mistake should be understood as a denial and frustration as a defence. Neither are we contending that the association between frustration and common mistake cannot be captured on certain views of defences. Our point is that invoking the language of defences might result in two rules that are related in some fundamental way being discussed, and perhaps even classified, separately, to the detriment of understanding regarding them.[78]

The second consideration we want to propose is that some moral features of the law might be missed if the language of defences is eschewed. In particular, the law's assessment of the moral character of certain acts might be overlooked. To understand what we have in mind here, it is important to distinguish the content of a legal rule from its moral implications. The precise same legal rule, or set of legal rules, can be more or less defensible depending on the language with which it is expressed. Consider, for example, the movement to recognise same-sex marriage. For many, an equivalent set of legal rules under the label of a 'civil partnership' would fail to treat same-sex partners in the same way as heterosexual partners. This suggests that the language used to create or discuss some legal rule can have moral implications: the implication of 'civil partnership' was widely thought to be an assessment that same-sex relations were qualitatively different from heterosexual relations even though they were accorded the same substantive legal rights.

If the language of defences carries with it moral connotations, we might have moral reasons to use (or avoid) this language. Consider John Gardner's claim that the 'consequences [of the contrast between offences and defences] extend not only to the organization of textbooks but also to the moral quality of the criminal law'.[79] He explains: 'In classifying some action as criminal, the law asserts that there are

[76] See Section II.A.

[77] Beale (n 2) ch 6.

[78] Our argument is subject to the caveat that the current method of presentation does not seem to have ensured rational thought about the law: common mistake and frustration are distinguished in the law in terms of their remedial consequences. See Law Reform (Frustrated Contracts) Act 1943 (UK).

[79] Gardner (n 60) 142. See also GP Fletcher, *Rethinking Criminal Law* (Boston MA, Little, Brown & Co, 1978) 555. There are numerous instances in the law of this phenomenon, where the way in which a body of rules is understood is important: for many, for example, an equivalent set of legal rules under the label of a 'civil partnership' would fail to treat same-sex partners equally with different-sex couples who are able to enter 'marriage'.

prima facie reasons against its performance—indeed reasons sufficient to make its performance prima facie wrongful'.[80] A prima facie wrong, for Gardner, is 'an *actual* wrong, not just an apparent or putative wrong'.[81] Defences are doctrines permitting the defendant, who has done something prima facie wrongful, to explain why she did it; she might, for example, be excused or justified in her wrongful act. The classification of some particular doctrine as an offence or defence, therefore, makes a moral claim about the character of the action-types in question.

These remarks bear on a prominent debate in the contract theory literature, in particular the extent to which any breach of contract is, in truth, a wrong. Oliver Wendell Holmes Jr famously pronounced that '[t]he duty to keep a contract at common law means a prediction that you must pay damages if you do not keep it—and nothing else'.[82] If this view is taken seriously, the language of defences arguably should be avoided entirely in the contract context.[83] Even if Holmes is wrong,[84] the justification of using the language of defences arises for individual doctrines. Consider frustration again. Suppose that an opera singer agrees to perform at an impresario's house during the course of a new production. The singer becomes ill and is unable to perform; the impresario replaces her and claims damages from the singer.[85] If the singer has a 'defence' of frustration, this might be thought to suggest that she has done something prima facie wrong, which requires justification. Whether she *has* done something prima facie wrong depends upon an independent theory of contractual obligation; our point here is that it might be thought important for the law to reflect the moral status of her action in its labelling of particular doctrines.[86]

V. CONCLUSION

The aim of this chapter has been to probe the resistance of contract lawyers to using the language of defences. By demonstrating that contract law clearly admits of numerous rules that answer to at least one of three popular definitions of the concept of a defence, we have shown that the resistance is real rather than apparent. Contract law undoubtedly has myriad doctrines that qualify as defences. This raises a puzzle—why are contract lawyers disinclined to think in terms of defences?—to which we drew attention. We endeavoured to explain exactly why this puzzle

[80] Gardner (n 60) 96.

[81] ibid (emphasis in original).

[82] OW Holmes, 'The Path of the Law' (1897) 10 *Harvard Law Review* 457, 462.

[83] We note that this would also make the language of defences inapposite in the unjust enrichment context.

[84] The claim has generated a vast literature, including as to what Holmes meant. For one treatment, see JM Perillo, 'Misreading Oliver Wendell Holmes on Efficient Breach and Tortious Interference' (2000) 68 *Fordham Law Review* 1085.

[85] This scenario is loosely based on *Poussard v Spiers and Pond* (1876) 1 QBD 410 (QBD).

[86] For a development of similar ideas, see Barker, Chapter 2 of this volume, p 22.

arises. Finally, we identified reasons for and against using the language of defences. The ideas that we canvassed are controversial. They are also far from fully developed, and intentionally so. This is because the puzzle with which this chapter engaged has gone unaddressed to date. In these circumstances, we have sought merely to isolate some possible lines of reasoning for future development.

2

What Is a Contractual Defence (and Does It Matter)?

KIT BARKER*

I. INTRODUCTION

ASK MOST LAWYERS to name defences in the criminal law, law or torts, or the law of unjust enrichments and they will readily be able to reel off a list with some confidence. Request from them instead a list contractual defences and they will probably pause longer for thought. The word 'defence' rarely features in the title, contents pages or indexes of modern works on the law of contract. In England, the 11th edition of Treitel[1] (chosen only because it lies close to hand and is broadly representative) contains but a single index entry. This is not to say that such works never contain the term, but they do not deploy it as an organisational idea. Nor are students generally taught the subject in a way that accords defences any explicit pedagogical importance. The purpose of this chapter is to explore why this might be so, and whether the reasons reveal anything significant about the law of contract, the idea of a defence in private law, or both.

My methodology is both historical and analytical, which is, I confess, a potentially unhappy marriage. History rarely respects the lines that analytical jurisprudence likes to draw, pursuing a freer, empirical path. In our particular case, it reveals the fact that the set of concepts categorised as 'defences' in contract law has been constructed in different ways at different times, and for different reasons. The likely consequence of this finding, I suggest, is that it is unlikely that we shall be able to attach a 'single' meaning to the idea of a contractual defence in the modern day, or that private lawyers will be disciplined into any one, discrete use of the term. Experience tells us otherwise, and the philosophy of language goes a long way to explaining why this is the case.[2] The big question is whether this really matters. I shall suggest that

* My great thanks to David McLauchlan, Warren Swain, Stephen Waddams and Fred Wilmot-Smith for their helpful comments on an earlier draft; and to Sam Walpole for his fabulous assistance in marshalling relevant material for this chapter. All remaining errors are mine.

[1] G Treitel, *The Law of Contract*, 11th edn (London, Sweet & Maxwell, 2003).

[2] Perhaps the most famous illustration of the impossibility of giving any term a single, essential meaning is that of L Wittgenstein, *Philosophical Investigations* (Oxford, Blackwell, 1953) 31e–32e. See also, rejecting essentialism in law, R Summers, 'The New Analytical Jurists' in R Summers, *The Jurisprudence of Law's Form and Substance* (Aldershot, Ashgate Publishing, 2000) 22–25.

it does not, provided communications around the definitional question and its consequences are made clear. I do not attempt here to answer the question of what constitutes the 'best' definition of a contractual defence, precisely because the answer to what is the 'best' category of anything assumes the resolution of too many prior, framework debates regarding the nature and ultimate purpose of taxonomy[3] (what is a good system of categorisation?), the surface of which one could barely hope to scratch in a contribution this modest. Instead, I shall focus on identifying the types of consideration that have proven influential in framing the various conceptions of a contractual defence that exist amongst legal writers. I shall also suggest that, for a number of reasons, it is best to frame our discussion of the idea of a contractual defence in such a way at to capture as many subtle distinctions as possible; and that, if we are to do so, we may need to take a less essentialist approach to the use of the term than some have suggested to be appropriate.

The chapter proceeds in two main parts. Section II examines the history of contractual defences as it is depicted in the writings of the various legal treatises that emerged in the eighteenth and nineteenth centuries, starting with Henry Ballow in 1737 and ending with Leake, Pollock and Anson. As a legal history, this is a partial treatment only and it leaves out of account the way in which courts themselves viewed matters during this critical developmental time. As we shall see, there was little juristic organisation of the law of contract around 'defence issues' in the subject's early period and very little unanimity in the way in which the language of defence was used. Such treatment of vitiating factors as became (increasingly) explicit during the period tended to occur under analytical headings related to agreement, assent, validity, evidence, or arguments bearing on the availability of certain types of remedy, such as rescission or specific performance. This changed to some extent towards the end of the period, when some vitiating factors were accorded their own, independent treatment and chapter headings. Other doctrines which are sometimes now referred to as defences, such as the doctrine of illegality, tend to emerge under their own headings, but not as illustrations of any higher-level 'defence' scheme. The most notable exception to the general refusal to elevate defences to any form of categorical status is to be found in the work of Joseph Chitty, who placed the word 'defence' in the sub-title of his work and who devoted a separate chapter to the topic. He was followed in this regard by Story in the United States. Both exceptions seem to have been born of the authors' procedural preoccupations and their desire to maximise their respective works' utility to practitioners. In Section III, I then turn to the

[3] The literature on taxonomy is vast. For some valuable contributions in the private law context, see P Birks, 'Equity in the Modern Law: An Exercise in Taxonomy' (1996) 26 *University of Western Australia Law Review* 1; N McBride, 'The Classification of Obligations and Legal Education' and P Birks, 'Definition and Division: A Meditation on Institutes 3.13' ch 4 and ch 1 respectively in P Birks (ed), *The Classification of Obligations* (Oxford, Clarendon Press, 1997); E McKendrick, 'Taxonomy: Does it Matter?' in D Johnston and R Zimmermann (eds), *Unjustified Enrichment: Key Issues in Comparative Perspective* (Cambridge, Cambridge University Press, 2002) 627; G Samuel, 'Can Gaius Really be Compared to Darwin?' (2000) 49 *ICLQ* 297; S Waddams, *Dimensions of Private Law: Categories and Concepts in Anglo-American Legal Reasoning* (Cambridge, Cambridge University Press, 2003) esp ch 11; S Hedley, 'Rival Taxonomies within Obligations: Is there a Problem?' in S Degeling and J Edelman (eds), *Equity in Commercial Law* (Sydney, Lawbook Co, 2005).

analytical question forming the kernel of this chapter's title. I do not in this section provide any, singular definition of the 'essence' of a contractual defence. Instead, I shall focus on the reasons why the provision of such an essentialist definition is likely to prove difficult, and reflect upon the implications of this fact.

II. INSIGHTS FROM LEGAL HISTORY

A. Forces of Suppression

It is a trite fact that, for a long period of time, there was no 'law of contract' in the modern sense,[4] let alone any coherent system of thinking around the idea of a contractual defence. This not to say that many of those ideas that are currently listed by writers as vitiating factors, remedial bars, or defences did not feature somewhere deep in the reasoning of the legal process, but they had very little visibility, or organisational purchase. There are several reasons for this.

The first and perhaps most significant reason is that before the nineteenth century, what we now think of as contract cases were mostly decided by juries. This kept reasoning off the formal record and inhibited the development of substantive legal doctrine, whether in relation to 'defences' in particular, or indeed to contract law as a whole.[5] A second factor was that, even as late as the eighteenth century, lawyers still thought in terms of forms, rather than causes of action. This stultified the analysis of substantive rights of all sorts and therefore of defences too—it was hardly likely that any substantive conception of a 'contractual defence' would emerge at this time when a substantive conception of 'contract' had not. Indeed, to the extent that the idea of a contractual defence existed at common law at all in this period, it seems likely to have been a procedural conception only. This hypothesis tends to be borne out by the writings of both Chitty and Story, to which we shall come in the next section.

A third and connected factor was that, until the rise of special pleadings in the 1830s, a defendant wishing to make out a contractual 'defence' based on the existence of a 'vitiating factor' such as mistake, incapacity or duress would generally have to raise the relevant facts and objections as part of the 'general issue' in any action in assumpsit.[6] That is to say, the matter would not be pleaded separately

[4] For the formative history, see AWB Simpson, *A History of the Common Law of Contract: The Rise of the Action of Assumpsit* (Oxford, Clarendon Press, 1975); D Ibbetson, *A Historical Introduction to the Law of Obligations* (Oxford, Clarendon Press, 1999); W Swain, *The Law of Contract 1670–1870* (Cambridge, Cambridge University Press, 2015).

[5] Simpson (n 4) 506; Swain (n 4) 3, 173–76; Ibbetson (n 4) 220. This was certainly the case at common law. Note, however, Ibbetson's observation that Chancery Courts—lacking the impediment of the jury in this regard—started to develop a 'taxonomy of vitiating factors' with a 'measure of definition' earlier than common law courts, in the seventeenth and eighteenth centuries: ibid 208.

[6] The objection on the general issue in an action of assumpsit is described by Chitty's father, Joseph Chitty (the elder), in *A Treatise on the Parties to Actions, the Forms of Actions and on Pleading*, 6th American from the 5th London edn (Springfield MA, G & C Merriam, 1833) 510 as 'that the defendant did not undertake or promise in manner and form as the plaintiff hath complained against him, and of this the defendant puts himself upon the country'.

as a legal issue in its own right, but evidence of its existence would simply be provided to rebut a plaintiff's allegation that a valid promise had been made: 'non-assumpsit'. This left such objections off the formal list of pleadings in rebuttal of many 'contractual' arguments.[7] In his work on pleadings,[8] Chitty's father, Joseph Chitty (the elder), identifies an extraordinarily extensive range of 'defence' matters that came to be argued *sub silentio* in this way in assumpsit actions, including not just most 'vitiating factors', but also assertions of: a contract's illegality; its violation of the formal requirements of the Statute of Frauds; the existence of a release, arbitrament or higher security for a debt; impossibility; a defendant's provision of performance; the making of accord and satisfaction; even bankruptcy. Joseph Chitty (the elder) was clearly critical of using the general issue to plead defences operating to 'discharge' a plaintiff's cause of action, rather than to 'deny' its existence (an analytical distinction adverted to further in Section III) but thought the practice 'perhaps too settled to be altered' at the time he was writing.[9] In fact, the practice did subsequently change around the same time that the nineteenth century treatises on contract gained real momentum[10] and it is interesting to note that many of the matters that the elder Chitty insisted ought to be pleaded 'specially' are precisely those that his more famous son, Joseph Chitty (the younger) lists in his contractual treatise[11] under the title of contractual 'defences'. In this one may divine the way that the latter's idea of a contractual 'defence' in the formal, categorical sense was most likely driven entirely by procedural prerogatives.

A fourth logistical factor operating to suppress the open discussion of 'defences', identified by Professor Swain in his excellent recent history of the law of contract, lies in the rules of evidence that operated in this, former age. Until 1851, the parties themselves (and anyone with a potential pecuniary interest in the suit) were incompetent to give evidence in civil actions. Moreover, where a contract was written, a very strict parol evidence rule precluded the contradiction of its terms in the absence of some serious ambiguity.[12] Both rules operated to hamper parties' ability to present

[7] Simpson (n 4) 579; Swain (n 4) 25, 174–75. On the various procedural factors inhibiting the development of mistake doctrine prior to the nineteenth century, see C MacMillan, *Mistakes in Contract Law* (Oxford, Hart Publishing, 2010) ch 4. The point made in the text only applies to actions in assumpsit, not to other types of 'contractual' claim such as actions for a debt on a bond. I am grateful to Warren Swain for this point and the latter example.

[8] Chitty (n 6) ch 7 ('Of Pleas in Bar') esp at 511–14. Sadly, Joseph Chitty (the elder)'s death in 1841 post-dated that of his more famous son, Joseph Chitty (the younger), who died in 1838 of an inflammation of the brain. All subsequent references in the text to 'Chitty' are references to Joseph Chitty the younger, save where otherwise clearly indicated.

[9] ibid 513–14.

[10] On the origins and process, see Swain (n 4) 174–75. A significant turning point appears to have been the adoption of the Hilary Rules in 1834, according to which the general issue could be used only to deny that there had in fact been a promise: ibid. What was gained in exposing defence issues more clearly via this process was arguably lost in the added technicality it spawned: W Holdsworth, 'The New Rules of Pleading of the Hilary Term, 1834' (1923) 1 *CLJ* 261; J Sorabji, *English Civil Justice after the Woolf and Jackson Reforms: A Critical Analysis* (Cambridge, Cambridge University Press, 2014) 50.

[11] J Chitty, *A Practical Treatise on the Law of Contracts Not Under Seal and Upon the Usual Defences to Actions Thereon* (London, S Sweet, 1826). All references in this chapter are to the 2nd American edn (1831), in which defences are itemised in ch VI.

[12] Swain (n 4) 208; MacMillan (n 7) 89. See further C Allen, *The Law of Evidence in Victorian England* (Cambridge, Cambridge University Press, 1997).

arguments about some of those matters that might otherwise vitiate a contract, such as a mistake or misrepresentation, even in the general issue. Since those most likely to be able to present convincing evidence of the existence of factors going to the existence of consent were precluded from giving it, there were correspondingly few occasions on which the arguments might be voiced.

A fifth factor highlighted by Professor Simpson, that drove many 'defence' considerations underground, was the dominance in English law of the doctrine of consideration. That doctrine was a powerful feature of the law from an early stage, and its effect in assumpsit actions through the sixteenth and seventeenth centuries was, Simpson reliably tells us, 'to exclude certain defences as independent grounds of invalidity'[13] in cases involving informal contracts. Consideration always needed to be *good* consideration to render a promise legally binding and any consideration that was tainted by some illegality, uncertainty, duress, mistake or fraud would simply not be regarded as 'good'. Simpson's conclusion is that the doctrine of consideration was so effective in sweeping up what would in the modern day be regarded as distinct doctrines of mistake and misrepresentation that it rendered their independent expression and development entirely otiose.[14] That impression is affirmed in Catharine MacMillan's recent work on the law of mistake.[15] To the extent, therefore, that these substantive doctrines may have had some spectral background existence and awaited the summons to a more formal life, their logical space was already occupied by another substantive idea.

Finally, it is easy to forget in modern conditions that the subject of law was only first taught, at the University of Oxford, as late in the day as 1850.[16] The sort of assimilation, filtration, rationalisation and re-ordering of legal ideas that takes place in University environments, as teachers and students experiment with new models of the intellectual world, was therefore entirely missing prior to the nineteenth century and made no contribution to the construction of the early conceptual landscape of the English law of contract. Whilst I hesitate to exaggerate the extent to which the teaching of law affects its ultimate construction by courts, I am mindful of the very significant impact that the teaching of Alan Griffiths, former fellow at Exeter College, had—and probably still has—on my own understanding of the subject and it must be that others who have gone on to high judicial office in the law have been similarly influenced by those from whom first they learned. Like the use of juries and the dominance of the forms of action, this factor also served to suppress thinking about defences in the law of torts and the law of unjust enrichments, of course.

The upshot is that, prior to the nineteenth century, explicit 'doctrinal' thinking about 'defences' in the substantive sense of doctrines operating either to 'deny' or 'confess and avoid' contractual causes of action was very much still a chemical suspension in a primordial broiling-pot of form, procedure and evidence. The pot contained many of the early ingredients of more modern thinking about these

[13] Simpson (n 4) 506.
[14] ibid 535.
[15] MacMillan (n 7).
[16] FH Lawson, *The Oxford Law School 1850–1965* (Oxford, Clarendon Press, 1968) 34–60. This was as part of a joint degree with history.

matters, but none of the ingredients had as yet been strained from the soup, at least by common law courts, and none of them had been formally conceptually labelled as substantive 'defence' matters. This process was to occur only as judges became more involved in the expression and development of legal doctrine in common law courts; as the doctrinal contributions of equity came to be directly applicable in these courts from 1854 onwards; as pleading rules changed; as the grip of the forms of action started to loosen; and as the writings of the nineteenth century treatise-writers began to make their mark upon legal consciousness. Many, but not all of the latter works were written by practitioners with professional readerships in mind and this in turn undoubtedly influenced their organisation and construction in many instances.

It is to these works we now turn. The treatment which follows is brief and designed merely to extract some of the principal features of the various works of the time as they bear upon the topic in question, not to give any more comprehensive account. The account is chronological, with a summation of thematic findings towards its conclusion. Throughout, the purpose is to divine the way in which the ideas that are currently sometimes referred to as defences of one sort or another were conceptualised in earlier, formative times.

B. The Treatise Writers from Ballow to Anson[17]

(i) The Eighteenth Century—Early Conceptions: Ballow, Blackstone and Powell

Henry Ballow's treatise of 1737, *A Treatise of Equity*,[18] has been described by Professor Ibbetson as 'the first published English work on contract with any pretension to treat the subject on an abstract basis'.[19] The author's abstract leanings were entirely foreign to the rough and tumble of the common law pleading system adverted to above and stemmed from the heavy influence of the Continental natural law theorists upon his thinking, in particular Samuel Pufendorf.[20] From that point of view, the work is remarkable and stands out as a landmark of its time. There is unsurprisingly no direct reference to defence terminology in the organisational structure of the work, nor in its index. The language surfaces in the text and footnotes on a very small number of occasions (three, by my reckoning)[21] and never in a way that accords it any real significance. The various doctrines that we might nowadays associate with the idea of a defence appear under the heading '*Of the Assent*

[17] The earliest 'detailed' work on the topic of contract in England is attributed by Swain to Jeffrey Gilbert, who died in 1724. I was unable to access the manuscript locally. Note also that the list of works that follows is incomplete, focusing on the more prominent works with distinctive features as regards defence discussions. Significant omissions include W Fox, *A Treatise on Simple Contracts and the Action of Assumpsit* (London, Stevens & Norton, 1842) and—very notably—C Addison, *A Treatise on the Law of Contracts and Rights and Liabilities Ex-Contractu* (London, Benning & Co, 1847). For an excellent overview of the full nineteenth-century panoply of works, see Swain (n 4) 177–80.

[18] H Ballow, *A Treatise of Equity* (London, Nutt & Gosling, 1737).

[19] Ibbetson (n 4) 218.

[20] ibid, 218–19. The 1793 edition (with notes by J Fonblanque) also contains marginal references to Grotius.

[21] The 1793 edition, with notes by J Fonblanque, contains seven.

Required in Agreements', or in his discussion of the '*Subject Matter of Contracts*'. The first of these sections provides a locus for the exposition of principles relating to incapacity (infancy, lunacy, drunkenness), ignorance and error, fraud, circumvention and unconscionable bargains; and the latter, for discussion of illegal and usurious contracts. Given the dominance of will theory in Ballow's thinking—as in the thinking of so many of the writers to whom we shall come—it is perhaps unremarkable that many of the nowadays familiar vitiating factors he discusses were given so little, independent space of their own, but rather tied into the governing, inception doctrine of 'assent'. On an approach which posits all contractual obligation to be the product of personal will, there is no obligation to undercut, rebut or resist, where will is undermined: there is no real 'case' to answer. Although most modern writers now accord the will theory of contracts less credence than Ballow did, many still adopt the analytical position implicit in his work, namely that arguments operating to negate or 'deny' a contractual 'claim' do not really warrant the distinct designation of a 'defence'. This is a controversy to which we shall return, but it is interesting to note that it was latent in discussions of the law of contract, right from the start.

Writing a little later, in 1765, William Blackstone was also influenced by natural law theory. His *Commentaries* devote very few pages to the law of contracts at all; and he discusses them overtly only in the context of analysing the various modes via which a person may acquire title to things.[22] His core conception of a contract was that of 'an agreement, upon sufficient consideration, to do or not do a particular thing'.[23] The language of defence is again nowhere used in the relevant section of the work and the only mention that I have been able to find of matters that we might now regard as pertaining to a contractual 'defence' features in his discussion of consideration, which he suggests can sometimes 'be set aside' when it 'tends in its consequences to defraud creditors or other third persons of their just rights'.[24] The small point of significance in this passage from our current point of view is that it illustrates nicely the way in which rebuttal arguments at common law tended to get wrapped up at the time in discussions about the validity of an agreement and whether or not *good consideration* existed for it. This bears out Professor Simpson's observations, alluded to above, about the conceptual dominance of these other, substantive inception doctrines at the time.

In 1790, John Joseph Powell published what Professor Gordley[25] has referred to as the first 'real'[26] treatise on contract law—an *Essay upon the Law of Contracts*

[22] W Blackstone, *Commentaries on the Laws of England*, 4 vols (Oxford, Clarendon Press, 1765–69) Book II ('Of the Rights of Things') Chapter XXX ('Of Title by Gift, Grant and Contract'). There is some debate about this issue, since it has sometimes been said that Blackstone simply provided a dispersed treatment of the subject matter of contracts throughout his work—see, eg, D Lieberman 'Contract Before "Freedom of Contract"' in H Scheiber (ed), *The State and Freedom of Contract* (Stanford CA, Stanford University Press, 1998) 89, 90. This is as may be, but the point for our purposes is that contracts were given no singular, distinct categorical or taxonomic place in the scheme of the work.

[23] Blackstone (n 22) 442.

[24] ibid 444.

[25] J Gordley, *The Philosophical Origins of Modern Contract Doctrine* (Oxford, Clarendon Press, 1991) 134.

[26] I assume that Gordley bypasses Ballow on the basis that the latter's focus was on 'Equity' and made no reference to contract as such in the title.

and Agreements.[27] As with Ballow and Blackstone before it and Colebrooke and Anson's later works of the nineteenth century, there is no explicit use of the word 'defence' anywhere in the publication's title, contents pages, or index. The bulk of discussion relating to what some might see as 'defence' arguments appears in three titles of the work—'*Of disannulling, discharging, rescinding, waiving, or altering Contracts or Agreements*', '*Of the Equitable Jurisdiction in relieving against unreasonable Contracts or Agreements*' and '*Of the Principles on which Courts of Equity refuse to Interfere in Cases of Contracts or Agreements*'. The first title covers matters such as release, accord and satisfaction, annulment by confusion, set-off, illegality and impossibility. The second examines many of the equitable doctrines of the age, with which we are now familiar, that served to relieve parties from a contract on grounds of fraud, inequality, oppression, threats of violence, mistake, illegality, breach of fiduciary duty and public policy, or which gave rise to some relief against forfeiture. The third sets out some of the grounds on which courts refused at the time to exercise their discretion to award specific performance—including misrepresentation, unilateral mistake, fraud, concealment and public policy. The title of the third section is of particular analytical interest again for our discussion in Section III, because some take the view that factors which simply lead a court to 'refuse to interfere' in a plaintiff's favour—illegality is often used as an example—are not really 'defences' to a contractual claim, but instances in which courts simply withhold their adjudicative powers in respect of a dispute.

(ii) The Dawn of the Nineteenth Century—Newland and Comyn

The turn of the nineteenth century saw a rapid rise in treatise production and the almost immediate emergence of two lengthy works of more than 500 pages—John Newland's *Treatise on Contracts Within the Jurisdiction of Courts of Equity*,[28] published in 1806; and John Comyn's *Treatise of the Law Relative to Contracts and Agreements Not Under Seal with Cases and Decisions Thereon in the Action of Assumpsit* (1807).[29] Both authors were barristers and their practical bent is purposefully reflected in the works' design. The former focuses almost exclusively on equitable doctrine and its modifying influence upon the common law,[30] whereas the latter claims in the advertisement that appears inside its inner cover to remedy a problem regarding the inaccessibility of decisions of the common law courts.[31] These differences in focus are likely to have made the works companions, rather than direct

[27] J Powell, *Essay Upon the Law of Contracts and Agreements*, 2 vols (London, Johnson & Whieldon, 1790).

[28] J Newland, *Treatise on Contracts within the Jurisdiction of Courts of Equity* (London, Butterworths, 1806).

[29] J Comyn, *Treatise of the Law Relative to Contracts and Agreements Not Under Seal: With Cases and Decisions Thereon in the Action of Assumpsit*, 2 vols (London, Strahan, 1807).

[30] In the preface, Newland describes his work as one on the 'Jurisdiction exercised by Courts of Equity, in compelling specific performance of contracts, and in rescinding them, as well as in relieving against their legal construction'.

[31] Comyn (n 29) A2.

competitors for the attention of practising lawyers. Neither contains any elevated discussion of the idea of contractual 'defences'. Newland was no theoretician and simply repeated Blackstone's definition of a contract without allusion to the philosophical thinking of Pufendorf that had inspired Ballow some 70 years earlier.[32] The word 'defence' appears to be used only four times in the book, but modern readers will still be able to find within it some familiar topics and principles regarding equitable relief. These include: transactions with infants; the principles and bars regulating the availability of the remedy of specific performance; improper contracts unenforceable for their 'inconsistency with the rules of public policy';[33] equitable relief against forfeiture and penalties; and the rescission of contracts in equity on a wide variety of grounds such as fraud, imposition, inequality, mistake, breach of fiduciary duty and 'turpitude'. Some of these (for example, rescission for 'imposition', inequality, advantage-taking or mistake) get their own substantive chapter headings, which is an advance on the status and importance they are accorded in Powell. This, more overt treatment of arguments relating to the various vitiating factors reflects, I would suggest, the more developed state of the equitable jurisprudence around topics of this sort at the time—equitable doctrine was, after all, not the focus of Powell's emphasis, but the main point of Newland's work. Unsurprisingly, given both the date of the book and the practical leanings of its author, Newland's attention is upon remedial principles and evinces little thinking about rights, causes of action and substantive 'defences' as such. This focus on remedies is again interesting in itself, because it raises the analytical question, considered further in Section III, whether arguments that bear upon the incidence of secondary rights and the exercise of discretionary court powers (what we usually refer to as 'bars' to the availability of an equitable remedy, or 'factors' and 'principles' negatively affecting the exercise of discretion) can legitimately be classified as arguments of 'defence' to a contractual claim. Pollock clearly thought so some 70 years later, as we shall see, but his appears to be a minority position these days.

John Comyn's treatise is far broader, encompassing even some claims in assumpsit that, in the modern era, would no longer be regarded as contractual at all, but which would instead be placed in the basket of unjust enrichment law. It contains many more references than Newland to the word 'defence' (I counted some 52 in total in the body of the text) but it never clarifies the sense in which the term is being used and one gets the impression that the designation of a matter as one of defence was very much a peripheral, if not an entirely irrelevant concern in terms of the scheme of the work. Some doctrines that might in a broad sense be regarded as defence doctrines, such as illegality, infancy, bankruptcy, wagers, and the restraint of trade do, again, receive their own chapter headings and get more overt recognition in this way, but these chapters are in turn generally still merely subtitles of bigger organisational themes that are related to the '*Nature and Requisites of a Contract*' (Vol 1, Part 1),

[32] Ballow was also a practitioner, but, interestingly, it seems he also occupied positions within the Exchequer. This may, it is sometimes suggested, have eased the practical financial pressures upon him and could perhaps explain the greater theoretical depth characterising his work.

[33] Newland (n 28) 157.

the '*Parties to a Contract*' (Vol 1, Part 2) and the examination of '*Particular [types of] Contract*' (Vol 2, Part 3).

(iii) Colebrooke

Professor Swain has observed that the contrast between Comyn's work of 1807 and that of Henry Colebrooke in 1818 'could hardly be greater'.[34] It is hard to dissent from this view. Colebrooke's *Treatise on Obligations and Contracts*[35] is a much shorter, designedly introductory work of a new style. It is also clear from the extensive marginal references it contains to Pothier (who was translated into English for the first time in 1806), Roman Law and even Hindu texts, both that it was premised upon more pedagogical[36] aims; and that it was very heavily influenced in its construction by the will theory of contracts.[37] It was not a practitioner text in the exhaustive style of Comyn or Newland and it tellingly (perhaps consequently?) has no index. The work is organised around the basic, logical structure that many modern contract courses now assume—*Definitions* (Book I), the *Validity of Agreements* (Book II), the *Interpretation and Effect of Contracts* (Book III) and the *Dissolution and Extinction of Contractual Obligations* (Book IV).

Defences do not therefore feature as a categorical feature of the work at any high level. There are some 15 or so direct references in the body of the text to the term and on some of those occasions the word is indeed directly linked to particular doctrines, in particular to ratification, set-off, rescission and insanity. At one point, when discussing the remedy of rescission, Colebrooke does appear to draw a set of conceptual distinctions between 'defences, exceptions, replies and answers' to claims,[38] but the exact nature of these distinctions goes unexplained. Indeed, he seems to assume that the reader is familiar with the terms and that their meanings are consequently self-evident and uncontroversial. Many familiar vitiating factors are now particularised and listed individually in Book I on the '*Validity of Agreements*' (error, compulsion, fraud, lesion and hardship), as is the doctrine of illegality, which gives them all a heightened degree of visibility. His final Book on '*Dissolution*' also contains a well-organised discussion of principles relating to compromise, satisfaction, performance, release, confusion, revocation, death and rescission (each of 12, distinct grounds of rescission being fully particularised).

It is worth pausing at this point to compare Colebrooke's work with that of Ballow in the previous century, since both were so strongly influenced by will theory

[34] Swain (n 4) 148.

[35] H Colebrooke, *A Treatise on Obligations and Contracts* (London, C Roworth, 1818).

[36] Swain (n 4) 148 refers to a suggestion made by Colebrooke's son and biographer that the work was intended to be an 'introduction on contract' for use in the Indian Service.

[37] An agreement is thus defined as an 'aggregation of minds': Colebrooke (n 35) 2.

[38] Colebrooke (n 35) 220. See also at 222, where he indicates that whilst one can bring an 'action for rescission' on grounds that a contract is voidable, the contract can also be 'defeated by exception and defensive plea' on similar grounds, such as force or fraud.

of one form or another (natural law in the latter case; and the work of Pothier[39] in the former). For reasons already mentioned, this probably explains why the conceptual role accorded to 'defences' in both works is so small. At the same time, whilst Ballow grouped vitiating factors like mistake under the title of '*Assent*', Colebrooke assembled them instead under the title of contractual '*Invalidity*'. There is, I think, a subtle difference in the two conceptualisations. To challenge a contractual claim for lack of party assent is one thing. To challenge it on the basis that assent is present, but the contract not 'valid' (for other reasons) is clearly another, adverting as it does to the importance of factors in the construction of contractual obligation that lie outside the parties' individual or collective wills. It seems possible that this difference in conceptualisation may itself be attributable to subtly different foundational views as to the type of 'assent' that counts in contract law—subjective or objective. That is a matter in respect of which there was clearly tension between the views of the natural lawyers (where subjectivity and the *actual* intent of the promisor was everything) and the more pragmatic approach of the English common law (where objective appearances counted, as indeed they still do today).[40] The more we objectivise the type of assent that counts as an inception doctrine in contract law, the more the various vitiating factors will feature as independent reasons to question the contract's bindingness or enforceability. By contrast, the more subjective our conception of the consent that is necessary to trigger contractual responsibility, the more we are likely to see such factors as simply part and parcel of the discussion as to whether a plaintiff has any 'prima facie claim'.

(iv) Chitty and Story—Procedural Conceptions of a Defence?

Whist there are significant differences between Chitty (the younger)'s *Practical Treatise on the Law of Contracts Not under Seal and Upon the Usual Defences to Actions Thereon*[41] (1826) and William Story's *Treatise on the Law of Contracts Not under Seal*,[42] first published in the United States in 1844, they are considered together here because they share an interesting and distinctive feature that has been lacking in all of the accounts hitherto mentioned. For the first time, both works contain a chapter specifically bearing the title of 'Defences' to contractual claims. Chitty is even bolder than Story and incorporates a reference to defences into the

[39] Pothier apparently became 'all the rage' in the nineteenth century. According to Bernard Rudden, cited in Swain (n 4) at 176, his work was cited some 400 times in court during the course of the century. He also became recommended reading for students at the Inns of Court at this time: S Warren, cited in Swain ibid, at 177.

[40] See generally, J Perillo, 'The Origins of the Objective Theory of Contract Formation and Interpretation' (2000) 69 *Fordham Law Review* 427. The precise time at which the objective approach became dominant in English law is disputed. Whilst some modern writers such as Friedman, Horwitz and Gilmore place this time in the late nineteenth and early twentieth centuries, and explain the objective approach as a function of the social transformation of contract from an instrument of fairness to one of commercial utility, Perillo convincingly demonstrates that objectivity was in fact evident in the English law from a much earlier time—in his words, 'from time immemorial'—albeit that there was some 'flirtation' with subjectivity in the mid-eighteenth century: at 428.

[41] Chitty (n 11).

[42] W Story, *Treatise on the Law of Contracts Not under Seal* (Boston, Little & Brown, 1844).

title of his work. His preface and the advertisement that appears inside the cover of the second edition, to which I had access for the purposes of this chapter, both stress the distinction in this regard from Comyn's earlier work (which is clearly seen as a market rival), highlighting the distinct treatment of defences and their pleading as a point of advantage. In both Chitty and Story, the range of matters that appear in the relevant defences chapter is narrow and excludes most of the customary vitiating factors, as well as illegality, all of which topics receive separate treatment under different headings. Chitty lists 14 specific 'defence' matters in total: lunacy, infancy, coverture, bankruptcy, insolvency, performance, payment, accord and satisfaction, the existence of security for a debt, release, the pending of another action, tender, limitation and set-off. Story's list is somewhat shorter, closely following Chitty's, but omitting lunacy, infancy, coverture, bankruptcy, insolvency and the existence of security for a contractual debt. The taxonomies of both writers have clear, procedural orientations. As mentioned above, most of the matters Chitty lists in his contractual defences chapter are those that his father considered, in his separate work on pleading, to be those that should be pleaded specially, rather than under the general issue in assumpsit.[43] Indeed, it is his clearly stated view at this time that matters which go to the '*confession and avoidance*' of a contract, as opposed to the *denial* of a plaintiff's prima facie claim, ought to be pleaded specially.[44] His inclusion amongst the list of defence matters of some arguments going to the existence of a claim, such as a defendant's incapacity or performance, reflects his pragmatic recognition of the historic practice of pleading on the general issue, not what he regarded as the ideal situation. The primary consideration at the heart of Chitty's preferred scheme was the practical one—of serious concern to lawyers at *nisi prius*—that a plaintiff should not suddenly be met at trial with arguments that do not 'come in contact with [his] … declaration' (claim) and which may therefore not be anticipated by him and 'take him by surprise'.[45]

In this distinction between 'avoidance' and 'denial' we see foreshadowed an analytical division that is now popular in the academic community and one that has a degree of coherence from a particular point of view, although it is not always straightforward to apply for reasons we shall come to in Section III. Unfortunately, however, Chitty never cleanly instated the line between 'avoidance' and 'denial' as the marker of defence arguments in his work. In this he followed his father, who, in his tome on pleadings, referred to both sorts of argument loosely as ones of 'defence' (although he still distinguished between them).[46] Indeed, some of the matters Chitty lists in the 'defences' chapter of his contract treatise include arguments that probably go to the denial of a cause of action—the failure of a plaintiff to fulfil a condition precedent to the defendant's obligation to perform being the most pointed example.[47] The reason for the blurring lies in the factor he himself identifies—the pleading

[43] See n 8 and text.
[44] Chitty (n 11) 251.
[45] ibid.
[46] Chitty (n 6) 505, 509, 511–12.
[47] Chitty (n 11) 271.

rules of the time permitted a host of 'defence' (confession and avoidance) as well as 'cause of action' (denial) matters to be argued by a defendant under the general issue. The same blurring of the language of defence occurs in Story, who indicates at the beginning of his defences chapter that 'a violation of the prerequisites of a contract' can be a 'defence' to a claim set up under it, just as much as any of the 'special' matters appearing under that title.[48] All of this reflects the pragmatic ambitions of two writers seeking to assist professional readers in negotiating the complexities of pleading practices. Their works do not purport to provide a fully consistent or coherent intellectual scheme.

(v) Later Nineteenth-century Modernisation: Leake, Pollock and Anson

As we approach the end of the nineteenth century, contractual works at last start to look much more like the texts of the modern day. Stephen Leake's *The Elements of the Law of Contracts*[49] (1867) was certainly a very different sort of book to Chitty and Story, aiming to provide an overview of the general principles relating to contracts, rather than to consider comprehensively the law relating to all of the different types of contract. It again does not accord defences any distinct treatment taxonomically and the 54 references to the term 'defence' in the text are indiscriminate in the sense that they refer to an exceptionally wide range of different matters, including: set-off, judgment, award and arbitration, informality, mistake, fraud, duress, infancy, incapacity, performance, abandonment, security, release and bankruptcy. Some vitiating factors, such as mistake, fraud, duress and incapacity are now given their own section headings in the work, as are defects of formality stemming from violations of the Statute of Frauds, but this always occurs under the higher rubric of chapters dealing with inception doctrines such as the '*Formation of Contracts*' and '*Parties to Contracts*'. There is a significant section on illegality, which appears in a chapter entitled '*The Matter of Contracts*'. Impossibility is discussed under the same chapter heading in the context of a discussion of the requirement of good consideration. Some of the matters that Chitty listed as specific defences in their own right—accord and satisfaction, release, arbitration and award, limitation, set-off and bankruptcy—are discussed at the end of the work in a chapter entitled '*Discharge*'. Although there is hence much greater visibility accorded to all of these matters than in the early treatises, the framework in which they are set is still heavily influenced by the governing idea of assent. Professor Swain points to several parts of the text in which Pothier is cited,[50] which goes some way to explaining this stance. Stepping away from the coalface of legal practice at which Chitty toiled and taking greater cognisance of the dominant abstract philosophical frameworks of the day, Leake covers much 'defence' material in a more overt way, without ever really alluding to

[48] Story (n 42) 403. Apparently Blackstone associated the idea of a defence entirely with denials of a cause of action: Blackstone, *Commentaries* (n 22) vol 3, 296–97, cited in J Goudkamp, *Tort Law Defences* (Oxford, Hart Publishing, 2013) 2.

[49] S Leake, *The Elements of the Law of Contracts* (London, Stevens, 1867).

[50] Swain (n 4) 203.

the idea of a defence itself as being conceptually significant, or assigning the word any particular meaning.

In Pollock's *Principles of Contract at Law and in Equity*,[51] published in 1876, we really begin to see clearly the classical framework that has come to dominate most modern contract texts. The reference to defence language is once more rare, muted and indiscriminate, the term being used variously to refer to issues such as the absence of consideration for a contract, illegality, impossibility, waiver, relief from catching bargains and error; and to refer to the basis on which remedies such as specific performance can be refused. Most obvious to anyone scanning the work's contents pages is the increased priority and visibility given to the discussion of matters such as capacity, illegality, impossibility, mistake, fraud and rescission, and duress and undue influence. Each of these topics now receives its own, full chapter and none of them appears under the rubric of any higher-level conceptual heading. They leap very clearly off the contents page. Although analytically the concept of a defence is given very little attention, the various 'defence matters' we have mentioned are therefore now very much at the fore of the subject's exposition and they are given a higher ranking than in Leake, along with increased independence and visibility. Interestingly, the fact that Pollock was (like his predecessors) heavily influenced by will theory[52] does not on this occasion seem to have led him to submerge these ideas under inception doctrine headings related to assent; although it undoubtedly did influence the way in which he understood those individual doctrines to work.[53] It seems that, despite holding the chair of Jurisprudence of Oxford University, Pollock's attitude toward legal theory was in fact rather ambivalent and he generally liked to keep it out of his analysis of the common law.[54] So the effect of will theory on the visibility of many contractual doctrines was not *always* wholly suppressive, especially as time wore on—this depended on the extent to which theory was permitted by the writer to dominate the mode of analysis. A further, interesting point to extract from the detail of Pollock's treatment of the language of defence, to which we shall return in section III below, is that he uses it to refer both to matters that negate secondary rights and/or affect judicial powers,[55] and to matters that bear upon primary contractual rights.

This brings us finally and briefly to Anson,[56] whose work also displays many of the divisions and features of modern works. Defence language is again sparse and indiscriminate and the various 'defence matters' (broadly conceived) that are discussed, whilst being accorded clear and visible treatment, are often considered at a

[51] F Pollock, *Principles of Contract at Law and in Equity: being a Treatise on the General Principles concerning the Validity of Agreements, with a special view to the Comparison of Law and Equity, and with references to the Indian Contract Act, and occasionally to Roman, American, and Continental Law* (London, Stevens, 1876).

[52] This time the dominant influence was Savigny, not Pothier.

[53] This is clearest in his treatment of the doctrine of mistake—Pollock (n 51) 357.

[54] N Duxbury, *Frederick Pollock and the English Juristic Tradition* (Oxford, Oxford University Press, 2004) ch 3, esp 88–89, 109–10.

[55] See, for example, his discussion of mistake as a 'defence' to the remedy of specific performance in equity—Pollock (n 51) 420.

[56] W Anson, *Principles of the English Law of Contract* (Oxford, Clarendon Press, 1879).

lower level than is the case in Pollock. Incapacity, Illegality and Discharge (including discharge for impossibility, by merger or through bankruptcy) hence get their own chapters, but mistake, misrepresentation, fraud, duress and undue influence all feature as subtitles in Anson's chapter on the '*Reality of Consent*'.

(vi) Summary: Two Thematic Observations

If there are two, generalised conclusions to be drawn from this overview they are as follows: first, there is a gradual emergence of visible thinking amongst treatise-writers about a variety of matters that can be broadly construed as 'defence' matters throughout the period upon which we have focused—in particular, clearer, more detailed and more independent consideration of discrete, substantive vitiating factors, as well as independent doctrinal consideration of public policy doctrines related to illegality. As we approach the end of the period, many of the ideas that were previously hidden from view by jury decisions and ancient pleading practices, or which were concertedly developed only in courts of equity, spring into conscious, formal life.

Secondly, and by dramatic contrast, there is very little usage of the *language* of defence amongst writers; and indeed little sign of any determined attempt to deploy the concept of a contractual defence as a *framework organisational idea* in any of the texts to which we have adverted, even the later ones. I have crudely tracked the frequency of textual reference to defence language across the various works in Figure 1 below, so as to give a sense of the overall pattern. The major exceptions to this rule are Chitty and Story, both of whom did accord defences a distinct analytical place in their schemes of thinking, but ironically the determination of these writers to elevate the idea of a contractual defence to a formal designation was born not of higher analytical or jurisprudential commitments, but of the pragmatics of pleading and the desire to appeal to the unfortunate practitioner audiences who were forced to deal with its intractable complications. If anything, the higher philosophical thinking of the age—classical 'will theory'—tended, I have suggested, toward the suppression, rather than the recognition of independent 'defence' doctrines and, although 'will theory' is no longer the force that once it was, it still has a hold over the modern imagination, at least in commercial contexts. I suspect that this difference in perspective (theoretical/pragmatic) persists today as between practitioners and members of the legal academy and subliminally influences their respective conceptions of what constitutes a 'defence' argument. I also suspect that, as the strains upon will theory became more apparent during the late nineteenth and twentieth centuries—as contracts came (once again)[57] to be seen less as the exclusive products

[57] There is much evidence that in the eighteenth century and indeed well before, courts were concerned about the distributive fairness of contracts; so that, for example, much greater scrutiny was placed on the adequacy of consideration. See PS Atiyah, *The Rise and Fall of Freedom of Contract* (Oxford, Clarendon Press, 1979) 146–49, 167–77. Evidence of this approach is found in Ballow (n 18) 11: '[I]n all contracts ... if there appear to be an inequality, although there was no deceit, and all the faults of the thing were exposed, yet, if the damage be considerable, the bargain ought to be made void. And this estimate of the damage is to be taken either from the exorbitance of the price, or the poverty of the party injured, for no man should be a gainer from another's loss'.

of individual or composite intentions and more as chosen arrangements that are subject to interventionist controls—the scope for admitting arguments 'in rebuttal' of contractual claims inevitably will have grown. After all, if contractual obligation is not just about what the parties genuinely intend, but about what society regards as a (procedurally or substantively) fair exchange, then greater conceptual scope is automatically available for arguments that deny *validity* or *legal effect* to terms which parties have in fact agreed. Whether such arguments should be referred to as ones of 'defence'—and if so when—is a separate and difficult matter. It goes to the heart of the question posed in the title of this chapter and it is the matter to which I now finally turn.

Treatise	Date	Title	Contents Pages	Text Body & footnotes	Index
Ballow	1736	0	0	3	0
Blackstone	1765	0	0	0[58]	0
Powell	1790	0	0	9	0
Newland	1806	0	0	4	0
Comyn	1807	0	0	52	4
Colebrooke	1818	0	0	15	No index
Chitty[59]	1826	1	1 (chapter title)	63	17
Story	1844	0	1 (chapter title)	71	23
Addison	1847	0	0	23	3
Leake	1867	0	0	54	3
Pollock	1876	0	2	15	1
Anson	1879	0	0	17	0

Figure 1: Number of search hits per publication on the word 'defence', analysed by sections of the work.

III. THE ANALYTICAL QUESTION

What then, is a contractual defence?[60] Were the early writers simply too ill-disciplined about this question? Is thinking about defences something that happens only long after the law has developed a stable conception of rights? Or is the absence of a

[58] Search made in Chapter 30 only.

[59] The text used for this search was that of the 2nd American edition (1831).

[60] For careful consideration of the same question in the context of tort defences, see Goudkamp (n 48) 1–7; A Dyson, J Goudkamp and F Wilmot-Smith (eds), *Defences in Tort* (Oxford, Hart Publishing, 2015) 5–11. See also, in the unjust enrichment context, A Dyson, J Goudkamp and F Wilmot-Smith, 'Defences in Unjust Enrichment: Questions and Themes' in A Dyson, J Goudkamp and F Wilmot-Smith (eds), *Defences in Unjust Enrichment* (Oxford, Hart Publishing, 2016). *cf* L Duarte d'Almeida, 'Defining "Defences"' in A Dyson, J Goudkamp and F Wilmot-Smith, *Defences in Tort* (above).

prominent, stable conception of a contractual defence in the modern day indicative not of early indiscipline and intellectual deficiency, nor of the law's continuing developmental immaturity, but rather of genuine disagreement about basic terms, systems of classification and the values underpinning contract law? I shall argue that the latter is more likely to be the case.

A. Terms and Classifications

All classifications are created by questions; and all questions are influenced by interests. Whether we regard an argument as a matter of 'defence' hence depends on the question (or set of questions) we are asking when we examine legal material and which we require to be satisfied before according the matter in question that label. Which question or set of questions we ask also depends on our own values and purposes. This may differ as between lawyers, sociologists, historians and natural scientists.[61] It may also differ—importantly for our purposes—as between those actually litigating cases in the courts and those who view their task as being to give the law a more coherent or intelligible construction, or to make it accessible to students.

There are a number of questions that analysts commonly ask when they seek to designate an argument as one of 'defence', all of which result in a different meaning for the term and a different 'taxonomy' of defence arguments. Sometimes, the classification of a matter as a 'defence' matter is made to depend on the answer to more than one of these questions. Dr James Goudkamp insightfully identifies several of these in his recent work on tort defences[62] and regards the lack of any clear definition of a defence that results from their complex interaction as intensely problematic. He encourages us to focus on a *single* question (and hence give the word defence a *single* meaning) in the hope that this will produce a clearer category of ideas and create a more coherent approach to the law as a whole. This is certainly a laudable aim, but I shall suggest that, as a pragmatic matter, the language may be too hard to control and that a better strategy may be simply to focus very clearly on the various distinctions that are explicit in each question. I adopt this approach on the basis that essentialism is likely to prove misguided when it comes to matters of classification. It is more likely, I suggest, that the idea of a contractual 'defence' as it exists in legal thinking stands for a *set* of ideas that bear family resemblances to one another, but not all of which share exactly the same feature, or set of features.[63]

[61] Samuel (n 3).

[62] Goudkamp (n 48) 1–7.

[63] This approach is similar to the one I have advocated in relation to the taxonomy of 'unjust enrichment' law, where the diversity of the relevant subject-matter has again caused some writers to doubt the propriety of using that term to refer to all of it. See K Barker, 'Understanding the Unjust Enrichment Principle in Private Law: A Study of the Concept and its Reasons' in J Neyers, M McInnes and S Pitel (eds), *Understanding Unjust Enrichment* (Oxford, Hart Publishing, 2004). This doubt is in my view unjustified, failing to appreciate that members of the same family can be different in important respects, as well as sharing similarities. For the same point made more recently, see K Barker, 'Centripetal Force: The Law of Unjust Enrichment Restated in England and Wales' (2014) 34 *OJLS* 155, 172.

The list of questions that have been suggested as bearing upon the classification of an argument or set of rules as a defence includes at least the following:

1. Does the argument provide a reason against the defendant's liability, as opposed to a reason for it?
2. Is it a response the defendant has made to an argument the plaintiff has raised in favour of that liability? (Does it 'answer' a claim the plaintiff has actually made?)
3. Does it 'deny' an element of the plaintiff's 'cause of action', or introduce an additional, countervailing reason why the claim should fail ('confess and avoid' the plaintiff's 'claim')?
4. Does it go to the defendant's primary or secondary obligations (to 'rights' or 'remedies')?
5. Does the argument articulate 'substantive' reasons against liability, or 'procedural' reasons?
6. Does the argument articulate 'moral' or 'corrective justice' reasons against liability that affect the balance of interpersonal justice between the parties, or does it extol an instrumental public 'policy' reason that extends beyond the parties' moral relationship?
7. Does the onus (legal or evidential) of establishing the argument lie upon the plaintiff or defendant?
8. Must the defendant, or the plaintiff, formally plead the argument?

Which question, or set of questions, is regarded as being of importance inevitably affects the definition and scope of one's category of defences. The first question yields the broadest category and incorporates some matters—such as illegality—that a court can raise and interject to defeat a plaintiff's claim of its own motion. It can also result in many arguments being dubbed 'defences' that go to the plaintiff's ability to make out his or her 'cause of action',[64] which is probably why writers committed to highlighting the importance of the third question tend to reject it. The second question, though narrowing the class of defence arguments to those formally 'raised' by a defendant in either pleadings or in the course of trial, also encompasses all forms of rebuttal argument, without regard to any further distinction or qualifying criterion. Like the previous question, it classifies as defences some arguments that apparently go to the existence of a contractual cause of action. On this approach, a defendant's objection to the admissibility of parol evidence regarding the proper meaning of an agreement would therefore count as a defence, just as much as arguments about the existence of duress, estoppel, or illegality.

The third question, favoured by James Goudkamp and others,[65] is popular amongst modern writers, although it was rejected by the late Professor Birks in

[64] An argument that D did not agree is hence clearly an argument against the liability of D. Similarly, in the law of negligence, many arguments against liability (eg the fact that it may undermine the purposes of a statutory scheme, or result in defensive practices) go to the question whether P can prove that D owes a duty of care. On the difficult question as to how to define a cause of action, see further n 68 below and the text thereto.

[65] See n 60.

his final exposition of unjust enrichment law.[66] If one understands a contractual cause of action as the set of facts both sufficient and necessary to meet the requirements of contractual inception doctrines (the 'elements' of a binding contract) then, on the third approach, it is pretty clear that no argument concerning agreement, consideration, intention to create legal relations or uncertainty of terms is really a defence argument, whereas arguments which accept the existence of these matters, but which add countervailing reasons why the plaintiff should nonetheless fail in a claim (such as illegality or limitation), are. This is probably the most popular of modern academic conceptualisations of the idea of a 'defence' and I suspect that I myself have until now subconsciously held it. Unfortunately, however, even if the third question creates a distinction that is both logical and normatively appealing,[67] it does not yield a clear, or uncontroversial definition of a defence, because opinions differ both as to what is meant by a 'cause of action' in private law generally[68] and

[66] See P Birks, *Unjust Enrichment*, 2nd edn (Oxford, Clarendon Press, 2005) Part 5, 'Defences'. This section relates each of the various restitutionary defences either to the 'enrichment', the 'at the expense of', or the 'unjust' part of causes of action in unjust enrichment law. See also, similarly, R Grantham and C Rickett, *Enrichment & Restitution in New Zealand* (Oxford, Hart Publishing, 2000) ch 14, 15, 16.

[67] Both propositions are contested by Duarte d'Almeida (n 60) 49 on consequentialist grounds (both 'denials' and 'avoidances' can equally cause a claim to fail). With respect, this may be too hasty a dismissal. It seems possible, for example, that the distinction approximately tracks the logical distinction in legal reasoning between positive and negative justifications. A positive justification describes a good reason *for* X (X in our example being D's liability). A negative justification identifies the *absence* of a reason *against* X. It is clearly logically and normatively important not to confuse the two types of justification for a liability; otherwise the mere absence of an argument against liability might wrongly be taken to be a reason for it. Unfortunately for those of us attracted to Goudkamp's distinction, however, arguments of negative justification quite often feature in private law in debates about the existence of causes of action—for example, courts often refer to the absence of a concern about indeterminate liability or the absence of conflict with a statutory regime when deciding whether or not to impose a duty of care on a defendant in cases of pure economic loss in tort. The upshot is that, although all 'defence' ('avoidance') arguments are arguments against liability, the absence of which is necessary for a claim's success, the same can be said of many other ('denial') arguments featuring within 'cause of action' inquiries. The tracking of the distinction between positive and negative justification that is produced by the distinction between denials and avoidances, whilst logical and normatively important, is therefore inexact. On the distinction between positive and negative justifications, see further J Raz, 'Promises in Morality and Law' (1982) 95 *Harvard Law Review* 916, 929. Rather oddly, given his criticism of Goudkamp, Duarte d'Almeida's own suggested definition of a defence is a 'merits-relative, liability-defeating consideration that is not a "denial": Duarte d'Almeida (n 60) 50. By excluding denials, this definition appears to endorse Goudkamp's own, albeit further qualifying it by narrowing the category of defences to those which relate to the 'merits' of a case.

[68] Goudkamp adopts a narrow definition of cause of action close to that set out in the text, but broader definitions are clearly possible and the broader the definition that is used, the narrower the corresponding class of 'defence' arguments gets, if one persists in asking the third question. For example, one might construe a cause of action as the entire set of conditions (both positive and negative) that is required to give rise to a Hohfeldian liability on the part of the defendant (i.e., the set of facts both necessary and sufficient to give a plaintiff the power to alter a defendant's legal rights and duties). On this approach, there would be no contractual defences at all—since the *absence* of a conclusive negating argument relating to limitation or illegality would be a precondition of the defendant's liability, just as much as an argument regarding the existence of consideration for the agreement in question. This broad approach to the definition of a cause of action appears implicitly to be taken by what Duarte d'Almeida (n 60) refers to as 'incorporationists'. Other conflicting definitions of a cause of action include the 'right to ask and obtain judicial aid', a 'statement of the facts showing cause for judicial action', the 'unlawful invasion of a right—the wrong committed'; the combination of a plaintiff's primary right and the relevant 'wrong' constituted by its invasion; and the group of operative facts supporting the award of a remedy. For discussion of all of these and the complications of choosing between them see S Harris, 'What is a Cause of Action?' (1928) 16 *California Law Review* 459. See also C Clark, 'The Cause of Action' (1934) 82

about the precise requirements of the various 'inception' doctrines that are thought to constitute such a cause of action in the law of contract. So, for example, even assuming the definition of a cause of action set out above to be correct, if one thinks that the existence of *objective* agreement between the parties is sufficient to bind the parties for the purposes of the inception doctrine of agreement (the basic position in English law), then the existence of duress, or some fundamental, common mistake as to the subject matter of a contract is clearly a 'defence'. If, however, the existence of *subjective*, *voluntary* or *autonomous* agreement were to be regarded as the necessary 'inception requirement' for the purposes of establishing a contractual cause of action,[69] then these vitiating factors would not warrant the designation of defence after all, since they would simply negate the inception doctrine's requirements. This point is important, because it illustrates the way in which the definition of a defence produced by the third question itself depends on one's definition of a contractual cause of action. And that definition is itself affected by one's conception of the normative foundations of contract law, which is a matter in respect of which views have changed over time as will theory has come to be supplanted, or (more realistically) adjusted by more distributive, welfarist conceptions of the contractual bond. We will return to this point in the next section.

The remaining questions (four to eight) are rarely used *in and of themselves* to generate a defence category, but are usually combined with one of the first three questions, so as to create a smaller category of defence argument. As regards the fourth question, many modern writers hence prefer to use the language of 'bars' or 'discretionary factors' to refer to arguments or principles affecting the availability of rescission or specific performance, rather than using the language of defence, on the basis that these matters operate differently and have different normative effects to factors bearing on a plaintiff's primary rights. Similarly, as regards the fifth question, the opinion has been voiced that arguments relating to procedure (such as the absence of court jurisdiction, or the expiry of a limitation period) do not warrant the designation of a defence because they do not logically relate to the *merits* of the *substantive* arguments that a plaintiff has put—and exceptions must be normatively linked to rules.[70] As regards the sixth, some legal theorists who are wedded to Kantian conceptions of the private law clearly think that 'defences' should be coherently modelled along corrective justice lines.[71] An extreme commitment to this approach might exclude from the ambit of the term 'defence' any rebutting argument that has an instrumentalist motivation external to the parties' own moral relationship. Taking that approach, the doctrine of illegality might be labelled less a 'defence' to a

University of Pennsylvania Law Review 354 and L Smith, 'Defences and the Disunity of Unjust Enrichment' in A Dyson, J Goudkamp and F Wilmot-Smith (eds), *Defences in Unjust Enrichment* (n 60) 29–39.

[69] See D McLauchlan, 'The Contract that Neither Party Intends' (2012) 29 *Journal of Contract Law* 26.

[70] Duarte d'Almeida (n 60) 48–49.

[71] See, for example, in the unjust enrichment context: R Grantham and C Rickett, 'A Normative Account of Defences to Restitutionary Liability' (2008) 67 *CLJ* 92. Note however, that the authors still use the language of defence in relation to policy-motivated defences. They do not therefore subscribe to the extreme position hypothesised in the text below.

contract claim, and more a legal 'ban' or rule against the *recognition* of certain types of socially harmful contracting practice.

Finally, as regards the seventh and eighth questions, we have seen from Chitty and Story that categorisations of arguments as ones of defence can turn on the pragmatic issues of how matters should be pleaded, or who should bear the onus of proof on a particular matter (which are connected, but still logically distinct questions). One needs to bear in mind in this regard that both pleading practice and the location of the onus of proof in respect of a particular matter can change over time. Professor Simpson notes, for example, that in mediaeval law, the onus regarding what many might regard as a core element completing the plaintiff's contractual cause of action—proof of breach—lay on the *defendant* in actions in debt.[72] The landscape of these matters is therefore always changing.

The list of analytical questions posed above is obviously not definitive—one might add further questions, so as to distinguish between different types of 'defence' in the broadest sense. A Hohfeldian, for example, might emphasise the difference between matters that affect contractual rights and bestow on defendants corresponding privileges (such as the absence of consideration) and those which negate a court's power to change a defendant's duties through the issue of a court order (such as the lack of jurisdiction in the court, the 'adequacy' of damages as a 'bar' to specific performance, the application of a limitation of actions provision, or the intervention of third-party rights as a principle limiting the award of rescission). One who is interested in the moral distinction between arguments of justification and excuse might seek to engage in further differentiation between different types of 'defence' that accord with the logic of that distinction.[73] A legal historian might distinguish between negating arguments recognised at law and those recognised in equity, and so on.

Is there a 'correct' analytical definition of contractual defence amongst the various usages suggested by the above set of questions? It seems unlikely. To maintain that thesis is to deny the validity of one or more of the questions asked and thereby categorically to prioritise one observer's question over that of another—the interest of the academic or legal theorist over the interest of the practising barrister, or judge, for example. It is also to slip into the trap of essentialism against which Wittgenstein wisely warned us.[74] The question whether there is a more *useful* definition of a defence for legal purposes is a better one, but again raises the question—useful from *whose point of view* and useful *for what ultimate purpose*? Are categorisations that are designed to highlight questions regarding the burden of proof, or the difference between substantive ('merits-based') and procedural arguments, or between arguments that may affect rights and remedies, more or less useful than one another? I doubt it, since each of these can be important to someone, whether at the coalface

[72] Simpson (n 4) 93. Note that the concept of a cause of action here is different to that stated above in the text—conceiving of a cause of action in contract as the facts that prove both the existence of a primary right and its violation by the defendant. This illustrates the fluid nature of the term—see Harris (n 68).

[73] For consideration of the difficult distinction in the tort context, see Goudkamp (n 48) 76–101.

[74] Wittgenstein (n 2).

of legal action, teaching, or academic construction. The best approach to this question, I suggest, is to recognise that within the grand family of arguments that are raised by defendants to defeat claims (call them what you will, but defence is surely as good a word as any), there are a number of important and potentially crucial differences that exist between its respective members and that the differences should be clearly marked, communicated and scrutinised for their utility and rationality. As part of this constant process of self-conscious, diligent scrutiny, it is therefore right to question, as some have done, whether the legal onus of proof regarding limitation matters should lie on the plaintiff, as it currently does in England.[75] At the same time, however, it would be wrong to attack the current rule simply on the basis that limitation is to be classified as a 'defence' in the broad sense. To do so would be to use its definition as a defence in one sense of the word (a negating argument, or an argument seeking to confess and avoid a cause of action) in order to conclude that it should be given the attributes of a defence in another, different sense (a negating argument, the onus of proving which lies on a defendant).

This is not, I stress, to deny the existence of a case for placing the legal onus of proof on a defendant in cases of limitation—but simply to say that the case must be made in terms other than classification. It must be made by addressing the question of onus in its own terms and by comparing the relative strength of the moral and pragmatic arguments in limitation cases with those that are used to justify the location of the onus of proof on defendants in other types of case in which negating factors are in play. These arguments might be arguments of distributive justice, based on the relative moral positions of the parties, one of whom has, after all, demonstrated that another has breached his or her promise; or they might take into account the parties' respective access to the information that is most relevant to the arguments placed in issue.

B. Values

It will be evident from the above that there are at least two serious instabilities that are likely to unhinge attempts to be essentialist about the definition of a defence from the analytical point of view. The first is the one surrounding linguistic meaning and taxonomy in law, which has proven highly problematic in a variety of contexts. This is an instability in the technique of classification—in the way we set about designing our observations and organising the material observed—and the choice of technique is ultimately value-driven. No universal, objective approach to taxonomy is possible because there is no single, interpretive truth (in this instance, any single category of 'defences' to be derived from the relevant material) that exists independently of our own evaluative premises. I rather suspect that, although practitioners and the legal academy share much, they may well remain divided over the proper

[75] *Haward v Fawcetts* [2006] UKHL 9; [2006] 1 WLR 682; *Roger Ward Associates Ltd v Britannia Assets (UK) Ltd* [2013] EWHC 1653 (QB). Both cases involved the application of s 14A of the Limitation Act 1980 in respect of tort claims.

definition of a defence for precisely this reason—some of us are more concerned with one set of questions (how do I plead this matter, who must prove it?) than another (does this matter deny the existence of consent, or provide a reason why that consent should not bind?).

The second problem is the foundational instability surrounding our understanding of the basis of contractual liability, which is a tale as old as the hills.[76] This instability, I have suggested at various points, has had an impact historically on the identification and construction of contractual defence concepts and will probably continue to do so. The way in which the contractual cause of action is understood inevitably affects the way in which 'defences' to that cause of action are identified and framed. Early will theories of contract probably played their own part, alongside the other systemic factors to which we alluded in Section II, in leading writers such as Ballow and Colebrooke to de-emphasise the role of defences. Their approach was understandable. After all, if a liability has truly been subjectively willed and that will is itself the dominant justificatory force behind contractual obligation, then it is only arguments that have no bearing upon the existence of that will that are to be regarded as 'avoidances' of a plaintiff's claim in the sense that has become academically popular. Furthermore, in a very strongly individualistic, libertarian society, the number of such reasons is likely to be small. By contrast, as will theories are tempered by greater objectivity in the construction of party intentions; and as the number of grounds upon which the state is prepared to intervene in commercial markets increases in accordance with modern distributive prerogatives in particular contexts in the twentieth and twenty-first centuries, the more contract becomes like tort law or unjust enrichment; and the more the range of reasons to 'avoid' claims based on an otherwise binding agreement increases.

It is thankfully not necessary for current purposes to decide which underlying theory of contractual liability is correct, or to choose between the various possible constructions of a contractual 'cause of action', which are several. It is sufficient to note that the extent to which contractual obligation is based on subjective or 'objective' intentions of the parties, and the extent to which such intentions can be set aside for social purposes, are both matters that are subject to regular revision and which continue to be the focus of heated debate in the modern day.[77] All we can perhaps say is that will theory still plays a significant role in the modern law (especially in commercial contexts between parties operating at arms' length), but that it is certainly more muted and more tempered by the conscience of social welfarism than

[76] For a comprehensive historical account of the traditions from Aristotle to the late nineteenth century, see Gordley (n 25). More modern landmarks (there are many more than listed) include: L Fuller and W Perdue, 'The Reliance Interest in Contract Damages' (1936) 46 *Yale Law Journal* 52; G Gilmore, *The Death of Contract* (Columbus OH, Ohio State University Press, 1974); C Fried, *Contract as Promise: A Theory of Contractual Obligation* (Cambridge MA, Harvard University Press, 1981); PS Atiyah, *Promises, Morals and Law* (Oxford, Clarendon Press, 1981); and J Raz, 'Is There a Reason to Keep a Promise?' in G Klass, G Letsas and P Saprai (eds), *Philosophical Foundations of Contract Law* (Oxford, Oxford University Press, 2014).

[77] For one modern manifestation of one aspect of this debate, see D McLauchlan, 'The "Drastic" Remedy of Rectification for Unilateral Mistake' (2008) 124 *Law Quarterly Review* 608. See also McLauchlan (n 69 above).

has been the case in former years. The renewed emphasis on objectivity and social welfarism may in turn explain why my trusty eleventh edition of Treitel, like Pollock at the end of the nineteenth century, has distinct chapters not just on inception doctrines such as agreement, consideration and form, but also chapters on mistake, misrepresentation, duress, illegality, statutory invalidity, (in)capacity, and frustration. These matters are now made more visible and more important precisely because they are seen to be substantive questions independent of the existence of agreement; and which need therefore to be considered in their own terms.

IV. CONCLUSION

There is less formal defence 'architecture' in texts on the law of contract than in the law of torts, or the law of unjust enrichments. This phenomenon is both current and historic. It appears to be related to the far greater role that party intentions have had to play in the construction of liabilities in contract law from the day the subject was formally born. When the idea that a contractual cause of action is based on the parties' wills is combined with the popular view that 'defences' avoid, rather than 'deny' a cause of action, the class of contractual 'defences' becomes very narrow. More radically, it might be suggested that there are simply fewer reasons to protect defendants against liabilities which they themselves have had a significant part in creating, than to protect them against liabilities that have been 'imposed' upon them, but that line of reasoning seems less secure and one must be hesitant about endorsing it without engaging in the further thinking that would be required to support its logic.[78]

At the same time, if we ask ourselves the question—'what is a contractual defence?'—we are most unlikely, I have suggested, to get a single, satisfactory answer. This is not necessarily because academics, judges or practitioners are confused, or have not thought hard enough about the matter, but rather because everyone who asks this question tends to focus on different 'essential' features of a doctrine or rule, when classifying and labelling it. They give the term their own interpretation that accords with their own, specific purpose, or set of purposes. The only solution to this definitional problem that I can usefully suggest is that we reject essentialism in matters of definition and meaning and accept instead that there exists in the law of contract a family of 'defence' ideas, the members of which bear significant resemblances to one another, but which also differ from one another in identified,

[78] There is some evidence in the law of tort that reasons that might ordinarily be sufficient to negate a liability are ignored where the liability has been 'voluntarily assumed': see, eg, the (to my mind, questionable) suggestion of Lord Goff in *Henderson v Merrett Syndicates Ltd* [1995] 2 AC 145 (HL) 181 that proof of an 'assumption of responsibility' eliminates the need to consider whether it would be 'fair, just and reasonable' to impose a duty of care on a defendant at the third stage of the *Caparo* test (on which see *Caparo Industries Plc v Dickman* [1990] 2 AC 605 (HL). However, one might well take the view that the fact that it is society that has seen fit to impose an obligation upon a defendant actually provides a stronger reason to hold the defendant forcibly to that obligation and therefore to admit fewer reasons for suspending or extinguishing it. The merits of these arguments sadly lie beyond the scope of the current chapter.

material aspects. If everyone is clear enough about the sense in which they are using the term 'defence'—and about identifying the question or set of questions that is at stake when they seek to classify a doctrine or rule as falling within the reach of that term, then the fact that they collectively use the word to mean different things is largely inconsequential. Our differences only have serious, negative consequences when they are unarticulated or improperly explained, for it is only then that we are at genuine risk of being misunderstood.

3

Good Faith Bargaining in the Shadow of a Form

DANIEL MARKOVITS*

I. INTRODUCTION

CONTRACTS OF ADHESION[1]—CONSUMMATED through standard forms drafted by one party (generally a repeat player) and offered to the other party (generally a less-frequent contractor) on a take-it-or-leave-it basis, without any opportunity for bargaining or negotiation[2]—dominate contemporary contractual practice.[3] It is impossible to say certainly or precisely what proportion of contracts today are contracts of adhesion, but a serious if speculative estimate puts the share at over 99 per cent.[4] And even if this exaggerates matters, contracts of adhesion surely represent a prominent face of contractual practice. Familiar examples include the 'boilerplate' contracts that govern mobile telephone and internet services, credit card and bank deposit agreements, tickets issued at theatres, parking garages, and other public facilities, and also the contracts that govern virtually all major retail purchases.

* This chapter elaborates on ideas first introduced in Chapter 20 of my *Contract Law and Legal Methods* (New York, Foundation Press, 2012). I would like to thank Andy Dyson, James Goudkamp, and Frederick Wilmot-Smith for inviting me to join the seminar out of which this volume has grown and the other participants in that seminar for lively and thoughtful engagement with the ideas in this chapter.

[1] An early discussion, which may have introduced the term 'contract of adhesion' to US lawyers, is E Patterson, 'The Delivery of a Life-Insurance Policy' (1919) 33 *Harvard Law Review* 198, 222. Patterson used the term 'adhesion' only once, and introduced it with the following footnote: 'This expressive term seems worthy of a place in our legal vocabulary. See RENÉ DEMOGUE in MODERN FRENCH LEGAL PHILOSOPHY, 472, 477; 2 M. PLANIOL, TRAITÉ ELÉMENTAIRE DE DROIT CIVIL, § 972. A similar usage occurs in international law. See I OPPENHEIM, INTERNATIONAL LAW, §§ 532, 533'.

[2] This feature likely gave this class of contracts its name. The term 'adhesion' was borrowed from French legal scholars who likely themselves borrowed from the law of treaties, and in particular the practice whereby a group of states negotiating a treaty leave the treaty open for adhesion by additional states, who must, however, take or leave its terms. See AL Corbin, *Corbin on Contracts*, vol 1, Joseph M Perillo (ed), rev edn (St Paul MN, West Publishing Co, 1993) § 1.14.

[3] This definition is standard in its substance. Its language closely tracks T Rakoff, 'Contracts of Adhesion: An Essay in Reconstruction' (1983) 96 *Harvard Law Review* 1173, 1177.

[4] See WD Slawson, 'Standard Form Contracts and Democratic Control Over the Lawmaking Power' (1971) 84 *Harvard Law Review* 529, 529; Slawson went on to say that '[t]he contracting still imagined by courts and law teachers as typical, in which both parties participate in choosing the language of their entire agreement, is no longer of much more than historical importance'.

But even as boilerplate has come to dominate contractual practice, the contract of adhesion lacks a secure theoretical or doctrinal foundation. The possibility thus arises that a party to a contract of adhesion might argue that the contract's adhesive form underwrites a defence against obligations that appear in boilerplate only. The arguments behind such a defence reach deep into the foundations of contract law, concerning both theory and practice. Attention devoted to boilerplate thus pays dividends for the broader agenda of understanding how contract functions in a modern economic and social order. The arguments against enforcing boilerplate also illuminate, by way of presenting an instructive case-study, the generic formal structure of defences in contract.

A brief and stylised account of the grounds of contract sets the stage for the problem with boilerplate. Contractual obligations arise, as chosen obligations, out of the intentions of the contracting parties.[5] This may be read off the face of doctrine: In the United States, for example, the Restatement defines both offer and acceptance in terms of intention or choice.[6] Moreover, theories of contract, whatever their other intramural differences, come together in affirming a close connection between contractual obligation and the free choice to be bound.[7] Theories that ground contract law in the morality of promise place choice at contract's core in order that the law might respect and indeed express human freedom and dignity.[8] And otherwise very different theories that ground contract law in efficiency also place choice at contract's core, this time out of the conviction that freedom of contract promotes efficient preference satisfaction.[9]

Choice's place among the grounds of contract explains why both fraud and duress negate contractual obligations that would otherwise arise. Where a party's consent to a contract is procured through fraud or duress, the consent no longer constitutes her free exercise of her normative powers and no longer reflects her informed and independent judgement that the contractual exchange will make her better off. Fraud and duress thus negate contractual liability because they break the connection between a party's intentions and the free exercise of her reason that ordinarily underwrites contractual obligations: enforcing contracts procured through fraud or duress neither respects rational freedom nor promotes efficient preference satisfaction. The

[5] For an account of the foundational role of party choice—of intentions—in both contract law and theory, see D Markovits, 'Theories of the Common Law of Contracts' (*The Stanford Encyclopedia of Philosophy*, 11 September 2015): plato.stanford.edu/archives/fall2015/entries/contracts-theories/, accessed 3 February 2016.

[6] An offer is thus 'the manifestation of willingness to enter into a bargain, so made as to justify another person in understanding that his assent to that bargain is invited and will conclude it': Restatement (Second) of Contracts § 24 (1981); An acceptance is 'a manifestation of assent to the terms [of the offer] made by the offeree in a manner invited or required by the offer': Restatement (Second) of Contracts § 50 (1981).

[7] Note that the intent to be bound need not involve the intent to establish specifically legal relations. US American law thus emphasises intent to be bound even though it does not require intent to be bound specifically at law. See Restatement (Second) of Contracts § 21 (1981).

[8] See, eg, C Fried, *Contract as Promise: A Theory of Contractual Obligation*, 1st edn (Cambridge MA, Harvard University Press, 1981); Daniel Markovits, 'Contract and Collaboration' (2004) 113 *Yale Law Journal* 1417.

[9] See, eg, A Schwartz and RE Scott, 'Contract Theory and the Limits of Contract Law' (2003) 113 *Yale Law Journal* 541.

unconscionability doctrine possesses a similar character. When a court declines to enforce an unconscionable contract or term, it asserts that (even without fraud or duress, properly-so-called) a combination of unequal or manipulative bargaining and oppressive substantive terms entails that a promisor lacks the relationship to her promise on which enforcing contracts generally depends.

Fraud, duress, and unconscionability thus constitute defences against contractual obligations that are infected by them, in two connected but formally very different senses of the term. Most fundamentally, all three doctrines assert that while the grounds of contractual liability appear to obtain, closer scrutiny dispels the illusion. Moreover, all three doctrines propose that the same basic values—concerning, variously, the connections between rational freedom and normative powers or between party sovereignty and economic efficiency—that generally recommend enforcing contracts counsel against liability when the defences apply. (To enforce a contract in the face of fraud, duress, or unconscionability would thus misappropriate contract law and apply the law against its own deeper purposes.) The defences acquire their character as *defences*, as opposed to being simple or direct *denials* that the elements of contractual liability obtain,[10] on account of this rhetorical structure—which turns precisely the considerations that ordinarily justify liability against liability in particular cases. (This is a matter of rhetoric rather than logic, as the distinction between defences and denials cannot be made out abstractly, in terms of the relations among concepts, but instead importantly invokes both commercial context and, derivatively, the habits of mind and speech adopted by well-socialised lawyers.) Finally, fraud, duress, and unconscionability constitute defences in a second sense also, which is much shallower: parties seeking to avoid contractual liability on account of these doctrines bear the burden of proof with respect to them.[11] The shallow sense in which these doctrines constitute defences follows from the deeper one. It is, in various ways, because efforts to avoid liability by arguing fraud, duress, or unconscionability redeploy the very considerations that ordinarily support contractual obligation in order now to undermine liability that the parties who would employ these defences must assert and prove them. To claim such a defence is, in effect, to concede a prima facie case that the obligation one wishes to avoid might be real.

Where do contracts of adhesion stand with respect to these matters? Might a party to a contract avoid enforcement of terms that appear only in boilerplate? And if she might avoid liability for boilerplate terms, might she proceed specifically on the model of a defence just outlined—that is, on the ground that the nature

[10] Earlier volumes in this series have also taken up this distinction. See, eg, A Dyson, J Goudkamp and F Wilmot-Smith, 'Central Issues in the Law of Tort Defences' and G Virgo, 'Justifying Necessity as a Defence in Tort Law' in A Dyson, J Goudkamp and F Wilmot-Smith (eds), *Defences in Tort* (Oxford, Hart Publishing, 2015) 6 and 139 respectively; A Dyson, J Goudkamp and F Wilmot-Smith, 'Defences in Unjust Enrichment: Questions and Theme' in A Dyson, J Goudkamp and F Wilmot-Smith (eds), *Defences in Unjust Enrichment* (Oxford, Hart Publishing, 2016) 3.

[11] For fraud, see, eg, *Duplisse v Devino*, 96 Conn App 673, 680, 902 A 2d 30 (2006). Indeed, the plaintiff must prove certain elements of fraud not just by a preponderance of the evidence but rather by clear and satisfactory or clear, precise and unequivocal evidence: *Duplisse v Devino*, 96 Conn App 673, 681, 902 A 2d 30 (2006). For duress, see, eg, *Mullins v TestAmerica, Inc*, 564 F 3d 386, 411 (5th Cir 2009). For unconscionability, see, eg, *RF Daddario & Sons, Inc v Shelansky*, 123 Conn App 725, 742 (2010).

of her engagement with a form contract (like assent procured by fraud, duress, or unconscionability) entails that enforcing boilerplate against her undermines rather than promotes the values that ordinarily sustain contractual obligations?

An august line of argument seeks to answer 'yes' to all these questions. As early as 1873, the United States Supreme Court, considering a form contract made between a drover and the New York Central Railroad, observed that the drover, being 'only one individual of a million', could not 'afford to higgle or stand out',[12] and, partly for this reason, struck down a contractual limitation on the Railroad's liability.[13] Moreover, although more recent decisions, especially in the United States, have become friendlier to boilerplate, scholars increasingly embrace and expand upon earlier doubts and reject contemporary doctrine. Prominent journals now devote entire issues to investigating the troubles with form contracts;[14] and prominent scholars devote entire books to attacking boilerplate.[15] The dispute about enforcing boilerplate has even escaped professional or elite discourse, as form contracts have become a potent political symbol for the corporate capture of public institutions and a broader neoliberal effort to displace democratic politics with economic power and then to naturalise resulting arrangements through a thin and formal conception of free choice.[16]

These pages reassess the lawyerly debate concerning boilerplate. They argue that the debate has reached an impasse because it is fundamentally misconceived. Both sides in the debate over enforcing form contracts imagine that boilerplate's function, within the logic of the contracting situations in which form contracts arise, is to fix contractual rights once-and-for-all, in a manner that might be either enforced or invalidated. Both sides in the debate agree, in other words, that where a party avoids liability for boilerplate, she does so on the model of a defence. In fact, however, the immanent logic of form contracting supports a structurally different account of boilerplate. On the correct view, a party that seeks to avoid enforcement of boilerplate does not offer a defence against contractual obligation so much as directly deny that the boilerplate belongs in the contract to begin with. This approach squares the legal regulation of boilerplate with both the formal logic of contractual doctrine and the economic and social logic of contractual practice. Theoretical clarity about the nature of defences in contract law thus promotes both doctrinal clarity about contracts of adhesion and, ultimately, better policies for regulating boilerplate.

II. THE PROBLEM OF THE FORM IN ITSELF

Contracts of adhesion seek, through boilerplate, to insert many and highly various substantive terms into the contractual relations that they establish. This is unsurprising,

[12] *Railroad Company v Lockwood*, 84 US 357, 379 (1873).

[13] ibid 384.

[14] See O Ben-Shahar, 'Boilerplate: Foundations of Market Contracts Symposium' (2006) 104 *Michigan Law Review* 821–1246.

[15] See MJ Radin, *Boilerplate: The Fine Print, Vanishing Rights, and the Rule of Law* (Princeton NJ, Princeton University Press, 2013).

[16] See, eg, Alliance for Justice, 'Lost in the Fine Print (2014)': www.afj.org/multimedia/first-monday-films/films/lost-in-the-fine-print, accessed 3 February 2016.

given boilerplate's widespread use. But the terms thus inserted vary so substantially that it is almost certainly a mistake to treat them all together, as instances of a single unified phenomenon.

On the one hand, boilerplate employs its dubious procedures to pursue arrangements whose substance is unseemly and quite possibly unacceptable entirely apart from, and indeed independent of, their adhesive form. Boilerplate thus sometimes seeks to alter and especially to limit a term-taker's procedural options in disputes regarding a form contract—by imposing forum selection clauses, mandating arbitration, and even precluding aggregation of claims.[17] Boilerplate may also seek to exculpate term-makers from liability for harms, including even personal injury, caused by their negligence.[18] Boilerplate may even seek to control a term-taker's statutory rights, including basic or otherwise quasi-constitutional rights, concerning for example anti-discrimination law, typically by compelling arbitration of claims in respect of such rights.[19] Indeed, contracts of adhesion can combine these schemes, as when they require term-takers wishing to contest the waivers that they impose to do so exclusively in arbitral fora rather than in courts. In these and other similar instances, it is reasonable to ask whether the legal effects that boilerplate seeks to accomplish might properly be brought about by contract at all, including even where contract proceeds by individuated bargaining. 'Rights deletion' of this sort,[20] especially when accomplished on a massive scale, is a serious business. The law should not rush to welcome it; and boilerplate's legitimacy is thus doubly undermined—by the concatenation of the procedural defects of bargaining associated with all form contracts and the substantive defects concerning inalienability associated with the particular clauses that the forms in question contain.

On the other hand, boilerplate also elaborates contractual terms that raise no substantive concerns at all and would unquestionably bind if produced through individually tailored bargains. In the consumer context, for example, contracts of adhesion familiarly disclaim warranties, forswear a seller's liability for consequential damages, and more generally limit a buyer's remedies to the repair or replacement of defective products.[21] Much less familiarly, adhesive licences of intellectual property abrogate licensees' rights to modify or copy, of a sort that intellectual property law would otherwise protect, including rights to derivative (even critical) and fair use.[22] And in the context of financial services, contracts of adhesion commonly bundle primary financial services such as credit cards or checking accounts with secondary services—such as delayed repayment plans or overdraft protection—that substantially increase the expected costs consumers of the primary services will bear.[23] These and

[17] On forum selection, see, eg, *Carnival Cruise Lines, Inc v Shute*, 499 US 585 (1991). On arbitration and aggregation, see, eg, *AT&T Mobility LLC v Concepcion*, 563 US 333 (2011).

[18] See, eg, *Jordan v Diamond Equip & Supply Co*, 207 SW 3d 525 (Ark 2005).

[19] See, eg, *Cooper v MRM Inv Co*, 367 F 3d 493 (6th Cir 2004).

[20] The term comes from Margaret Jane Radin: see Radin (n 15).

[21] Such limitations of remedy are so common that they have triggered a statutory response, designed to deal with cases in which a remedy so limited 'fails of its essential purpose'. See *Uniform Commercial Code* § 2–719(2).

[22] For a discussion, see Radin (n 15) 168–70.

[23] These secondary services have become so prevalent in the United States that they have triggered a substantial regulatory and publicity response from the new Consumer Financial Protection Bureau.

myriad similar adjustments of interests between contracting parties—reallocations of contractual surplus between buyers and their sellers—might uncontroversially be achieved by individually dickered, bespoke contractual bargains. Indeed, it belongs to the essence of contract that contracting parties might adjust their bargains to reallocate gains from trade, however—given their creativity and relative bargaining power—they agree. Contracts of adhesion that belong to this second class thus squarely pose the question whether the adhesion form in itself undermines contractual authority and underwrites a case against enforcing form contracts.

This is a case, therefore, in which substantive variety requires drawing formal distinctions. Some mass-produced form contracts catalyse or, to change metaphors, leverage already and independently dubious contractual practices to transform otherwise narrow encroachments on important but isolated rights into wide-ranging schemes of rights deletion. Evaluating these contracts of adhesion therefore requires coming to grips with the problem of market-inalienability, both in the individual instance and, especially, where coordinated patterns of conduct cause the costs of collective alienation to exceed the sum of the cost of individual alienation, taken one-person-at-a-time. But other contracts of adhesion merely regularise and generalise arrangements that would be individually unobjectionable if struck as dickered bargains. And a defence against enforcing a form contract of this sort must meet the more demanding burden of objecting against adhesive arrangements directly and narrowly and on account specifically of their formal character.

Form contracts of this variety thus raise what might be called the problem of the form in itself: when and how might the adhesive form in itself underwrite scepticism about enforcing the otherwise legitimate substantive obligations that form contracts seek to establish?

III. BEGUILED BY FORM

Conventional analyses of this problem, whatever their many and wide-ranging disagreements, all focus exclusively on the forms through which contracts of adhesion operate—on the processes that generate agreement on the form and on the terms by which the form structures the contractual relationship. Some views regard a term-taker's agreement on or consent to a form contract as fundamentally inauthentic and thus ineffectual; other, contrary views regard agreement on the form as perfectly valid and indeed as effective in the ordinary way in which bespoke agreement (or consent) might adjust legal rights. Similarly, some views regard contracts of adhesion as naturally and indeed almost inevitably exploitative and thus insist that un-dickered terms be displaced by more fair-minded alternatives; other, contrary views regard form contracts as solving genuine problems of administrative and contractual coordination and thus incline to grant un-dickered terms precisely the same respect that contract law grants bespoke bargains.

See, eg, D Rutherford, 'Consumer Advisory: You've Got Options when it comes to Overdraft' (*Consumer Financial Protection Bureau*, 28 April 2015): www.consumerfinance.gov/blog/category/overdrafts/, accessed 3 February 2016.

All these views, however, remain beguiled by the form, in the sense that they regard the contractual relationships established by contracts of adhesion as encapsulated in, and indeed exhausted by, the forms that these contracts employ. Whatever intramural differences separate these familiar views, they thus all operate in the thrall of the form. In the end, this prevents analyses of contracts of adhesion, as commonly conceived, from settling on a satisfactory conclusion.

Begin to see this by considering the quality of a term-taker's consent to a form contract. The conventional framing of disputes concerning the term-taker's consent precludes any non-conclusory disposition of the disputes so framed.

The term-taker will typically know and understand a few of the form's most salient terms—the price in a contract for consumer goods, for example, or the primary interest rate in a financial services contract. Her consent to these terms is as full-throated and therefore effective as consent in archetypical bespoke contracts, and the adhesive form will underwrite no defence against their enforcement. (The fact that she could not dicker over these salient terms—because the term-maker flatly refused, including through its organisational structure, even to engage in bargaining over them[24]—does not by itself underwrite a defence against enforcement. After all, it is no defence against a conventional, bespoke contract that the offeror refused to adjust to, or even to entertain, counteroffers but instead insisted on his terms or none. Consent may be real even where the alternatives are stark.) However, the term-taker typically will not understand or even know of the form's remaining terms—concerning warranties, perhaps, and certainly concerning limitations of remedy, or secondary financial services, or myriad other matters. Indeed, these terms will—for the term-taker—typically be not just known but rather unknown unknowns: she will not know even that terms of this sort exist or indeed that they could exist. She cannot, therefore, full-throatedly consent to these hidden terms, at least in the ordinary, affirmative sense in which the parties to bespoke contracts consent to the terms that they mutually create and on which their minds meet.

Some critics of contracts of adhesion argue, from these facts, to a blanket defence against enforcement of a form contract's unknown terms.[25] According to this argument, the consent to the unknown terms is improperly induced by the term-maker, and the principles of contract law that generally connect consent to obligation thus

[24] Often, a term-taker confronting a contract of adhesion cannot even find an agent of the term-maker who is authorised to bargain over or otherwise vary the terms in the term-maker's form.

[25] Analogous considerations have led others, including some scholars who favour enforcing contracts of adhesion, to proceed under a banner other than contract proper. Indeed, it is by now a banality that, 'on a theoretical level, boilerplate is a legal phenomenon different from contract': O Ben-Shahar, 'Preface Or: A Boilerplate Introduction' in O Ben-Shahar (ed), *Boilerplate: The Foundation of Market Contracts* (New York, Cambridge University Press, 2007) ix, xiv; Instead, contracts of adhesion have been variously analogised to statutes: see Slawson (n 4) 529; products: see A Schwartz and L Wilde, 'Intervening in Markets on the Basis of Imperfect Information: A Legal and Economic Analysis' (1979) 127 *University of Pennsylvania Law Review* 630; and even property: see H Smith, 'Modularity in Contracts: Boilerplate and Information Flow' in O Ben-Shahar (ibid) 163–75. Indeed, boilerplate's departure from the contract form is self-consciously celebrated in the interstices of some analyses, for example in the thought that boilerplate's efficiency is a direct result of its abandoning the intensiveness of communication that characterises contract-proper in favour of a more extensive form of expression: see H Smith, 'Modularity in Contracts: Boilerplate and Information Flow' (ibid) 163.

mitigate against obligation with respect to the unknown terms. The merely verbal formulations favoured by those who would enforce form contracts in full—under headings such as 'assent' and 'constructive' or 'hypothetical' consent[26]—cannot sustain an inference from factual ignorance of terms' very existence to normative endorsement of their enforcement. Instead of being the subject of an agreement, a form's unknown terms are flatly and unilaterally imposed by term-makers, the critics say. Accordingly, contract terms that never escape the form into the consciousness (no matter how attenuated) of the term-taker quite simply carry no contractual weight. The unknown terms are at most suggestions for how courts might fill the contractual gaps that lie between a form contract's salient terms, and they should have no bearing on contractual obligation save insofar as the court independently endorses them on first principles. Some prominent critics, who follow this line of thought, have gone so far as to propose that the portions of contracts of adhesion that the term-taker cannot reasonably be expected to read and understand should be treated as 'presumptively unenforceable',[27] so that they become binding only insofar as they comply with standards in the 'public interest'.[28]

Those who would fully enforce contracts of adhesion, for their part, flatly reject these arguments.[29] These champions of form contracts insist that nothing in the nature of the general normative power to consent precludes effectively consenting generically to whatever obligations a contractual text contains, including obligations that are unknown and even unsurmised. There is, moreover, nothing hypothetical or implied about such consent; on the contrary, the consent (including to the unsurmised terms) is as actual and express as any consent can be. Indeed, consent to these terms, and not just to the salient terms, may be read off the face of the form, as it were. A term-taker confronted with boilerplate cannot reasonably conclude anything other than that she is being presented with terms whose content she does not know and indeed whose nature she does not know of. Moreover, boilerplate contract terms do not differ, in this respect, from any number of physical properties of goods sold on mass markets. A consumer who buys a toaster, for example, does not know the wattage of its heating element and knows still less respecting the resistance of the element's metal or its stability in the face of repeated heating and cooling (indeed, she likely will not know even that such properties of heating elements exist and are measurable). But her ignorance, standing alone, cannot defeat contractual obligations that are cast and calibrated in terms of these features. (And physical properties that surprise a consumer but do not defeat a good's merchantability cannot

[26] For a criticism of these efforts, see Radin (n 15) 82–84, 93–96.

[27] This was Todd Rakoff's view. See Rakoff (n 3). He continues to stand by it today and the quoted language was written recently. See TD Rakoff, 'The Law and Sociology of Boilerplate' in Ben-Shahar (ed), *Boilerplate: The Foundation of Market Contracts* (n 25) 200, 200.

[28] Slawson (n 4) 566.

[29] See, eg, RE Barnett, 'Consenting to Form Contracts' (2002) 71 *Fordham Law Review* 627. Moreover, champions of form contracting point out that those who object to contracts of adhesion on the grounds that term-takers do not consent nevertheless gravitate towards alternative regimes—most notably, replacing adhesive terms with terms provided by law, in the public interest—that retreat from contract entirely and merely substitute one non-contractual order for another. As Randy Barnett has observed, this approach, if anything 'moves an agreement much further from the consent of the parties and towards a regime in which the legal system supplies terms that others think best': RE Barnett (ibid) 734.

underwrite a defence against her own performance obligations.) Unknown terms in form contracts are no different.

Finally, form contracts' champions may observe that the distinction between reasonable and unreasonable terms—or the related idea of the term-taker's reasonable expectations—does little to advance the argument at this point. There exists, familiarly, a wide range of reasonable diversity in contract terms. Where within this reasonable diversity a particular contract falls might materially, and indeed even dominantly, determine the division of contractual surplus between buyer and seller (term-taker and term-maker) that the contract establishes. (Moreover, as past practice informs present consumer expectations, term-makers may move terms around within this reasonable range almost at their discretion and so capture surplus for themselves over time.) The range of reasonable expectations, in a form contract, thus expands to cover effectively the entire range of outcomes that might be enforced if achieved through bespoke contracting (which, by construction, is the entire range of outcomes in issue). Accordingly, boilerplate should be unenforceable only when it is sufficiently substantively oppressive or outrageous as to exceed the limits of freedom of contract, which is to say that the adhesive form should never itself constitute a defence against contractual obligation.

The debate concerning boilerplate, framed in this fashion as a dispute about the effectiveness of consent, admits no stable resolution. Indeed, the familiar frame frustrates progress. The grounds of the frustration, moreover, sound in contract law's deepest foundations. It has been familiar at least since the realist critique of classical formalism's subjective approach to offer and acceptance (and the related insistence that offers and acceptances constitute mirror images of each other) that contract law cannot possibly require contracting parties' minds actually to meet on all particulars of their agreements. (The classical formalists in fact also understood this well and embraced quasi-contract as a release valve when the pressure created by their overly narrow and rigorous conception of orthodox contractual intent became unbearable.)[30] Instead, contractual intentions—including consent to contractual terms—must be constructed according to a rule of reason, which imputes intent to be bound to terms that never penetrate contracting parties' actual consciousness. This straightforwardly entails that boilerplate's champions are right in theory—in respect of the concepts out of which contract law builds obligations. There is no qualitative difference—or difference in kind—between a term-taker's consent to a contract of adhesion and the consent that parties' ordinarily and uncontroversially give in bespoke contracts. But the general, abstract victory has no value in deciding particular, concrete cases and thus will hardly move those who doubt the validity of contracts of adhesion in practice. To show that contracts of adhesion can bind without doing violence to the most abstract form of contract obligation is necessary but hardly sufficient for showing that any particular contract of adhesion does bind a term-taker, when the methods of imputing intent that govern bespoke contracting are applied to boilerplate. Boilerplate's champions in the end achieve nothing more than a possibility theorem, and this advances the case for enforcing particular contracts

[30] See, eg, *Plate v Durst*, 24 SE 580 (W Va 1896).

of adhesion hardly at all. Certainly boilerplate's critics remain free to advance their reform projects undaunted.

Perhaps for this reason, the conventional dispute concerning contracts of adhesion shifts to a second, parallel ground, which sets aside form—and formal concepts such as consent—in order expressly to take up contractual function. Boilerplate's critics thus argue—often vehemently—that contracts of adhesion permit term-makers to exploit term-takers, in a fashion that contract law should not permit (even acknowledging that a deep commitment to freedom of contract precludes imposing any comprehensive standard of substantive justice on contracts). Boilerplate's defenders answer by questioning whether term-makers really possess the exploitative agenda that boilerplate's critics suppose and by elaborating a counter-narrative of boilerplate's appeal that sounds in more salutary motives.

Critics of boilerplate thus emphasise bargaining inequalities between term-makers and term-takers that find their roots in the transactions costs of drafting and understanding agreements, especially in their technical details. Because the repeat-players (typically firms) who draft forms can spread these costs out over many contracts (and because they may antecedently have expertise and education that anyway lowers these costs for them), they may craft forms to incorporate contract terms that favour their own interests. And because the one-shot players (typically natural persons) who receive form contracts do so rarely, or at least only intermittently, they cannot afford the costs of identifying or negotiating for alternative terms that better promote their interests. In many cases, term-takers cannot afford even the costs of reading and understanding all but a few of the terms (price, quantity) in the forms that they receive. Repeat players can therefore use forms to increase their share of the contractual surplus, including perhaps even in exploitative ways. Moreover, these methods of capturing surplus may be privately profitable for the repeat players even though they are inefficient and therefore socially undesirable—the increase in the share of contractual surplus that these terms allocate to the term-maker may outweigh the decrease that the terms impose on the overall size of the surplus to which this share is applied. Finally, the mechanisms through which bargaining ordinarily polices the contents of agreements—the back-and-forth by which self-interested parties ensure that their contracts' terms maximise joint surplus and divide surplus in a fashion that makes both parties better off than any available alternative—do not apply in form contracting. The transactions costs of reading and understanding complex forms are too high for term-takers effectively to assess or to police their bargains. Accordingly, even if term-takers' consent is normatively effective (see the earlier discussion), it cannot play its conventional instrumental role in promoting severally acceptable and jointly optimal contract terms. Transactions costs permit term-makers to behave unfairly and inefficiently against term-takers, and contract quality consequently goes down.

Form contracting's champions acknowledge that this can happen, and every lawyer knows of cases involving form contracts that are indefensibly one-sided and inefficient.[31] But it is far from clear that contracts of adhesion should be expected

[31] A prominent US American example is the disclaimer of warranty and limitation of liability discussed in *Henningsen v Bloomfield Motors, Inc* 32 NJ 382, 161 A 2d 69 (NJ 1960).

generally to display these vices or, in particular, to display them to a greater degree than bespoke contracts do (as the functionalist critique of boilerplate requires). To begin with, many of the same mechanisms that discipline mass-markets in other respects may also serve to discipline form contracts, in ways that limit exploitation and inefficiency. Competition among term-makers—which naturally extends not just to product but also to contract quality—exerts pressure to craft forms that maximise surplus and also drives down the share of surplus that the term-makers keep for themselves. (Real-world cases of this mechanism exist, moreover: modern car manufacturers thus expressly and prominently compete in their warranties, offering much more generous terms than the law requires.) Furthermore, many aspects of product quality—concerning the durability of hidden internal parts, for example—are no more salient to consumers than contract quality is. Finally, a relatively small proportion of sophisticated term-takers—who read and understand form contracts and thus accurately value their terms—can under certain conditions sustain market equilibria in which term-makers provide efficient and fair terms for all term-takers.[32] Form contracting thus does not entail and need not invite that term-makers distinctively exploit term-takers.

Moreover, nothing in the market structures in which form contracts flourish suggests that the balance of these considerations more naturally favours exploitation there than elsewhere. Although both courts and commentators who object to form contracts often emphasise a term-makers' monopoly power,[33] monopolists in fact have no special reason to draft sub-optimal non-salient contract terms. A monopolist, unlike a seller in a competitive market, can extract surplus from her customers. Her profits depend on demand rather than just costs, and she therefore wishes to face as large an aggregate demand as she can, in order to maximise the surplus out of which she may extract her monopoly rents. Typically, the monopolist will do so by making her product as appealing to her customers as she can, including by making her contracts as appealing to term-takers as she can. None of this denies that the monopolist seeks to exploit her customers. But there is no simple, general reason to think that contracts of adhesion add to her exploitative powers or that their use indicates that exploitation is occurring. And insofar as a monopolist's form contracts do exploit term-takers, they will likely do so through the price term, whose high salience defeats the conventional criticisms of contracts of adhesion.

Finally, and perhaps most importantly, contracts of adhesion have an appealing side that directly counterbalances their demerits. To begin with, they are 'a rational and economically efficient response to the rapidity of market transactions and the high cost of negotiations'[34] in a mass-consumption economy. Moreover, reduced direct transactions costs–reduced costs of fixing the terms of a bargain—do not exhaust the benefits offered by form contracts. Thus, as has long been familiar, form contracts also serve much more generally to 'stabilise [firms'] market relationships

[32] See A Schwartz and L Wilde, 'Imperfect Information in Markets for Contract Terms: The Examples of Warranties and Security Interests' (1983) 69 *Virginia Law Review* 1387.

[33] See, eg, *Henningsen v Bloomfield* (n 31).

[34] Corbin (n 2). This has not been lost on a wide range of courts. See, eg, *Lackey v Green Tree Fin Corp*, 330 SC 388, 395–96 (SC Ct App 1998).

and serve the needs of a hierarchical and internally segmented [firm] structure'.[35] They are a technique of firm management: for example, form contracts facilitate coordination among a firm's several departments (sales, collection, customer service, and so on), and they help to control wayward agents who might otherwise bind a firm in undesirable ways.[36] And customers, all else being equal, prefer to deal with well-managed rather than poorly managed firms, as good management reduces firms' costs and increases the quality of their outputs and thus increases the contractual surplus out of which customers take their shares. These considerations may be compounded—so much so that it seems plausible that bespoke contracting is just as inefficient in a mass-market economy containing large and complex firms as bespoke manufacturing. The benefits of contracts of adhesion, moreover, redound not only to term-makers but to term-takers also. Indeed, it is tempting to say that contracts of adhesion permit term-takers—perhaps even knowingly—to exploit mechanisms whose details they do not fully understand in order to reduce the costs of achieving their ends. At the very least, these benefits offset the costs that form contracts impose on term-takers, so that the balance of benefit and burden favours embracing the adhesion form in many contexts and may even favour embracing contracts of adhesion quite generally. Even as boilerplate's critics advance a serious argument against contracts of adhesion, boilerplate's champions mount a serious reply.

Arguments about contracts of adhesion that focus narrowly on the form itself thus draw to a standstill. Critics of form contracting cannot discern a categorical distinction between adhesive and bespoke arrangements, in respect either of consent to enter them or exploitation in their operation. At the same time, contracts of adhesion's champions cannot fully or conclusively dispel the critics' sense—which endures even though it finds no precise objection to latch onto—that something remains amiss in form contracting. Debates about form contracts thus reach a familiar impasse: contracts of adhesion may be correlated with contractual infirmities that must be identified without reference to the adhesion form, but they are not constitutive of any distinctive infirmities in their own right. There is thus no intrinsic or general defect in contracts of adhesion, so that whatever objections arise in particular cases must be subsumed under other contract-law defences for non-performance in circumstances that are identified, finally, on independent grounds.[37] Indeed, the

[35] Rakoff (n 3) 1220.

[36] These examples come from Rakoff (n 3) 1222–23.

[37] Richard Posner has gone so far as to observe that '[i]f a clause really is buried in illegible "fine print"—or if it plainly is neither intended nor likely to be read by the other party—this circumstance may support an inference of fraud, and fraud is a defence to a contract. There was no burial in fine print here. The print is small, but it is not fine; it is large enough that even the pale copies in the appendix on appeal can be read comfortably by the author of this opinion, with his heavily corrected middle-aged eyesight': *Northwestern National Ins Co v Donovan*, 916 F 2d 372, 377 (7th Cir 1990). Other courts have adopted a similar approach. See, eg, *Seus v John Nuveen & Co*, 146 F 3d 175, 184 (3d Cir 1998); *Morris v Snappy Cart Rental, Inc*, 84 NY 2d 21, 30 (1994); *Aviall, Inc v Ryder System, Inc*, 913 F Supp 826, 832 (SDNY 1996) ('A court may refuse to enforce an agreement only if the contract is the product of procedural unfairness and suffers from one of the enumerated substantive defects. If either feature is absent, the court will enforce the contract.') See also Restatement (Second) of Contracts s 211 cmt c (1981). Thus Farnsworth notes that '[t]he mere fact that [a] contract is one of adhesion is not generally regarded as fatal': EA Farnsworth, *Contracts*, 4th rev edn (New York, Panel Publishers, 2004) § 4.28, 585.

correlation may turn out to be so weak as to make it a mistake to give the category *contracts of adhesion* any free-standing doctrinal status in the law.

IV. BARGAINING IN THE SHADOW OF A FORM

The two sides in the conventional dispute over contracts of adhesion, whatever their subsequent differences, set out from a shared premise: they each treat the form itself as the alpha and the omega of the legal relationship that a contract of adhesion establishes. That is, they each conceive of the parties' contract-making as constituted and exhausted by the form. Once again, both sides of the conventional dispute over contracts of adhesion proceed in the thrall of the form.

The lived experience of form contracting is very different, however. Indeed, economic and social life under form contracts in fact involves substantial bargaining, and even bespoke adjustment of exchange relations … only not in connection with the boilerplate form. To make headway in understanding and regulating form contracts, legal theory and doctrine must catch up and attend to this lived experience.

Begin by revisiting the different paths along which bespoke and adhesive contracts are made. In bespoke contracting, the parties' minds meet on many terms—in principle on all terms recorded in a contractual writing; in form contracting, by contrast, the parties' minds meet on only a very few of their writing's terms—price, perhaps, and quantity. Moreover, the processes that generate contracts of adhesion fail quite generally to trigger the relational morality of negotiations. Term-makers and term-takers do not participate in any processes of reciprocal adjustment in forming contracts of adhesion, or indeed engage each other at all. Instead, each party to such contracts acts purely unilaterally, and they make their contracts of adhesion not together, but severally.[38] It is almost, although of course not precisely, as if contracts of adhesion lack offer and acceptance. Perhaps more helpfully put, contracts of adhesion involve offer and acceptance not concretely, through the interlocking and thus reciprocally adjusting intentions of actual contract partners, but in a purely abstract sense only. Term-makers' offers are not directed at concrete term-takers (they neither engage any particular term-takers nor are the products of a prior engagement with term-takers) but are in substance just general statements of terms on which the term-makers are willing to proceed. And term-takers' acceptances arise without any sense that that they have had a hand in creating the arrangement that they are accepting. The parties thus proceed to performance before they have completed contracting, in the conventional sense. This is perhaps most vividly illustrated by the case in which contracts of adhesion arise between two term-makers who each treat the other as a term-taker, a scenario commonly called the battle of the forms. In this case, the offer and acceptance quite literally fail to engage each other, and the parties commence performance even though they each openly deny, through their forms, that their

[38] This is not to deny that term-makers, in particular, take into account the desires of term-takers when they draft contract terms. Of course they do, and they may even compete with other term-makers to draft attractive terms. But term-makers do not respond to individual term-takers or indeed enter into any pre-contractual relations with individual term-takers.

efforts at contract formation have been successful. If a contract arises at all in such cases, it arises only on the model of two ships crashing in the night.[39]

Next consider the performance of form contracts. Concrete relations nevertheless do arise in and around contracts of adhesion, even in cases in which the parties display the most extreme asymmetries of sophistication and scale. Both consumers and the companies whose customers they are commonly conceive of themselves as in a (commercial) relationship—just ask any depositor and her bank, tenant and her landlord, or subscriber and her mobile telephone company. Indeed, these relationships commonly involve individual adjustments and even extensive individualisation. Consumers return unwanted or defective goods, request exemptions from or contest fees and other fines, and seek early cancellations of subscriptions or even renegotiations of prices. Sellers, for their parts, establish entire departments or divisions—typically called 'customer service' or 'customer complaints'—dedicated to answering (sometimes to satisfy and sometimes to disappoint) consumers' demands.

This raises the question how to understand what goes on between customer service departments and the consumers whose demands and complaints they engage. Those who proceed in the thrall of the form understand customer service departments as providing a kind of in-house adjudication of contractual rights that are conclusively established by boilerplate. This view naturally invites scepticism about the performance of the complaints process, on the grounds that firms serve as judges in their own cases. But actual behaviour in these engagements—including by firms' customer service agents—rejects this view in favour of another. Firms commonly grant customer requests that boilerplate forms expressly repudiate, and they do so following a process that much more nearly resembles the constituting of new rights than the identification of rights already fixed by the form.[40] The best account of this back-and-forth thus understands it as an instance of bargaining—now bespoke—between the firm and its customers.[41] This is bargaining in the shadow of the form.

Moreover, bargaining in the shadow of the form typically takes up precisely those matters—warranties, fees and fines, early cancellation—that were earlier relegated

[39] Recent empirical work suggests that the commonplace morality of contract reflects this characterisation. When ordinary people contract, they view bespoke bargaining as a substantial source of an agreement's authority. Thus in one recent experiment, subjects who were more actively engaged in the pre-consent phase of contract-making were more motivated to perform their contracts than subjects who had made contracts of adhesion. See Z Eigen, 'When and Why Individuals Obey Form-Adhesive Contracts: Experimental Evidence of Consent, Compliance, Promise, and Performance' (2012) 41 *The Journal of Legal Studies* 67. Moreover, appeals to morality generated performance more effectively when contracts were dickered than when they arose through adhesion.

[40] Astonishingly little is known about the workings of customer service departments. The best current treatment is R Van Loo, 'The Corporation as Courthouse' (2016) *Yale Journal on Regulation* (forthcoming). Van Loo observes that in spite of all the attention paid to consumer arbitration, the number of claims processed by customer complaints departments exceeds the number processed by arbitration by many orders of magnitude.

[41] One must resist the urge to characterise in-firm complaint resolution on the model of adjudication—that is, as a process that takes the boilerplate terms to establish the parties' respective rights and seeks to determine what these terms require when they are applied to the facts that have developed. The firm's customer complaints department is itself a party with interest in the dispute rather than a neutral judge or arbitrator. Further, as the discussions that follow reveal, adjudication is simply not how customer complaints are in fact processed.

to the fine print of the form. This suits the functionalist logic of form contracting—in particular by conserving the transactions costs required for negotiation. A form contract's few salient terms—the prices and quantities that are bargained for ex ante—are cheaply arrived at and suffice to govern the overwhelming majority of the relations that these contracts establish. In these cases, the term-taker pays the price and receives satisfactory goods or services in exchange, and nothing further needs to be arranged. Accordingly, rather than incurring the much greater transactions costs required to reach actual, bespoke agreement on the non-salient boilerplate terms ex ante in every instance, including in the majority of cases in which they prove irrelevant, the contracts instead displace bargaining concerning these terms to renegotiation, ex post, where they can concentrate negotiating resources on the instances in which the terms become actually relevant. At the same time, the negotiations that this regime requires—and the return to individual tailoring that it involves—arises against a richer informational backdrop than was reasonably available at earlier stages in the contracting process. One might thus say that instead of *concluding* bargaining, as the model of bespoke contracting supposes, a form contract *initiates* bargaining, at least concerning these non-salient terms. In practice, then, the substantive content of a contract of adhesion is fixed not just by the form itself, but also by subsequent bargaining in the shadow of the form.

The ex post negotiations associated with customer complaint resolution are both common and complicated. Once again, just as retailers commonly reject reasonable consumer complaints, so they also commonly acquiesce to complaining consumers' demands, including when doing so provides consumers with benefits that the boilerplate in sales contracts expressly denies them.[42] The liberal return policies adopted by many retailers represent only the most obvious example of this practice. Others include policies that waive published change fees for airline ticket holders, relieve complaining credit card holders of fees triggered by occasional and accidental late payments, and enable credit card holders to renegotiate repayment schedules (and even interest rates) on their debt and patients to negotiate ex post price reductions for medical care.[43] In some firms, customer service policies are astonishingly liberal: Ritz-Carlton hotels permit every employee to spend up to US$2,000 to satisfy a complaining guest.[44] And in some industries, such liberality appears to be pervasive: according to one report, nearly 90 per cent of credit card holders who seek waivers of late-payment fees receive relief.[45]

The sociological fact of renegotiation has recently been noticed by some contracts scholars, who have sought to incorporate it into functionalist analyses of contracts of

[42] An early and prominent study of related behaviour is S Macaulay, 'Non-Contractual Relations in Business: A Preliminary Study' (1963) 28 *American Sociological Review* 1.

[43] These examples come from JS Johnston, 'Cooperative Negotiations in the Shadow of Boilerplate' in Ben-Shahar (ed), *Boilerplate: The Foundation of Market Contracts* (n 25) 14–16. See also JS Johnston, 'The Return of Bargain: An Economic theory of How Standard-Form Contracts Enable Cooperative Negotiation between Business and Consumer' (2006) 104 *Michigan Law Review* 857.

[44] See Van Loo (n 40) (text accompanying n 57).

[45] Van Loo documents these incentives, and firms' awareness of them, in considerable detail: ibid.

adhesion.[46] These analyses emphasise that when consumer opportunism is difficult for courts to verify, firms may wish to retain broad discretion to deny certain benefits to consumers whom they regard as behaving opportunistically or in some other way in bad faith. On the other hand, insofar as firms have a reputational interest in appearing fair or even generous, they may wish to extend discretionary benefits to consumers whom they regard as proceeding in good faith or in some other way as desirable future customers. These reputational interests may be immensely weighty; and new technologies, including most notably social networking, that give customers a megaphone for ventilating their dissatisfactions only increase firms' sensitivities to these interests.[47] When firms' customer relations (or complaints) departments restore some of the benefits to consumers that the firms' contracts of adhesion remove, they promote the bottom line.

A question concerning norms remains, however, and the widespread practice of bargaining in the shadow of the form raises the stakes. How should the ex post negotiations that contracts of adhesion invite proceed? And how should law regulate them? In particular, to what extent should courts permit term-makers to insist on the non-salient terms included in their boilerplate, by enforcing these terms in case bargaining ex post fails? Put the other way around: to what extent should term-takers be able to assert the adhesion form in order to resist boilerplate in this case?

Functionalist analyses disagree about what attitude courts should take to this feature of contracts of adhesion. Some argue that judicial intervention to give consumers a legally protected contractual interest in firms' generous practices—for example, by treating common practice as establishing an implicit promise that consumers will enjoy whatever benefits firms typically provide—would undermine the point of the firms' policy of granting benefits in excess of their written promises. It would place courts in the position of policing firm-discretion by reference to their own judgments of consumer good faith, judgments whose cost and unreliability led firms—efficiently—to seek to retain discretion to begin with.[48] Others argue that, at least where there exists strong evidence that a firm has adopted a practice of providing benefits in excess of those specified by a written form, preventing firm opportunism requires that courts compel the firm to grant 'discretionary' benefits in at least some cases in which it wishes not to.[49]

Both sides of this debate take an all-or-nothing approach to boilerplate. One side would enforce boilerplate against complaining consumers whenever firms request it, so that whenever firms confer benefits on complaining consumers that boilerplate would permit the firms to withhold, they do so as a matter of unilateral grace.

[46] See LA Bebchuck and R Posner, 'One-Sided Contracts in Competitive Consumer Markets' in Ben-Shahar (ed), *Boilerplate: The Foundation of Market Contracts* (n 25) 3–11; JS Johnston, 'Cooperative Negotiations in the Shadow of Boilerplate' (n 43) 12, 14–16.

[47] See Van Loo (n 40) (text accompanying n 57).

[48] See LA Bebchuck and R Posner (n 46) 3, 9–10.

[49] JS Johnston, 'Cooperative Negotiations in the Shadow of Boilerplate' (n 43) 12, 25. Johnston acknowledges Bebchuck's and Posner's concern about the non-verifiability of consumer opportunism. But he also worries, as Bebchuck and Posner seem not to, about firm opportunism, specifically that firms (especially when they are short-run players) may seek to 'creat[e] a false appearance of pursuing a policy of forgiveness by mimicking the behaviour of a firm that really does implement these strategies': ibid 12, 23.

The other side would refuse to enforce boilerplate, at least against consumers who complain in good faith, and so would vindicate good faith consumer complaints as a matter of right. Both positions thus in effect deny that the consumer complaints process represents a genuine negotiation: they treat the rights of the parties as fixed by their contract, ex ante, and disagree only about how they are fixed, because they disagree about whether or not the firms' boilerplate reservations are enforceable.

The account of contracts of adhesion just rehearsed opens up a profoundly different possibility. Courts might regulate contracts of adhesion in order to ensure that the customer complaints process proceeds as a genuine, good-faith negotiation. Boilerplate that does not undermine this negotiating posture would be respected and enforced. But boilerplate clauses would not be permitted to give term-makers bargaining advantages ex post that they could not have acquired through bespoke negotiations ex ante. In particular, courts would refuse to allow boilerplate to enable retailers to exploit the fact that consumers, having begun to deal with the retailers with whom they have become dissatisfied, can no longer credibly threaten, ex post, to take their custom elsewhere. (Note the analogy between this approach and the duty of good faith in performance: both focus on cases in which one party uses strategic vulnerabilities associated with entering a contract relation to extract surplus ex post that would not have been given up in an ex ante negotiation.)

Courts taking this general approach might proceed down any number of more particular paths. One such path would seek to structure the ex post renegotiation so that it approximates, as nearly as possible, to the negotiation that would have occurred ex ante, had the contracting parties possessed the negotiating resources to dicker over the contingency that has generated their dispute. Boilerplate would be enforced insofar as it promotes such renegotiations (for example, by protecting term-makers against the vulnerabilities to opportunistic consumers that the functionalist analysis just rehearsed emphasise); it would be rejected insofar as it hinders them. Such a case-by-case assessment might overtax courts' adjudicative capacities or even their expertise, however.

An alternative elaboration of the basic insight that contracts of adhesion invite bargaining in the shadow of the form therefore asks courts to assess not the treatment of particular term-takers' individual complaints but rather the general structure and culture of a term-maker's customer service department.[50] Under this approach, a firm whose customer service department met certain guidelines might enter a safe-harbour that allowed it to enforce boilerplate where bargaining in the shadow of the form failed. These guidelines might require the customer service department to stand in a certain relationship to the rest of the firm—as sustaining goodwill rather than just immediate cash revenues in the firm's internal business plans, for example; or they might require the department to keep records of the shares of complaints that have been satisfied and the ratios of monies paid out to complainants to sums requested but retained; or they might require the departments to adopt certain internal procedures designed to promote good faith engagements with complaining customers (and to abjure certain procedures that constitute obvious bad faith);

[50] Rory Van Loo proposes a similar approach: see Van Loo (n 40).

or they might require the departments to employ leaders or even line workers who have been certified by customer service trade associations to satisfy professional norms.[51] Each of these approaches elaborates an aggregative account of good faith, which rejects assessing individual cases directly in favour of evaluating the faith of the institutions, procedures, and rules that determine the individual outcomes. This transformation in the object of good faith suits the current context: the aggregative approach to good faith ex post matches boilerplate's aggregative approach to contract drafting ex ante.[52]

These ideas bring customer service departments out of the shadows and into the limelight of contract theory, studying their potential to function as sites of productive exchange and even social solidarity—as analogues to the village market for bespoke contracts that are adapted to the needs of a mass-contracting age. At the same time, they match the legal regulation of contracts of adhesion to the legal wrong that generates the concern about form-contracting to begin with. Where a term-maker deploys boilerplate to shift a contractual settlement within the range of outcomes that a bespoke contract might legitimate (as the argument here assumes is the case), then any wrong that she commits must be a bargaining wrong. The argument just rehearsed identifies this wrong in terms that do not reduce it to other, more familiar bargaining wrongs, such as fraud. And the proposed legal regulation of bargaining in the shadow of a form treats the wrong with a bargaining remedy.

These ideas also emphasise the essential role that law might play in eliminating the most alienating feature of adhesive consumer contracts: the experience (all-to-familiar) of consumers who complain to customer service departments that operate in bad faith, employing unresponsive bureaucratic administration to insist on boilerplate terms that could never have been reached by negotiation ex ante. The alienation arises not simply because the complaining consumers do not receive substantive satisfaction; it arises because they cannot manage to get heard. A regime that gave consumers legal entitlements to complaints procedures structured as good faith negotiations might not cause all their complaints to be satisfactorily answered, but it would require them all to be engaged. It would, in this way, contribute to the practices of reciprocal recognition by which contract, writ large, helps to sustain social solidarity in open, cosmopolitan societies.[53]

V. DEFENCES REVISITED

The case of the form contract thus provides an object-lesson in the general structure of defences in contract law.

[51] In the United States, the two leading associations of customer service professionals are the Society of Consumer Affairs Professionals in Business and the American Council on Consumer Interests: Society of Consumer Affairs Professionals in Business (SOCAP International): www.socap.org/about-SOCAP, accessed 3 February 2016; American Council on Consumers Interests (*ACCI*): www.consumerinterests.org/about, accessed 3 February 2016.

[52] This formulation responds and owes a great deal to an exchange with Frederick Wilmot-Smith.

[53] See generally D Markovits, 'Contract and Collaboration' (2004) 113 *Yale Law Journal* 1417; Daniel Markovits, 'Market Solidarity' Inaugural Lecture as Guido Calabresi Professor of Law, 9 April 2012 (Yale Law School, Newhaven CT).

The conventional account of contracts of adhesion—on both sides of the dispute about enforcing boilerplate—evaluates arguments against liability for boilerplate on the model specifically of a defence. Conventional arguments thus ask whether boilerplate sufficiently closely approaches fraud or duress so that the values that generally underwrite enforcing contracts, when applied in boilerplate's case, support relief from liability. Often, the arguments formulate this question in terms of unconscionability. This is a natural move within the conventional frame, as the unconscionability doctrine is itself best understood to complete the defences in contract law, by granting relief in cases that fall within the span of fraud and duress—as the gravamen of these traditional common law defences obtains—but in which certain technical requirements of the traditional defences (often reflecting epistemic or institutional limitations of courts, as traditionally conceived) cannot be made out. It should therefore come as no surprise that courts that are sceptical of contracts of adhesion sometimes associate boilerplate terms that fall outside the reasonable expectations of consumers with unconscionability.[54]

This formal framing—in terms of a defence—explains why the conventional dispute about boilerplate ends at an impasse. Unconsionability—as the idea that the doctrine completes common law defences emphasises—already lives at the outer boundary of judicial competence to override contract law's baseline presumption in favour of party-sovereignty and to void an obligation on account of fraud or duress. Arguments against enforcing boilerplate—understood, in the commonplace way, to assert a defence—live at the outer bounds of unconscionability. They thus pile speculation atop speculation. The conventional dispute about boilerplate remains unsettled because it is framed in a way that places it, inevitably, at the very limit of what the doctrinal resources from which it is built can sustain. The unconscionability of boilerplate will thus be forever contested.

The account developed here takes a structurally very different approach to boilerplate. On this account, a promisor who seeks to avoid liability for terms included in boilerplate makes an argument that more nearly resembles a denial of liability than a defence. Contract theory and orthodox contract doctrine both typically imagine that contracts are negotiated agreements struck between parties who each possess the capacity to propose and to alter their contracts' terms. This model—of the individually tailored, or bespoke, contract—is implicit in any number of academic and doctrinal discussions. Standard accounts of offer and acceptance, for example, largely imagine parties who adjust reciprocally to one another as they negotiate towards agreement. Without such bespoke adjustments, it becomes difficult to make sense of so basic a notion as the meeting of minds. Once again, it is almost, although not precisely, as if contracts of adhesion lack offer and acceptance, at least with respect to boilerplate terms. The parties to a contract of adhesion agree to the salient terms and agree to reach future agreement on the subjects covered by the non-salient terms. But the second agreement remains abstract and does not settle on any concrete content, and therefore never reaches the concrete terms set forth in the boilerplate. Rather

[54] See, eg, *Armendariz v Foundation Health Psychcare Services, Inc*, 24 Cal 4th 83 (2000); *Graham v Scissor-Tail, Inc*, 28 Cal 3d 807 (1981); *A & M Produce Co v FMC Corp*, 135 Cal App 3d 473, 486–87 (Cal App, 4th Dist 1982).

than calling for a judgment of whether bargaining inequalities render boilerplate unenforceable even though part of the contract, the approach developed here denies that boilerplate ever makes it into the parties' bargain.

Finally, the formal differences between these two approaches—the difference between treating arguments against enforcing boilerplate as asserting defences and as denying liability—makes a substantive difference to the law's capacity to resolve disputes about boilerplate. A party seeking to avoid liability for boilerplate nevertheless accepts a contractual obligation even as she denies that the particular terms set out in the boilerplate have got into her contract. This is the obligation to proceed in good faith in the ex post negotiation that her broader contract, including through its boilerplate, contemplates. By refocusing attention on the displaced bargaining that boilerplate invites, the law can avoid the impasse that plagues conventional approaches and instead intervene on questions that it is equipped to decide. When a party asks a court for relief from boilerplate, this no longer requires the court to place a particular form contract on one or the other side of the nearly invisible line separating free contracting from oppressive advantage-taking. Instead, the court can ask whether the party seeking to enforce boilerplate is doing so only after good faith efforts to reach a bespoke agreement ex post have failed. And courts have for decades been willing and able to adjudicate agreements to bargain in good faith. Commercial context—and in the particular case of boilerplate the professional and institutional culture of customer service divisions—provides the normative and epistemic resources required to identify concrete cases of oppression even where abstract judgement fails.

The discussion of boilerplate rehearsed here thus reaches beyond the particular problem of judicial regulation of contracts of adhesion. It also illustrates that the doctrinal distinction between a defence against and a direct denial of contract liability, although largely rhetorical when stated as a matter of general theory, can make a difference to outcomes when embedded in a particular sphere of commercial and legal practice.

4

Good Faith, Good Conscience, and the Taking of Unfair Advantage

STEPHEN WADDAMS*

I. INTRODUCTION

WHEN THE JUDICATURE Acts came into force in 1875 it was provided that 'generally, in all matters not herein-before particularly mentioned, in which there is any conflict or variance between the rules of Equity and the Rules of the Common Law with reference to the same matter, the Rules of Equity shall prevail'.[1] This was an integral feature of the reform. By 1870 there was a consensus that the separate jurisdiction of the Court of Chancery should be abolished, but if this was to be done without altering the juridical position on thousands of questions where law and equity had interacted (on which there could be no political consensus), it was essential that the new court should have both the power and the duty of administering both law and equity.[2] Before the Judicature Acts equity had, as a practical matter, prevailed in case of conflict with the common law by means of the common injunction, restraining a person from exercising legal rights where such exercise was judged to be inequitable. If the common injunction was to be abolished, as it had to be if the courts were to be effectively combined, and the substantive juridical position on multiple legal questions was to remain unaltered by the reform, it was essential to provide that the new court should administer both law and equity, with equity to prevail.

The modern court has, therefore, both the power and the duty to administer equity. In attempting to determine precisely what this means in practice, some attention to the past is unavoidable. This is not of merely antiquarian interest. If it can be shown that the Court of Equity before 1875 had certain powers, it follows that the modern court received at least the same powers. It has often been observed that the prevailing mood of the late nineteenth century was unfriendly to the granting of relief against unfair contracts, but not all the judges held this opinion, as will appear from the discussion of Lord Selborne's and Sir George Jessel's decisions, below. Even

* I am grateful to Fred Wilmot-Smith, to the other participants in the workshop, and to Spencer Robinson for helpful suggestions.

[1] Judicature Act 1873, s 25(11).

[2] For a fuller discussion, see Waddams, 'Equity in English Contract Law: the Impact of the Judicature Acts (1873–75)' (2012) 33 *The Journal of Legal History* 185.

supposing the observation to be largely correct, it does not follow that the modern court need be equally unfriendly: older equitable practices and traditions can be revived. Moreover, since equity need not be supposed to have been frozen in 1875, the modern court may, for sufficient reason, develop equitable principles to deal with new circumstances in the same way in which judge-made law generally has developed. Not every modern court has recognised the full implications of these powers, and some courts and commentators have sought to restrict them, but a recent decision of the Privy Council, to be discussed below,[3] indicates a lively consciousness of the court's equitable inheritance, and of its power to develop equitable principles in order to do justice in modern circumstances.[4]

For all these reasons, attention to the past is necessary, but it is not necessary to take sides in the 'fusion' debate—or, rather, it is not necessary to take one side only in that debate, for there is truth both in the proposition that equity has its own history and traditions, and in the proposition that equity cannot now be disentangled from the common law. Nor is it necessary to retain all the language of the past, and sometimes it may be undesirable to do so. Words change their meanings over time, and a word, such as 'conscience' and its derivatives ('unconscientious', 'unconscionable'), or 'fraud,' though well understood in former times, may be ambiguous, or positively misleading to modern readers. A recent decision of the Supreme Court of Canada, also to be discussed below, raises the possibility of approaching problems of contractual unfairness through the concept of good faith.[5]

'Conscience' as a legal concept has mediaeval roots, and the word was still in frequent use in the courts of equity in the seventeenth century. A recent study has shown that seventeenth-century usage was somewhat ambivalent, the word signifying often an objective, legally cognisable standard, but sometimes seeming to import the personal opinion of the judge.[6] The statement of Finch LC (later Lord Nottingham) in 1676 in *Maynard v Moseley*[7] that 'the Chancery mends no man's bargain' is readily—perhaps rather too readily—memorable, and has often been quoted, or alluded to, in modern cases with the implication that the meaning of the statement is that equity lacked power to modify contractual obligations. But, when the words are read in context, it is apparent that this was not their meaning. *Maynard v Moseley* involved a claim by a purchaser of land, where the vendor had not warranted title and had made no misrepresentation. The purchaser was a lawyer (Serjeant Maynard) more knowledgeable than the vendor on matters of land law, who had examined the title, and had himself initiated the transaction (which would have been very profitable if the title had been good) in the interest of a member of his own family.

[3] See the text accompanying nn 79–89.

[4] *Çukurova Finance International Ltd and another v Alfa Telecom Turkey Ltd (Nos 3 to 5)* [2013] UKPC 2, [2013] UKPC 20, [2013] UKPC 25; [2016] AC 923.

[5] *Bhasin v Hrynew* 2014 SCC 71; [2014] 3 SCR 494.

[6] D Klinck, *Conscience, Equity and the Court of Chancery in Early Modern England* (Farnham, Ashgate, 2010).

[7] *Maynard v Moseley* (1676) 3 Swans App 653, 655; 36 ER 1010, 1011—DEC Yale (ed), *Lord Nottingham's Chancery Cases* vols I and II (Selden Society vols 73 and 79, 1957 and 1961) vol I, 400–401 (No 537).

The transaction had been completed, and Serjeant Maynard, having paid the price in full, and having been later evicted by the holder of a paramount title, sought to recover back the price from the vendor. Finch LC, in refusing the assistance of equity, said:[8]

> Possibly there may be equity to stop the payment of such purchase money as is behind, but never to recover what is paid; for the Chancery mends no man's bargain, though it sometimes mends his assurance ... Wherefore, upon the whole matter, though if the defendants had been plaintiffs for the money, his Lordship would hardly have decreed for them, as they are defendants and in possession of money upon an agreement executed, his Lordship saw no cause to decree against them.

It will be seen that the phrase 'the Chancery mends no man's bargain' is qualified by both the immediately preceding and by the immediately subsequent clause, and by the concluding sentence, all of which suggest that Finch might well have granted relief if the agreement had been still executory. Finch is (unsurprisingly, in the circumstances) denying an equitable right to set aside a completed transaction and to recover back the purchase price, but he implies that equity might grant relief to a purchaser who had promised to pay the price but had not yet paid it. In 1680 he did grant relief in such a case,[9] criticised in 1701[10] and subsequently,[11] as showing *too great* a readiness to relieve against contractual obligations. This case, reported anonymously, is probably the same case as *Skip v Rich*, found in Yale's edition of *Nottingham's Chancery Cases*, in which the purchaser had given a bond of £100 to secure payment of the balance of the price of land to which the title had proved defective. Finch said:[12]

> I granted a perpetual injunction against the bond of 100 *l.*, for though I could not relieve the plaintiff for the money he had paid down, it being his own folly to take no better covenants, yet for so much of the purchase money as was unpaid, I thought fit to help him. For it seemed to me against equity to let loose the bond of 100 *l.*, against him who had already paid too much for nothing.

Plainly this was a modification of a legal contractual obligation. The question addressed here is not whether Finch's holding in *Skip v Rich* was correct or wise (it was rejected by later courts and commentators), but what he meant by saying in *Maynard v Moseley* that 'the Chancery mends no man's bargain'. The clauses before and after those words in *Maynard*, together with the later decision, indicate that Finch did not intend to exclude the power of equity to grant relief against contractual obligations that had not been fully performed. The case is also interesting as suggesting that what made the transaction unfair, in Finch's opinion, was primarily the factor of unjust enrichment ('to let loose the bond ... against him who had already paid too much for nothing').

[8] ibid, Swans App 655, 657, ER 1011.

[9] *Anon* (Hilary Term, 1679/80) 2 Chan Cas 19; 32 ER 826. (The calendar year began on March 25; 1679/80 signifies dates between Jan 1 and March 24: 1679, old style; 1680, new style).

[10] ibid, Chan Cas C 20 (reporter's note) (the report was published in 1701).

[11] E Sugden, *Practical Treatise of the Law of Vendors and Purchasers of Estates* (London, Butterworth, 1805) 241.

[12] *Skip v Rich*, *Lord Nottingham's Chancery Cases* (n 7) vol II, 805 (February 1679/80, No 1007). In vol I, xcii–cvii, Yale discusses several other cases in which Finch granted relief against contractual obligations.

Finch's reluctance to set aside a completed contract and to order repayment of a money sum is related to the restricted role of the court of equity in his time. A modern court undoubtedly has power, in a proper case, to set aside a completed sale and to order restitution of the price. From one point of view the use of such a power may be regarded as a defence to contractual obligation; from another point of view it is an action for restitution of an unjust enrichment.

A strong unjust enrichment perspective also appears half a century after Lord Nottingham's time in Henry Ballow's *A Treatise of Equity*:[13]

> But further, in all Contracts purely chargeable, if there appears to be an Inequality, altho' there was no Deceit on either Side ...: Yet if the Damage be considerable, the Bargain ought to be made void. And this Estimate of the Damage is to be taken, either from the Exorbitance of the Price, or the Poverty of the Party injured; for no Man should be a Gainer by another's loss ... it is a certain Rule, that where the Bargain is plainly iniquitous, and it is against Conscience to insist upon it, as forty Years Purchase for Lands; or an extravagant Price for Stock, as was given in the *South-Sea* Year, Equity can't support it; for that would be to decree Iniquity.

It is clear from this passage that Ballow recognised a jurisdiction to set aside contracts that had the effect of bringing about very large enrichments. It is notable also that what was against conscience was not to have entered into the bargain in the first place ('no deceit on either side'), but to 'insist upon' the bargain when it was *now* clear (at the time of potential enforcement) that enforcement would be inequitable.

II. FRAUD

The court of equity relieved against forfeitures of all kinds, especially in mortgages, against penal bonds, against improvident sales of future expectancies, against contracts obtained by undue influence, and, more generally, against highly disadvantageous contracts made by persons of weaker bargaining power. The first published treatise on English contract law (by John Joseph Powell, 1790) included a long chapter entitled 'Of the Equitable jurisdiction in relieving against unreasonable Contracts or Agreements'.[14] Powell stated that the mere fact of a bargain being *unreasonable*[15] was not a ground to set it aside in equity, 'For, contracts are not to be set aside, because not such as the wisest people would make; but there must be fraud to make void acts of this solemn and deliberate nature, if entered into for a consideration'.[16]

[13] H Ballow, *A Treatise of Equity* (London, D Browne and J Shuckburgh, 1737) ch 11, sections 9–10. The phrase 'purely chargeable', ie, 'burdensome', derived from Pufendorf, seems to be intended by Ballow to exclude contracts containing a gift element. The phrase 'no man should be a gainer by another's loss' alludes to the Digest, D.12.6.14.

[14] J Powell, *Essay upon the Law of Contracts and Agreements*, vol ii (London, J Jonhson, 1790) 143.

[15] ibid 144.

[16] ibid.

But Powell went on to point out that 'fraud' in equity had an unusual and very wide meaning:[17]

> And agreements that are not properly fraudulent, in that sense of the term which imports deceit, will, nevertheless, be relieved against on the ground of inequality, and imposed burden or hardship on one of the parties to a contract; which is considered as a distinct head of equity, being looked upon as an offence against morality, and as unconscientious. Upon this principle, such courts will, in cases where contracts are unequal, as bearing hard upon one party ... set them aside.

Powell gave as an example the very common provision in a mortgage (which might have been called boilerplate, if the word had been then in use) that unpaid interest should be treated as principal and should itself bear interest until paid. Powell wrote that 'This covenant will be relieved against as fraudulent, because unjust and oppressive in an extreme degree'.[18]

The very wide meaning thus given to the concepts of 'fraud' and 'fraudulent' indicates that the power to set aside contracts was much larger than might at first appear. Frederick Pollock, in his chapter on duress and undue influence in his treatise of 1876, also explained that 'fraud' could not be taken at face value:[19]

> The term fraud is indeed of common occurrence both in the earlier and in the later authorities: but 'fraud does not here mean deceit or circumvention; it means an unconscientious use of the power arising out of these circumstances and conditions': and this does not come within the proper meaning of fraud, which is a misrepresentation ... made with the intent of creating a particular wrong belief in the mind of the party defrauded. Perhaps the best word to use would be imposition, as a sort of middle term between fraud, to which it comes near in popular language, and compulsion, which it suggests by its etymology.

It is significant that Pollock, in seeking to elucidate the meaning of the word fraud, should consciously look for an equally ambiguous word (imposition), suggesting, on the one hand, the taking of unfair advantage, and, on the other hand, actual compulsion.

III. FORFEITURES

The court of equity commonly gave relief against forfeitures, particularly in mortgages. Mortgage documents usually provided that, on default in repayment, the land should be forfeited. The courts of equity consistently refused to enforce this simple provision, despite the fact that it was well known and perfectly clear. Whatever form of words was used—even if the document evidenced an outright conveyance of the land—the court, if convinced that the substance of the transaction was

[17] ibid 145–46.
[18] ibid 146.
[19] F Pollock, *Principles of Contract: at Law and in Equity* (London, Stevens, 1876) 527.

a mortgage, refused to enforce the document and permitted the borrower to redeem the land:[20]

> [S]o that in every mortgage the agreement of the parties upon the face of the deed, seems to be, that a mortgage shall not be redeemable after forfeiture … and a mortgage can no more be irredeemable, than a distress for a rent-charge can be irrepleviable. The law itself will control that express agreement of the party; and by the same reason equity will let a man loose from his agreement, and will against his agreement admit him to redeem a mortgage.

No restriction, even by express agreement, was permitted on the right to redeem. In *Spurgeon v Collier* (1758) Sir Robert Henley, later Lord Northington, said that 'a man will not be suffered in conscience to fetter himself with a limitation or restriction of his time of redemption. It would ruin the distressed and unwary, and give unconscionable advantage to greedy and designing persons'.[21] A few years later the same judge again linked the concepts of reason, justice, freedom of consent, and deterrence of trickery:[22]

> This court, as a court of conscience, is very jealous of persons taking securities for a loan, and converting such securities into purchases. And therefore I take it to be an established rule, that a mortgagee can never provide at the time of making the loan for any event or condition on which the equity of redemption shall be discharged, and the conveyance absolute. And there is great reason and justice in this rule, for necessitous men are not, truly speaking, free men, but, to answer a present exigency, will submit to any terms that the crafty may impose upon them.

The rule was that the mortgagee could stipulate for no collateral advantage, and so strict was this rule that it came to be applied so as to cause the setting aside of agreements that were perfectly fair and reasonable. It was easier for the nineteenth-century English legal mind to accept a rigid rule that in no circumstances might a mortgagee stipulate for a collateral advantage (a rule that, for better or worse, happened to be the law) than a general power to relieve against unfair transactions. So, ironically, in an era when sanctity of contracts was paramount, transactions were set aside that were *not* unfair. In a decision of the House of Lords in 1904 Lord Halsbury remarked, with evident irritation, that '[a] perfectly fair bargain made between two parties to it, each of whom was quite sensible as to what they were doing, is not to be performed because at the same time a mortgage arrangement was made between them'.[23] Ten years later the House of Lords restored some flexibility by appealing to the underlying original reason for the intervention of the courts:[24]

> It was, in ordinary cases, only where there was conduct which the Court of Chancery regarded as unconscientious that it interfered with freedom of contract. The lending of money, on mortgage or otherwise, was looked on with suspicion, and the Court was on the

[20] *Howard v Harris* (1683) 1 Vern 190, 192; 23 ER 406, 407. This passage from the argument of successful counsel was cited, with page reference and near quotation, as stating the law on the point, by R Coote, *A Treatise on the Law of Mortgage* (London, Butterworth, 1821) 22.

[21] *Spurgeon v Collier* (1758) 1 Eden 55, 59; 28 ER 605, 606.

[22] *Vernon v Bethell* (1762) 2 Eden 110, 113; 28 ER 838, 839.

[23] *Samuel v Jarrah Timber and Wood Paving Co Ltd* [1904] AC 323 (HL) 325.

[24] *G&C Kreglinger v New Patagonia Meat and Cold Storage Co Ltd* [1914] AC 25 (HL) 36–38 (Lord Haldane).

> alert to discover want of conscience in the terms imposed by lenders … [I]t is inconsistent with the objects for which they [the rules of equity] were established that these rules should crystallise into technical language so rigid the letter can defeat the underlying spirit and purpose.

This is a persuasive argument for enforcing agreements that are fair; it gives no support whatever to the proposition that all agreements should be enforced, *even if unfair*.

IV. PENALTIES

Forfeiture in its various forms has obvious advantages to the secured party, and the penal bond represented an attempt to secure equivalent advantages without the immediate transfer of the property to be forfeited. A common form of the bond was a covenant to pay a fixed sum of money unless some other act was performed by a certain date. The effect was to secure the performance of the other act, which might itself be the payment of a sum of money lent by the obligee to the obligor.

The court of equity gave relief from such bonds on much the same principle as in mortgages. The bond was, in substance, a device to secure repayment of a loan, and the legitimate interest of the lender was in repayment of the principal (together with interest and costs) and no more. In 1880 the law on the point, out of keeping though it was with the spirit of the nineteenth century, was explained by Bramwell LJ (who, though not himself sympathetic, accepted that this was the law) as follows:[25]

> [T]he Court of Chancery said that a penalty to secure the payment of a sum of money or the performance of an act should not be enforced; the parties were not held to their agreement; equity in truth refused to allow to be enforced what was considered to be an unconscientious bargain.

Another judge said, in 1900:[26]

> The Court of Chancery gave relief against the strictness of the common law in cases of penalty or forfeiture for nonpayment of a fixed sum on a day certain, on the principle that failure to pay principal on a certain day could be compensated sufficiently by payment of principal and interest with costs at a subsequent day.

Important also was the obvious factor that a borrower in urgent need was apt to sign too readily an extravagant penal bond: the need for the funds was always immediate, and the possibility of enforcement of the bond remote.

The law relating to penalties has been recently reviewed by a seven-judge panel of the UK Supreme Court in *El Makdessi v Cavendish Square Holding BV*.[27] In one of the judgments the law in this area was described as 'an ancient, haphazardly constructed edifice which has not weathered well'.[28] The court, however, rejected arguments for abolition of the doctrine, or for confining it to consumer transactions.

[25] *Protector Endowment Loan and Annuity Co v Grice* (1880) 5 QBD 592 (CA) 596.
[26] *Heynes v Dixon (Re Dixon)* [1900] 2 Ch 561 (CA) 576 (Rigby LJ).
[27] *El Makdessi v Cavendish Square Holding BV* [2015] UKSC 67; [2015] 3 WLR 1373.
[28] ibid [3] (Lord Neuberger PSC and Lord Sumption JSC, Lord Carnwath JSC concurring).

But the court also rejected (as decisive tests) whether the clause was a genuine pre-estimate of loss and whether the clause was designed to have a deterrent effect, preferring the more flexible tests of whether the clause was extravagant, exorbitant or unconscionable. This greater flexibility will enable clauses that are not unreasonable to be enforced, as in the two cases decided in *Cavendish Square* (where the clauses might have failed the former tests based on genuine pre-estimate of loss and deterrent effect), while maintaining judicial control over clauses that would have the effect of causing excessive enrichment. Although the court declined directly to extend the law of penalty clauses to cases where there was no breach of contract, the indirect effect of the case seems likely to support a flexible test of enforceability that would be capable of application to penalty clauses, to 'near penalty' clauses, and to the other aspects of contract law discussed in this chapter.[29]

V. PERSONS BORROWING ON THE EXPECTATION OF FUTURE OWNERSHIP OF PROPERTY

The English courts of equity granted relief against transactions entered into by persons expecting to own property in the future. The typical case was of the 'expectant heir', and this phrase, together with the otherwise obsolete phrase 'catching bargain', is often used to denote this branch of English law, but the jurisdiction was not restricted to heirs: it extended to every kind of case in which the borrower expected to become the owner of property in the future. Commonly the substance of the transaction was a loan, but the transaction took the form of a sale of the expectancy, or of the reversion. The court would set aside the transaction unless the purchaser proved that he had given full value. As in the case of mortgages and penalties, the situation is one in which experience shows that a person, pressed with the immediate need for money, is apt to sell a future interest at an undervalue—sometimes at a gross undervalue: again, the need for money is immediate, and the interest given up seems remote. So ready was the court to set aside such transactions that the rule came to seem, in the intellectual climate of the nineteenth century, too rigid: a statute of 1867 provided that such transactions should not 'be opened or set aside merely upon the ground of undervalue'.[30] The statute, however, did not affect the general jurisdiction of the court to set aside unconscionable transactions,[31] and this line of cases supplies an important illustration of that wider jurisdiction, before and after 1867.[32] Frederick Pollock, in his first edition, recognised the wide powers of the court of equity, saying that '[p]ractically the question is whether in the opinion of the Court the transaction was a hard bargain'.[33]

[29] If 'near penalty' clauses were not included, there would be anomalous distinctions based on fine variations in wording (overdraft prohibited: penalty $1,000 per day; overdraft permitted: fee $1,000 per day).

[30] Sales of Reversions Act 1867, 31 & 32 Vic (c 4).

[31] *Earl of Aylesford v Morris* (1873) LR 8 Ch App 484, 490.

[32] See the passages quoted at nn 39, 45 and 62.

[33] Pollock (n 19) 534–35. See n 46.

Equitable jurisdiction in this area was affirmed by the Lord Chancellor, Lord Selborne, on the eve of the Judicature Acts in *Earl of Aylesford v Morris*.[34] The case involved a foolish and extravagant spendthrift, just over the age of majority, who had incurred heavy debts, and had raised money at a high rate of interest, not by actually selling a future property interest, but generally on the strength of his prospects of inheritance. The transaction was set aside by the Chancery court at first instance, a common injunction was issued to restrain the legal proceedings instituted by the lender, and the lender appealed. The appeal was heard by Lord Selborne, sitting with one other judge (Mellish LJ), at almost exactly the same time as the Judicature Bill—for which Lord Selborne, as Lord Chancellor, was primarily responsible, and which he introduced with a long speech—was being debated in the House of Lords.[35] The future relation between law and equity, the central feature of the Bill, must have been in the forefront of Lord Selborne's mind when he heard the arguments and gave the judgment (with which Mellish LJ agreed) in *Aylesford v Morris*.

Recent statutes repealing the usury laws[36] and providing that sales of reversions were not to be set aside on the ground of undervalue alone[37] had lent support to an argument that modern equitable jurisdiction in this area was very narrow, or even obsolete.[38] Lord Selborne's judgment firmly rejected any such idea, and sought to explain and consolidate the equitable jurisdiction. The judgment has something of a didactic tone, as though instructing a common law reader in basic equitable principles, showing that Selborne expected that his words would, in the near future, be interpreted and applied by judges not familiar with the equitable sources. Selborne stressed that this was a well-established jurisdiction ('There is hardly any older head of equity'),[39] and that the statute dealing with sales of reversions did not repeal the equitable jurisdiction, but restored an earlier flexibility, which he linked with the general concept of unconscionability:

> the arbitrary rule of equity as to sales of reversions was an impediment to fair and reasonable, as well as to unconscionable, bargains … [T]he Act … leaves under-value still a material element in cases in which it is not the sole equitable ground for relief.[40]

Selborne explained carefully that equitable references to 'fraud' did not have the same meaning as at common law ('Fraud does not here mean deceit or circumvention; it means an unconscientious use of the power arising out of these circumstances and conditions').[41] Selborne stressed that the lender 'is not alleged or proved to have

[34] *Earl of Aylesford* (n 31). See C MacMillan, '*Earl of Aylesford v Morris* (1873)' in C Mitchell and P Mitchell (eds), *Landmark Cases in Equity* (Oxford, Hart Publishing, 2012).

[35] *Earl of Aylesford* (n 31) argued 17 and 18 February; judgment 5 March 1873. First reading of Judicature Bill, 13 February 1873.

[36] Usury Laws Repeal Act 1854, 17 & 18 Vic (c 90).

[37] Sales of Reversions Act (n 30).

[38] A leading article in the *Law Times* manifested a commonly held, and very narrow, view of the proper scope of relief for unconscionability in the light of the statutes just mentioned, (1870) 49 *Law Times* 223.

[39] *Earl of Aylesford* (n 31) 489.

[40] ibid 490.

[41] ibid 490–91.

been guilty of deceit or circumvention',[42] and costs in the court of first instance were refused to the successful plaintiff for this reason:

> the Plaintiff has no merits of his own to plead. He comes into Court to be relieved from the consequences of a course of very willful and culpable folly and extravagance. I think him entitled to the relief which he asks; but I think it is not unjust that he should obtain it at his own expense.[43]

The equitable jurisdiction was not to be explained away or marginalised as resting on policy considerations relating to the preservation of family estates ('Whatever weight there may be in such collateral considerations, they could hardly prevail, if they did not connect themselves with an equity more strictly and directly personal to the Plaintiff in each particular case').[44] Lord Selborne was not obliged to hear this case personally, or to reserve judgment; neither was he obliged to write such an elaborate judgment as he did. Taken as a whole, and considering its timing in relation to the Judicature Bill, the judgment suggests a deliberate attempt by Selborne to solidify this branch of equitable jurisprudence before the Judicature Acts should come into effect.

In 1875, just before the Acts came into force, Sir George Jessel MR, in another case of moneylending at high interest rates, spoke in potentially even wider terms about the jurisdiction of equity to set aside unfair contracts, again stressing that fraud (in the usual, or common law, sense) was not relevant:[45]

> The point to be considered is, was this a hard bargain?[46] The doctrine has nothing to do with fraud ... It has been laid down in case after case that the Court, wherever there is a dealing of this kind, looks at the reasonableness of the bargain, and if it is what is called a hard bargain, sets it aside.

An appeal was summarily dismissed by James and Mellish LJJ, who called it 'a perfectly idle appeal'.[47] These decisions suggest that some, at least, of the equity judges were conscious, on the eve of the Judicature Acts, that the rather specialised equitable meaning of 'fraud' was likely to be misunderstood, and that they were anxious to correct that misunderstanding and to secure the jurisdiction of the old court, and therefore of the new court, to set aside contracts for unfairness. Jessel gained something of a reputation as a champion of equity in the new court: Sir William Brett (Lord Esher), Jessel's successor as Master of the Rolls, was supposed to have said 'that Jessel MR had been sent to dragoon the Court of Appeal into substituting equity for Common Law, but that he (Esher) and his Common Law colleagues would not have it'.[48] Though the occasion is not identified, the anecdote

[42] ibid 499.
[43] ibid.
[44] ibid 492.
[45] *Beynon v Cook* (1875) LR 10 Ch App 389, 391.
[46] The expression 'hard bargain', though used here to mean 'unconscionable bargain', came, both in general and in legal usage, to signify a contract that, though disadvantageous, was nevertheless enforceable. See *Middleton v Brown* (1878) 47 LJ Ch 411, 413 (Jessel MR, but refusing relief), *Nevill v Snelling* (1880) 15 Ch D 679 (Ch D) 704 (Denman J), *Multiservice Bookbinding Ltd v Marden* [1979] Ch 84 (Ch D) 112 (Browne-Wilkinson J).
[47] *Beynon* (n 45) 393.
[48] A Underhill, *Change and Decay* (London, Butterworths, 1938) 87.

was evidently thought to be plausible, and some further credibility is lent to it by the noticeably didactic tone of Jessel's judgment in *Beynon v Cook* ('nothing to do with fraud' ... 'laid down in case after case').

If it was the purpose of the equity judges—or of some of them—to establish and to solidify unfairness as a ground of contractual relief, it must be concluded that the purpose was attained only in part. After the Judicature Acts, writers on English contract law emphasised the enforceability of contracts, and tended to marginalise the instances in which contracts had been set aside for unfairness. In dealing with consideration it was common to point out that inadequacy of consideration is not, in itself, a defence to contractual obligation, and from this 'elementary principle', as Pollock called it, it was inferred that, if there is sufficient consideration to meet the test of contract formation, the contract must be enforceable. Pollock in his first edition (1876) wrote that it was[49]

> a distinguishing mark of English jurisprudence that the amount of the consideration is not material. 'The value of all things contracted for is measured by the appetite of the contractors, and therefore the just value, is that which they be contented to give'. It is accordingly treated as an elementary principle that the law will not enter into an inquiry as to the adequacy of the consideration.

Anson (1879) followed the same line, and made the point more forcefully:[50]

> So long as a man gets what he bargained for Courts of law will not ask what the value may be to him, or whether its value is in any way proportionate to his act or promise given in return. This would be 'the law making the bargain, instead of leaving the parties to make it'.

As both writers were aware, however, this was not a complete account, because courts of equity had often set aside contracts on a variety of grounds related, in general terms, to unfairness. Pollock mentioned this aspect of English law with an awkward side-note in his chapter on consideration (Chapter IV): 'Inadequacy *plus other things* in Equity: see chap. XI'.[51] In the body of the text, he wrote:[52]

> Inadequacy of consideration coupled with other things may however be of great importance as evidence of fraud, &c., when the validity of a contract is in dispute: and it has been considered (though, it is believed, the better opinion is otherwise) to be of itself sufficient ground for refusing specific performance. This subject, which is by no means free from difficulty, will be examined under the head of Undue Influence, Ch XI., *post*.

When he came to the matter in the later chapter, Pollock stressed the exceptional nature of relief for unfairness. The matter was dealt with, very artificially, as subsidiary to the topic of undue influence, with the side-note: 'Other circumstances from which undue influence inferred'.[53] The next side-notes read: 'As to

[49] Pollock (n 19) 154, quoting T Hobbes, *Leviathan or The Matter, Forme and Power of a Common Wealth Ecclesiasticall and Civil* (London, 1651) part 1 ch XV 'Of Other Laws of Nature: Justice Commutative and Distributive'.

[50] W Anson, *Principles of the English Law of Contract* (Oxford, Clarendon Press, 1879) 63, quoting Alderson B in *Pilkington v Scott* (1846) 15 M & W 657, 660; 153 ER 1014, 1015.

[51] Pollock (n 19) 156 (emphasis in original).

[52] ibid.

[53] ibid 518. Warren Swain is critical of Pollock's treatment of the subject, W Swain, 'Reshaping Contractual Unfairness in England 1670–1900' (2014) 35 *The Journal of Legal History* 120, 140.

undervalue … General rule: undervalue has *of itself* no effect'.[54] *Aylesford v Morris* and related cases were marshalled by a side-note calling them 'exceptional cases of expectant heirs and reversioners'.[55] All this suggested that relief for unfairness was anomalous, exceptional, and, impliedly, rather regrettable.

Anson, closely following both the form and the substance of Pollock's work, but with less nuance, dealt with the matter as follows:[56]

> Equity so far takes adequacy of consideration into account in dealing with contracts, that if a contract is sought to be avoided on the ground of Fraud or Undue Influence, inadequacy of consideration will be regarded as strong corroborative evidence in support of the suit.

One of the principal stated purposes of Pollock's book, just after the Judicature Acts, was to consider English law and equity as a whole. But his approach to this question, followed in starker form by Anson, tended to marginalise the power of the court to set aside disadvantageous contracts. The statement of the general principle of law, followed by mention two pages later of a power to set aside contracts in 'equity' suggested that the power was exceptional. The categories of 'fraud, &c.', and 'fraud or undue influence' suggested rare and closely defined instances, scarcely affecting the general principles of contract law, though Pollock's very awkward phrase 'fraud, &c.' shows the difficulty of any such definition. The reference to inadequacy of consideration as a matter only of *evidence* tended to suggest that it has little effect on substantive law, and the emphasis of both writers on the power of the court of equity to refuse specific performance (leaving the promisee with a right to full damages) tended to distract the reader from the far more significant power of the court of equity to *rescind* the contract (leaving the promisee with no remedy at all). The postponement of the subject to a later chapter also tended to suggest that it was not directly relevant to the most basic principles of contract law, and that relief on the ground of unfairness was conceptually exceptional; within the later chapter, entitled 'Duress and Undue Influence', cases resting on inequality of exchange were further marginalised by their subordination to the topic of undue influence. The tendency to marginalise the issue reached a peak in Halsbury's *Laws of England* (1907–17) where unconscionable contracts were excluded altogether from the article on Contract, and dealt with, anomalously, in a different volume in the article on Fraudulent and Voidable Conveyances (a quite separate topic). In the case of moneylending contracts, the equitable jurisdiction was, in one sense, confirmed by statute at the beginning of the twentieth century,[57] but, in another sense, displaced, so that, ironically, the statutory confirmation of equitable power in respect of one particular kind of contract tended to weaken support for a general judicial power to set aside other kinds of contracts for unfairness.

[54] Pollock (n 19) 519.

[55] ibid 527.

[56] Reference followed to what Anson, like Pollock, considered the doubtful power of the court to deny specific performance on this ground. Anson, *Principles of the English Law of Contract* (n 50) 65.

[57] Money Lenders Act 1900, 63 & 64 Vic (c 51). Significantly, the old equitable word 'unconscionable' was used in the statutory test: s 1(1).

VI. UNDUE INFLUENCE

Disadvantageous contractual transactions have frequently been set aside for 'undue influence'. This phrase covers a number of different circumstances. It may apply to an openly hostile relationship where one party threatens the other with adverse consequences if the agreement is not made. Such a case was *Williams v Bayley*[58] where a son had forged his father's signature to promissory notes, and the creditor threatened to prosecute the son unless the father agreed to pay the debt. More commonly the phrase has been applied to situations related to fiduciary duties where one party reposes trust in the other.[59] Certain categories of case have been said to give rise to a presumption of undue influence, but it is not necessary for the weaker party to bring his case into a recognised category: any case in which there is a relationship of trust or confidence may qualify for relief. A modern case that does not readily fall into any pre-existing category is one where an employee guaranteed her employer's debts. The guarantee was set aside by the English Court of Appeal. Millett LJ used strong language, very reminiscent of the older equity cases:[60]

> This transaction cannot possibly stand ... It is an extreme case. The transaction was not merely to the manifest disadvantage of Miss Burch; it was one which, in the traditional phrase, 'shocks the conscience of the court'. Miss Burch committed herself to a personal liability far beyond her slender means, risking the loss of her home and personal bankruptcy, and obtained nothing in return beyond a relatively small and possibly temporary increase in the overdraft facility available to her employer, a company in which she had no financial interest. The transaction gives rise to grave suspicion. It cries aloud for an explanation.

VII. UNFAIR TRANSACTIONS

The courts of equity exercised a general jurisdiction to set aside transactions that they regarded as very unfair. In 1818 it was said that:[61]

> [A] Court of Equity will inquire whether the parties really did meet on equal terms; and if it be found that the vendor was in distressed circumstances, and that advantage was taken of that distress, it will avoid the contract.

In 1888, summarising the cases, Kay J said:[62]

> The result of the decisions is that where a purchase is made from a poor and ignorant man at a considerable undervalue, the vendor having no independent advice, a Court of Equity will set aside the transaction.
>
> This will be done even in the case of property in possession, and *a fortiori* if the interest be reversionary.

[58] *Williams v Bayley* (1866) LR 1 HL 200.
[59] See *Lloyds Bank Ltd v Bundy* [1975] QB 326 (CA).
[60] *Credit Lyonnais Bank Nederland NV v Burch* [1997] 1 All ER 144 (CA) 152.
[61] *Wood v Abrey* (1818) 3 Madd 417, 423; 56 ER 558, 560 (Leach VC).
[62] *Fry v Lane* (1888) 40 Ch D 312 (Ch D) 322. Lord Selborne's words were from *Earl of Aylesford* (n 31) 491.

> The circumstances of poverty and ignorance of the vendor, and absence of independent advice, throw upon the purchaser, where the transaction is impeached, the onus of proving, in Lord Selborne's words, that the purchase was 'fair, just, and reasonable'.

Was undervalue alone a sufficient ground for relief? This question is not easy to answer because of the elusive meaning of 'fraud', mentioned above. There are, indeed, many statements by courts and commentators to the effect that undervalue alone was insufficient, but these cannot be taken at face value because of frequent indications that a gross undervalue created a 'presumption of fraud': where there was a large inequality of exchange the court could presume, without any separate proof, that the disadvantaged party must have been labouring under some sort of mistake or disability, or else must have been influenced by necessity, or by some sort of pressure, or by a relationship with the stronger party.[63] Some cases suggest that the presumption was practically irrebuttable: Joseph Story (1836) spoke in this context of 'the most vehement presumption of fraud'.[64] An Irish Lord Chancellor (Hart), summarising the practical effect, said, in 1828: 'Inadequacy of price is not in itself sufficient, but the Court has got at it by indirect means—it has been astute, as it is said to infer fraud from inadequacy, so as to raise it indirectly into a ground for relief'.[65]

Inequality of exchange was not, in itself, conclusive, but it does not follow that it was irrelevant: a large inequality of exchange often seems to have called for some sort of explanation (which might be that a part-gift was intended, or that the inequality was caused by risks fairly allocated by the transaction).[66] An attempt in the twentieth century by Lord Denning[67] to restate a general principle in terms of unfairness and inequality of bargaining power was rejected by the House of Lords,[68] but the older cases were not overruled. The use of the word 'unconscionablity', though common in this context and not in itself erroneous, has led to the supposition that proof is required of some kind of misconduct at the time of the transaction. As indicated earlier,[69] unconscionability, as used by the courts of equity, denoted not misconduct at the time of the transaction, but a judicial conclusion that enforcement would be inequitable. However, the use of the word is significant as signifying a judicial power to grant relief against contracts on grounds of extreme unfairness.

[63] *Earl of Chesterfield v Janssen* (1751) 2 Ves Sen 125; 28 ER 82, *Heathcote v Paignon* (1787) 2 Bro CC 167; 29 ER 96.

[64] J Story, *Commentaries on Equity Jurisprudence: as administered in England and America* (Boston, Hillard Gray & Co, 1836) 250.

[65] *Drought v Eustace* (1828) 1 Molloy 328, 335, cited by L Sheridan, *Fraud in Equity: A Study in English and Irish Law* (London, Pitman, 1957), and by Swain (n 53) 133.

[66] *Rotheram v Browne* (1747) 8 Bro PC 297; 3 ER 594 (part gift), *Mortimer v Capper* (1782) 1 Bro CC 156; 28 ER 1051 (inherent risk).

[67] *Lloyd's Bank Ltd v Bundy* [1975] QB 326 (CA).

[68] *National Westminster Bank Plc v Morgan* [1985] AC 686 (HL).

[69] See the text accompanying n 13.

VIII. RELATION OF JUDICIAL DEVELOPMENT TO LEGISLATION

It has sometimes been suggested that reform of the law is for the legislature, and that, if no legislation is applicable the court is bound to enforce contracts without regard to considerations of unfairness. In *Seidel v Telus Communications Inc*[70] the Supreme Court of Canada held that an arbitration clause was not effective to exclude a class action under the British Columbia Business Practices and Consumer Protection Act, but the reasoning of the majority turned on the precise wording of the statute, and included the following:[71]

> The choice to restrict or not to restrict arbitration clauses in consumer contracts is a matter for the legislature. Absent legislative intervention, the courts will generally give effect to the terms of a commercial contract freely entered into, even a contract of adhesion, including an arbitration clause.

It is true that this comment is obiter, and it does suppose a contract 'freely' entered into, but it seems to contemplate that a standard form contract, even in the consumer context, and even if very burdensome, will normally be binding. The comment on 'legislative intervention' might be read to suggest that all contractual clauses are valid unless explicitly prohibited by legislation. An alternative, more realistic, more historical, and more flexible view would (it may be suggested) be that the court may develop equitable or common law doctrines, such as unconscionability or public policy, by analogy with legislation, even though legislation in the relevant jurisdiction is not precisely applicable. It is not realistic to suppose that legislative silence on the question of arbitration clauses in consumer contracts, for example, is equivalent to a statute positively requiring enforcement of such clauses in all circumstances; nor could it be supposed that the prohibition of one kind of potentially abusive clause is equivalent to an explicit legislative command that all other imaginable clauses, however unfair, must positively be enforced. As the Chief Justice of Canada has said, extrajudicially:[72]

> [L]egislatures only rarely intervene to correct anomalies in the law of private obligation ... there is a broad sphere of private action which is untouched by [legislative] constraints and which is regulated only by the common law of tort, contract and equity. Change in this area, if it is to be made at all, must be made by the courts.

More generally, it might be said that if the courts require legislative authority for granting relief against unfair contracts, they already have it in the form of the Judicature Act provision that the modern court must administer equity, and, in case of conflict with the common law, equity is to prevail.

The need for a general power to control unfair contracts is illustrated by such cases as *Credit Lyonnais Bank Nederland NV v Burch*, mentioned above. Another recent

[70] *Seidel v TELUS Communications Inc* 2011 SCC 15; [2011] 1 SCR 531.

[71] ibid [2]; see also [160].

[72] B McLachlin, 'The Evolution of the Law of Private Obligation: The Influence of Justice La Forest' in R Johnson and J McEvoy (eds), *Gerard V La Forest at the Supreme Court of Canada, 1985–1997* (published for the Supreme Court of Canada Historical Society by the Canadian Legal History Project, University of Manitoba, 2000) 21, 23.

case that would astonish observers in most European jurisdictions is the decision of the British Columbia Court of Appeal in *Loychuk v Cougar Mountain Adventures Ltd.*[73] The plaintiffs were injured while engaging in a recreational activity known as zip-lining, which involves sliding at high speed along a steeply-inclined wire to which the participant is strapped in a harness. A collision occurred when one of the plaintiffs was stopped between platforms and, due to miscommunication between those operating the system, the other plaintiff was released onto the same stretch of line. The defendant 'admitted that the accident was caused by the negligence of its employees'[74] but *summary judgment* was given for the defendant, and upheld by the Court of Appeal, on the basis of a standard-form signed waiver. The granting of summary judgment implies that no degree of negligence, however egregious, could entitle the plaintiff to a remedy. The waiver was found not to be unconscionable, either in equity or under the relevant consumer protection legislation. In English or European law, and probably in the law of many other jurisdictions, the waiver would have been invalid insofar as it attempted to exclude liability for negligence causing personal injury.[75] The waiver is objectionable from the perspective of unjust enrichment: the claimant has given up a very valuable right (the right to compensation for potentially serious injury caused by negligence) in exchange for something of little value (a brief thrill). The objectionable aspects of the contract are increased when it is considered that such exclusions of liability may be hidden in fine print standard forms, or imposed in computer-generated transactions, and waiver forms are often presented to participants at a point when it is difficult, as a practical matter, for the participant to withdraw (after travelling to the site, or waiting in line with companions, for example). Another aspect of such cases is that anyone advertising and profiting from a potentially dangerous recreational activity can reasonably be taken to be representing to participants that the activity will be conducted with at least minimal attention to safety.

The phrase 'sanctity of contract', which still appears in modern judicial opinions, seems scarcely appropriate in a secular era (when practically nothing remains sacred). Let us allow that enforcement of contracts is a highly beneficial principle; it does not follow that it must outweigh every other human value and every other consideration of justice. Equity, while generally respecting contracts, nevertheless intervened in a variety of circumstances to prevent very unfair consequences. Attention to the past is important in this context, for neglect of legal history may foster a simplistic formalism, ironically more rigid than anything that the American legal realists sought to displace.[76] Practical considerations also are important: Margaret

[73] *Loychuk v Cougar Mountain Adventures Ltd* 2012 BCCA 122; 347 DLR (4th) 591.

[74] ibid [1].

[75] Unfair Contract Terms Act 1977 (UK) s 2(1), now in Consumer Rights Act 2015 (UK) ss 16(3)(b), 17(4), European Directive, art 3(3) and Annex, and *Principles, Definitions and Model Rules of European Private Law: Draft Common Frame of Reference*, C von Bar and others (eds), (6 vols, Sellier, 2009) II.–9:410(1).

[76] It has been suggested in a recent article that there is a political aspect to this tendency, in that the practical effect is to enable business interests to impose terms beneficial to themselves: J Feinman, 'The Duty of Good Faith: A Perspective on Contemporary Contract Law' (2015) 66 *Hastings Law Journal* 937.

Jane Radin, in a recent book,[77] has rightly objected to a form of reasoning that leads judges to turn a blind eye to the realities of commercial practice in the computer age, where submission to standard form terms is a practical necessity. It remains true, as was said 250 years ago, that 'necessitous men are not, truly speaking, free men, but, to answer a present exigency, will submit to any terms that the crafty may impose upon them'.[78]

IX. GOOD CONSCIENCE

As indicated above, the power of the court of equity to grant relief against unfair contracts was often expressed by reference to the concept of conscience, and by use of the words 'unconscientious', and 'unconscionable' to denote transactions against which the court would grant relief. As the discussion of *Aylesford v Morris* has shown, the word 'unconscionable' did not imply any wrongdoing on the part of the stronger party at the time of entering into the transaction. What was unconscionable was not the conduct of the defendant *then*, but the attempt *now* to enforce a transaction that the court had judged to be unfair. It was the transaction or its enforcement that was unconscionable, not the conduct of the defendant. Karl Llewellyn successfully introduced the concept of unconscionability into the American Uniform Commercial Code, in the expectation that this would enlarge the power of the courts openly to engage with the issues of fairness and justice that Llewellyn thought were at the heart of the matter. However, unconscionability has been given a narrow interpretation in many American, and in some English and Canadian cases, partly due to its modern meaning in common usage of 'disgraceful'. The attempt to define unconscionability, for example, as requiring proof of wrongdoing on the part of the stronger party, or proof of inequality of bargaining power, while understandable, is unhistorical, and has been unduly restrictive. It was not in the tradition of equity to limit its jurisdiction by laying down rigid prerequisites to its exercise. Not all cases of unfairness involve misconduct, nor do all cases of unfairness involve inequality of bargaining power.

Several courts and commentators have suggested that the cases of relief against forfeitures and penalties may be regarded as cases of 'unconscionability'. This appeared to offer an intellectually satisfying explanation of apparently disparate and anomalous cases, and so has had a natural attraction to the legal mind (academic and judicial), but, ironically, it may lead to a restriction on the powers of the courts. One commentator (favouring expansive powers of relief) may say that the forfeiture and penalty cases are instances of unconscionability, with the idea of showing that a general power to grant relief against unfair contracts has been, and should be widely recognised, but another (seeking to restrict the court's power) may accept that forfeitures and penalties are aspects of unconscionability but conclude that therefore relief should be *withheld* unless the supposed strict criteria of unconscionability are

[77] M Radin, *Boilerplate: The Fine Print, Vanishing Rights, and the Rule of Law* (Princeton NJ, Princeton University Press, 2013).

[78] Lord Northington in *Vernon v Bethell* (n 22) 113.

established, ie, proof of wrongdoing, or of inequality of bargaining power. The latter approach would not be expansive, but restrictive: the old cases on mortgages and penalties did not require proof of wrongdoing, or of inequality of bargaining power. Relief was granted because strict enforcement of contractual provisions would sometimes result in awards that were perceived as disproportionate and extravagant, given that the claimant's real interest was the enforcement of security for the debt (in the case of a mortgage) or for the performance of the main contractual obligation (in the case of a penalty). Relief was independent of any question of inequality of bargaining power. The unjust enrichment perspective was prominent: it was unjust to confer an extravagant windfall on one party at the expense of the other, when the claimant's legitimate expectation could be satisfied by a more moderate award.

X. THE *ÇUKUROVA* CASE

These reflections provide a convenient introduction to the recent case of *Çukurova Finance International Ltd v Alfa Telecom Turkey Ltd.*[79] This was not a case of inequality of bargaining power. The sums of money involved were very large, and the case was argued several times before the Judicial Committee of the Privy Council. Simplifying the facts, a loan was made of US$1.352 billion at a high interest rate, the loan being secured by shares that represented a controlling interest in a very profitable Turkish cell phone company (Turkcell). On the occurrence of certain events of default the lender was entitled to immediate repayment of the loan, and, on default of immediate repayment, entitled to appropriate the shares. An event occurred that was found to be an 'event of default', and the lender demanded repayment, which was tendered, but rejected on the ground that it was too late, the lender's real motive being not to recover the loan but to take control of the cell phone company. The borrower then paid the amount into an interest-bearing escrow account.

In the Privy Council the principal question was whether the borrower was entitled to relief from forfeiture. The Court held unanimously that relief from forfeiture was available, that such relief was not confined to mortgages of real property,[80] that it was available in commercial cases, and that the Court would exercise a broad and flexible discretion in setting the precise terms of relief. On the subsequent hearing to settle the terms of relief the Court held, by a majority, that, though normally a party seeking relief from forfeiture would have to comply with all the terms of the original contract, this was not an inflexible rule, and in this case, where the lender had rejected the tender of repayment, and the borrower had paid the money into an escrow account, it was appropriate to grant relief from the high interest required under the contract during the period when the escrow account had existed. An order was made permitting redemption of the shares on payment of the appropriate sum by a certain date. The lender then took steps, including obtaining an injunction in New York, designed to prevent the borrower from raising the necessary sum, the

[79] *Çukurova (No 3)* (n 4).
[80] Cited with approval on this point in *Cavendish Square* (n 27) [17].

motive again being to obtain control of the cell phone company. On a further hearing, the Judicial Committee held, unanimously, that a further extension of time for repayment would be allowed.

This complex case manifests a dynamic and flexible approach to the court's equitable jurisdiction. The unanimous holding that the jurisdiction to grant relief extends beyond mortgages of land is significant,[81] as is the reaffirmation that 'the mere fact that the transaction is commercial in nature does not preclude the jurisdiction to grant relief from forfeiture, provided that the forfeiture is of possessory or proprietary rights'.[82] In the second of the three cases reported in the Law Reports, *Çukorova (No 4)*, the majority of the Board adopted a flexible approach to setting the terms of relief, with frequent references to equity and unconscionability.[83] On the question of the need for certainty (an understandable reason for restraint in the use of judicial discretion, and a central concern of the minority in this case), the majority quoted Oliver Wendell Holmes Jr, with approval:[84]

> The language of judicial decision is mainly the language of logic. And the logical method and form flatter that longing for certainty and for repose which is in every human mind. But certainty generally is an illusion and repose is not the destiny of man.

On the relation of equity to the powers of the modern court, the majority said, quoting the Australian authors Meagher, Gummow and Lehane, 'that what was really involved was "a return to the more remote past when equity jurisprudence had dynamism lost with the attainment of the rigidity for which Lord Eldon was so praised by nineteenth century positivists"'.[85] The approving reference to 'dynamism' is significant.

The majority added the words:[86]

> Nevertheless, the Board emphasises that it is in no way suggesting that equity recognises any general or open-ended discretion. The Board's reasoning and decision in this case are based on and confined to what it sees as an exceptional situation, in which it would, in the Board's view, be both inequitable and unconscionable to ignore the background and circumstances of the tender.

further adding that 'The unusual facts of this case are in this respect probably unlikely to be repeated'.[87] These words indicate the understandable concern of the majority, as well as of the minority, to preserve a measure of certainty and predictability. But it may be observed that these words are unlikely, in practice, to restrict greatly the future exercise of discretion, for in any case in which the court will be inclined to grant relief it will not be difficult to describe the circumstances as 'inequitable', 'unconscionable,' or 'exceptional'. This observation is not intended as a

[81] *Çukorova (No 3)* (n 4) [92].
[82] ibid [95].
[83] *Çukorova (No 4)* (n 4) [13], [17], [26], [44], [45].
[84] ibid [43], Oliver Wendell Holmes Jr, 'The Path of the Law' (1897) 10 *Harvard Law Review* 457, 461.
[85] *Çukorova (No 4)* [43].
[86] ibid [44].
[87] ibid.

criticism of the majority decision; rather it recognises the force of what they had implied in the previous paragraph, that certainty, though important, cannot be a consideration that overrides every other value in legal decision-making. Lord Neuberger of Abbotsbury PSC, one of the two dissenting judges in *Çukorova (No 4)*, has spoken more recently of 'the familiar tension between the need for principle, clarity and certainty in the law with the *equally important* desire to achieve a fair and appropriate result in each case' (emphasis added).[88]

Another significant feature of the majority judgment in *Çukorova (No 4)* is the recognition of the link between the forfeiture and the penalty cases:[89]

> Likewise, Nicholls LJ ... treated forfeiture of a lease on non-payment of rent and forfeiture of a mortgage together and both as stemming from the same underlying principle as that governing penalty clauses. For centuries, he said, 'equity has given relief against such provisions by not permitting the innocent party to recover ... more than his loss'.

This comment recognises the force of the unjust enrichment perspective. The fundamental objection to strict enforcement of the contractual provisions is, both in forfeiture and in penalty cases, the undue enrichment of the claimant, who may recover far more by strict enforcement than could reasonably have been expected from the ostensible purpose of the forfeiture or penalty clauses (that is, to give security for performance of the other party's principal obligation). It is true that judgment is required to determine the 'ostensible purpose' of the transaction, and in some cases this might present difficulties, but often it does not: the substance of an ordinary mortgage, for example, is generally perceived as a way of giving security for repayment of a loan, not as a kind of wager permitting the lender to make random and disproportionate profits from trivial breaches.

XI. GOOD FAITH

The facts of the *Çukurova* case naturally prompt the thought that the lender was not acting in good faith in rejecting—indeed in actively impeding—the borrower's attempts to repay the loan, the lender's true motive being not to secure repayment but to gain control of the cell phone company. The question of bad faith was argued before the Privy Council in *Çukurova (No 3)*, and rejected (unanimously) as a ground of relief:[90]

> The acquisition of control was a necessary incident of a permitted mode of satisfying the debt. The fact that it was an incident which was highly attractive to [the lender] does not mean that the right of appropriation was exercised in bad faith ... More generally ... the Board considers that if a chargee enforces his security for the proper purpose of satisfying the debt, the mere fact that he may have additional purposes, however significant, which are collateral to that object, cannot vitiate his enforcement of the security. If the law were

[88] *Jetivia SA v Bilta (UK) Ltd* [2015] UKSC 23; [2016] AC 1 [13].

[89] *Çukurova (No 4)* (n 4) [19] quoting Nicholls LJ in *Jobson v Johnson* [1989] 1 WLR 1026 (CA) 1038. In *Cavendish Square* (n 27) however, distinctions were drawn between penalty clauses and relief against forfeiture.

[90] *Çukurova (No 3)* (n 4) [77]–[78].

> otherwise, the result would be that the exercise of the right to enforce the charge for its proper purpose would be indefinitely impeded because of other aspects of the chargee's state of mind which were by definition irrelevant.

This passage demonstrates one of the recurrent difficulties in seeking to employ the concept of good faith in order to control unfair contractual provisions: if the claimant has a contractual right, it cannot be bad faith to seek to enforce it, and if the contractual right is to be limited, there must be a reason for the limitation independent of the claimant's motive. Nevertheless, although the Privy Council rejected a direct appeal to considerations of good faith, the Board was evidently influenced, from beginning to end of the three cases (Nos 3 to 5), by the consideration that the purpose of the transfer of the shares was to secure repayment of the loan, whereas the lender's real motive was not to secure repayment, but to gain control of the cell phone company.

The recent decision of the Supreme Court of Canada in *Bhasin v Hrynew* raises directly the possibility of dealing with cases of contractual unfairness through the concept of good faith. The case involved an agreement between Bhasin and a company called Can-Am for the marketing of educational savings plans. The contract included a clause providing for renewal at the end of a three-year period unless one of the parties gave six months' notice to the contrary. Can-Am formed the intention to give such notice, but concealed its intention from Bhasin, dealt secretly with a competitor of Bhasin's, and misled Bhasin into thinking that the contract would be renewed. The court of first instance had held that this was a breach of an obligation of good faith. When the case reached the Supreme Court of Canada, the Court held that there was a duty in every contract to act honestly in its performance, and that Can-Am was in breach of this duty. The Court also said that good faith 'is a general organizing principle of the common law of contract which underpins and informs the various rules in which the common law, in various situations and types of relationships, recognizes obligations of good faith contractual performance'.[91]

The Court then gave various instances of the recognition in existing law of this 'general organizing principle'. The significant aspect of the judgment in the present context is that relief for unfairness was included as such an instance. The Court said:[92]

> Thus we see, for example, that good faith notions have been applied to particular types of contracts, particular types of contractual provisions and particular contractual relationships. It also underlies doctrines that explicitly deal with fairness in contracts, such as unconscionability …
>
> Considerations of good faith are apparent in doctrines that expressly consider the fairness of contractual bargains, such as unconscionability. This doctrine is based on considerations of fairness and preventing one contracting party from taking undue advantage of the other.

[91] *Bhasin v Hrynew* (n 5) [33].
[92] ibid [42]–[43].

In dealing with the power to exclude the obligation of honesty the Court said:[93]

> I am at this point concerned only with a new duty of honest performance and, as I see it, this should not be thought of as an implied term, but a general doctrine of contract law that imposes as a contractual duty a minimum standard of honest contractual performance. It operates irrespective of the intentions of the parties, and is to this extent analogous to equitable doctrines which impose limits on freedom of contract, such as the doctrine of unconscionability ...
>
> Because the duty of honesty in contractual performance is a general doctrine of contract law that applies to all contracts, like unconscionability, the parties are not free to exclude it.

In another significant paragraph the Court referred to the civil law:[94]

> The *Civil Code of Québec* recognizes a broad duty of good faith which extends to the formation, performance and termination of a contract and includes the notion of abuse of contractual rights ... While this is not the place to expound in detail on good faith in the Quebec civil law, it is worth noting that good faith is seen as having two main aspects. The first is the subjective aspect, which is concerned with the state of mind of the actor, and addresses conduct that is, for example, malicious or intentional. The second is the objective aspect which is concerned with whether conduct is unacceptable according to the standards of reasonable people. As J-L Baudoin and P-G Jobin explain ... 'a person can be in good faith (in the subjective sense), that is, act without malicious intent or without knowledge of certain facts, yet his or her conduct may nevertheless be contrary to the requirements of good faith in that it violates objective standards of conduct that are generally accepted in society'.

This objective standard of good faith is, in effect, an objective standard of fairness. In referring to it in this way the Court might be taken to imply that the common law could, with advantage, adopt a similar approach.

The Court also referred at several points to the duty of good faith in American law. The duty of good faith has been very narrowly construed by many American courts, so as to require actual misconduct, or conduct close to fraud, in order to establish a breach of the duty.[95] Probably the Supreme Court of Canada did not intend to import such a narrow interpretation into Canadian law, but the matter is not entirely free from doubt, as the judgment contains some internal tensions.[96] Part of the difficulty in formulating a single principle is that the concept of good faith has

[93] ibid [74]–[75].

[94] ibid [83].

[95] P McMahon, 'Good Faith and Fair Dealing as an Underenforced Legal Norm' (2015) 99 *Minnesota Law Review* 2051; Feinman, 'The Duty of Good Faith' (n 76).

[96] The overall tone is expansive in the direction of granting relief for unfairness, but the Court says that 'experience in Quebec and the United States shows that even very broad conceptions of good faith have not impeded contractual activity or contractual stability: see, e.g., J Pineau ...' [85], and a US decision refusing to find a breach of the duty of good faith is cited with approval at [87]. This might suggest approval of United States experience. However, the amalgamation of Quebec and United States experience, and the immediate reference to a Quebec author, point towards an objective standard of good faith. At one point [65] the Court says that appropriate regard for the other party's legitimate contractual interests 'merely requires that a party not seek to undermine those interests in bad faith', but this comment was made in the context of distinguishing good faith from the exceptional obligations associated with fiduciary duty, and presumably was not intended to require proof of (subjective) bad faith in determining relief for unfairness, or in implying terms.

been used for several entirely different purposes, including imposition of a requirement of actual honesty (as in *Bhasin* itself), interpretation of contractual obligations, supplementing contractual obligations, controlling unfair agreements, restricting the exercise of contractual rights, imposing a duty of disclosure in pre-contractual negotiations, imposing a duty not to break off negotiations prematurely, awarding punitive damages, determining when a contract induced by misrepresentation or mistake can be enforced, and determining when a buyer of property can acquire title from a non-owner. Good faith may be welcomed, not as supplying a single simple solution to all these problems (this is not attainable), but as recognising a residual power in the court to do practical justice where doctrines of contract law of general application would otherwise lead to an unjust result.

XII. CONCLUSION

Conscience and its verbal derivatives have deep historical roots, but have not proved wholly satisfactory for dealing in modern times with unfairness in contracts. The concept of conscience is not a persuasive basis for the imposition or modification of legal obligations in the twenty-first century: the word has religious overtones, and it suggests a matter that is for the private consideration only of the individual whose conscience might be affected. Moreover, 'unconscionability' has been taken sometimes to imply the need for proof of some highly objectionable conduct, and sometimes to imply the need to establish, as a prerequisite to relief, proof of inequality of bargaining power. Good faith can offer an alternative approach, but carries the danger that the ordinary, or subjective, meaning of those words would be too narrow as a test of unfairness, and might actually restrict the existing powers of the court to grant relief. In many cases in which equitable relief has traditionally been given, the advantaged party cannot be shown to have had any sort of improper, dishonest or corrupt motive, and the cases on implied terms (often identified as a method of securing standards of good faith in the common law)[97] have never required proof of bad motive. This danger can be avoided by giving to good faith a specialised and objective meaning, as the Supreme Court of Canada implies might be done by its reference to Quebec law. No doubt legal phrases can be given, and have been given, special meanings, and no doubt the concept of good faith, or that of abuse of rights, also mentioned by the Supreme Court of Canada, could be used to control unfairness in the common law,[98] as they have done in the civil law. But once it is recognised that the court's power to grant relief is, in the words of the Supreme Court, 'based on considerations of fairness and preventing one contracting party from taking undue advantage of the other',[99] it would seem simpler to grasp the nettle, and to adopt a test along the lines of taking unfair advantage, or imposing an unfair burden.

[97] *Bhasin v Hrynew* (n 5) [44]; *Energy Fundamentals Group Inc v Veresen Inc* 2015 ONCA 514.

[98] See *Tercon Contractors Ltd v British Columbia (Transportation and Highways)* 2010 SCC 4; [2010] 1 SCR 69 [118], where Binnie J (dissenting, but not on this point) said, 'Freedom of contract, like any freedom, may be abused'.

[99] *Bhasin v Hrynew* (n 5).

It would certainly be possible to conceptualise such a test as an aspect of good faith, but, if so, this must be good faith in the objective sense of conformity to 'the standards of reasonable people'.[100] If the proposition came to be accepted that it is contrary to the requirements of good faith to seek to enforce a contractual obligation that is very unfair, good faith might, indeed, come to be understood as a modern version of equity. As with conscience in equity, the lack of good faith would occur, conceptually, not at the formation of the obligation, but in the attempt to enforce it when it has been determined by a court of justice to be very unfair. The comparison with equity was made by a leading civilian academic, Professor Martijn Hesselink, who wrote:[101]

> Good faith does not differ much from what the English lawyers have experienced with equity ... It does not make any more sense for a common lawyer to fight the concept of good faith than it would have been to fight the whole of equity.

But if the civilian concept of good faith is to be embraced as equivalent to equity it is essential to note, as Hesselink also explained, that the concept is widely understood in civilian systems in an objective sense.

I would suggest that we should be more open to the exercise of judgement by the courts, even if the criteria by which judgement is exercised are flexible. A 'general or open-ended discretion'[102] is apt to arouse suspicion, but the proposition that the court has a residual power to avoid results that are very unjust might be more readily accepted. At least, few would wish to affirm the contrary, ie, that the court is powerless to restrain itself from making orders that are very unjust, or, in the words of the UK Supreme Court, 'extravagant, exorbitant or unconscionable'.[103] It might be objected that recognition of such a power would lead to uncertainty, or that reform should be left to legislation. As to uncertainty, two responses may be suggested: first, that certainty is not the only objective of a court of justice; and second, that if results are perceived to be unduly harsh certainty will not in practice be attained, because ingenious ways of avoiding injustice are likely to be devised. Leaving the matter to legislation is not a satisfactory response, particularly in jurisdictions with weak consumer protection legislation but also in all jurisdictions in respect of matters falling nearly but not quite within relevant legislation, or not quite within applicable judge-made categories. The modern court has ample powers, derived from equity and affirmed by the Judicature Acts, to modify contracts in order to avoid injustice.

[100] ibid [83].

[101] M Hesselink, 'The Concept of Good Faith' in A Hartkamp and C Bar (eds), *Towards a European Civil Code*, 4th edn (Alphen ann den Rijn, Kluwer Law International BV, 2010) 648. See also H Schulte-Nolke and others (eds), *Principles Definitions and Model Rules of European Private Law: Draft Common Frame of Reference*, vol I (Munich, Sellier European Law Publishers, 2009) 677, where an objective standard seems to be contemplated ('community standards of decency and fairness'). The comparison between good faith and equity is also made by M Chen-Wishart, 'The Nature of Vitiating Factors in Contract Law' in G Klass, G Letsas and P Saprai (eds), *Philosophical Foundations of Contract Law* (Oxford, Oxford University Press, 2014) 296, 313.

[102] *Çukurova (No 4)* (n 4) [44].

[103] *Cavendish Square* (n 27) [152].

5

Undue Influence and Unconscionability

HUGH BEALE

BOTH UNDUE INFLUENCE and unconscionability are grounds on which a claimant may seek to undo a transaction and recover the money or other property that the claimant has transferred to the defendant. Either doctrine can also be used as a defence.[1] This is particularly common with undue influence, for example where a surety resists enforcement of a guarantee that she has given to a bank on the basis that either the bank itself[2] or a third party[3] obtained the guarantee by undue influence. There does not seem to be any difference in the rules applicable according to whether the relevant doctrine is used as a ground for restitution or as a defence. Nor do the formal doctrines appear to differ according to whether the transaction was an inter vivos gift[4] or an onerous contract,[5] though I argue below that the nature of the transaction is relevant to the way in which the doctrines apply.

In this chapter a central question I address is whether relief can be given for undue influence or unconscionability if the defendant has not deliberately exploited the claimant. The discussion is limited to English authorities. This is because Commonwealth courts have taken a more liberal approach.[6] This may well be part of the development of a law of contract that is more suited to conditions in the relevant jurisdiction than the rather rigid and limited approach of the English courts, which may not be prepared to follow the Commonwealth leads.[7]

[1] Purely for convenience, in both types of case I will refer to the party against whom undue influence or unconscionable behaviour is alleged as the defendant and male, and the party seeking to avoid the transaction or to use the relevant doctrine as a defence as the claimant and female.

[2] As in *Lloyds Bank Ltd v Bundy* [1975] QB 326 (CA) (successfully) and in *National Westminster Bank Plc v Morgan* [1985] AC 686 (HL) (unsuccessfully, because there was no relationship of trust and confidence between the wife who gave the guarantee and the bank).

[3] As in the 'surety wife' cases exemplified by *Royal Bank of Scotland v Etridge (No 2)* [2001] UKHL 44; [2002] 2 AC 773.

[4] The doctrine on undue influence that applies to testamentary gifts is different: see N Enonchong, *Duress, Undue Influence and Unconscionable Dealing*, 2nd edn (London, Sweet & Maxwell, 2012) ch 13. I do not consider it in this chapter.

[5] See A Burrows, *The Law of Restitution*, 3rd edn (Oxford, Oxford University Press, 2011) 289.

[6] See D Capper, 'The Unconscionable Bargain in the Common Law World' (2010) 126 *LQR* 403.

[7] cf P Ellinghaus, 'An Australian Contract Law' (1989) 2 *Journal of Contract Law* 13.

I. UNDUE INFLUENCE

A. Deliberate Exploitation?

The debate over whether undue influence necessarily involves dishonest exploitation is well-known. It is helpfully described, for example, in *Goff & Jones: The Law of Unjust Enrichment*.[8] There are a number of cases since *Royal Bank of Scotland v Etridge (No 2)* in which the courts have held that the doctrine exists to protect the claimant and that, as Mummery LJ put it in *Pesticcio v Huet*, 'a transaction may be set aside by the court even though the actions or conduct of [the defendant] could not be criticized as wrongful'.[9] The balance of judicial opinion, however, seems to be that undue influence involves victimisation and exploitation.[10] Similarly there is a variety of views in the academic and extra-judicial writing, ranging from Birks and Chin's account of the doctrine as 'plaintiff-sided'[11] through to Sir Kim Lewison's 'we are concerned ... with tyranny, trickery and fraud'.[12] It has been cogently argued that neither position is correct, and that the English law of undue influence is best explained in relational terms.[13]

A great deal depends on the meaning of words like 'wrongful'—did Mummery LJ mean to include unintentional wrongs? And when in *CIBC Mortgages plc v Pitt*[14] Lord Browne-Wilkinson described undue influence as a species of fraud, was he referring only to dishonest conduct? *Goff & Jones*[15] points out that he may have been referring to a wider notion in equity, summarised by Viscount Haldane LC in *Nocton v Ashburton*[16] thus:

> It must now be taken to be settled that nothing short of proof of a fraudulent intention in the strict sense will suffice for an action of deceit ... But when fraud is referred to in the wider sense in which the books are full of the expression, used in Chancery in describing cases which were within its exclusive jurisdiction, it is a mistake to suppose that an actual intention to cheat must always be proved. A man may misconceive the extent of the obligation which a Court of Equity imposes on him. His fault is that he has violated, however

[8] C Mitchell, P Mitchell and S Watterson (eds), *Goff & Jones: The Law of Unjust Enrichment*, 8th edn (London, Sweet & Maxwell, 2011) paras 11-08 ff. See also M Chen-Wishart, 'Undue Influence: Vindicating Relationships of Influence' (2006) 59 *Current Legal Problems* 231, 236–39.

[9] *Pesticcio v Huet* [2004] EWCA Civ 372 [20]. See also *Hammond v Osborn* [2002] EWCA Civ 885; [2002] WTLR 1125 [32] (Sir Martin Nourse) and other cases cited in *Goff & Jones* (n 8) at para 1-08, fn 10.

[10] A very clear example, quoted by *Goff & Jones* (n 8), is Lord Millett in *National Commercial Bank (Jamaica) Ltd v Hew* [2003] UKPC 51; [2004] 2 LRC 396 [28]–[33], discussed at the text to n 59. See also the many other authorities cited by *Goff & Jones* (n 8) para 11-09 fn 12.

[11] P Birks and NY Chin, 'On the Nature of Undue Influence' in J Beatson and D Friedmann (eds), *Good Faith and Fault in Contract Law* (Oxford, Clarendon Press, 1995) 57

[12] K Lewison, 'Under the Influence' [2011] *Restitution Law Review* 1, 3. The academic debate is helpfully set out by J Morgan, *Great Debates in Contract Law* (Basingstoke, Palgrave Macmillan, 2012) 196–200.

[13] See in particular Chen-Wishart (n 8) and the same author's 'Undue Influence: Beyond Impaired Consent and Wrongdoing towards a Relational Analysis' in A Burrows and A Rodger (eds), *Mapping the Law: Essays in Memory of Peter Birks* (Oxford, Oxford University Press, 2006) 201.

[14] *CIBC Mortgages plc v Pitt* [1994] 1 AC 200 (HL) 209.

[15] *Goff & Jones* (n 8) para 11-24.

[16] *Nocton v Ashburton* [1914] AC 932 (HL) 953–54.

> innocently because of his ignorance, an obligation which he must be taken by the Court to have known, and his conduct has in that sense always been called fraudulent, even in such a case as a technical fraud on a power. It was thus that the expression 'constructive fraud' came into existence. The trustee who purchases the trust estate, the solicitor who makes a bargain with his client that cannot stand, have all for several centuries run the risk of the word fraudulent being applied to them. What it really means in this connection is, not moral fraud in the ordinary sense, but breach of the sort of obligation which is enforced by a Court that from the beginning regarded itself as a Court of conscience.

It also depends on whether we are referring to the general aim of the doctrine or the requirements for relief. Some judicial statements[17] may be read as saying that only active and deliberate abuse of influence amounts to undue influence, but can also be read as stating the primary aim of the doctrine, without excluding relief being given in some cases even if deliberate exploitation has not taken place. That might be justified, for instance, on the basis that it is hard to detect whether the defendant was consciously seeking to exploit the claimant.

The central question is whether the defendant must knowingly and dishonestly have taken advantage of the claimant, or does it suffice that the defendant unthinkingly failed to take steps to ensure that the claimant was sufficiently informed and free of influence? I will argue that if we take seriously what was said by the House of Lords in *Etridge*—that there is only one type of undue influence—and if we then re-examine *Allcard v Skinner*[18] and other cases in which the claimant succeeded on the basis of a presumption, then it cannot be correct that deliberate exploitation is a sine qua non for relief.

There are other issues to consider along the way. (1) Is active exploitation needed, or does it suffice that the defendant was more-or-less the passive recipient of a gift or, when the transaction was a contract, had accepted an offer which he had not manipulated the claimant into making? (2) Must the transaction be one that was evidently disadvantageous to the claimant at the time that it was made? And (3), what is the defendant required to do to prevent the transaction being voidable for undue influence? I will argue that undue influence may involve merely passive behaviour; that in some cases it may suffice that the transaction did not at the time appear to the defendant to be against the claimant's interests if it has unforeseeably turned out badly for her; and that in cases in which the defendant was not acting dishonestly, it may suffice to rebut the presumption that the steps taken gave the claimant a reasonable opportunity to act in a free and fully informed way, even if she chose not to do so.

B. One Kind of Undue Influence

In *Etridge*[19] their Lordships were agreed that there are not two kinds of undue influence, one actual and one presumed. Rather, there are two ways of proving that

[17] E.g., Lord Nicholls in *Royal Bank of Scotland v Etridge (No 2)* [2001] UKHL 44; [2002] 2 AC 773 [6]–[7].

[18] *Allcard v Skinner* (1887) 36 Ch D 145 (CA).

[19] *Royal Bank of Scotland v Etridge (No 2)* [2001] UKHL 44; [2002] 2 AC 773.

there was undue influence, one by direct evidence and one by means of an evidential presumption that arises when the claimant and the defendant are in a relationship, normally described as a relationship of trust and confidence,[20] and the transaction between them is one that requires explanation. Relief will then be given unless the defendant can provide an explanation or show that the claimant acted freely and independently. The normal way to seek to rebut the presumption is to show that the defendant had independent advice, though this may not be sufficient.[21] However, the presumption is only an evidential one. At the end of the day the court must be satisfied that the transaction resulted from undue influence.

Lord Nicholls said:[22]

> Proof that the complainant placed trust and confidence in the other party in relation to the management of the complainant's financial affairs, coupled with a transaction which calls for explanation, will normally be sufficient, failing satisfactory evidence to the contrary, to discharge the burden of proof. On proof of these two matters the stage is set for the court to infer that, in the absence of a satisfactory explanation, the transaction can only have been procured by undue influence. In other words, proof of these two facts is prima facie evidence that the defendant abused the influence he acquired in the parties' relationship. He preferred his own interests. He did not behave fairly to the other. So the evidential burden then shifts to him. It is for him to produce evidence to counter the inference which otherwise should be drawn.
>
> ... This use of the term 'presumption' is descriptive of a shift in the evidential onus on a question of fact. When a plaintiff succeeds by this route he does so because he has succeeded in establishing a case of undue influence. The court has drawn appropriate inferences of fact upon a balanced consideration of the whole of the evidence at the end of a trial in which the burden of proof rested upon the plaintiff. The use, in the course of the trial, of the forensic tool of a shift in the evidential burden of proof should not be permitted to obscure the overall position. These cases are the equitable counterpart of common law cases where the principle of res ipsa loquitur is invoked. There is a rebuttable evidential presumption of undue influence.[23]

In other words, even when the presumption of undue influence has arisen, the court must be satisfied that the claimant was the victim of undue influence. As was said in *Royal Bank of Scotland plc v Chandra*,[24] 'the issue for the Court is whether on

[20] I will not deal with the criticisms made in *Etridge* of the notion of 'Class 2B cases', nor with the other presumption—the presumption that the relationship was one of trust and confidence—that is said to arise in Class 2A cases, save to note that Lewison (n 12) 10 and others have correctly pointed out that an automatic presumption in these cases seems to reflect social conventions that disappeared long ago. In addition the limits of some of the classes are so circular (eg 'there is an irrebuttable presumption of influence of parent over child unless the child was emancipated') or vague that in reality the Class 2A relationships give rise to no more than rebuttable presumptions of trust and confidence. See also H Beale (ed), *Chitty on Contracts*, 32nd edn (London, Sweet & Maxwell, 2015) para 8-082; A Burrows, *A Restatement of the English Law of Contract* (Oxford, Oxford University Press, 2016) 203.

[21] See below.

[22] *Royal Bank of Scotland v Etridge (No 2)* [2001] UKHL 44; [2002] 2 AC 773 [14].

[23] ibid [16]. See also Lord Clyde at [93] and Lord Scott at [158].

[24] *Royal Bank of Scotland plc v Chandra* [2010] EWHC 105 (Ch); [2010] 1 Lloyd's Rep 677 [121], cited by E Peel, *Treitel The Law of Contract*, 14th edn (London, Sweet & Maxwell, 2015) para 10-028 (on appeal, see text to nn 62–65 below).

the totality of the evidence, including any appropriate inference, it finds that the transaction was in fact brought about by undue influence'. It follows that if dishonest exploitation—tyranny, trickery, fraud or the like—is required, it should be possible to rebut the presumption not only by showing that the claimant was acting in a free and informed way but by simply showing that the defendant was not consciously exploiting her.

C. Directly Proven Undue Influence

In principle there are two types of cases in which undue influence can be proved directly: the 'pressure' cases and the 'trust me' cases.

(i) 'Pressure' Cases

I agree with the widely held view[25] that some cases in which the defendant pressurised the claimant into making a payment are properly categorised as duress, namely cases in which there was a wrongful threat to prosecute a relation of the claimant, such as *Williams v Bayley*,[26] *Mutual Finance Ltd v John Wetton & Sons Ltd*[27] and *Kaufman v Gerson*.[28] These do not involve a relationship between the claimant and the defendant; the only link to relationships is that the defendant is able to apply pressure because of the relationship of the claimant to the person to be prosecuted. Cases in which the defendant makes any threat of physical violence can also be dealt with under the heading of duress—and as it is established that the victim of physical threats may have relief unless the threat had no effect whatever on her,[29] relief should be readily available.

Cases in which the defendant uses his own relationship with the claimant—whether it be a question of emotional ties, of financial dependence, of physical dependence ('who else will look after me?')[30] or of the social and cultural context—to pressurise her into a transaction to which she is unwilling to agree should be treated differently.[31] These cases should continue to be treated as within undue influence, if only for the pragmatic reason that often there will be both emotional or other ties and a relationship of trust and confidence. In the context of the relationship between a member of the SAS and a senior officer it was said that a claimant cannot plausibly argue both that 'I was coerced' and that 'I trusted him',[32] but in emotional

[25] Birks and Chin (n 11) 63–65; A Burrows, *The Law of Restitution*, 3rd edn (Oxford, Oxford University Press, 2011) 280–82.
[26] *Williams v Bayley* (1866) LR 1 HL 200.
[27] *Mutual Finance Ltd v John Wetton & Sons Ltd* [1937] 2 KB 389 (KBD).
[28] *Kaufman v Gerson* [1904] 1 KB 591 (CA).
[29] *Barton v Armstrong* [1976] AC 104 (PC).
[30] Cf *Simpson v Simpson* [1992] 1 FLR 601 (Ch D) or *Langton v Langton* [1995] 2 FLR 890 (Ch D).
[31] Birks and Chin (n 11) 63 suggest that all pressure cases should be dealt with under duress, but they refer principally to cases dealt like *Williams v Bayley*; their position on the cases discussed in this paragraph is less clear. See also Chen-Wishart (n 8) 262.
[32] Lord Hoffmann in *R v Attorney-General for England and Wales* [2003] UKPC 22. See also *Etridge* (n 19) [314].

relationships it is perfectly possible for both emotional pressure and trust to operate simultaneously and often it will be almost impossible to tell how far the claimant was acting under pressure and how far she was trusting the other party.[33] In such cases the presumption is particularly useful.

Obviously the 'pressure' cases involve the defendant taking active steps; and at least in these cases of deliberate pressure, relief should be given however the defendant viewed the transaction at the time and even if as things turned out it is not evidently to the claimant's disadvantage: it is enough that the claimant was unwilling to enter it.[34] In *Etridge* Lord Nicholls said that[35]

> It is not essential that the transaction should be disadvantageous to the pressurised or influenced person, either in financial terms or in any other way. However, in the nature of things, questions of undue influence will not usually arise, and the exercise of undue influence is unlikely to occur, where the transaction is innocuous. The issue is likely to arise only when, in some respect, the transaction was disadvantageous either from the outset or as matters turned out.

In cases of deliberate pressure it also seems appropriate to apply the limited causation requirement that is applied in cases of fraud and duress to the person: the claimant should obtain relief unless the defendant shows that the pressure had no effect at all on her.[36] Below I argue that neither granting relief irrespective of whether the transaction seemed disadvantageous to the claimant, nor the relaxed causal requirement, is appropriate in all cases.

(ii) 'Trust me' Cases

Where the parties are in a relationship of trust and confidence it will seldom be necessary for the claimant to offer direct proof of undue influence because in most cases in which a claimant seeks relief the transaction will be one that requires explanation. However, a claimant is entitled to relief if she can show that she relied on the defendant, at least if the court concludes that he deliberately took advantage of her trust to prefer his own interests. That was accepted in *Dunbar Bank plc v Nadeem*,[37] though as we will see below the Court of Appeal held that there was no actual undue

[33] Eg *Hammond v Osborn* [2002] EWCA Civ 885.

[34] It is true, as Professor Chen-Wishart pointed out in the discussion of this chapter, that pressure is not necessarily dishonest, in that the defendant may honestly believe that what he is forcing the claimant to do is in her interest; but at least if the defendant must have known that he got his way only by pressure it is justifiable to treat such cases in the same way as dishonest pressure, in order to safeguard the claimant's right of self-determination.

[35] *Etridge* (n 19) [12]. See also Lord Scott at [156].

[36] As decided in *UCB Corporate Services Ltd v Williams* [2002] EWCA Civ 555; [2003] 1 P & CR 12 [86] (a case in which the husband 'had fraudulently procured the consent of his wife'. The reference may be to the wider concept of equitable fraud, see above at n 16, but the husband had certainly made fraudulent misrepresentations). I do not however accept the argument (at [91]) that this followed from Lord Browne-Wilkinson's statement in *CIBC Mortgages plc v Pitt* [1994] 1 AC 200 (HL) 209 that the victim has the right to the transaction have set aside 'as of right': his Lordship's point may have been merely that once undue influence has been established, rescission is not a matter for the court's discretion.

[37] *Dunbar Bank plc v Nadeem* [1998] 3 All ER 876 (CA).

influence because the defendant had not preferred his own interests. It was also in effect accepted by the House of Lords in *Barclays Bank v Coleman* (heard with *Etridge*): there was no transaction requiring explanation but a presumption arose out of the relationship, as[38] 'Mrs Coleman was not merely disinclined to second-guess her husband on matters of business, but appears to have regarded herself as obliged not to do so'. It is less clear whether unthinking action or passive acceptance on the defendant's part will suffice. At this point we need to consider the presumption cases, and in particular *Allcard v Skinner*.

D. *Allcard v Skinner*

In *Etridge* their Lordships referred frequently to *Allcard v Skinner*[39] without any apparent criticism of the decision. In that case, relief was refused on the ground that the plaintiff had waited too long before trying to recover her property; but it seems clear that, had she acted more promptly, she would have recovered any property that remained in the hands of the order. So it is worth looking again at the facts. In brief, the plaintiff had joined an Anglican religious order, established by the Reverend D Nihill and under the leadership of Miss Skinner, that involved taking a vow of poverty. She knew the rules of the order before she joined it and at that time she was still living at home (albeit possibly not happily) and was in contact with her brother and others who gave her advice, even if she did not follow it. It was not found that the Reverend Nihill had influence over her at that stage. While she was a member of the order she made substantial transfers to it; after she left it and joined the Church of Rome she tried to recover what the order had not expended, though she waited a considerable time before making her claim. At first instance Kekewich J held that she was not the victim of undue influence because when she joined the order and took the vow of poverty she was both fully aware of what she was doing and had advice, even if she did not follow it. The subsequent transfers 'were simply ministerial [ie administrative] acts required to perfect a gift already made' and it was not necessary for her to be advised again.[40]

The Court of Appeal took a different approach: in effect, there must be a lack of undue influence at the time of each transfer. But the Court specifically acquitted Miss Skinner of any wrongdoing. What weighed most heavily with the court is that the rules of the order prevented the plaintiff from taking any outside advice. Now it is quite true that once she had joined the order the plaintiff would have come under pressure from the rules that demanded a life of poverty, but that the plaintiff had freely consented to. I cannot see that she was the victim of tyranny, trickery or fraud. Rather, the defendant had failed to give the plaintiff the opportunity or a warning to seek and follow advice on whether further gifts were sensible.

In other words, at least in some circumstances I cannot see that dishonest exploitation is a sine qua non of relief on the ground of undue influence.

[38] *Etridge* (n 19) [291].
[39] *Allcard v Skinner* (1887) 36 Ch D 145 (CA).
[40] ibid 165–68.

E. Other Presumption Cases

It is not necessary to go through all the cases on presumed undue influence. The point I want to make can be stated shortly. If dishonesty is a requirement, then even before *Etridge* there should have been cases in which the defendant succeeded in rebutting the presumption, not by showing that the claimant had sufficient independent advice that her consent was adequately informed and not reliant on him (or was free of his influence), but simply by convincing the court that he was not dishonest—even if he was careless of the claimant's interests. But we do not see such cases. Indeed, *Cheese v Thomas*[41] points the other way. Nicholls VC began his judgment (with which the other LJJ agreed) by saying that the case[42] 'arises out of the all too familiar situation where different generations of a family join to provide the older member with a home. Both sides have the best of intentions, but the arrangement breaks down'.

Later he stated categorically that there had been no dishonesty:[43]

> the only issue the judge was called upon to decide on this part of the claim was whether or not the transaction was clearly disadvantageous to Mr Cheese. I mention this in fairness to Mr Thomas. Otherwise one might think Mr Thomas had behaved improperly, and sought to trick or take advantage of his aged uncle. No conduct of this sort occurred.

By the same token, it would not seem to matter that the defendant did not take active steps to further the transaction but merely accepted the gift or offer to enter a transaction, at least if the defendant knew that the claimant was relying on him to advise against it. Passive acceptance seems to be enough.[44] A parallel can be drawn to the case of entering a transaction with a person suffering from mental incapacity. In *Hart v O'Connor*, in which the Privy Council held that the claimant's incapacity would be relevant only if it were known to the defendant at the time, Lord Brightman (delivering the Privy Council's reasons) said that equitable fraud means[45] 'victimisation, which can consist either of the active extortion of a benefit or the passive acceptance of a benefit in unconscionable circumstances'.

It is less clear that 'passive acceptance' will suffice in the case where the claimant makes a gift as the result of emotional ties which the defendant has not played on. (I have in mind a claimant making an absurdly generous gift as the result of the kind of infatuation seen in *Louth v Diprose*,[46] though in that case the claimant had been manipulated by the defendant; or a case in which the claimant was acting from an

[41] *Cheese v Thomas* [1994] 1 WLR 129 (CA).

[42] ibid 132.

[43] ibid 135.

[44] Chen-Wishart (n 8) 253, 264, citing Lord Hobhouse in *Etridge* (n 19) [107]. I find that passage equivocal—Lord Hobhouse was addressing a different point. However, it is clearly enough that the defendant invited the claimant to enter the transaction without putting pressure on her: that was decided in *Bank of Credit & Commerce International SA v Aboody* [1990] 1 QB 923 (CA) 968–69 and I am not aware that this aspect of the case has even been doubted. But it would not seem to matter that (as in *Hammond v Osborn* [2002] EWCA Civ 885; [2002] WTLR 1125) the initiative has come from the claimant.

[45] *Hart v O'Connor* [1985] AC 1000 (PC) 1024. Similarly, J Devenney and A Chandler, 'Unconscionability and the Taxonomy of Undue Influence' [2007] *Journal of Business Law* 541, 569 have noted that in many of the unconscionable bargain cases the defendant's conduct amounted to no more than passive acceptance.

[46] *Louth v Diprose* (1992) 175 CLR 621 (HCA).

overwhelming sense of gratitude.)[47] On existing authority, the presumption seems to arise only when the relationship is one of trust and confidence. But I can envisage that relief might be given, if the defendant took knowing advantage of the claimant's emotional state of mind; and possibly even if he did so not dishonestly but simply without thinking about the consequences for the claimant—for example, without thinking that a gift would leave the claimant without means of support or the wherewithal to pay the tax bill that would arise.[48]

The other question is the defendant's knowledge. It is hard to think that the kind of relationship required in pressure cases could be unknown to the defendant, and similarly in Class 2A cases. In contrast, in what formerly were labelled Class 2B cases,[49] it seems now to be necessary to show that there was a relationship of trust and confidence in respect of the particular transaction, and it may be necessary to show that the defendant was aware that the claimant was relying on him on for the relevant purpose.[50] In most cases the defendant knew or 'must have known', but this may not always be the case. Possibly it will suffice that the reasonable person with the same knowledge as the defendant would have realised. It seems unlikely, however, that relief will be given if the defendant had no reason to know that the claimant was looking to him for advice or accepting his word without question.

F. Counter-examples

It is quite true that some cases[51] do seem to suggest that exploitation is required. One example is *Dunbar Bank plc v Nadeem*.[52] In this case, which preceded *Etridge*, presumed undue influence was not made out, on the ground that the transaction was not manifestly to the wife's disadvantage. On appeal it seems not to have been argued that this was case of actual undue influence[53] but Millett LJ said he need not decide the question whether[54]

> although the pen may have been the pen of Mrs Nadeem, the mind was the mind of Mr Nadeem ... because of the judge's clear finding that Mr Nadeem did not take unfair advantage of his position. Seen through his eyes, the transaction was obviously beneficial to his wife and was intended by him to be for her benefit. She was obtaining a beneficial interest in the matrimonial home for the first time. Far from seeking to exploit the trust which she reposed in him for his own benefit, he was seeking to give her an interest in the matrimonial

[47] This seems to have been a large part of the explanation for the gift in *Hammond v Osborn* [2002] EWCA Civ 885, though in that case the defendant was arranging the claimant's financial affairs, so that there was trust and confidence also, and she and her son took active steps to realise the claimant's investments. On mixed cause cases, see above.

[48] As in *Hammond v Osborn* (n 47), but as already noted, in that case there were elements of trust and confidence.

[49] And if the earlier points made about Class 2A are correct, possibly also in Class 2A cases.

[50] See Lord Hobhouse's reference in *Etridge* (n 19) [105] to the wife leaving particular decisions to the husband; *Chitty* (n 20) para 8-084.

[51] I leave aside the cases in which the point did not arise for decision.

[52] *Dunbar Bank plc v Nadeem* [1998] 3 All ER 876 (CA).

[53] See Morritt LJ, ibid, 886

[54] *Dunbar Bank plc v Nadeem* [1998] 3 All ER 876 (CA) 883.

> home 'because he was getting on'. … In my judgment, his own evidence, coupled with the situation in which he found himself, and, to my mind, objective criteria, he was not exploiting the trust reposed in him for his own benefit but seeking to turn an opportunity of his own, at least in part, to his wife's advantage.

It is not clear what Millett LJ meant by 'objective criteria' but I think that this passage should be read as saying that the husband was neither deliberately exploiting his wife's trust nor making an unreasonable choice on her behalf. So on this approach, even if the defendant did not set out to exploit the claimant's trust but acted carelessly—he should have realised that the transaction might easily work against her interest and should not have let her sign without taking steps to try to ensure that she was fully informed and willing to take the risk—then undue influence may be established. So the case seems to show that, on the one hand, deliberate exploitation is not required, but on the other hand, that in 'trust me' cases influence will not be treated as undue if the defendant acted in a way that seemed reasonable in order to promote the claimant's interests.

I believe that the decision of the majority[55] in *R v Attorney General for England and Wales*[56] may also be explained in a way that is consistent with such an objective standard. The case does not seem to have been one of deliberate exploitation, any more than *Allcard* was; but the difference is that the majority seemed to think it was not 'unfair' exploitation because they saw nothing untoward in the soldier having to enter a confidentiality agreement.[57] They also doubted if the lack of advice would have made a difference.[58] I have to admit, however, that I think the case may have been wrongly decided. Lord Hoffmann said

> If facing him with such a choice was not illegitimate for the purposes of duress, their Lordships do not think that it could have been an unfair exploitation of a relationship which consisted in his being a member of the SAS.

I do not believe the standard required to avoid a finding of undue influence is, or should be, merely that there was no blackmail.

In *National Commercial Bank (Jamaica) Limited v Hew*[59] an elderly man was given a large bank loan in order to develop a property. The lower courts held that there was a relationship of trust and confidence between the borrower and the bank. The Privy Council were clearly skeptical about this but proceeded on the assumption that there was such a relationship.[60] The Privy Council held that there was no undue influence. Lord Millett said:[61]

> it must be shown that the ascendant party has unfairly exploited the influence he is shown or presumed to possess over the vulnerable party. It is always highly relevant that the transaction in question was manifestly disadvantageous to the person seeking to set it aside;

[55] Lord Scott held that advice should have been given to the soldier; the case was in effect the same as *Allcard v Skinner* (n 18).

[56] *R v Attorney General for England and Wales* [2003] UKPC 22; [2003] EMLR 24.

[57] ibid [24].

[58] ibid [27].

[59] *National Commercial Bank (Jamaica) Limited v Hew* [2003] UKPC 52; (2004) 79 BMLR 1.

[60] ibid [31].

[61] ibid [33]–[34].

> though this is not always necessary: see *CIBC Mortgages plc v Pitt* ... But 'disadvantageous' in this context means 'disadvantageous' as between the parties. Unless the ascendant party has exploited his influence to obtain some unfair advantage from the vulnerable party there is no ground for equity to intervene. However commercially disadvantageous the transaction may be to the vulnerable party, equity will not set it aside if it is a fair transaction as between the parties to it.
>
> Their Lordships have looked in vain for any evidence that the transaction of loan was unfair as between the Bank and Mr Hew. The Bank derived no unfair advantage from it, nor any benefit which it would not have sought to obtain from an ordinary arms' length transaction with a commercial borrower.

While Lord Millett certainly speaks of unfair exploitation, 'unfair' is not necessarily 'deliberate'. But in any event, the gist of the decision seems to have been that there was nothing wrong or even risky in the loan itself, and Hew was not relying on the bank to advise him on the wisdom of the scheme for which he wanted it. The Privy Council had already dismissed an argument that the bank had been negligent in failing to advise against the scheme.

Perhaps the most difficult case for my argument that deliberate exploitation is not required is *Royal Bank of Scotland v Chandra*,[62] in which Patten LJ, with whom the other members of the court agreed, said:[63]

> As Lord Nicholls explained in *Etridge* at paragraphs [6]–[12], it is impossible adequately to classify every type of situation in which improper or undue influence can be said to have been used to persuade a person to enter into the transaction under review. But for a person's conduct to fall into this category it must, on established principles, make it unconscionable for that person and any who have notice of his conduct to seek to rely on the effect of what has been done. Conscious deception obviously satisfies this test as does an abuse of confidence in the form of a breach of loyalty or good faith of the kind described above. The trusted adviser who chooses to prefer his own interests over those of the person who confides in him is a classic example of this.
>
> The language of the decided cases summarised by Lord Nicholls in the passage I have referred to is replete with references to abuse of trust, exploitation and domination of the injured party. All of these characterise some conscious act of wrong-doing on the fiduciary's part. But it is much more difficult to apply these notions to cases of innocent misrepresentation where the highest it can be put is that more care should have been taken in giving the information or advice which was relied on. To elevate such a failure into a breach of fiduciary duty or abuse of confidence is to fall into the very trap exposed by Millett LJ in his judgment in *Mothew*.[64]

I have two points about this. The first is that even if a fiduciary who acts negligently but in good faith is not unfaithful and commits no equitable wrong,[65] I wonder

[62] *Royal Bank of Scotland v Chandra* [2011] EWCA Civ 192; [2010] 1 Lloyd's Rep 677.

[63] ibid [26]–[27].

[64] *Bristol & West Building Society v Mothew* [1998] Ch 1 (CA) 18 (where Millett LJ said, 'not every failure by the fiduciary party will amount to a breach of these core obligations. The defining characteristic of a fiduciary relationship is loyalty. A fiduciary who acts negligently but in good faith is not unfaithful and commits no equitable wrong'.

[65] *Chandra* (n 24) [24], referring to *Mothew* (n 64).

if it follows that a defendant in whom trust and confidence is reposed should be excused when he was negligent. Will not the fiduciary normally also owe a duty of care?[66] Should not the same in effect apply when there is a relationship of trust and confidence? Secondly, on its facts the *Chandra* case does not seem to be one in which the transaction called for an explanation; and though the wife reposed trust and confidence in the husband, he seems to have consulted her. The problem was that he was overoptimistic—but it was held that his optimistic statements did not a misrepresentation. So it is not a strong case from which to argue that deliberate exploitation is always necessary.

G. The Nature of the Transaction

At least since the decision in *Etridge*, it has been clear that the presumption of undue influence will not arise unless the transaction is one that is not explicable by ordinary motives. Normally this will mean a transaction that is obviously against the claimant's interests, such as a large gift or a guarantee of the defendant's business debts given when the business is already in trouble or is about to be expanded in a very risky way. But a transaction that at the time appeared to be to the claimant's disadvantage is not essential in cases in which the claimant does not need to rely on the presumption. Earlier I argued that if the undue influence takes the form of pressure, it should make no difference that the defendant did not think the transaction was against the claimant's interests.[67] I think the same should apply in cases where the claimant shows that she trusted the defendant to the extent that she simply signed whatever the defendant put in front of her and the defendant knew that if the transaction in question was explained fully to the claimant, and she were left to follow her own inclination, she would not agree to it. But it seems more problematic to say that in all the proven 'trust me' cases the claimant can have relief from a transaction she would now like to avoid if at the time, the defendant believed it was in both their interests, and particularly if the case is not one of deliberate advantage-taking but one of making a choice on her behalf. So in 'unthinking or careless failure' cases I would not expect a court to find undue influence without a finding that at the time the transaction was evidently disadvantageous, or at least potentially disadvantageous, to the claimant. This, I suggest, is consistent with the argument I made above,[68] that influence will not be treated as undue if the defendant acted in a way that seemed reasonable in order to promote the claimant's interests.

So if the defendant was deliberately using pressure or preferring his own interests, the transaction does not have to be evidently disadvantageous to the claimant; but in cases of a failure to meet an objective standard, the nature of the transaction is

[66] Cf Enonchong, *Duress, Undue Influence and Unconscionable Dealing* (n 4) para 14-035.

[67] Unless perhaps the defendant was not dishonest and was unaware that the claimant was agreeing only because of the pressure (see n 34).

[68] After discussing *Nadeem* (n 37).

relevant. In other words, there is a balance: the less blameworthy the defendant's conduct, the more important the apparent disadvantage or risk to the claimant.[69]

There are cases in which the defendant may be under a stricter duty: namely, when there is a fiduciary relationship between the claimant and the defendant. The fiduciary must not only use care and skill but is strictly liable to disclose any material fact. If he fails in the latter, the transaction 'may be set aside even if it was not disadvantageous to the principal or even if the fiduciary was motivated by good intention'.[70] The closer relationship and the obvious need to trust the fiduciary seem to justify a heavier duty.

H. Rebutting the Presumption

Earlier I argued that if deliberate exploitation were a sine qua non of undue influence, and the presumption that is raised by the combination of a relationship of trust and confidence and a transaction calling for an explanation is merely an evidential one, we would expect to find cases in which the defendant is able to rebut the presumption by showing that he was not acting dishonestly. How does my argument that there will be no 'undue' influence if the defendant was acting reasonably in attempts to further the claimant's interests fit with the presumption? I think the answer is simple: if the defendant shows that he was trying to promote the claimant's interests,[71] then the transaction has been explained and the presumption falls away.[72]

I. What the Defendant Is Supposed to Do

If the transaction is not explained in terms of ordinary motives, then to save the transaction the defendant will have to rebut the presumption of undue influence. The classic description of how to rebut it is that the defendant must show that the claimant's decision was in fact fully-informed and free of the defendant's influence—'emancipated', as Mindy Chen-Wishart puts it.[73] It sometimes appears that liability for achieving this emancipation is strict. Thus it is not necessarily sufficient that the claimant had legal advice—certainly not if it is likely that the legal advice was not fully independent, nor when the defendant knows that transaction is against the claimant's interests and that the claimant will do what the defendant has suggested,

[69] This appears to fit with the finding in *Etridge*'s case itself that there was no undue influence: 'there was no evidence of abuse ... or of bullying' and the transaction had some benefits for the wife: see *Etridge* (n 19) [221].

[70] Enonchong, *Duress, Undue Influence and Unconscionable Dealing* (n 4) para 14-028.

[71] The same might be argued in a 'pressure' case if the defendant was acting honestly and was unaware that the claimant was agreeing only because of the pressure: see n 34.

[72] See Buxton LJ in *Turkey v Awadh* [2005] EWCA Civ 382; [2005] 2 P & CR 29 [15] (the evidential burden shifts if the transaction calls for an explanation that is not forthcoming); *Chitty* (n 20) para 8-092.

[73] Chen-Wishart (n 8) 260.

advice or no advice.[74] Possibly the Privy Council case of *Inche Noriah v Shaik Allie bin Omar*[75] goes even further. There the gift was set aside even though the claimant had taken independent advice, on the ground that the advice had not been adequate—the lawyer had not known that the gift comprised almost the whole of the claimant's estate and he had not advised her that she could achieve what she wanted by a gift in her will rather than an inter vivos gift. But the case must be read in context: it was almost certainly a case of 'wicked' exploitation and the defendant had given the lawyer very little information.

In this context, *Allcard v Skinner*[76] itself is a puzzle. What might the Mother Superior (Miss Skinner) have done that would have rebutted the presumption? Or was it in effect a case in which the transaction could not be allowed stand, whatever steps she had taken? What if the Mother Superior had exceptionally suggested that despite the rules of the order, before making the transfer Miss Allcard should obtain legal advice, and (to meet Lindley LJ's point that she must also be free to act on the advice)[77] that she should feel free to follow it—that, in effect, her vows did not require her to give up all her wealth? Kekewich J said it would have made no difference, as she would not have followed the advice. The Court of Appeal did not address this. One possibility is that they saw the gifts as so contrary to the claimant's long-term interests that they could never be upheld. Even in the light of all the contemporary concerns about religious orders so well described by Smith,[78] this does not seem right. First, it is directly contrary to the spirit of Lindley LJ's dictum that the court does not set aside gifts on the grounds of 'folly, imprudence or want of foresight'[79]—I think he might have added 'eagerness to the point of obstinacy'. Secondly, on the facts it is not clear that the gift would have left the claimant unable to pursue a worthwhile life-style. She still had an income of at least £5,000 a year (that is, something over £500,000 a year today)[80] and it seems unlikely her new life-style would be so very different that this would not see her through. At a guess she wanted to recover the assets held by her former Mother Superior in order to devote them to other, probably Roman Catholic, good causes. Rather, it seems likely that the Court of Appeal thought that it would suffice that the defendant gave the claimant the opportunity to take advice that she would regard as independent (perhaps from her barrister brother or some other trusted relation, if she had one) and did their best to persuade her that she need not follow her vow of poverty on this occasion if she did not want to. If they had done both and the claimant had persisted in the gift, I strongly suspect it would have been upheld. There will be some gifts that the defendant simply cannot accept, because no reasonable adviser could ever agree to them—gifts, for example, that will evidently leave the claimant destitute. But in cases like *Allard v Skinner* where the result of the gift would be less disastrous for

74 *Bank of Montreal v Stuart* [1911] AC 120 (PC).
75 *Inche Noriah v Shaik Allie bin Omar* [1929] AC 127 (PC).
76 *Allcard v Skinner* (1887) 36 Ch D 145 (CA).
77 ibid 184.
78 C Smith, '*Allcard v Skinner*' in C Mitchell & P Mitchell (eds), *Landmark Cases in the Law of Restitution* (Oxford, Hart Publishing, 2006) ch 8.
79 *Allcard v Skinner* (1887) 36 Ch D 145 (CA) 183.
80 See: inflation.stephenmorley.org.

the claimant, while the doctrine may require the defendant to take steps to guard against the claimant's imprudence or lack of foresight, I do not think the defendant is required to refuse the gift. Not only would that impose a kind of strict liability on the defendant, it would impinge too much on the claimant's autonomy.

J. Causation

There is another way to put much the same point that the defendant is not in effect strictly liable: causation. Earlier I argued that if the defendant was dishonestly exploiting the claimant, then it is right to apply the relaxed rule of causation applied in cases of fraud and duress to the person. The defendant's influence is treated as sufficiently linked to the transaction unless it is shown that it had no effect at all. But in cases in which the defendant was thoughtless rather than dishonest, as I have argued was the view of the Court of Appeal took of the Mother Superior in *Allcard v Skinner*, it seems inappropriate to apply a causal test that is justified by a need to deter fraud.[81] It is more appropriate to apply the standard 'but for' test.[82] If the defendant were able to show that even if the claimant had taken the steps suggested in the last paragraph, she would still have made the gift—in other words, she would have made it even if emancipated from the influence—relief should not be given. It follows that although when presumption of undue influence arises, it includes an evidential presumption that the relationship caused the claimant to enter the transaction, the presumption of causation is also rebuttable.[83]

K. Conclusions

Thus I argue that, reading *Allcard v Skinner* and other cases of presumed undue influence in the light of the decision in *Etridge* to the effect that there is only one class of undue influence, with two methods of proof, it becomes clear that to insist that undue influence is limited to cases of wicked exploitation would involve at least a substantial re-working of the authorities. It may be that the primary purpose is to prevent 'tyranny, trickery and fraud' but those are not requirements. First, exploitation may be passive. Secondly, the defendant's behaviour need not be dishonest: it can consist of a failure to ensure that the claimant was properly informed, was thinking through the consequences and was acting free of the defendant's influence. Thirdly, the transaction need not always be apparently to the claimant's disadvantage at the time. Fourthly, however, the requirements vary according to the circumstances. If the defendant has deliberately exploited his relationship with the claimant (whether it

[81] This seems to have been one reason why in *Bank of Credit and Commerce International SA v Aboody* [1990] 1 QB 923 (CA) 971 the Court of Appeal suggested that the 'but for' test should apply: it refers to the fact that the bank was not personally responsible for the influence.

[82] However Burrows' *Restatement of the English Law of Contract* (n 20) 201 seems to apply the relaxed test to all cases.

[83] This also appears to be consistent with the decision on the facts in *Etridge*'s case: even if the documents had been explained to her, Mrs Etridge would have signed them: see *Etridge* (n 19) [223].

be one of emotional dependence or one of trust and confidence, or a mixture) then it is immaterial whether the defendant thought the transaction was for the benefit of the claimant; the transaction will be avoidable unless the defendant can show that the relationship had no influence at all on the claimant's decision to enter it. If the defendant had merely failed to take adequate steps to safeguard the claimant, then probably relief will be given only if the transaction appeared an unwise one for the claimant to enter, the defendant's failure was unreasonable, and if the claimant would not have entered it but for the defendant's failure.

In other words, we may be dealing with a doctrine that is deliberately over-broad because of the difficulty in proving wicked intent or because it aims, as Bigwood has argued,[84] to act as a prophylactic against it; but I would argue that undue influence encompasses not just dishonest behaviour but also a form of what Bigwood aptly calls 'transactional neglect', which will disable the defendant from enforcing or retaining the benefit of the transaction.[85] These special rules of undue influence are dependent on and justified by the relationship.

This means that the doctrine cannot be viewed as entirely 'claimant sided': we are dealing with, I argue, a combination of impaired consent and deliberate or neglectful behaviour on the part of a defendant; and it is the relationship of trust and confidence that in 'trust me' cases puts an onus on the defendant. The defendant must either act in what he reasonably thinks is the claimant's interest or, in the case of a transaction that cannot be explained other than in terms of the relationship with the defendant (or, in cases like *Allcard v Skinner*, with the institution the defendant represents), show that the claimant was acting independently of the relationship. So I am firmly in the 'relational' camp.[86] Nor is it surprising to find that English law looks for something more than impaired consent on the part of the claimant. It does not give relief for other kinds of impaired consent unless this was somehow the fault of or caused by the other party. So, a contract is voidable for duress only if the other party has used an illegitimate threat. English law does not give relief for mistake simply because the claimant was mistaken. If I have made a mistake in the terms of my offer, the other party can hold me to it unless it was unreasonable for him to rely on what I said because he knew[87] (or possibly should have known)[88] that I did not mean what I said or wrote. If I have made a mistake as to the facts, I will only get relief if my mistake was caused by a misrepresentation by the other party.[89] It is true that the misrepresentation may have been an innocent one;[90] but an innocent

[84] R Bigwood, 'Contracts by Unfair Advantage: from Exploitation to Transactional Neglect' (2005) 25 *OJLS* 65.

[85] English seems to lack an appropriate word to describe this situation—the defendant is not under an obligation that he can be required to carry out, nor a duty breach of which may render him liable in damages, but his rights are conditional on his avoiding certain behaviour. I believe German lawyers might classify this as an *Obligienheit.*

[86] cf Chen-Wishart (n 8).

[87] *Hartog v Colin and Shields* [1939] 3 All ER 566 (KBD).

[88] See *Chitty* (n 20) para 3-023.

[89] *Smith v Hughes* (1870–71) LR 6 QB 597 (QBD); *Statoil ASA v Louis Dreyfus Energy Services LP (The Harriette N)* [2008] EWHC 2257 (Comm); [2008] 2 Lloyd's Rep 685 (QBD).

[90] *Redgrave v Hurd* (1881) 20 Ch D 1 (CA).

misrepresentation probably must have been as to something material,[91] and misrepresentation requires an active statement, not mere silence. It is logical that relief on the ground of undue influence should be available only if there was deliberate exploitation or a failure by a person who knew he was trusted to take adequate steps to safeguard the claimant.

II. UNCONSCIONABILITY

The most obvious difference between undue influence and unconscionability is that that unconscionability does not involve a relationship of trust and confidence or an emotional relationship. Though some older cases seem to have applied the unconscionability doctrine on the basis that the claimant has a particular status[92]—'poor and ignorant'—I think it is now widely accepted that it applies when the claimant suffers from an identifiable bargaining weakness that was taken advantage of by the defendant. In *Blomley v Ryan*[93] Fullagar J listed as examples: 'poverty or need of any kind, sickness, age, sex, infirmity of body or mind, drunkenness, illiteracy or lack of education, lack of assistance or explanation where assistance or explanation is necessary'. In *Chitty* it is suggested that[94]

> The doctrine of unconscionable bargains seems to be limited in three ways. The first is that the bargain must be oppressive to the complainant in overall terms; the second that it may only apply when the complainant was suffering from certain types of bargaining weakness; and the third that the other party must have acted unconscionably in the sense of having knowingly taken advantage of the complainant.

It has been argued that undue influence can be treated merely as a sub-category of unconscionability,[95] but that was on the basis that undue influence involved wicked exploitation. If I am correct that undue influence does not require wicked exploitation, that seems to set it apart from unconscionability at least as currently conceived, especially by the Privy Council in *Boustany v Piggott*.[96] In that case their Lordships were in general agreement with the following propositions (citations omitted):

> (1) It is not sufficient to attract the jurisdiction of equity to prove that a bargain is hard, unreasonable or foolish; it must be proved to be unconscionable, in the sense that 'one of the parties to it has imposed the objectionable terms in a morally reprehensible manner, that is to say, in a way which affects his conscience'.

91 See *Chitty* (n 20) para 7-042.

92 See Devenney and Chandler, (n 45) 549.

93 *Blomley v Ryan* (1956) 99 CLR 362 (HCA) 405.

94 In *Irvani v Irvani* [2000] 1 Lloyd's Rep 412 (CA) 424, Buxton LJ, delivering the only full judgment in the Court of Appeal, said that this paragraph (in the 28th edn of *Chitty*) accurately sets out the limitations on the doctrine of unconscionability. In *Strydom v Vendside Ltd* [2009] EWHC 2130 (QB), Blair J said (at [36]): 'one party has to have been disadvantaged in some relevant way as regards the other party, that other party must have exploited that disadvantage in some morally culpable manner, and the resulting transaction must be overreaching and oppressive'.

95 D Capper, 'Undue Influence and Unconscionability: A Rationalisation' (1998) 114 *LQR* 479.

96 *Boustany v Piggott* (1995) 69 P & CR 298 (PC).

(2) 'Unconscionable' relates not merely to the terms of the bargain but to the behaviour of the stronger party, which must be characterised by some moral culpability or impropriety.
(3) Unequal bargaining power or objectively unreasonable terms provide no basis for equitable interference in the absence of unconscientious or extortionate abuse of power where exceptionally, and as a matter of common fairness, 'it was not right that the strong should be allowed to push the weak to the wall'.
(4) A contract cannot be set aside in equity as 'an unconscionable bargain' against a party innocent of actual or constructive fraud. Even if the terms of the contract are 'unfair' in the sense that they are more favourable to one party than the other ('contractual imbalance'), equity will not provide relief unless the beneficiary is guilty of unconscionable conduct.[97]
(5) 'In situations of this kind it is necessary for the plaintiff who seeks relief to establish unconscionable conduct, namely that unconscientious advantage has been taken of his disabling condition or circumstances'.

These propositions have justifiably been criticised,[98] but they do seem to make it clear that unconscionability depends on there being deliberate exploitation. They also suggest that the defendant must have taken active steps to exploit the claimant. With respect, the latter may be doubted: it is inconsistent with Lord Brightman's statement in *Hart v O'Connor* quoted earlier and probably also with what took place in some of the early cases such as *Evans v Llewellin*.[99] But leaving aside the question of 'passive exploitation', the doctrine of unconscionability seems to rest on deliberate exploitation; and it may also require that the bargain overall be oppressive to the claimant. I will return to these points later.

It is hard to get excited about the type of case to which the doctrine has traditionally been applied, sales of land at an undervalue by the poor and ignorant. With constant talk about the price of houses and land on the one hand, and on the other, improved education and better protection for those who, though not mentally incapacitated, are suffering from general bargaining weaknesses, it is at least to be hoped that such cases will be rare today. However, the doctrine may still have significant bite if the idea of bargaining weakness is more precisely defined and developed.

A. Identifiable Bargaining Weakness

Fullagar J refers to bargaining weaknesses of general kinds such as lack of education, and he may have had in mind the 'poor and ignorant persons' cases. But in cases like *Cresswell v Potter*[100] relief has been given when the claimant's 'weakness' was not so much lack of education as a failure to appreciate what she was giving up—in that case that she was surrendering a valuable share in the property to her

[97] *Nichols v Jessup* [1986] 1 NZLR 226 (CA).
[98] Eg N Bamforth, 'Unconscionability as a Vitiating Factor' [1995] *Lloyd's Maritime & Commercial Law Quarterly* 538, 550.
[99] See the discussion of the case in Devenney and Chandler (n 45) 546–51.
[100] *Cresswell v Potter* [1978] 1 WLR 255 (Ch D) (decided in 1968). In *Backhouse v Backhouse* [1978] 1 WLR 243 (Fam Div), Balcombe J said he would be willing to follow this case.

ex-husband—perhaps coupled with lack of experience of transactions of the type (conveyances and post-divorce settlement). Something similar seems true in *Credit Lyonnais v Burch*,[101] in which the Court of Appeal suggested the bank was guilty of unconscionable conduct; the claimant, a junior employee, seems not to have understood the risk that she was running by acting as surety for her employer, nor was she experienced enough to get advice before she signed. The updated version of the old 'poverty and ignorance' requirement—a 'less highly educated member' of 'a lower income group'—might have been considered relevant to explain how it came about that the plaintiff did not consider more carefully what was going on or take advice, so it might have been relevant also that there were circumstances that explained why she did not get independent advice before signing (in *Cresswell v Potter* she was dealing with an experienced lawyer who was representing the ex-husband, in *Burch* with her employer's bank); but in *Cresswell v Potter* Megarry J stated specifically that it did not matter that she *could have* got legal advice; what was important was whether she *had it*. So it seems that lack of understanding of the particular transaction, at least if coupled with inexperience and a lack of advice, is a sufficient bargaining weakness.

Ignorance of the value of other rights is also a problem. In Canada one of the main applications of the doctrine has been to agreements under which a person who has been injured has released the defendant in exchange for a paltry sum.[102] In this country the Court of Appeal in *Bank of Credit and Commerce International SA v Ali (No 1)*[103] held (Buxton LJ *dubitante*) that equity can give relief against a release of a claim on the ground of unconscionability where the release was procured by the other party's deliberate concealment of facts, if that party knew or believed that the party giving the release could not discover the facts and the releasing party had not in fact known of them. In the House of Lords,[104] the case was decided on construction of the agreement, but there is a suggestion by Lord Nicholls that in extreme cases, unconscionability might have a part to play.[105] Now, I doubt Mr Ali was suffering from any general bargaining weakness. So the suggestion again seems to be that it is unconscionable to take deliberate advantage of the claimant's ignorance of his claim. It may be that Mr Ali was not sufficiently experienced to realise that he should get advice before signing; but if Megarry J's dictum in *Cresswell v Potter* is followed, what matters is that the defendant knew that the claimant did not receive it, whether or not the claimant could have got it.

A further possible use of the doctrine arises as the result of the recent decision of the Supreme Court in *Cavendish Square Holding BV v El Makdessi* and *ParkingEye Ltd*

[101] *Credit Lyonnais Bank Nederland NV v Burch* [1997] 1 All ER 144 (CA).

[102] eg *Black v Wilcox* (1976) 70 DLR (3d) 192 (Ont CA); *Stephenson v Hilti (Canada) Ltd* (1990) 63 DLR (4th) 573 (NS SC); and other cases listed in S Waddams, *Law of Contracts*, 6th edn (Toronto, Canada Law Book, 2010) para 518.

[103] *Bank of Credit and Commerce International SA v Ali (No 1)* [2000] IRLR 398; [2000] ICR 1410 (CA).

[104] *Bank of Credit and Commerce International SA v Ali (No 1)* [2001] UKHL 8; [2002] 1 AC 251 (HL).

[105] ibid [32]–[33].

v Beavis.[106] A clause that requires a party who has broken the contract to pay a sum of money, to forgo a payment that would otherwise be due or to transfer property for less than its value, may be valid even if it does not represent a genuine pre-estimate of the loss, and even though it is aimed at deterring a party from breaking the contract. The other party must, however, show a legitimate commercial interest[107] in deterring the breach rather than simply being entitled to damages and that the clause is not disproportionate, extravagant or unconscionable in proportion to that interest.

The interesting question is whether the word 'unconscionable' has any independent role to play here. The point is that the new test requires only consideration of the non-breaching party's interest in securing performance rather than claiming damages. A clause that is not extravagant in relation to that interest might still operate very harshly to the disadvantage of the breaching party. Is there are requirement to consider the breaching party's interests?

Lord Toulson clearly thought 'unconscionable' added nothing to 'extravagant'.[108] He claimed that he was agreeing with Lord Mance on the point, but I read the relevant paragraph of Lord Mance's judgment as saying something different. Lord Mance said:[109]

> What is necessary in each case is to consider, first, whether any (and if so what) legitimate business interest is served and protected by the clause, and, second, whether, assuming such an interest to exist, the provision made for the interest is nevertheless in the circumstances extravagant, exorbitant or unconscionable. In judging what is extravagant, exorbitant or unconscionable, I consider (despite contrary expressions of view) that the extent to which the parties were negotiating at arm's length on the basis of legal advice and had every opportunity to appreciate what they were agreeing must at least be a relevant factor.

And Lords Neuberger and Sumption said:[110]

> the circumstances in which the contract was made are not entirely irrelevant. In a negotiated contract between properly advised parties of comparable bargaining power, the strong initial presumption must be that the parties themselves are the best judges of what is legitimate in a provision dealing with the consequences of breach. In that connection, it is worth noting that in *Philips Hong Kong* ...,[111] Lord Woolf specifically referred to the possibility of taking into account the fact that 'one of the parties to the contract is able to dominate the other as to the choice of the terms of a contract' when deciding whether a damages clause was a penalty.

[106] *Cavendish Square Holding BV v Makdessi* and *ParkingEye Ltd v Beavis* [2015] UKSC 67; [2015] 3 WLR 1372 1 Lloyd's Rep 55.

[107] This is not the place to explore what will count as a legitimate commercial interest. It presumably refers to an interest for which the claimant cannot be adequately compensated (for example, because the loss would be very hard to prove), rather than to merely to obtaining more money if the defendant breaks the contract. Compare the meanings attached to similar phrases in the contexts of (1) whether a party can ignore a repudiation, complete its performance and sue for the price, as in cases such as *White and Carter (Councils) Ltd v McGregor* [1962] AC 413 (HL) and its progeny (on which see *Chitty* (n 20) paras 26-104–26-106); and (2) whether the victim of a breach of contract may recover an account of profits: see *Attorney General v Blake* [2001] 1 AC 268 (HL).

[108] *Cavendish* (n 106) [293].

[109] ibid [152].

[110] ibid [35].

[111] *Philips Hong Kong Ltd v Attorney General of Hong Kong* (1993) 61 BLR 41 (PC) 57–59.

The 'disproportion' or 'extravagance' of the clause compared to the innocent party's legitimate interest in getting actual performance seems to me to be purely substantive, but these references to 'unconscionable' suggest that procedural issues are relevant also. Now it is possible that all their Lordships meant was that if the parties meet on more-or-less equal terms, the non-breaching party is less likely to get away with a provision that is disproportionate to what it needs if there is at least some bargaining pressure from the other party. But it is certainly possible that their Lordships saw a particular role for unconscionability in 'legitimate deterrent clause' cases, when the breaching party was somehow taken advantage of—even though the breaching party will seldom be suffering from a general bargaining weakness.

Even if this is not what the Justices of the Supreme Court had in mind, there is scope for the general doctrine of unconscionability to apply here. It is quite plausible that an unsophisticated breaching party, one who is certainly not poor or ignorant in general but who does not know of the clause, or who does not appreciate its possible effect, may be taken advantage of in one of two ways. First, if he has not taken into account the risk that he may commit a breach triggering the clause, he may not realise that the contract is worth a great deal less to him than he thinks and has agreed to accept or pay, as the case may be. That would be the direct equivalent of the sale at an undervalue. Secondly, even if the price offered by the non-breaching party was in fact adjusted to compensate for the risk (this might result, for example, from the pressure of competition from other potential counter-parties), so that the sale was not at under or over-value or on terms that are oppressive overall, the 'legitimate deterrent clause' may make the deal a very unwise one for the particular party, for example if the party has very limited resources with which to pay the sum or if it will not be able to absorb losing the further instalments of the price. This is no more than the commercial equivalent of those transactions in undue influence cases that are property sales which are not unfair in terms of market price but which will leave the claimant with nowhere she can afford to live. I think either situation could be accommodated within the current doctrine, provided (1) that the requirement of bargaining weakness is interpreted, as I think it should be, in relation to the particular aspect of the transaction rather than generally (and I take both the 'release' and the 'legitimate deterrent clause' cases to point this way); and that (2) the non-breaching party, at the time of the contract, was aware that the breaching party did not know of or did not understand the implications of the clause and was not advised, and the non-breaching party deliberately took advantage of the breaching party's lack of knowledge or understanding.

Indeed it may be that these situations are within Fullagar J's words as they stand: he included 'lack of assistance or explanation where assistance or explanation is necessary'. If the breaching party was patently not aware of the clause or patently did not understand it, explanation or assistance is needed.

B. Deliberate Exploitation

I am not seeking to argue that the unconscionability doctrine imposes a positive duty on the non-breaching party to ensure that the breaching party did know of and understand the clause. Authority is clearly against allowing the defence of unconscionability in the absence of dishonest advantage-taking: quite apart from the Privy Council's views in *Boustany v Piggott*, the point was clearly decided by the Court of Appeal in *Portman Building Society v Dusangh*.[112] Consistently with a requirement of deliberate exploitation, I think relief should be given only if the defendant 'knew or must have known' of the claimant's lack of understanding. It should not suffice that he 'ought to have known', even if the weakness would have been spotted by the reasonable person without further enquiry being needed.[113] In relationship cases there may be a requirement to ensure that the non-breaching party did know of and understand the clause; but the absence of a relationship between the parties, and particularly the absence of a relationship of trust and confidence, suffices to distinguish the policy we should pursue in unconscionability cases from that in undue influence. I argue, however, that deliberate exploitation of other party's lack of knowledge or understanding of one or more terms of the agreement may amount to unconscionability.

C. Exploitation of the Claimant's Need

Many laws, under one guise or another,[114] allow for relief where one party has deliberately exploited a situational monopoly to extort a high price. Thus the UNIDROIT Principles of International Commercial Contracts (2010) provide:

> Article 3.2.7
>
> *(Gross disparity)*
>
> (1) A party may avoid the contract or an individual term of it if, at the time of the conclusion of the contract, the contract or term unjustifiably gave the other party an excessive advantage. Regard is to be had, among other factors, to
>
> (a) the fact that the other party has taken unfair advantage of the first party's dependence, economic distress or urgent needs, or of its improvidence, ignorance, inexperience or lack of bargaining skill, and
>
> (b) the nature and purpose of the contract.

English law gives relief in '£1000 or no rope' cases[115] but this may be a peculiarity of Admiralty law that applies only on salt water.[116] If relief were generally available

[112] *Portman Building Society v Dusangh* [2000] 2 All ER (Comm) 221 (CA). A plea of undue influence failed because the judge found that there was no relationship of trust and confidence between the father and the son, and because in any event the transaction was not of a nature as to put the building society 'on notice'. Burrows' *Restatement of the English Law of Contract* (n 20) 211 states that the better view is that 'blameworthy' exploitation is required.

[113] cf *Chitty's* criticisms of the dicta in the recent case of *Dunhill v Burgin* [2014] UKSC 18; [2014] 1 WLR 933: see *Chitty* (n 20) paras 9-078 ff.

[114] In French law exploiting the defendant's need has been treated as a form of duress—'*violence par circonstances*': see B Nicholas, *The French Law of Contract*, 2nd edn (Oxford, Clarendon, 1992) 108–10. See now Art 1143 of the Code civil as revised by Ordonnance No.2016-131 of 10 February 2016. Such a conception is possible only in a system that in duress cases looks at the claimant's consent rather than the defendant's behaviour.

[115] eg, *The Port Caledonia and The Anna* [1903] P 184 (HC). See now the Salvage Convention 1989, given force of law by Merchant Shipping Act 1995 (UK), s 224.

[116] See Burrows, *Law of Restitution* (n 5) 306–7; *Chitty* (n 20) paras 8-048 and 8-135.

for this type of case, it might also apply to a 'legitimate deterrent clause' to which the breaching party had objected but which it did not have sufficient bargaining power (ie was not a sufficiently important customer) to persuade the other party to remove. I cannot imagine the Supreme Court wanting to grant relief in such a case, at least when the claimant is a business—which may be a very good reason for limiting exploitation of circumstances to the salvage cases.[117]

III. CONCLUSION

So I see a clear distinction between unconscionability and undue influence. Unconscionability involves the defendant's deliberate exploitation of a bargaining weakness on the part of the claimant,[118] albeit that this can include simple ignorance or lack of understanding of the relevant term of the contract, and that exploitation can also include passive acceptance of an offer from the claimant. In undue influence, the relationship between the parties is the justification for requiring more than that the defendant should not deliberately exploit the claimant. In effect, undue influence occurs when the parties are in a relationship in which the claimant is not likely to think through what she is agreeing to, whether because she leaves everything to the defendant, because she is in a situation where she is constrained by a system or simply because of emotions that are likely to mean that 'she is not thinking straight'. But the defendant who was not acting dishonestly, in the sense of deliberately exploiting the claimant's condition, is not a guarantor that the claimant was fully informed and completely independent.

What the defendant is required to do will vary according to the apparent nature of the transaction and its likely impact on the claimant; and it is suggested that the honest defendant has no more than a kind of duty of care. It is perhaps not too different to the notion of good faith employed in many continental systems, as exemplified in the Principles of European Contract Law[119] or (in a more defined form) the former proposal for a Common European Sales Law:[120]

> *Article 2*
>
> ***Definitions***
>
> …
>
> (b) 'good faith and fair dealing' means a standard of conduct characterised by honesty, openness and consideration for the interests of the other party to the transaction or relationship in question;

[117] Burrows, *Restatement of the English Law of Contract* (n 20) 210 argues that the fact that the cases are Admiralty ones is not a rational reason for ignoring them; but it may be a reason for not applying the principle broadly.

[118] cf Bamforth (n 98) 557.

[119] See O Lando and H Beale (eds), *Principles of European Contract Law: Parts I and II* (London, Kluwer, 2000) Art 1:201.

[120] Proposal for a Regulation on a Common European Sales Law, 11 October 2011, COM(2011) 635 final, withdrawn by Commission Work Programme 2015: A New Start, COM(2014) 910 final (16 December 2014), Annex II item 60, p 12.

Annex

Article 2 ***Good faith and fair dealing***

1. Each party has a duty to act in accordance with good faith and fair dealing.

2. Breach of this duty may preclude the party in breach from exercising or relying on a right, remedy or defence which that party would otherwise have, or may make the party liable for any loss thereby caused to the other party.

This of course requires the defendant to refrain from deliberate, unjustified harm to the claimant but also requires him to have reasonable regard to the claimant's interests, judged by an objective standard.

Somewhat closer to home, it is also fairly closely parallel to what is required of a party dealing with another group which commonly suffers from bargaining weakness, namely consumers. In the *Aziz* case[121] the Court of Justice said[122]

> With regard to the question of the circumstances in which such an imbalance arises 'contrary to the requirement of good faith', having regard to the sixteenth recital in the preamble to the directive and as stated in essence by the Advocate General … the national court must assess for those purposes whether the seller or supplier, dealing fairly and equitably with the consumer, could reasonably assume that the consumer would have agreed to such a term in individual contract negotiations.

Those who deal with consumers but who take it upon themselves to fix the terms of the contract unilaterally have a duty to consider what the consumer would have agreed to. Similarly, I submit, those who know or should know that they are being trusted, or their relationship may mean that the other party's judgement may be impaired, should have a duty towards the other. In contrast, in the absence of a relationship, a defendant should not be allowed to get away with deliberately exploiting claimants who suffer from bargaining weaknesses of various other kinds, but, particularly in a system whose general contract law is oriented towards commercial cases,[123] it would almost certainly be too much to require care on the part of those who deal with them.

[121] Case C-415 *Aziz v Caixa d'Estalvis de Catalunya, Tarragona i Manresa*, EU:C:2013:164; [2013] 3 CMLR 5.

[122] ibid [69].

[123] See H Beale, 'The Impact of the Decisions of the European courts on English contract law: the limits of voluntary harmonisation' (2010) 18 *European Review of Private Law* 501; *Mistake and Non-disclosure of Facts: Models for English Contract Law* (Oxford, Oxford University Press, 2012) 103–8.

6

Should Consideration Be Required for the Consensual Discharge of an Agreement By Part Payment?

MARY ARDEN

THE LAW REFLECTS a number of different values by which it has been thought right that society should be governed. These values may apply to the law generally, or they may be refined for use in a specific area where particular problems arise. To take an obvious example, the law must be fair ('the fairness principle') but in the specific context of agreements fairness may well mean fulfilling your commitments and not resiling from them.[1] To take a value at a more general

[1] Compare Lord Hoffmann's explanation in *O'Neill v Phillips* [1999] 1 WLR 1092 (HL) 1098 of the word 'unfair' as used in the unfair prejudice remedy for members in the Companies Act 1985 (UK), s 459: 'In section 459 Parliament has chosen fairness as the criterion by which the court must decide whether it has jurisdiction to grant relief. It is clear from the legislative history (which I discussed in *Re Saul D Harrison & Sons plc* [1995] 1 BCLC 14 at 17–20) that it chose this concept to free the court from technical considerations of legal right and to confer a wide power to do what appeared just and equitable. But this does not mean that the court can do whatever the individual judge happens to think fair. The concept of fairness must be applied judicially and the content which it is given by the courts must be based upon rational principles. As Warner J said in *Re JE Cade & Son Ltd* [1992] BCLC 213 at 227: "The court ... has a very wide discretion, but it does not sit under a palm tree".

Although fairness is a notion which can be applied to all kinds of activities, its content will depend upon the context in which it is being used. Conduct which is perfectly fair between competing businessmen may not be fair between members of a family. In some sports it may require, at best, observance of the rules, in others ("it's not cricket") it may be unfair in some circumstances to take advantage of them. All is said to be fair in love and war. So the context and background are very important ...

In the case of s 459, the background has the following two features. First, a company is an association of persons for an economic purpose, usually entered into with legal advice and some degree of formality. The terms of the association are contained in the articles of association and sometimes in collateral agreements between the shareholders. Thus the manner in which the affairs of the company may be conducted is closely regulated by rules to which the shareholders have agreed. Secondly, company law has developed seamlessly from the law of partnership, which was treated by equity, like the Roman *societas*, as a contract of good faith. One of the traditional roles of equity, as a separate jurisdiction, was to restrain the exercise of strict legal rights in certain relationships in which it considered that this would be contrary to good faith. These principles have, with appropriate modification, been carried over into company law.

The first of these two features leads to the conclusion that a member of a company will not ordinarily be entitled to complain of unfairness unless there has been some breach of the terms on which he agreed that the affairs of the company should be conducted. But the second leads to the conclusion that there will be cases in which equitable considerations make it unfair for those conducting the affairs of the company to rely upon their strict legal powers. Thus unfairness may consist in a breach of the rules or in using the rules in a manner which equity would regard as contrary to good faith'.

level, there is a principle that a person should not damage the interests of someone whom he has led to believe they may rely on his actions ('the reliance principle'). This principle may have its roots in the distant past in Roman law. In the specific context of contract law, two particular values stand out: autonomy, meaning here the right of a person to make his own decisions, or 'party autonomy' where both parties to a contract agree on a particular course of action; and certainty, that is, clarity and predictability in the law. And, finally, the law should generally be kept in line with society's expectations (the 'expectations principle').

Once you have identified the values or principles at play in any area of law, the next step of applying them should in theory be straightforward. But that is not always so because sometimes the values conflict, or there are different views as to the weight to be given to them. Then it is a question, to adapt Humpty Dumpty's words:

> 'When *I* use a value,' Humpty Dumpty said, in rather a scornful tone, and adjusting his curial wig 'it means just what I choose it to mean—neither more nor less'. 'The question is,' said Alice, 'whether you *can* make values mean so many different things'. 'The question is,' said Humpty Dumpty, 'which is to be master—that's all'.

The truth of this can be seen in the context of arguments to discharge the whole of an existing debt by payment of a lesser amount.

I. *FOAKES V BEER*

A. Imagine someone in debt whose creditor agrees to accept part of what the debtor owes—is that agreement binding?

In my example, the creditor and debtor get together. The creditor for whatever reason decides to accept part payment from his debtor in satisfaction of the whole debt. The debtor acts on his promise and pays the agreed amount. Later the creditor changes his mind and seeks to recover the unpaid balance.

B. Enter Julia Beer…

Along comes Julia Beer. She obtained judgment against John Weston Foakes for £2,090. When he failed to pay she agreed to give him time to pay by instalments, which he duly paid. Julia Beer (or possibly her legal adviser if she had assigned him her rights) promptly sued for what appears to have been statutory interest on the judgment. Interest for late payment had formed no express part of the parties' agreement either when originally made or when it was varied by agreement. The House of Lords agreed with Julia Beer that she was entitled to interest.[2] There was an issue as to the meaning of the parties' variation agreement but we are not concerned with that.

[2] *Foakes v Beer* (1884) 9 App Cas 605 (HL).

C. What was the reasoning on this point in *Foakes v Beer*?

The majority relied on Lord Coke's ruling in *Pinnel's Case*: 'payment of a lesser sum … in satisfaction of a greater, cannot be any satisfaction for the whole'.[3] Lord Coke had added that 'the gift of a horse, hawk, or robe, etc in satisfaction is good for it shall be intended that a horse, hawk, or robe, etc might be more beneficial to the plaintiff than the money'.[4]

How did the House of Lords reach that result? Ostensibly the majority were applying *Pinnel's Case*. They were not bound by that case. Lord Coke's observations in *Pinnel's Case* were in any event only obiter dicta. The explanation may be that the Rule in *Pinnel's Case* had been assumed to represent the law ever since that case was decided, and perhaps the majority took the view that it was important not to disturb the dust of generations on the peculiarly English doctrine of consideration.

Obviously the House of Lords were persuaded that certainty and traditional views as to consideration were all important. They did not consider any alternative to *Pinnel's Case* or any qualification to it. So the decision was that consideration was needed to discharge a contract as much as to make a contract.

D. Lord Blackburn—rumblings from Olympus?

Lord Blackburn, a Scotsman and senior wrangler and one of the greatest exponents of the common law, was more free-thinking. He was minded to dissent. Dissenting judgments are very important in the common law system because they demonstrate that the majority's view was not obvious or without its own inherent uncertainty. Lord Devlin once said that obiter dicta are 'rumblings from Olympus' which 'give warning of uncertain weather'.[5] The same applies to dissenting judgments. But, in the event, Lord Blackburn's dissent was inchoate. He expressed the view that Lord Coke was mistaken in saying that there could never be any benefit to a creditor in receiving part payment, though early payment or payment in a different place might be. Lord Blackburn took the view that Lord Coke was mistaken in his perception of benefit. But what started as loud rumblings ended up as agreement with the majority. Lord Blackburn did not think this was a matter on which it was worth going so far as to dissent:[6]

> What principally weighs with me in thinking that Lord Coke made a mistake of fact is my conviction that all men of business, whether merchants or tradesmen, do every day recognise and act on the ground that prompt payment of a part of their demand may be more beneficial to them than it would be to insist on their rights and enforce payment of the whole. Even where the debtor is perfectly solvent, and sure to pay at last, this often is so. Where the credit of the debtor is doubtful it must be more so. I had persuaded myself

[3] *Pinnel's Case* (1602) 5 Co Rep 117a, 117a; 77 ER 237, 237.
[4] ibid.
[5] P Devlin, *The Judge* (Oxford, Oxford University Press, 1979) 7.
[6] *Foakes v Beer* (n 2) 623.

> that there was no such long-continued action on this dictum as to render it improper in this House to reconsider the question. I had written my reasons for so thinking; but as they were not satisfactory to the other noble and learned Lords who heard the case, I do not now repeat them nor persist in them. I assent to the judgment proposed, though it is not that which I had originally thought proper.

E. Is the decision in *Foakes v Beer* logical?

Dear, dear!—as Tony Weir would say—come back, logic! However, the truth is that *Foakes v Beer* was not decided on the basis of logic but on the basis that the House (except Lord Blackburn) thought the ground was covered by *Pinnel*'s *Case*, which had been there since the sixteenth century. They did not see it as distinguishable. Lord Blackburn pointed out that there was no reported case in which the courts had held that if parties agreed on part payment there had to be consideration for making a contract. The majority of the House were not impressed by this, possibly because *Pinnel's Case* had always been treated as law. Is the outcome logical? I put forward four reasons why not.

First, in *Foakes v Beer*, the questions of making and renegotiating a contract were simply treated as one and the same without any analysis of why contract law has a doctrine of consideration and when it should apply. If that had been done, it might have been found that consideration is a doctrine of a highly technical nature, designed to restrict legal enforceability of an agreement to cases where both parties had got something out of the transaction, whatever the value of what they got. It is not necessarily intended to provide safeguards for parties in an existing contractual relationship who wish to vary their arrangements by agreeing on a part payment in discharge of the whole of the debt due.

Secondly, the law does not concern itself with the adequacy of consideration. So the Rule in *Pinnel's Case* does not apply if the debtor gives his creditor a peppercorn. This is artificial. Thus the House extended the operation of this anomaly and moved the common law's disregard of the adequacy of consideration into a new area. True, courts have done their best to find peppercorns in all sorts of surprising places, but the anomaly was now applied to a wholly different subject area.

Thirdly, the House of Lords' decision allowed Julia Beer *to change her mind*, which is wholly contrary to the fairness principle. They provided the ways and means for one party to an existing contract to break his word if the parties had agreed on a variation of their contract involving a part payment only of the whole debt.

Fourthly, the Rule in *Pinnel's Case* does not apply to an assignment by way of trust of part of a debt, so the creditor could have made a gift of part of the debt to the debtor by declaring himself a trustee of that part. That trust would have been enforceable at the instance of the debtor even though he was a volunteer.[7] The creditor's overall intention in this situation is the same as it would be in an agreement

[7] See, generally, *Milroy v Lord* (1862) 4 De GF & J 264; 45 ER 1185.

for part payment of a debt in settlement of the whole. The law of contract would simply be insisting on a more cumbersome way for him to achieve the objective of a binding agreement.

I would add that the outcome can also be analysed as unprincipled in its approach if it is assumed that the starting point for a court in any dispute about an agreement should be that a person is bound by what he has freely and obviously agreed. But, if that is the principle, it seems to have been lost sight of in *Foakes v Beer.*

Humpty Dumpty, reading *Foakes v Beer*, would have been unable to tell which important value of the law of contract should be the master. In the forest of consideration, he would have been unable to see the wood for the trees.

II. WHAT SHAPE SHOULD ANY LEGISLATIVE REFORM TAKE?

There have been proposals to abolish consideration altogether but the relevant question for present purposes is about legislative reform on the basis that the legislature would deal only with *Foakes v Beer*.

Any law reform measure has to contain safeguards against abuse. Otherwise there could, for example, be wicked insurance companies who put pressure on, for example, tort claimants, to accept part only of their claim. But, as *Chitty* points out, the law on economic duress could be used for this purpose.[8]

In the 1930s, the Law Revision Committee was asked to consider reform of the Rule in *Pinnel's Case* and no less a commercial lawyer than Lord Wright was appointed to chair it.[9] In its report,[10] Lord Wright's Committee proposed that the rule should be repealed by statute and replaced by a rule that, if parties did agree to settle a debt by part payment, the creditor should thereupon have no further claim unless the debtor failed to pay.[11] Lord Wright's proposal was obviously a pragmatic compromise but it would to some extent have restored party autonomy and mitigated the draconian effects of the bright-line approach of *Foakes v Beer.*

Unhappily the legislature took no note. Perhaps some powerful business group lobbied against it. I do not know. Happily, agreements to accept part payment do not come before the courts every day. But Lord Blackburn's inchoate dissent, Lord Wright's recommendation and *Chitty's* reference to economic duress suggest that it is quite absurd these days to think that, if the law were changed, creditors would suddenly be oppressed by debtors who try to twist their creditors' arms.

8 H Beale (eds), *Chitty on Contracts*, 32nd edn (London, Sweet & Maxwell 2015) para 4-119.

9 He went on (it is said) to disagree the with the decision of the Privy Council rejecting the Canadian New Deal, which was one of the factors which led Canada to abandon appeals to the Privy Council (*Attorney General for Canada v Attorney General for Ontario* [1937] AC 326 (PC)) and he had the very doubtful honour of being a member of the majority in *Liversidge v Anderson* [1942] AC 206 (HL).

10 Sixth Interim Report of the Law Revision Committee, *Statute of Frauds and Doctrine of Consideration* (Cmnd 5449, 1937).

11 ibid, para 35.

III. THE COURTS HAVE SOUGHT TO DEVELOP THE LAW IN WAYS THAT MITIGATE THE EFFECT OF *FOAKES V BEER*

Judges have sought to develop the law in ways that mitigate the consequences of *Foakes v Beer.* The principal doctrine invoked is that of promissory estoppel, which the House did not have to consider in *Foakes v Beer*. Under this doctrine, when the creditor makes a representation to his debtor that he will not require immediate payment of the debt, and the debtor relies on that representation, the courts have held that the obligation to repay the debt is suspended. The reliance may not have to be detrimental.[12] The period of suspension could be brought to an end by giving reasonable notice. This was the effect of the famous judgment of Denning J in *Central London Property Trust Ltd v High Trees House Ltd.*[13]

In *D & C Builders Ltd v Rees*,[14] Lord Denning MR and Dankwerts LJ went further and held (obiter) that courts could prevent a creditor from going back on an agreement for acceptance of part payment in satisfaction of the whole debt where that result was inequitable. According to Denning J in the *High Trees* case,[15] it would be inequitable where there had been a true accord between the parties and the debtor had relied on the promise. In that event, the effect of promissory estoppel would not be merely suspensory but would in effect extinguish the balance of the debt, provided that there was true accord between the parties. But this point did not form part of the ratio of *D & C Builders Ltd v Rees*.

So far, the question of permanent suspension has only arisen in the Court of Appeal in the context of a summary judgment application. On such an appeal the only question is whether a point is reasonably arguable. In *Collier v P & MJ Wright (Holdings) Ltd*,[16] the allegation was that the creditor, a Mr Wright, had orally agreed to accept part payment. There was a dispute about exactly what had been said. Mr Wright then (according to Mr Collier) changed his mind. Mr Collier's case was that he had acted in reliance on Mr Wright's promise in making the part payment. The Court of Appeal set aside the summary judgment so that Mr Collier's defence based on promissory estoppel could be tried.

[12] See Beale (n 8) para 4-095 (footnotes omitted): 'There is sometimes said to be a further requirement, namely that the promisee must have suffered "detriment" by acting in reliance on the promise. This may mean that the promisee must have done something that he was not previously bound to do and as a result have suffered loss: for example, by incurring some expenditure in reliance on the promise. This alleged requirement of "detriment" is based on the analogy of the doctrine of estoppel by representation. But that analogy is (as we shall see) inexact, and the equitable doctrine may be applied even though there is no "detriment" in this sense. It is enough if the promisee has altered his position in reliance on the promise so that it would be inequitable to allow the promisor to act inconsistently with it: for example, if the promisee has forborne from taking steps that he would otherwise have taken to safeguard his legal position (as in *Hughes v Metropolitan Ry.* itself); or if he has performed, or made efforts to perform the altered obligation (for example, where a seller after being promised extra time for delivery has continued his efforts to perform after the originally agreed delivery date had gone by). However, the fact that the promisee has not suffered any prejudice by acting in reliance on the promise may be relevant … for in such circumstances it may not be "inequitable" for the promisor to go back on his promise'.

[13] *Central London Property Trust Ltd v High Trees House Ltd* [1947] KB 130 (KBD).

[14] [1966] 2 QB 617 (CA).

[15] See n 13.

[16] *Collier v P & MJ Wright (Holdings) Ltd* [2007] EWCA Civ 1329; [2008] 1 WLR 643.

In my judgment in that case I pointed out that the effect of promissory estoppel is usually suspensory only but that, if the effect of resiling was sufficiently inequitable, the unpaid balance of the debt might be extinguished.[17] At the end of my judgment, I said this:[18]

> The facts of this case demonstrate that, if (1) a debtor offers to pay part only of the amount he owes; (2) the creditor voluntarily accepts that offer, and (3) in reliance on the creditor's acceptance the debtor pays that part of the amount he owes in full, the creditor will, by virtue of the doctrine of promissory estoppel, be bound to accept that sum in full and final satisfaction of the whole debt. For him to resile will of itself be inequitable. In addition, in these circumstances, the promissory estoppel has the effect of extinguishing the creditor's right to the balance of the debt. This part of our law originated in the brilliant obiter dictum of Denning J, as he was, in the *High Trees* case [1947] KB 130.[19] To a significant degree it achieves in practical terms the recommendation of the Law Revision Committee chaired by Lord Wright MR in 1937.

I was careful to say in (2) that the creditor must voluntarily accept *the offer* ie, the offer to make part payment in settlement of the debt. Longmore LJ made the point that if the creditor agrees only to give the debtor time to pay, there would not be true accord.[20] The terms of the parties' agreement were one of the major areas of dispute.[21] The Court of Appeal was not finding the facts, because they would have to be proved at trial.

Before the trial judge, there was an issue as to whether there was detrimental reliance. There was evidence from Mr Collier on that point,[22] but the judge had on the summary judgment application rejected that evidence without hearing any oral evidence, and decided that issue against Mr Collier.[23] That was one of the issues which had to be tried (see also per Longmore LJ).[24] Mr Collier's counsel argued that, in promissory estoppel, the reliance need not be detrimental[25] but none of the judgments in terms addresses that submission.

Collier v Wright illustrates the presence and interaction of each of the values mentioned in the first paragraph of this chapter: the fairness, reliance, autonomy, certainty and expectations principles.

17 ibid, 658 [37].
18 ibid, 659 [42].
19 The *High Trees* case (n 13) and the obiter dictum of Denning J referred to in the last three lines of that paragraph were explained in 655 [29]–[30] of my judgment as follows: 'This case concerns a rent reduction given by concession during the Second World War. After that war, the landlord sought to recover the difference between the reserved rent and the concessionary rent for the period following the war. Denning J held that the agreement to reduce the rent was intended to apply only while the war lasted. It was not intended to run for the full term of the lease. Accordingly the landlord could recover the full rent for the post-war period.

Denning J went on to hold (obiter) that the landlord was bound by the earlier agreement as a result of what we now call promissory estoppel: the landlord had made a representation on which the tenants relied and it would be inequitable for the landlord to be allowed to resile from his promise'.
20 ibid, 660 [47]
21 ibid, 653–54 [22]–[24].
22 ibid, 649 [14].
23 ibid, 650 [19], 653 [22]–[23].
24 ibid, 660 [48].
25 ibid, 656 [32].

IV. *WILLIAMS V ROFFEY*: THE COURT OF APPEAL HOLDS THAT PRACTICAL BENEFIT TO THE CREDITOR IS GOOD CONSIDERATION

My next case is *Williams v Roffey Bros & Nicholls (Contractors) Ltd*,[26] a case where the Court of Appeal found consideration in the form of the practical benefit of a promise to pay a sum in excess of the contract price, which was given in exchange for a promise to perform the existing contract. The promise to perform an existing obligation is not of itself sufficient consideration in law.[27]

In that case, the contractor for the refurbishment of a block of flats agreed to pay a carpenter an additional sum for each flat on which he completed the carpentry work he had contracted to do. The carpenter did not finish the carpentry work on all the flats as he promised, but claimed the additional sum for each flat on which he had completed the work. The contractor refused to make the additional payments on the basis that the performance of an existing contractual duty was not good consideration. The Court of Appeal found that the carpenter not only agreed to perform his contract but provided a practical benefit to the contractor by reaffirming his agreement to do the work. Among other things, his newly-incentivised enthusiasm for performing his obligations reduced the risk that the contractor would incur liability under a penalty clause with the main contractor. The Court of Appeal reached its conclusion without expressly referring to *Foakes v Beer*.

Roffey opened the door on a new era: that of consideration consisting of a practical benefit to the party receiving a promise as opposed to detriment to the person making the promise. The question was, however, whether that would affect agreements for part payment of debt, a question considered in the next two cases which I shall discuss.

V. *RE SELECTMOVE LTD*: THE COURT OF APPEAL HOLDS THAT *ROFFEY* REASONING DOES NOT APPLY TO DEBT RESCHEDULING

In *Re Selectmove Ltd*,[28] the Court of Appeal was concerned with an appeal by a company against a winding up order obtained by the inland revenue for non-payment of tax and national insurance contributions. The company contended the order should not have been made because it had a binding agreement with the revenue for payment of what it owed by instalments and it was honouring that agreement. The Court of Appeal did not accept that the officer of the revenue whom the company said had made the instalment agreement had any authority to do so, and held that the agreement was not binding. The Court went on to deal with a further argument by the company that the revenue had received benefit from this agreement and that, on the basis of *Roffey*, there was therefore good consideration in law for the instalment agreement. The company argued that the revenue was likely to recover more

[26] *Williams v Roffey Bros & Nicholls (Contractors) Ltd* [1991] 1 QB 1 (CA).

[27] *Stilk v Myrick* (1809) 6 Esp 129; 170 ER 851. This may be yet another principle grandfathered by *Pinnel's Case*.

[28] *Re Selectmove Ltd* [1995] 1 WLR 474 (CA).

from the instalment agreement than it would by liquidating the company. The company also argued that, although in *Roffey* the contract was one for services, the same principle should apply to a money obligation. Peter Gibson LJ, with whom Stuart Smith and Balcombe LJJ agreed, rejected this argument on the grounds that it would leave *Foakes v Beer* without any application.

VI. *MWB V ROCK*: THE COURT OF APPEAL DISTINGUISHES *SELECTMOVE* WHERE ADDITIONAL PRACTICAL BENEFIT IS FOUND

In *MWB Business Exchange Centres Ltd v Rock Advertising Ltd*,[29] the claimant (MWB), operated serviced offices in central London. The defendant (Rock) was in the business of providing marketing services. Rock had occupied the claimant's offices as a licensee for seven or eight years. Hoping to expand its business, Rock agreed a one-year contract with the claimant for larger accommodation at an increased rent. The licence period began on 1 November 2011. The licence fee was £3,500 for first three months, then £4,433.34 from February 2012 onwards. Rock overstretched itself financially and by February 2012 it had incurred arrears of over £12,000. On 30 March 2012 MWB exercised its right under the licence agreement to lock Rock out of the premises. On 2 April 2012 MWB served a termination notice, with the effect that the licence terminated on 4 May 2012. MWB brought proceedings against Rock to recover the arrears of the licence fee plus charges and damages for other losses. Rock counterclaimed, saying it was wrongly excluded and claiming damages.

The trial judge, HHJ Moloney QC, found that on 27 February 2012 the parties had made an oral agreement ('the variation agreement') rescheduling the licence fee so that Rock would pay less than the agreed amount in the first few months (increasing the arrears) followed by more than the agreed amount for the rest of the year. This was designed so that the arrears would have been cleared by the end of the contract. Rock had immediately paid MWB £3,500, which it said was the first instalment due under the variation agreement. The judge held that there was just enough 'practical benefit' to MWB in retaining Rock as a tenant to constitute adequate consideration for the variation agreement. However, he dismissed Rock's defence because of a 'no-oral variation' clause in the licence, which said that the licence agreement set out all of the terms of the agreement and that any variations to the agreement had to be agreed in writing.

Rock appealed, among other matters, against the judge's conclusion on the no-oral variation clause. MWB contended on appeal, again among other matters, that there was no consideration adequate in law for the variation agreement, relying on the Rule in *Pinnel's Case*. It was common ground that the Rule applied to an agreement deferring payment of a debt as much as it did to an agreement for part payment of a debt.

[29] *MWB Business Exchange Centres Ltd v Rock Advertising Ltd* [2016] EWCA Civ 553.

The Court of Appeal (Arden, Kitchin and McCombe LJJ) allowed the appeal.[30] The lead judgment was given by Kitchin LJ, with whom the other members of the Court agreed. The Court of Appeal held that the no-oral variation clause did not have the effect which the judge had held that it had. On the question whether the Rule in *Pinnel's Case* applied, Kitchin LJ held that practical benefit to the creditor could in the circumstances be good consideration in law for an agreement for payment of part of an existing debt in discharge of the whole, and that *Re Selectmove* was therefore distinguishable.[31]

> [U]pon reflection, I have come to the conclusion that [MWB's submissions] fail to take proper account of the full extent of the factual findings of the judge. He was clearly of the view that the oral variation agreement would have a number of beneficial consequences for MWB. First, MWB would recover some of the arrears immediately and would have some hope of recovering them all in due course. But secondly and importantly, Rock would remain a licensee and continue to occupy the property with the result that it would not be left standing empty for some time at further loss to MWB.
>
> There has been no suggestion that MWB was at any material time operating under any kind of duress. Rather, acting by Miss Evans, it had for some time been trying to find a way to accommodate Rock's financial difficulties. There was, so it seems to me, a commercial advantage to both MWB and Rock in reaching an agreement if that could be achieved. MWB would receive an immediate payment of £3,500, it would be likely to recover more from Rock than it would by enforcing the terms of the original agreement and it would also retain Rock as a licensee. Rock would remain in occupation of the property, continue its business without interruption and have an opportunity to overcome its cash flow difficulties. Accordingly this is not a case in which the only benefits conferred on MWB by the oral variation agreement were benefits of a kind contemplated by Lord Blackburn in *Foakes v Beer* and by this court in *In re Selectmove*. MWB derived a practical benefit which went beyond the advantage of receiving a prompt payment of a part of the arrears and a promise that it would be paid the balance of the arrears and any deferred licence fees over the course of the forthcoming months. This is therefore a case where, as in *Williams v Roffey*, Rock's immediate payment of £3,500 and its agreement to perform its obligations under the revised payment schedule conferred a practical benefit on MWB which amounted to good consideration, so rendering the oral variation agreement enforceable.
>
> I conclude that the judge was right to find that the payment by Rock of the £3,500 and its promise to make further payments in accordance with the revised payment schedule conferred upon MWB a benefit which constituted sufficient consideration to support the oral variation agreement. In my judgment the oral variation agreement thereupon became binding upon MWB and it would remain binding for so long as Rock continued to make payments in accordance with the revised payment schedule.

I gave a concurring judgment in which I summarised my conclusions on adequacy of consideration in these terms:[32]

> In agreement with Lord Justice Kitchin, I consider that [the contention that the judge was wrong in law to hold that the variation agreement was supported by consideration] is

[30] MWB asked for permission to appeal to the Supreme Court but the Court of Appeal refused permission. It is open to the respondent to make an application for permission directly to the Supreme Court.

[31] *MWB* (n 28) [47]–[49].

[32] ibid [70].

unsound. In summary, the practical benefit which the judge found that MWB derived from the variation agreement constituted good consideration: see *Williams v Roffey Bros & Nicholls (Contractors) Ltd*. Neither the Rule in *Pinnel's* case nor *Foakes v Beer* nor *Re Selectmove* prevents that conclusion. Furthermore, the variation agreement may be a contract between the parties which is properly analysed as a collateral unilateral contract.

McCombe LJ agreed with both judgments, but neither he nor Kitchin LJ expressed any view on my additional (provisional) analysis of the variation agreement as a 'collateral unilateral contract':[33]

Rock was not bound to continue as licensee of its unit for more than the contractual term, which was shorter than the period over which its arrears were rescheduled. The variation agreement, conferring as it did on MWB the advantage of 'avoiding a void' meant that Rock had to be the occupier. Rock did continue to occupy its unit until the licence was terminated. To reconcile the parties' legal positions, my provisional view (in the absence of argument) is that Rock's acceptance of MWB's promise gave rise to a 'collateral unilateral contract,' meaning that, collaterally to the licence, for so long as Rock was entitled to and did occupy the unit and paid the licence fee as renegotiated, MWB would be bound on payment of the initial £3,500 to accept the deferral of the arrears in accordance with the variation agreement. This seems to me to be the legal effect of what the parties agreed, which was confirmed by Rock's immediate payment of £3,500 to MWB. Although the effect of the variation agreement if it was supported by consideration was not the subject of submissions, it was not suggested by either party that Rock could take the benefit of the variation agreement without performing its side of the bargain, or that MWB could withdraw from the variation agreement so long as Rock was complying with it.

I gratefully adopt the concept of 'collateral unilateral contract' in this context from a helpful article: M Chen-Wishart, *Reforming Consideration—No Greener Pastures* in S Degeling, J Edelman and J Goudkamp (eds), *Contract in Commercial Law* (Sydney, Thomson, 2016) (Publication pending). Since writing this judgment I have also seen *A Bird in the Hand: Consideration and Contract Modifications* (Andrew S Burrows and Edwin Peel (eds) *Contract Formation and parties* (OUP, 2010) page. 89–113) by the same author, which also discusses this point.

There may be no difference in a particular case (and none in *MWB*) whether there is a unilateral contract or a bilateral contract in the terms found by Kitchin LJ. The importance of the unilateral contract analysis is that it facilities the result which is likely to have been what the parties intended, namely, that the creditor should only be bound to accept the reduced debt in discharge of the payment of the whole debt when he had actually received the appropriate part payment. If the debtor wants to bind a creditor to his promise he has to deliver on his promise, and the creditor must allow him to set about doing so within the agreed timetable.

VII. CONCLUSION

The title to this chapter asks whether the law should require consideration where parties agree to the discharge of an existing debt by part payment. We have seen

[33] ibid [89]–[90].

that this would involve a departure from the unanimous decision of the House of Lords in *Foakes v Beer* in 1884. A promise of a lesser amount than was originally due is not enough to make the new exchange of promises binding on both parties. Something extra is required.

Subject to any appeal from the Court of Appeal's decision in *MWB*, that something extra may take the form of a practical benefit received by the creditor. That practical benefit must be over and beyond the benefit of receiving some part of the debt. It must be a consequence of the new agreement, and the creditor must have wanted to receive this benefit. But it need not be consideration which comes from the promisor or involve detriment to him.

Roffey and *MWB* must be seen in their historical context. They are another episode in the refinement of the law of consideration. They can be called the 'practical benefit' cases. In this, they provide a contrast with the nineteenth-century cases about seamen's wages which established that performance of an existing obligation was not good consideration in law.[34] And, as we have seen, the doctrine of promissory estoppel has in several cases been invoked in this area, and has had a supporting role to play in the development of practical benefit as a form of consideration for part payment agreements.

The development of a practical benefit as a form of consideration improves the chances of there being consideration in law for an agreement for part payment of a debt in discharge of the whole. To succeed in establishing that such an agreement is binding, debtors now have the possibility not only of showing that there was traditional consideration for the agreement (including a peppercorn), but also that the creditor received a practical benefit which he had been seeking. To that extent it may reduce the number of situations in which *Foakes v Beer* will be relevant in the future. So, while the decision in *Foakes v Beer* continues to be binding on all courts save the Supreme Court, it may become increasingly isolated in practice.

The final bridge of re-examining *Foakes v Beer* has not been crossed. That re-examination might lead to a wider examination of the role of the doctrine of consideration in the modern world, but that is outside the scope of this chapter.

Should the bridge be crossed? In the opening paragraphs of this chapter I referred to the values and principles which underlie any area of the common law. Of course, courts generally use the language of past precedents, rather than these values or principles. The Court of Appeal in *MWB* made no radical departure from this conventional approach.

Nonetheless those values and principles are necessarily there. Even a minor development of the law can reflect a subtle change in the balance between underlying values and principles. Despite unstated, they are there to be excavated and mined in future cases.

And they are, I suggest, the right place to start when considering whether there should be any change in the law. Like Humpty Dumpty, we should aim to know which is to be master. That does not mean applying the values and principles in the same way in every case in the future: social or economic needs may have moved on

[34] See, eg, *Stilk v Myrick* (n 27).

and we may need to give different weight to different principles to accommodate those changed needs. Nor does it mean that the courts can always apply what they may consider to be the appropriate values and principles, because the law may have been established in cases which are binding on them.

The law as established by the practical benefit cases (as I have called them), when examined in the future against the relevant values and principles, may be considered to strike an acceptable balance for modern times between creditors and debtors in a situation where the debtor cannot pay his debt in full and, if the creditor is to get what may be the best recovery from this situation, the debt needs to be rescheduled. If that balance has been struck, there is likely to be less demand for, and less point in, rethinking the requirement for consideration when parties make an agreement for the discharge of a debt by part payment, which was established by *Foakes v Beer*. But there is food for further thought and study here.

7

Not Waiving but Drowning

ROBERT STEVENS

I. THE CLAIMS

FIRST, THAT WAIVER is central to what it is to have a right. Second, that it is possible to waive all of our rights, including those arising in contract. Third, that it is possible to be estopped from asserting two things: facts and rights. Fourth, estoppel properly so-called is never a cause of action (although it may allow a claim that would otherwise fail to succeed). Fifth, that equitable estoppel prevents the assertion of rights, and is an equitable extension of the common law doctrine of waiver. Sixthly, that those cases which have puzzlingly described estoppel as a cause of action are better explained in other ways, primarily as based upon either constructive trusts or unjust enrichment.

II. TERMINOLOGY

The largest hurdle in understanding waiver is terminological. First the same concept is given many different labels. Second, the best available label, 'waiver', is also used in other different senses.

At common law it is possible to waive all of our rights. So if I step into a boxing-ring wearing gloves, my opponent commits no battery by hitting me. My guests are not trespassing when I invite them into my home, and I will not be falsely imprisoning if I lock the door behind them. Rights to bodily safety, to exclude others from your property, not to be detained and not to be defamed can all be waived. Waiver needs to be differentiated from alienation or transfer. Many rights are inalienable, none are unwaivable. In none of these examples has there been a transfer of a right. Rather, the right-holder's manifestation of consent has conferred a privilege. Exceptionally, the right-holder has no right in relation to that person with respect to whom he has waived his right.

In the law of torts we commonly refer to this concept using a Latin tag in order to confuse the young: *volenti non fit injuria*. *Volenti* is not a defence to a wrong, in the same way that contributory fault is. Rather once the right is waived there can be no breach of a duty, and hence no wrong to commit.

In the context of land law the same idea is commonly referred to as the conferral of a non-contractual licence (licence being synonymous with privilege). As licences can arise in other ways (for example if my football is kicked without my fault on to your land I have a licence to enter and retrieve it) this is not a particularly helpful label either.

Precisely the same principles apply to contractual rights. If a carrier has contracted to deliver goods to me on 1 April, and I state that it is fine if they deliver the next day, they will not be in breach of contract if they deliver on 2 April. Waiver is effective without the necessity of proving a contract or an estoppel. So, it is wholly unnecessary to show that the carrier has accepted my offer of a delay, it need not be shown that I have been provided any consideration for it, and proof of reliance by the carrier is wholly unnecessary. The effect of the waiver is not to vary the contract, any more than my consent to be punched destroys my right to bodily safety, but rather to prevent there from being a wrong committed by the non-performance.[1] A contractual variation is unnecessary for purposes of waiver, just as a contract is unnecessary in order to waive any other of the rights we have. Consideration is no more required than it is for consent to be kissed to prevent a battery.

For waiver to be effective there must be a manifestation of a *current* intention to waive the right. If I initially consent to painful surgery and then communicate my change of mind, or if I agree to stay in the Big Brother House for a series but ask to leave after a couple of days, the surgeon would be committing a battery if they go ahead anyway, and the producers of the programme would be falsely imprisoning if they refused to release me. The centrality of the right-holder's ability to control the right is shown reflected in the ability to retract consent.

Again, precisely the same is true in contract. An initial waiver may be withdrawn, so long as reasonable notice is given. So if the carrier is initially told that delivery the next day is fine, but is then immediately told that that actually the goods are needed on 1 April after all, delivery on 2 April will constitute a breach of contract.

If you grant me permission to enter your property I am not a trespasser if I do so. It does not matter that I would have entered without permission in any event. Similarly the carrier who is granted permission to deliver at a later date than stipulated in the contract is not in breach if he delivers on that later date, regardless of whether he would have delivered on that day in any event. No reliance is required.

Other labels used in the cases and literature for the doctrine I have called 'waiver' are consent, acquiescence and forbearance. English is not always a good language for conducting the business of law.

Waiver is in fact the distinguishing feature of private rights. Many duties in law have no correlative right-holder (ie public duties, my duty not to break the speed limit is not owed to anyone in particular). Hohfeld called rights 'properly so-called' claim-rights, but this is misleading as some rights are valid but unenforceable (because for example of the expiry of a limitation period). They cannot be claimed. That the right-holder has control over a duty,[2] through the ability to consent to an act that

[1] *Hartley v Hymans* [1920] 3 KB 475 (KBD).

[2] HLA Hart, *Essays on Bentham: Jurisprudence and Political Philosophy* (Oxford, Clarendon Press, 1982) 183. Confusion is caused because sometimes by 'right' we mean an interest of an individual sufficient to ground a duty. This is just a difference in usage, and neither one nor the other is incorrect.

would otherwise be wrongful,[3] distinguishes rights-based duties from both mere duties of virtue and public duties. Confusion is caused because some (but not all) public wrongs (eg battery) depend upon the existence of a private wrong. Waiver will mean that the latter does not occur, and as a result nor will the former.

Notice that there is nothing historically 'equitable' about this form of waiver. This is a common law principle applicable across all of private law.

III. OTHER USES OF 'WAIVER'

In contract law, waiver is used in different senses which can cause confusion.[4]

First it has been used to mean variation of a contract. Sometimes this entails a change to the parties' contractual rights;[5] in others, it entails the complete release of the parties. For a variation, an agreement and consideration is required, and the language of waiver is unhelpful.

Second, where one party has the power to terminate for a breach of contract but elects not to do so by indicating that he will continue to perform, this has been described as a waiver of the right to terminate.[6] Such an election is irrevocable. Here the wrong (the breach of contract) is not waived, damages are still payable, and the language of affirmation is to be preferred.

IV. IS IT A DEFENCE?

In private law, a defence is a reason that the defendant must assert in his pleadings that will defeat an otherwise good claim.[7] Ordinarily, the application of the principle *semper necessitas probandi incumbit ei qui agit* (roughly, 'he who asserts must prove') entails that the burden of proving the defence will fall on the defendant, but this is not necessarily so, and in fact is not in relation to proving whether a limitation period has expired.

Generally therefore, waiver operates as a defence to a claim that would otherwise succeed. Three examples illustrate why this is not always true.

First, in the case of battery, conduct may not be prima facie wrongful without the absence of consent. Although pleading 'you punched me on the nose' ought to be sufficient to make out a cause of action, 'you kissed me' should not. In the latter case it should be for the claimant to plead 'you kissed me without consent'.

[3] See generally, R Stevens, 'Private Rights and Public Wrongs' in M Dyson (ed), *Unravelling Tort and Crime* (Cambridge, Cambridge University Press, 2014).

[4] Using the same word to mean more than one thing seems to be a feature of the common law of contract. See also 'rescission'.

[5] *Brikom Investments Ltd v Carr* [1979] QB 467 (CA) 488 (Roskill LJ), 491 (Cumming-Bruce LJ).

[6] *Bentsen v Taylor* [1893] 2 QB 274 (CA).

[7] R Stevens, 'Should Contributory Fault be Analogue or Digital?' in A Dyson, J Goudkamp and F Wilmot-Smith (eds), *Defences in Tort* (Oxford, Hart Publishing, 2014); *cf* J Goudkamp, *Tort Law Defences* (Oxford, Hart Publishing, 2013). This wholly formal approach does not work well in the criminal law, which does not have a formal system of pleading.

Second, in contract the effect of a waiver is not only to bar a claim for damages for non-performance by the party who has waived his rights, but also where such counter-performance constitutes a condition precedent to his obligation to perform, it ceases to constitute such a condition. So, in a contract for the purchase of first grade durum wheat, if the buyer consents in advance to the contract being performed with either first or second-grade wheat, the buyer cannot refuse to pay on the basis that the wheat was second grade and not that which had been originally contracted for.[8] However, it would not be possible to waive altogether the promised counter-performance, as if this were done no consideration would remain. So the buyer could not waive entirely the seller's obligation to deliver wheat, and thereby bind himself to pay the price in return for nothing. Put another way, it is possible by a waiver to give effect to what Professor Treitel has called a 'decreasing pact' (accepting less than what had been bargained for) but where it is sought to show that there is an 'increasing pact' (eg upgrading a contract for the sale of second-grade wheat to first grade) it would be necessary to show a contractual variation. A decreasing pact cannot, however, entail no consideration at all.

It is not, therefore, the case that a waiver only operates as a 'shield not a sword', as its effect may be to enable a contractual claim which would otherwise fail to succeed, but it is no more a cause of action in its own right than the maxim *volenti non fit injuria* is within the law of torts. There must, therefore, be some kind of pre-existing contractual right to waive.[9]

Third, and most importantly, if a right has been waived by a defendant he cannot invoke it as grounding a defence. If, for example, you enter my property without permission I may be justified in using reasonable force in excluding you. If however I have waived my right to exclude you, I cannot invoke my right to my land as conferring upon me the privilege to use force until I have revoked my permission and you have been given a reasonable opportunity to leave.

V. EVIDENTIAL ESTOPPEL (OR ESTOPPEL BY REPRESENTATION)

Before coming to the equitable extension of the doctrine of waiver, it is necessary to briefly distinguish evidential estoppel. Where A makes a clear and unambiguous statement of fact to B, intending B to rely upon such statement, and B believed the truth of the statement and acted upon it, A is estopped from proving that the fact is false.

This is a rule of evidence. It is neither a cause of action nor a defence, although it may allow a cause of action or a defence that would otherwise fail to succeed. There is nothing specifically equitable about this rule, it is common to all courts and all private law claims.

[8] See Sale of Goods Act 1979 (UK), s 11(2).

[9] *cf Pacol Ltd v Trade Lines Ltd (The Henrik Sif)* [1982] 1 Lloyd's Rep 456 (QBD) 466.

VI. EQUITABLE ESTOPPEL

If I am invited into All Souls College for a conference by one of those authorised to do so, I am not a trespasser when I enter. If, however, I behave appallingly, by swearing at the judges in attendance perhaps, my licence to enter may be withdrawn. Do I immediately become a trespasser? The answer is of course no. I have a reasonable opportunity to leave. If I fail to leave with reasonable despatch, then I will become a trespasser, but not before. It is no longer fair for the right-holder to revoke the consent that has been given and immediately return to the pre-waiver situation.

The same idea underlies the expansion of the doctrine of waiver by the courts of equity. The leading and usefully illustrative case is the decision of the House of Lords in *Hughes v Metropolitan Railway Co.*[10] The defendant leased premises from the claimant. On 22 October 1874 the claimant, as they had the power to do under the terms of the lease, served notice on the defendant to repair the premises within six months, the lease being forfeitable upon failure to comply. The defendants replied that the repairs would be carried out but that the plaintiff might wish to buy their interest, and proposed the deferral of the repairs until they had heard back from the claimant. In November 1874 the claimant entered into negotiations with the defendant for the surrender of the lease. The negotiations broke down on 31 December. The original notice to repair expired in April 1875, and the claimant served a writ of ejectment on the defendant. The defendant completed the repairs in June 1875. The House of Lords granted the defendant relief from forfeiture. Bowen LJ subsequently described the principle as being that[11]

> if persons who have contractual rights against others induce by their conduct those against whom they have such rights to believe that such rights will either not be enforced or will be kept in suspense or abeyance for some particular time, those persons will not be allowed by a Court of Equity to enforce the rights until such time has elapsed, without at all events placing the parties in the same position as they were before.

No member of the House of Lords described the principle they were invoking as based upon 'estoppel', this was the label coined 70 years later,[12] but it is an apt description. The claimant is estopped, or barred from asserting his legal rights. It is equitable in its form in the sense that it is form of meta-law, or a rule that governs another rule. The archetypal form of equitable rule is the trust, which involves rights to other rights. Equitable estoppel involves a restriction on a right-holder's ability to reassert his rights.

We may summarise the position as follows. Where one party has told the other that he need not perform an obligation, and the other does not perform, it is not possible to treat the non-performance as a breach of contract, as no wrong has been committed, nor can such non-performance be treated as a default entitling termination of the contract. Where non-performance is consented to, it does not constitute default. This form of estoppel is accurately described as 'promissory estoppel' not

10 *Hughes v Metropolitan Railway Co* (1877) 2 App Cas 439 (HL).
11 *Birmingham District Land Co v L & NW Railway* (1888) 40 Ch D 268 (CA).
12 By Denning J in *Central London Property Trust Ltd v High Trees House Ltd* [1947] KB 130 (KBD).

because it requires a promise to have been made, but rather because the right that is barred from assertion is a promissory right.

Enter Denning J. Most of Lord Denning's novel innovations within the law of contract have not survived. So, his attempt to expand the doctrine of frustration to cases of uncontemplated turns of events,[13] the separate legal doctrine of fundamental breach[14] (twice),[15] the category of 'equitable mistake',[16] his novel approach to offer and acceptance,[17] and his attempt to explain away the doctrine of privity of contract at common law,[18] have all now been rejected. The one offspring within contract law which lives on is the doctrine of 'promissory estoppel'. The romance of Denning J's creativity in this area is increased when it is realised that its unpromising birth occurred in an obiter dictum of a first instance judge, in a judgment delivered on the day of the conclusion of oral argument. In *Central London Property Trust Ltd v High Trees House Ltd*[19] a block of flats had been let to the defendants in 1937 for a rent of £2,500 per annum. In 1940 the landlords agreed to reduce the rent to £1,250 as many of the flats were unlet during wartime. After the war had ended the landlords demanded that the full rent be paid for the last two quarters of 1945. This claim was upheld. Denning J also stated that they would have been prevented from claiming the full rent for the period covered by the agreement (ie 1940–45).

That this doctrine was, and is still claimed by some to have been discoverable in the equitable cases exemplified by *Hughes* is somewhat surprising. First, waiver in both its common law and equitable forms is not based upon one party having been promised anything. If I kiss you with your consent I commit no battery. This is not because you have promised me anything, but rather because of your manifestation of consent to the kiss. Similarly, if the employer of a carrier consents to the goods being delivered a day late, there is no necessity to make out any promise in order to make out a waiver. There was no promise discernible in the conduct of the landlord in *Hughes*: rather they consented to a delay in the work being done. To take another example, it is sometimes said that the House of Lords in *Woodhouse v Nigerian Produce* required that before a promissory estoppel could be made out, it was necessary to show a clear and unequivocal promise.[20] In fact, their Lordships did not say this. The case concerned an obligation to pay in Nigerian pounds, with it being alleged that the promisee had consented to being paid in Sterling as an alternative. It was not alleged that there was any promise, but merely the consent to be paid in another currency. The question was whether the consent was merely to the denomination

[13] *British Movietone News Ltd v London and District Cinemas* [1952] AC 166 (HL), rejecting [1951] 1 KB 190 (CA) 201 (Denning LJ).

[14] *Karsales (Harrow) Ltd v Wallis* [1956] 1 WLR 936 (CA), overturned *Suisse Atlantique Societe d'Armement Maritime SA v NV Rotterdamsche Kolen Centrale* [1967] 1 AC 361 (HL).

[15] *Harbutt's 'Plasticine' Ltd v Wayne Tank and Pump Co Ltd* [1970] 1 QB 447 (CA); *Levison v Patent Steam Carpet Cleaning Co Ltd* [1978] QB 69 (CA); overturned *Photo Productions Ltd v Securicor Transport Ltd* [1980] AC 827 (HL).

[16] *Solle v Butcher* [1950] 1 KB 671 (CA), rejected *Great Peace Shipping Ltd v Tsavliris Salvage (International) Ltd (The Great Peace)* [2002] EWCA Civ 1407, [2003] QB 679.

[17] *Gibson v Manchester City Council* [1978] 1 WLR 520 (CA), overturned [1979] 1 WLR 294 (HL).

[18] *Beswick v Beswick* [1968] Ch 538 (HL) 557, rejected *Beswick v Beswick* [1968] AC 58 (CA).

[19] *High Trees* (n 12).

[20] *Woodhouse v Nigerian Produce Marketing Co Ltd* [1972] AC 741 (HL).

in which payment was actually made, or whether it also went to its quantification, so that a fall in Sterling meant that less was payable. As the consent was ambiguous, it did not amount to a consent to accept a lesser sum.

Second, there is no necessity to show any reliance to make out the waiver in a case like *Hughes*. If the employer of a carrier consents to later delivery, it is irrelevant that the carrier has not changed his position based upon the consent in any way. It is unnecessary for the carrier to demonstrate that he has rendered a different performance than that he would otherwise have done. If the analogy between waiver of contractual rights and other rights is correct, it must be doubtful whether it is necessary to show any link at all between the defendant's conduct and the claimant's consent. If I kiss Lord Hoffmann with his consent I commit no battery, even if I would have kissed him regardless of consent. The doctrine created by Denning J in *High Trees* by contrast does require reliance by the promisee.

The doctrine in *High Trees* cannot be supported as an extension of waiver. If without consideration I consent to your using my car, walking on my land, kissing me, locking me up or speaking ill of me, when you do these things you are not converting the car, trespassing on the land, battering me, falsely imprisoning or defaming me. However, once I no longer consent, you no longer have the privilege to ignore my right that you once had. This is so, even if I purport to waive my right irrevocably. The same is true of the waiver of a contractual right, so that the giving of reasonable notice will enable the promisor to once again assert his contractual entitlement. The withdrawal of consent cannot make wrongful what was not so at the time. So my withdrawal of permission to kiss does not make an earlier kiss a tort, nor does my subsequent change of mind make a late delivery a breach of contract if I consented at the time to accept such late performance.

Waiver cannot bar the claim for the rent during the war years. Waiver does not destroy the underlying primary right, except insofar as it is now impossible to respect it. So, in *High Trees* the claim was not that the tenant had wrongfully failed to pay the rent during the war. This was not a claim for a past breach of contract, but rather a claim to enforce the tenant's primary obligation to pay the money owing under the lease. The waiver of the right to payment during the war should not have prevented it from being claimed afterwards. The doctrine of waiver does not destroy the underlying right, whether contractual or otherwise.

To his credit Denning J did not claim that the doctrine he sought to introduce was an estoppel 'properly so-called', although he did insist that the basis for the equitable doctrine was promissory, which is doubtful.

Once we have understood that 'promissory estoppel' is properly understood as an equitable extension of the doctrine of waiver, the limits upon its scope become readily explicable. If instead we see 'promissory estoppel' as a full-scale cause of action, a little brother to the law of contract, its rules appear completely mysterious. So, the Court of Appeal in *Combe v Combe*[21] held that it is only a 'shield not a sword'.

[21] *Combe v Combe* [1951] 2 KB 215 (CA). See also *Baird Textile Holdings Ltd v Marks and Spencer plc* [2001] EWCA Civ 274, [2002] 1 All ER (Comm) 737.

On one view this is a more or less arbitrary limitation to prevent the wholesale destruction of the doctrine of consideration. Once promissory estoppel is understood as a species of waiver, this limitation follows as a matter of course. It is a bar to the assertion of a right, not a cause of action. The Australian decisions to the contrary are inconsistent with the historical and doctrinal bases of the rule.[22] Similarly that the doctrine requires a pre-existing contractual relationship between claimant and defendant makes sense if it is part of the law of waiver. Without a right, there is nothing to waive. Further, that the doctrine is generally 'suspensory not extinctive'[23] of legal rights derives from its doctrinal basis. Where the right-holder can return the duty bearer without prejudice to the pre-waiver position (or perhaps more accurately the position that would have obtained if no waiver had been made), he should be allowed to do so.

Until recently appellate authority for Denning J's extension of *Hughes* was missing. In *Collier v Wright*[24] the Court of Appeal endorsed Denning J's views, and refused to follow the House of Lords decision as to whether part payment of a debt could operate as a discharge in *Foakes v Beer.*[25] It may be noted in conclusion that this is a much more radical step than that taken by the Court of Appeal in *Williams v Roffey.*[26] There is no necessity under the *High Trees* principle to show that the part payment conferred a benefit upon the promisor, practical or otherwise, that they would not otherwise have received.

VII. PROPRIETARY ESTOPPEL

There is no reason why equitable estoppel should be confined to restricting the assertion of contractual rights. It has, for example, been applied to a statutory right to compensation against a director for signing a bill of exchange without the company's name legibly appearing upon it.[27] The recognition of a separate doctrine of 'proprietary estoppel' is even more recent than its 'promissory estoppel' sibling. In *Inwards v Baker*[28] the Court of Appeal rejected a claim for eviction on the basis of what Danckwerts LJ described as 'equitable estoppel'. Old Mr Baker was the owner of six acres of land. His son lived nearby, and had his eye on a piece of land to buy on which to erect a bungalow. His father said to him 'Why not put the bungalow on my land and make it a little bigger?', which is what the son did. The son then lived in the erected bungalow for over 30 years. The father died, leaving the property to others, who then sought to evict the son. The court concluded that it would now be inequitable to allow the assertion of the right to exclude from the premises, allowing the defendant to remain for the rest of his life. This caused the authors of

[22] Exemplified by *Walton Sores (Interstate Ltd) v Maher* (1988) 164 CLR 387 (HCA).
[23] *Tool Metal manufacturing Co Ltd v Tungsten Electric Co Ltd* [1955] 1 WLR 761 (HL).
[24] *Collier v Wright* [2007] EWCA Civ 1329, [2008] 1 WLR 643.
[25] *Foakes v Beer* (1884) 9 App Cas 605 (HL).
[26] *Williams v Roffey Bros & Nicholls (Contractors) Ltd* [1991] 1 QB 1 (CA).
[27] *Durham Fancy Goods Ltd v Michael Jackson (Fancy Goods) Ltd* [1968] 2 QB 839 (QBD).
[28] *Inwards v Baker* [1965] 2 QB 29 (CA).

Snell's Equity to employ, for the first time, the term 'proprietary estoppel'.[29] This refusal to allow the right-holder to return to the pre-waiver position is consistent with the principle in *Hughes*.

In more recent years, however, 'proprietary estoppel' has been used to create a much more expansive liability-creating rule which is nothing to do with anyone being estopped from asserting anything. The beginning of this process was the decision of the Court of Appeal in *Crabb v Arun*.[30] Mr Crabb bought a property which had Arun District Council as his neighbour to the west. Crabb had two routes of access to the highway, one by way of a formal easement, the other by way of an informal licence granted to him by the Council. Crabb sold the portion of land over which he had a formal easement, the council subsequently blocking off his access over the other route. Mr Crabb claimed a right of access on the basis of equitable estoppel.

A 'right of access' is, more accurately, a privilege of access. If all that had been recognised was a privilege to cross the land, there would be no problem with describing the result as based upon estoppel: the council would be estopped from asserting their right to exclude Mr Crabb from the land. The court went further than this, however, and granted Mr Crabb an easement over the Council's land (ie a property right binding upon all others). How, absent the conditions necessary for the creation of an easement, could such a proprietary right be recognised?

Subsequent to *Crabb* this promise-based liability has 'developed with remarkable speed'.[31] A few short years after *Crabb*, the Court of Appeal in *Pascoe v Turner*[32] ordered the conveyance of a fee simple estate in land based upon an 'estoppel', and many cases since then have proceeded upon the same assumption that 'proprietary estoppel' is a special liability rule.

For a brief moment it appeared as if proprietary estoppel would be (re-)confined to operating as an estoppel, and that the cases that had employed it as operating as a freestanding cause of action would either have to be justified on different doctrinal bases, or dismissed as wrong. This happy prospect seemed to have been achieved by the decision of the House of Lords in *Yeoman's Row v Cobbe*,[33] in particular in the speech of Lord Scott.[34] The defendant was the owner of land with potential for redevelopment as residential properties. It entered into negotiations for sale of the land to the claimant. They reached an oral agreement in principle, but never entered into a formal bargain of sufficient certainty to be enforced. The claimant was to pursue the application for planning permission at his own expense, once this was granted the land was to be conveyed to him, developed at his expense, the residential properties sold off, and the profits divided between the parties. The claimant

[29] R Megarry and PV Baker (eds), *Snell's Equity*, 26th edn (London, Sweet & Maxwell, 1966) 629. See B McFarlane, *The Law of Proprietary Estoppel* (Oxford, Oxford University Press, 2014) 1.

[30] *Crabb v Arun District Council* [1976] 1 Ch 179 (CA).

[31] McFarlane, *Proprietary Estoppel* (n 29) 8.

[32] *Pascoe v Turner* [1979] 1 WLR 431 (CA).

[33] *Yeoman's Row Management Ltd v Cobbe* [2008] UKHL 55; [2008] 1 WLR 1752.

[34] With which Lords Hoffmann, Brown and Mance agreed. Lord Walker gave a concurring speech, with which Lord Brown agreed.

incurred time and expense in successfully obtaining planning permission, at which point, the defendant sought better terms. Negotiations broke down, and with no enforceable contract between them the claimant sought relief on a number of different grounds.

The trial judge, Etherton J, and the Court of Appeal had granted relief on the basis of proprietary estoppel. The House of Lords rejected this basis for the claim (whilst accepting others). Lord Scott stated[35]

> An 'estoppel' bars the object of it from asserting some fact or facts, or, sometimes, something that is a mixture of fact and law, that stands in the way of some right claimed by the person entitled to the benefit of the estoppel. The estoppel becomes a 'proprietary' estoppel—a sub-species of a 'promissory' estoppel—if the right claimed is a proprietary right, usually a right to or over land but, in principle, equally available in relation to chattels or choses in action. So, what is the fact or facts, or the matter of mixed fact and law, that, in the present case, the appellant is said to be barred from asserting? And what is the proprietary right claimed by Mr Cobbe that the facts and matters the appellant is barred from asserting might otherwise defeat?

There are some infelicities in this paragraph. First it sees proprietary estoppel as a sub-species of promissory estoppel, which it is not. We may be estopped from asserting either a proprietary or promissory right, but both are species of a wider genus. Second, it confuses the procedural or evidential question of whether one party may be estopped from asserting a *fact* with the substantive law doctrine that estops one party from asserting a *right* against another. However, the final point is a good one. The claimants were not arguing that the defendants were estopped from asserting anything. How then could there be any claim based upon 'proprietary estoppel'?

VIII. CONSTRUCTIVE TRUSTS

The academic reaction to *Yeoman's Row v Cobbe* was a furious one.[36] In the years after *Crabb v Arun* proprietary estoppel had been successfully used as a cause of action at Court of Appeal level many times.[37] These cases ordering the conveyance of land on the basis of an 'estoppel' could not be justifiable on Lord Scott's more traditionalist understanding of what an estoppel is. Because no serious analysis was undertaken in *Yeoman's Row v Cobbe* of the wealth of case law that had adopted the expansive approach to proprietary estoppel since the 1970s, the question arose of whether it had all been implicitly overruled.

Much of this case law could be justified, but not on the basis of a so-called 'estoppel'. An early case often given as an example of the operation of proprietary estoppel is the decision in *Dillwyn v Llewelyn*.[38] Unsurprisingly that term does not appear in

[35] *Cobbe* (n 33) [14].

[36] See B McFarlane and A Robertson, 'The Death of Proprietary Estoppel' [2008] *Lloyd's Maritime and Commercial Law Quarterly* 449.

[37] eg *Pascoe v Turner* (n 32); *Gillett v Holt* [2001] Ch 210 (CA); *Jennings v Rice* [2002] EWCA Civ 159; [2003] 1 P & CR 100.

[38] *Dillwyn v Llewelyn* (1862) 4 De GF & J 517, 45 ER 1285, relied on in the *Pascoe* and *Jennings* cases (ibid).

a decision of its vintage. A father wished to make a gift of land to his youngest son, and thought he had done so by signing a memorandum and presenting it to him 'for the purpose of furnishing himself with a dwelling house'. Unfortunately the gift was not in the requisite form to constitute a deed. The son incurred expense in building himself a house on the land. Two years later after the father died the eldest son who had inherited his father's estate disputed his younger brother's title to the land. Lord Westbury LC held that the younger son was entitled to call for a conveyance of the fee simple promised.

If the decision had merely been that the younger son could not be evicted by the eldest, it could be justifiable on the basis of estoppel. As the result was not so confined, what is its justification? In order to understand the result it is necessary to understand what a trust is, and as a result how and why they can arise by operation of law.

If A, the owner of Blackacre, declares himself a trustee of the right to his land in B's favour, the law (by which is meant here law and equity together) does 'not say that [B is] the owner of the land, it says that the trustee was the owner of the land, but adds that he is bound to hold the land for the benefit of [B]'.[39] This may be illustrated by the fact that B has no standing to sue for violation of the right to the land itself: only A may sue a trespasser or the creator of a private nuisance.[40] B has no right in relation to the land exigible against the rest of the world, but only one as against the person with title to Blackacre from time to time. B does not, therefore, acquire in the narrow sense employed by the Romans, a right *in rem*.

B's right that A hold the title to the land for his benefit (which is simply the converse of A's duty to hold the title to the land for B's benefit) is not simply a right against A personally, a right *in personam* in the traditional sense. Rather the subject matter of B's right is A's *right* to the land.[41] If, therefore, A gives the (right to) Blackacre to his son, C, B's right will bind C because B's right is in relation to the right C has acquired. Similarly, if A goes into bankruptcy, B's right against A's right will bind

[39] FW Maitland, *Equity: A Course of Lectures*, 2nd edn (Cambridge, Cambridge University Press, 1936) 17–18.

[40] The decision of the Court of Appeal in *Shell UK v Total UK* [2010] EWCA Civ 180, [2011] QB 86 is, in part, inconsistent with this proposition, as beneficiaries under a trust of the title to an oil refinery were allowed to claim for consequential loss they suffered as a result of the defendant's negligent damage of the refinery, provided that the trustee was joined as a party to the proceedings. The prior authorities do not support this proposition and the dismissal of arguments to the contrary as 'legalistic' (at [132]) is not a highpoint in English jurisprudence. The better view is that the case is rightly decided because the claimants were in joint possession of the land (and therefore had title) through the agency of those who operated the refinery on their behalf.

[41] See also R Chambers, *An Introduction to Property Law in Australia*, 2nd edn (New South Wales, Law Book Co, 2008) [13.90]; L Smith, 'Unravelling Proprietary Restitution' (2004) 40 *Canadian Business Law Journal* 317; L Smith, 'Philosophical Foundations of Proprietary Remedies' in R Chambers, C Mitchell and JE Penner (eds), *Philosophical Foundations of The Law of Unjust Enrichment* (Oxford, Oxford University Press, 2009); L Smith, 'Trust and Patrimony' (2008) 38 *Revue générale de droit* 379; 'Trust and Patrimony' (2009) 28 *Estates, Trusts and Pensions Journal* 332; W Swadling, 'Property: General Principles' in A Burrows (ed), *English Private Law*, 2nd edn (Oxford, Oxford University Press, 2007) 4.140–4.153; B McFarlane and R Stevens, 'The Nature of Equitable Property' (2010) 4 *Journal of Equity* 1; cf R Nolan, 'Equitable Property' (2006) 122 *LQR* 232.

A's trustee in bankruptcy and hence will be protected in this event.[42] Because of these characteristics, we are content to describe B's right as proprietary, although it is not of the same kind as a right *in rem* strictly so called.

Whenever one party is obliged to another not to use a right for his own benefit[43] a trust arises, because that is, as a matter of definition, what a trust is. So, if A makes a binding contract to transfer specific shares, or receivables, or title to land, or an intellectual property right, or an equitable interest that he owns, to B, A becomes a trustee of this right even though the requisites of transfer have not been fulfilled. Similarly if A sells and conveys land to B, subsequently discovers that B has committed a misrepresentation in negotiations, and rescinds, B is under an obligation to re-transfer back the right to the land, and as a result holds the title to the land on trust for A.

However, the occasions when A is under a duty to B not to use a right for his own benefit are not confined to those categories of obligation recognised by the common law (eg contract, unjust enrichment, etc). This is most obvious in cases of express trusts. If A declares himself a trustee of a right in B's favour, the trust is complete, despite the assumption of the obligation being entirely gratuitous. Another category of case is where one party receives a right having made an undertaking to the transferor to use it for the benefit of a third party, giving rise to a trust in favour of the third party.[44]

Where therefore A has promised B an interest in land (or indeed any right capable of being held on trust) and B has relied upon that promise, a constructive trust may arise despite the absence of any consideration for the promise. As a result, B as beneficiary may call for the conveyance of the right to him. This provides a more satisfactory explanation for the line of cases exemplified by *Dillwyn v Llewelyn* than does the invocation of estoppel.

The only decision of the United Kingdom's appellate court where a claim based upon proprietary estoppel has succeeded is best explained on this same basis. In the House of Lords' decision in *Thorner v Major*,[45] David Thorner worked on his second cousin Peter's farm for 30 years unpaid. From 1990 to 2005 Peter encouraged David to believe that he would inherit the farm and other assets, and David acted on this assurance. The trial judge ordered the farm and other assets to be conveyed to David. If the analysis provided above is correct, a constructive trust should arise over the farm at the point at which the duty fell to be performed (Peter's death). This trust may be described as 'remedial' in the sense that it was not expressly intended by the parties (it does not arise at the time of the court's judgment). The analysis of the result in terms of a constructive trust was adopted by Lord Scott, consistently with what he had said in *Yeoman's Row v Cobbe*.

[42] For bankrupt individuals this is expressly stated in the Insolvency Act 1986 (UK), s 283(3)(b). It is also true of insolvent companies despite the absence of expression in legislation: see eg *Barclays Bank Ltd v Quistclose Investments Ltd* [1970] AC 567 (HL).

[43] This appears to be the minimum.

[44] See generally B McFarlane, 'Constructive Trusts Arising on Receipt of Property Sub Conditione' (2004) 120 *LQR* 667.

[45] *Thorner v Major* [2009] UKHL 18, [2009] 1 WLR 776.

The majority[46] preferred to base their decision upon there being a 'proprietary estoppel' that justified liability.

If the majority are right, this would be significant in two ways. First if promises that are reasonably relied upon can be enforced as a 'proprietary estoppel', either to the extent of the claimant's reliance loss or, where appropriate, what is expected to be received, there seems to be no good reason to confine such a principle to promises in relation to land or other property. Professor McFarlane boldly takes this principle to its logical conclusion and argues that the liability rule should not be confined to promises in relation to land or other property and that there should be a claim in all circumstances where there has been a promise that has been relied upon. If this were to be adopted, not only would the 'estoppel' part of the label be inapt, so too would be the 'proprietary' qualifier.[47] By contrast if we see the claim as arising under a trust, the fact that the promise relates to particular rights is crucial. Only rights can be held on trust. Promises to pay money or provide services should not suffice. A promise to convey or confer an entitlement to particular rights would, on this view, be crucial.

Second, the remedial response to a 'proprietary estoppel' could be more flexible (uncertain?) than is true for a constructive trust. If the promise is that a particular right be held on trust, the court's response should be that that right is held on trust. The court's response should track the underlying obligation. If by contrast, the estoppel claim is based upon the reliance by the claimant on the promise, then the claim should usually be confined to the reliance expense incurred.[48] However, the courts have generally not adopted this approach, instead preferring in almost all cases to give effect to the promise to convey.[49] This is the law of constructive trusts under a different label.

IX. UNJUST ENRICHMENT

An alternative analysis that is also commonly available is based upon unjust enrichment. Where there is a transaction between A and B, under which A renders performance to B, if that performance was conditional (usually upon some counter-performance by B) and that condition fails, B must make restitution to A of the performance received. For this principle to operate there is no requirement that the transaction be sufficiently certain to itself be enforced. Rather, all that is required is an agreement that the performance rendered is conditional. The claim for restitution is not a claim to enforce a contract, but rather to unwind its performance.[50] The late development of the law of unjust enrichment in England may partially explain the growth of idiosyncratic liability rules to fill the gap.

[46] Lord Hoffmann, Lord Rodger, Lord Walker and Lord Neuberger.

[47] eg B McFarlane, 'Equitable Estoppel as a Cause of Action: Neither One Thing Nor one Other' in S Degeling, J Edelman and J Goudkamp (eds), *Contract in Commercial Law* (Sydney, Thomson Reuters, 2016).

[48] See *Jennings v Rice* (n 37).

[49] *Suggitt v Suggitt* [2012] EWCA Civ 1140, [2012] WTLR 1607.

[50] For an excellent example see *Deglman v Guaranty Trust* [1954] SCR 725 (SCC).

This principle was applied by the House of Lords in *Yeoman's Row v Cobbe*. Unfortunately, Lord Scott identified three separate possible principles in play: quantum meruit, unjust enrichment, a consideration that has wholly failed. These are, at least on these facts, three different ways of saying the same thing. The defendant was unjustly enriched, because the condition to which performance was subject under the transaction failed, entitling the claimant to a quantum meruit for the service provided.

X. PROPRIETARY ESTOPPEL AND CONTRACT

The expansive liability rule that 'proprietary estoppel' has become appears to be a mistake that originated in decisions of the Court of Appeal in the 1970s. Instead of an equitable extension of the doctrine of waiver, a species of estoppel has become transformed into a liability rule of uncertain scope. Although alternative grounds for recovery are often available (either by way of trust or unjust enrichment) this will not always be so, and the remedial response for the (relatively) new liability rule may not be the same.

Is this new rule capable of being reconciled with the law of contract, in particular with the doctrine of consideration, especially if it is not confined to promises relating to property?

At a formal level, the answer is yes.

First the remedies available may, in some cases be different. The claimant may in some case be confined to her reliance expenditure (although the circumstances in which this will be so are currently obscure).[51] Second, the defences may differ. Third, some kind of reliance is required for a 'proprietary estoppel', whereas it is not for a contract.

At a substantive level, the real problem is not whether the proprietary estoppel liability rule can be made to fit, but what the normative justification for it may be. It does not involve enforcing an agreement. It is not a remedial response to wrongdoing. It is not the reversal of unjust enrichment. It has no obvious analogue with the private law rules in other legal systems.

It is natural for lawyers to think in terms of liability formulas. When we learn law we often do so as if learning spells at Hogwarts. So, we are taught that negligence involves a duty, breach, causation and remoteness. We learn that we can resist these claims by asserting counteracting magic spells which themselves have their own formulas. The most extreme form of this way of thinking arises in the area of the economic torts, where we seem to be presented by a host of spells that have neither rhyme nor reason to them. Some require intent, whilst others do not. Some require some independent kind of (varying) unlawfulness, whilst others do not. Some can only be committed by more than one person acting together, whilst others can be committed alone. Some other liability rules are named after cases

[51] For discussion see McFarlane, *Proprietary Estoppel* (n 29) 431–85.

(*Rylands v Fletcher*,[52] *Wilkinson v Downton*).[53] For all that tells us about what the justification for the rule, we might as well call them *expelliarmus*, *petrificus totalus* or *incendio*.

This is the way I was taught the law of torts 25 years ago and it is also how I was taught constructive trusts and proprietary estoppel. As I have a reasonable memory for cases and rules, and could list off the distinguishing feature of one liability spell from another, I did reasonably well.

Law cannot, however, be understood like this. (Indeed a few months after sitting finals I could not have told you how the unlawful means conspiracy spell differed in its requirements from the procuring a breach of contract potion. It took me years, and Peter Birks, to realise that what I had been taught about constructive trusts made little sense.)

On its face those who incur reliance expenditure on the basis of an expectation created by another have suffered *damnum sine injuria*. That is, they have suffered a loss, but have not had any right violated. We know that being caused a loss by another is not, alone, in English law a good enough reason to justify a claim, even where the loss is inflicted deliberately.[54] In many cases, such as in *Thorner v Major* itself, the defendant is not guilty of a high degree of blame. Why is this particular category of claimant deserving of the law's assistance?

XI. WHAT TO DO?

The giveaway symptoms of a mistake are that the label ('proprietary estoppel') no longer describes the rule, and the source of the error is both relatively recent and easy to spot. The original doctrinal basis of equitable estoppel as an expansion of the doctrine of waiver has been lost sight of.

Three options seem open.

The first is to allow this novel development to grow. Not all new growths are cancerous. Sometimes mistakes can be productive. This is the view of the author of the largest and best book covering proprietary estoppel (although he may be thought to have a vested interest).[55]

The second option is to confine the anomaly within more or less arbitrary limits. There are suggestions of this in the speech of Lord Neuberger in *Thorner v Major*, where he suggested that what distinguished the case from the earlier decision in *Yeoman's Row v Cobbe* was that it was non-commercial. Attempts to confine the operation of the principle to promises concerning land (or other property?) as contract texts attempt to do are similarly artificial barriers to stop the spread of contagion.

The third option is to operate, and remove the error. Although there recently seemed hope that this could be done, and that we could return to the world where estoppels estopped, this looks like it cannot be done in the immediate future.

[52] *Rylands v Fletcher* (1868) LR 3 HL 330 (HL).
[53] *Wilkinson v Downton* [1897] 2 QB 57 (QBD).
[54] *Allen v Flood* [1898] AC 1 (HL).
[55] McFarlane, *Proprietary Estoppel* (n 29).

8

Frustration: Automatic Discharge of Both Parties?

EWAN McKENDRICK

I. INTRODUCTION

AS LORD WRIGHT observed in *Joseph Constantine Steamship Line Ltd v Imperial Smelting Corp Ltd*,[1] the doctrine of frustration is 'generally relied on as a defence to a claim for failure to perform a contract'.[2] Typically, a party (the claimant) who has not received the performance promised by its counterparty (the defendant) brings an action for damages for breach of contract. In such a case it is for the claimant to prove that a contract has been concluded between the parties, that the defendant has failed to perform according to these terms and that that failure amounts to a breach of that contract. It is then for the defendant to rely on frustration as a defence to the claim and the defendant must prove that the events which happened amounted in law to frustration.[3] There are two essential elements to a plea that a contract has been frustrated. The first, which it is for the party relying on the doctrine to establish, is that[4]

> there must be some outside event or extraneous change of situation, not foreseen or provided for by the parties at the time of contracting, which either makes it impossible for the contract to be performed at all, or at least renders its performance something radically different from what the parties contemplated when they entered into it.

The second element is that the 'the outside event or extraneous change of situation concerned, and the consequences of either in relation to the performance of the contract, must have occurred without either the fault or the default of either party to the contract'.[5] The onus of proof in relation to this second element of the doctrine of frustration has proved to be more contentious. The authorities establish the following proposition: in the case where the defendant has made good the first

[1] *Joseph Constantine Steamship Line Ltd v Imperial Smelting Corp Ltd* [1942] AC 154 (HL).
[2] ibid 192. See, to similar effect, *Kodros Shipping Corporation of Monrovia v Empresa Cubana de Fletes (The Evia) (No 2)* [1983] 1 AC 736 (HL) 751–52 (Lord Roskill).
[3] *Eliab v Attorney General* [2011] UGSC 12; [2012] 3 LRC 481 (Uganda SC) 487–88.
[4] *Paal Wilson & Co A/S v Partenreederei Hannah Blumenthal (The Hannah Blumenthal)* [1983] 1 AC 854 (HL) 909 (Lord Brandon).
[5] ibid.

element of the doctrine, and established a prima facie case that an external event has frustrated the contract, but the claimant alleges that the event cannot in law amount to a frustrating event because it was caused by the fault or default of the defendant, it is then for the claimant to prove that the defendant was at fault such as to deprive the defendant of its entitlement to rely on the defence of frustration, on the ground that the event alleged to have frustrated the contract was 'self-induced'.[6]

However, not all cases in which frustration is invoked are cases in which frustration is invoked by way of defence. A party who has entered into a bargain which has proved to be disastrous may seek to invoke frustration for the purpose of setting aside the contract so that it can then recover the market value of the services it has rendered.[7] Admittedly, a party seeking to invoke frustration in such a context is likely to find that the courts are not receptive to the submission that the contract has been frustrated; it may be more onerous to perform but it has not been frustrated. But as a matter of principle, the doctrine of frustration can be invoked by a claimant; it is not a doctrine that can only be invoked by defendants.

It is not the aim of this chapter to examine the general question whether frustration is correctly characterised as a defence, or the extent to which it can be so characterised. Rather, it is concerned with a narrower issue, namely the proposition that frustration operates to bring 'the contract to an end forthwith, without more and automatically, in the sense that it releases both parties from any further performance of the contract'.[8] The point is well-established in the authorities in England but it is not a view shared in all common law jurisdictions, nor is it to be found in many civilian legal systems or international re-statements of contract law.[9] Why is it that English law has developed this rule that frustration operates to discharge both parties, and that it does so automatically?

There are at least three features of English law that are worthy of note in this context. First, the discharge is automatic in the sense that it does not depend upon the action or conduct of the parties. So the fact that the parties might have intended to keep their contract alive is not a relevant consideration. Of course, if the parties did in practice wish to keep their relationship in existence, there is nothing to prevent

[6] *Joseph Constantine* (n 1) 174, *cf FC Shepherd & Co Ltd v Jerrom* [1987] QB 301 (CA) 319 (Lawton LJ) who stated that the burden of proof was on the party invoking frustration. However, this dictum cannot be reconciled with the decision of the House of Lords in the *Joseph Constantine* case and so should not be regarded as good law.

[7] An example in this category is *Davis Contractors Ltd v Fareham Urban District Council* [1956] AC 696 (HL). It is also the case that the occurrence of a frustrating event can confer new rights on the parties, in the sense that it may confer on the parties a right to recover benefits conferred upon the other party prior to the discharge of the contract. This of course is a claim in restitution or, as it is more commonly described today, unjust enrichment. It is not the purpose of this chapter to examine the scope of these restitutionary rights of action. In some Commonwealth jurisdictions the frustration of a contract can also give rise to a claim to recover wasted expenditure incurred prior to the frustration of the contract. But the source of these rights is the intervention of Parliament, not the development of common law rights.

[8] H Beale (ed), *Chitty on Contracts*, 32nd edn (London, Sweet & Maxwell, 2015) [23-071].

[9] See generally E Hondius and HC Grigoleit (eds), *Unexpected Circumstances in European Contract Law* (Cambridge, Cambridge University Press, 2011).

them from doing so. They can simply enter into a fresh contract to replace the one that has been discharged by the frustrating event. Second, the doctrine does not take the form of a right that is given to one of the parties to the contract to bring the contract to an end.[10] Rather, it is a legal doctrine according to which it is for the court to decide as a matter of law whether the contract has been frustrated and it is open to either party to the contract to submit that the contract has been frustrated. Although it is generally the case that the doctrine is invoked by the party whose performance has become significantly more onerous, there is no formal requirement to this effect. The doctrine can be invoked by either party to the contract and, where the court is satisfied that the contract has been frustrated, both parties are thereafter discharged from their obligations to perform under the contract. Third, it should be noted that the response of the law to the frustration of a contract is to discharge the contract between the parties and not to permit or enable its adaptation. English law prefers the nuclear option of termination (at least as regards obligations to perform in the future) to the more nuanced response of adaptation. Had English law sought to develop a more liberal doctrine of 'impracticability' or 'hardship' it almost certainly would have been accompanied by a more flexible remedial regime.[11] This is the approach which has been adopted in those legal systems which have developed a doctrine of hardship and it is also apparent in international re-statements of contract law.[12] But it has not been the English way. To the extent that there is flexibility in English law, it is derived from the express terms of parties' contracts, in the form of force majeure and hardship clauses,[13] not from the black-letter rules of English contract law.

The approach which will be adopted in this chapter is to begin by examining two of the leading cases which are the source of the rule that frustration operates to discharge both parties from the obligation further to perform their contractual obligations and that it does so automatically. The proposition that frustration operates to discharge both parties can be gleaned from the leading case of *Taylor v Caldwell*,[14] and the rule that it does so automatically from the decision of the Privy Council in *Hirji Mulji v Cheong Yue Steamship Co Ltd*.[15] It is to these cases that we must now turn before seeking to explore why English law might have developed in this way and whether it should continue to retain these rules or should develop a more nuanced remedial regime for frustrated contracts.

[10] *BP Exploration Co (Libya) Ltd v Hunt (No 2)* [1979] 1 WLR 783 (QBD) 810.

[11] While in theory it is possible for automatic termination to be the remedial response even in a more liberal regime, there is little in practice to commend such a solution because it would extend the nuclear option of automatic termination to a significantly wider range of transactions. It is therefore no surprise to note that legal systems that do recognise a broader doctrine of 'commercial impracticability' also typically give to their courts greater flexibility in terms of the available remedies.

[12] On which see Section VI of this chapter.

[13] On which see generally E McKendrick, 'Force Majeure Clauses: The Gap between Doctrine and Practice' in A Burrows and E Peel (eds), *Contract Terms* (Oxford, Oxford University Press, 2007).

[14] *Taylor v Caldwell* (1863) 3 B & S 826, 122 ER 309.

[15] *Hirji Mulji v Cheong Yue Steamship Co Ltd* [1926] AC 497 (PC).

II. *TAYLOR V CALDWELL*

The facts of *Taylor v Caldwell*[16] are well known. The defendants granted to the claimants a licence to use the 'Surrey Gardens and Music Hall' for a series of four concerts at a fee of £100 per concert. After the contract had been concluded, but before the first concert was performed, the music hall was accidentally destroyed by fire so that it became impossible to stage the concerts. The claimants brought a claim against the defendants on the basis that the defendants were in breach of contract in failing to supply the hall, and sought to recover their wasted advertising expenditure. The claim was dismissed and it was held that the contract had been frustrated because the destruction of the music hall rendered performance of the contract impossible. The frustrating event was held to have released both parties from their obligations under the contract. The essence of the reasoning of the court is to be found in the following passage from the judgment of Blackburn J:[17]

> In the present case, looking at the whole contract, we find that the parties contracted on the basis of the continued existence of the Music Hall at the time when the concerts were to be given; that being essential to their performance. We think, therefore, that the Music Hall having ceased to exist, without fault of either party, both parties are excused, the plaintiffs from taking the gardens and paying the money, the defendants from performing their promise to give the use of the Hall and Gardens and other things.

It is clear from this passage that 'both parties' were excused from their prospective contractual obligations. Two points can be made in relation to this proposition. First, it was not strictly necessary for the court to reach this conclusion in order to decide the case. It would have sufficed to conclude that the defendants had a defence to the claim for damages. The existence of such a defence would not have required the court to conclude that 'both' parties were excused; it would have sufficed to conclude that the defendants were excused from the liability in damages which otherwise would have accrued as a result of their non-performance. Second, the court provided little by way of reasoning in support of its conclusion that both parties were excused other than to state that the continued existence of the Music Hall was essential to both parties in the sense that they had both contracted on the basis of its continued existence.

While it is clear that impossibility of performance discharged the defendants from their obligation to provide the Music Hall for the series of concerts, why were the claimants discharged from their obligation to make payment? The answer cannot be that it was impossible for them to make payment given that there was no legal impediment to them doing so. The most careful consideration of this issue has been provided by Professor Treitel. He provides us with three options, two of which are derived from explanations adopted in the United States and the third is his preferred

[16] *Taylor v Caldwell* (n 14). On the background to the case itself, see C Macmillan, '*Taylor v Caldwell* (1863)' in C Mitchell and P Mitchell (eds), *Landmark Cases in the Law of Contract* (Oxford, Hart Publishing, 2008).

[17] ibid 839–40.

option which is derived from the judgment of Lord Sumner in *Hirji Mulji v Cheong Yue Steamship Co Ltd* to which we shall turn in the next section.

The first explanation which Professor Treitel outlines and which is derived from the United States is that adopted by Corbin, namely that the defendants were discharged by impossibility but the claimants were discharged 'because their purpose in entering into the contract (ie to secure the use of the Hall) [was] frustrated'.[18] The principal difficulty created by this explanation is that it uses 'frustration of purpose' in a different sense from that traditionally used in English law. The context in which it is typically used is in the case where performance remains physically possible but the common purpose of the parties can no longer be achieved.[19] In such cases it is the frustration of the parties' common purpose which brings about the discharge of the contract. But this doctrine operates within very narrow confines in English law,[20] reflecting the courts' concern not to allow the doctrine to become an excuse for a party who has simply entered into an improvident bargain. However, it is not this 'frustration of purpose' which is being invoked in order to explain the decision in *Taylor v Caldwell*, where it was the impossibility of performance which was at the root of the claim that the contract had been frustrated. As a consequence of that impossibility, the claimant's purpose could no longer be achieved but the mere fact that the purpose of one party can no longer be achieved does not of itself provide that party with an excuse for its failure to perform its contractual obligations. Something more is required.

The second explanation which Professor Treitel derives from American jurisprudence is that the claimants were discharged by 'failure of consideration' or by 'failure in performance'.[21] As Professor Treitel points out, the former term is unhelpful to the extent that it has the potential to draw us into a discussion as to the nature of the claim to recover a payment on the ground that the consideration for it has totally failed. The issue with which we are here concerned is a different one and so the language of 'failure of consideration' in this context is unhelpful and will not be further pursued.[22] The term 'failure in performance' is more promising provided that it is realised that it is not be equated with a breach of contract. The defendants in *Taylor v Caldwell* were not in breach of contract in failing to provide the Music Hall. But it can be argued that their inability to provide the claimants with

[18] GH Treitel, *Frustration and Force Majeure*, 3rd edn (London, Sweet & Maxwell, 2014) [2-042], citing AL Corbin, *Corbin on Contracts*, rev edn (St Paul MN, West Publishing, 1993) [1322].

[19] As in the coronation cases, such as *Krell v Henry* [1903] 2 KB 740 (CA).

[20] See, eg, *Herne Bay Steam Boat Co v Hutton* [1903] 2 KB 683 (CA); *Amalgamated Investment and Property Co Ltd v John Walker & Sons Ltd* [1977] 1 WLR 164 (CA); *North Shore Ventures Ltd v Anstead Holdings Inc* [2010] EWHC 1485 (Ch) [310].

[21] Treitel (n 18) [2-044]. See also EA Farnsworth, *Contracts*, 4th edn (New York, NY, Aspen, 2004) § 9.9, where it is stated that the effect of supervening impracticability or frustration on the excused party is usually to discharge that party's remaining duties of performance, and the excusal of those duties of performance 'affects the other party's duties of performance in the same way as if the excused party had broken the contract'.

[22] A further difficulty is potentially created by the fact that the House of Lords in *National Carriers Ltd v Panalpina (Northern) Ltd* [1981] AC 675 (HL) held that 'failure of consideration' did not provide a satisfactory juridical basis for the doctrine of frustration. Given its rejection in that context, its possible use in the present context does not seem helpful, and this provides a further reason for its rejection.

the performance which they had promised operated to discharge the claimants from their obligations under the contract. We shall return to this explanation at a later point in this chapter.

Before we leave *Taylor v Caldwell* one final observation can be made. There is no suggestion in the judgments that the discharge of both parties operated automatically, irrespective of their intention. On the contrary, the court attributed the discharge of the contract to the implied intention of the parties and it is likely that the court was of the opinion that the discharge of the contract also flowed from the intention of the parties. In other words, both parties were discharged because that was the outcome which the parties would have intended. There was no question of the court imposing upon the parties a discharge which neither of them intended or wished for. Unequivocal authority for the proposition that frustration automatically brings a contract to an end had to wait until the decision of the Privy Council in *Hirji Mulji v Cheong Yue Steamship Co Ltd*, to which we now turn.

III. *HIRJI MULJI V CHEONG YUE STEAMSHIP CO LTD*

The leading authority which is generally cited for the proposition that frustration operates automatically to discharge both parties prospectively from their obligations to perform, irrespective of their intention, is the decision of the Privy Council in *Hirji Mulji v Cheong Yue Steamship Co Ltd*.[23] The parties entered into a time charter on 17 November 1916 under which it was agreed that a steamship, the *Singaporean*, would be placed at the disposal of the charterers on 1 March 1917 and that it would be employed by them for a 10-month period. Prior to 1 March 1917 the *Singaporean* was requisitioned by the government. On 5 April 1917 the owners, believing that the *Singaporean* would be returned to them within a few months, wrote to the charterers and asked them whether they would be willing to take up the vessel after its release. The charterers responded positively to this request on 12 May 1917. In the months that followed there was some sporadic correspondence between the parties. In particular, the charterers inquired as to when the *Singaporean* might be available to them. This correspondence came to an end in October 1917 and there was no further communication between the parties until March 1919 when, the *Singaporean* having been released by the government in late February 1919, the owners' agent wrote to the charterers on 2 March 1919 asking them who would take delivery of the ship. The charterers responded to the effect that it was now 'useless'[24] to offer delivery given that the charter had long since expired.

The owners brought a claim against the charterers invoking the arbitration clause in the contract. The arbitration clause provided that 'any dispute arising under this charter shall be referred to the arbitration of two persons in Hong Kong, one to be nominated by owners' agents, and the other by the charterers'. The charterers declined to appoint an arbitrator but the arbitrator appointed by the owners

[23] *Hirji Mulji* (n 15).
[24] ibid 500.

proceeded nevertheless to hear the claim and made an award in favour of the owners in the sum of HK$162,584. The charterers appealed against the award and it was this appeal that made its way through the Hong Kong courts to the Privy Council. The charterers maintained that the arbitrator had no jurisdiction to decide the dispute which had been referred to him because, at the time at which the dispute arose between the parties in 1919, the time charter had already been frustrated with the consequence that no dispute 'arising under this charter' could be referred to him. The Privy Council agreed with this submission and held that the time charter, including the submission to arbitration, had been frustrated, with the consequence that the arbitrator did not have jurisdiction to make the award which he had made.

In reaching the conclusion that the requisition of the *Singaporean* had frustrated the time charter, Lord Sumner identified in the case law 'an almost continuous series of expressions to the effect that such a frustration brings the contract to an end forthwith, without more and automatically'.[25] The cases which he cited in support of this proposition included *Jackson v Union Marine Insurance Co Ltd*,[26] *FA Tamplin Steamship Co Ltd v Anglo-Mexican Petroleum Co Ltd*[27] and *Bank Line Ltd v Arthur Capel & Co*.[28] From these and other cases he derived the following proposition:[29]

> Language is occasionally used in the cases which seems to show that frustration is assimilated in the speaker's mind to repudiation or rescission of contracts. The analogy is a false one. Rescission (except by mutual consent or by a competent Court) is the right of one party, arising upon conduct by the other, by which he intimates his intention to abide by the contract no longer. It is a right to treat the contract as at an end if he chooses, and to claim damages for its total breach, but it is a right in his option and does not depend in theory on any implied term providing for its exercise, but is given by the law in vindication of a breach. Frustration, on the other hand, is explained in theory as a condition or term of the contract, implied by the law ab initio, in order to supply what the parties would have inserted had the matter occurred to them, on the basis of what is fair and reasonable, having regard to the mutual interests concerned and of the main objects of the contract: see per Lord Watson in *Dahl v. Nelson, Donkin & Co.* It is irrespective of the individuals concerned, their temperaments and failings, their interest and circumstances. It is really a device, by which the rules as to absolute contracts are reconciled with a special exception which justice demands.

A number of points should be noted about this paragraph. First, a contrast is expressly drawn between the case of a repudiatory breach and the frustration of a contract. The term 'rescission' as used by Lord Sumner is a difficult one in English law, in that it is used in different senses. However, it is clear that its use in this context is to describe the setting aside of a contract following the acceptance of a repudiatory breach where discharge operates prospectively and not retrospectively, as would be the case where a contract is set aside because of a vitiating factor, such

[25] ibid 505.
[26] *Jackson v Union Marine Insurance Co Ltd* (1874–75) LR 10 CP 125.
[27] *FA Tamplin Steamship Co Ltd v Anglo Mexican Petroleum Products Co Ltd* [1916] 2 AC 397 (HL).
[28] *Bank Line Ltd v Arthur Capel & Co* [1919] AC 435 (HL).
[29] *Hirji Mulji* (n 15) 509–10 (footnotes omitted).

as misrepresentation. Frustration also operates to discharge a contract prospectively, not retrospectively, and so in this sense at least it operates in a manner similar to the discharge of a contract following the acceptance of a repudiatory breach.[30]

The second point is that the real ground of distinction between discharge for breach and discharge following the frustration of the contract is that breach gives to the innocent party an option which it is for that party to decide whether or not to exercise. The innocent party can choose either to accept the breach and bring the contract to an end or to affirm the contract so that it continues in existence for the benefit of both parties. The question whether or not a repudiatory breach of itself brings a contract to an end was authoritatively re-considered in the context of a contract of employment by the Supreme Court in *Geys v Société Générale, London Branch*,[31] where it was affirmed that a repudiatory breach of contract by the employer did not have the automatic consequence of bringing to an end the contract of employment. Rather, it gave rise to an option on the part of the innocent party either to affirm or to bring the contract to an end.

The position is otherwise where the contract is frustrated. In this situation the parties do not have an option to exercise. The contract is terminated automatically and both parties are discharged from further performance. Why did the Privy Council reach this conclusion? A number of answers can be given to this question.

First, as has been noted, it was held to be consistent with the authorities.[32] Second, frustration was held to be different from breach in that it arises from an event for which neither party is responsible and it makes it impossible for the parties to achieve their common object in entering into the contract. A repudiatory breach, by contrast, confers a right upon only one party to the contract, namely the innocent party, and it is for that party to decide whether or not to exercise it. In the case of the frustration of a contract, Lord Sumner observed that[33] it is the parties'

> common object that has to be frustrated, not merely the individual advantage which one party or the other might have gained from the contract. If so, what the law provides must be a common relief from this common disappointment and an immediate termination of the obligations as regards future performance. This is necessary, because otherwise the parties would be bound to a contract, which is one that they did not really make. If it were not so, a doctrine designed to avert unintended burdens would operate to enable one party to profit by the event and to hold the other, if he so chose, to a new obligation.

This reference to the 'common object' of the parties is picked up by Professor Treitel to support the conclusion that frustration operates to discharge both parties because it defeats or frustrates their 'common object'. In his view the parties' common object is defeated even though one party expected to benefit from the contract by receiving

[30] ibid 510.

[31] *Geys v Société Générale, London Branch* [2012] UKSC 63; [2013] 1 AC 523.

[32] There was some authority from which it might have been inferred that frustration did not arise automatically but from the exercise of an option by one or other party to the contract (see, e.g, the judgment of Lord Blackburn in *Dahl v Nelson, Donkin and Co* (1881) 6 App Cas 38 (HL) 53) however these dicta were later held not to support the view that termination did not occur until a party said so: see *Hirji Mulji* (n 15) 507–08.

[33] *Hirji Mulji* (n 15) 507.

a sum of money and the other by receiving the promised counter-performance. Thus he concludes that[34]

> whenever such common objects are defeated, it makes practical sense to say that performance of the contract has been frustrated. It follows that both parties will be discharged even though the supervening event directly affects only the performance to be rendered by one of them.

Third, automatic discharge was believed to be a 'fair and reasonable' solution which, in the judgment of Lord Sumner, was what the parties would have provided as reasonable people had the matter occurred to them. It should be noted that Lord Sumner does not state that the rule of automatic discharge is implied into the contract as a matter of fact: rather, it is implied 'by the law' in order to provide a fair and reasonable solution that is believed to be consistent with what the parties would have provided had they thought about the matter. Is it open to the parties to show that they had a different intention from that which the law attributes to them as reasonable people? It would appear not. Lord Sumner stated that the legal effect of frustration 'does not depend on their intention or their opinions, or even knowledge, as to the event, which has brought this about'.[35] Their intention is of some relevance when considering whether the event amounted in law to frustration[36] but, once it has been decided that the contract was frustrated, the parties' intention in relation to the discharge of the contract is not relevant because discharge follows automatically from the conclusion that the contract was frustrated. That said, it remains open to the parties to enter into a fresh contract after the discharge of the contract (except in the case of supervening illegality, at least where the illegality remains operative). This might have been of some significance on the facts of *Hirji Mulji*. The correspondence between the parties in April and May 1917 demonstrated a willingness to continue with the contract but it was conceded that these communications 'did not amount to a new contract or in any way vary the contract contained in the charterparty'.[37] It therefore could not be said on the facts of the case that the parties had entered into a fresh contract.

But the decision of the Privy Council did not escape criticism. On the particular point in issue in the case, namely that the frustration of the charter had the effect of depriving the arbitrator of jurisdiction, doubt was cast on its authority in strong obiter dicta by the House of Lords in *Heyman v Darwins Ltd*,[38] and in the light of these doubts Pilcher J declined to follow *Hirji Mulji* on this point in *Kruse v Questier & Co*.[39]

[34] Treitel (n 18) [2-044].

[35] *Hirji Mulji* (n 15) 509.

[36] 'What the parties say and do is only evidence, and not necessarily weighty evidence, of the view to be taken of the event by informed and experienced minds': ibid.

[37] *Hirji Mulji* (n 15) 500.

[38] *Heyman v Darwins Ltd* [1942] AC 356 (HL). The consideration of *Hirji Mulji* was technically obiter. The strongest criticism is to be found in the judgments of Lord Simon LC (at 366) and Lord Porter (at 401), but it is also apparent in the judgment of Lord Wright (at 383). Lord Macmillan reserved his opinion (at 373), the issue not having been fully argued before the court.

[39] *Kruse v Questier & Co* [1953] 1 QB 669 (QBD) 679. The High Court of Australia also declined to follow *Hirji Mulji* in this respect: see *Codelfa Construction Pty Ltd v State Rail Authority of New South Wales* (1982) 149 CLR 337 (HCA) 365 (Mason J). And see now Arbitration Act 1996 (UK), s 7, which confirms the separability of arbitration agreements.

But the doubt cast on the conclusion in relation to the jurisdiction of the arbitrator did not extend to Lord Sumner's conclusion that frustration operates to discharge a contract automatically, which Viscount Simon LC in *Heyman* described as a 'pronouncement of the highest authority'.[40]

The principal critic of the proposition that frustration operates automatically to discharge the contract between the parties is probably Dr McElroy whose book, *Impossibility of Performance*,[41] based on his doctoral thesis and edited by Glanville Williams, was published in 1941. While Dr McElroy acknowledged that it was 'quite easy'[42] to apply the automatic theory of discharge to the facts of *Taylor v Caldwell*, he argued that there were 'obvious difficulties'[43] with the proposition that frustration operated automatically, and concluded by suggesting that the automatic theory 'should not be further pursued'.[44] His principal criticism was that automatic discharge had the potential to create 'suspense and uncertainty'.[45] The particular context in which he alleged that such uncertainty might arise was the case of delay. Thus he argued that a rule which holds that frustration operates automatically gives no incentive to either party to inform the other of his belief that the contract between them has come to an end. Rather, it entitles the parties to remain silent and then, when it suits one or other of them, submit that the contract had come to an end at some earlier point in time even though no attempt had been made at that time to invoke the doctrine of frustration or even to suggest that the contract between them had come to an end. In theory, this invocation of frustration could occur a long time after the frustrating event occurred because, given that its effect is automatic, the entitlement to invoke frustration cannot be lost by lapse of time, in contrast with the position that obtains in relation to a repudiatory breach. Rather than invoke automatic discharge, Dr McElroy preferred the following solution[46]

> when the circumstances of delay have lasted so long that a presumption can be drawn that it will prove inordinate, *either* party may take the initiative and declare the contract at an end (irrespective of the consent of the other) and then *both* are free. The date of dissolution, then, is the date when one party (ie either party) makes an intimation to that effect. If the matter is disputed, the party making the intimation has the burden of establishing that, at the time when he declared the contract to be at an end, the facts amounted to 'frustration'.

The rule put forward by Dr McElroy does give comfort to the parties that their contract remains binding until notice is given by one party, but it is unlikely to remove all 'suspense and uncertainty'. As Glanville Williams pointed out in an editorial insert to Dr McElroy's text, 'the party seeking to get out of the contract is

[40] *Heyman* (n 38) 365.
[41] RG McElroy, *Impossibility of Performance: A Treatise on the Law of Supervening Impossibility of Performance of Contract, Failure of Consideration, and Frustration* (Cambridge, Cambridge University Press, 1941).
[42] ibid 223.
[43] ibid.
[44] ibid 231.
[45] ibid 227.
[46] ibid 229 (footnotes omitted).

not absolutely safe until he gets a pronouncement of the court that the contract is discharged'.[47]

These criticisms of *Hirji Mulji* were also picked up in the nineteenth edition of *Anson*, edited by Brierly. He points out that some of the results produced by the application of the theory of automatic discharge are 'rather curious'.[48] In addition to supporting Dr McElroy's view that the automatic theory of discharge can 'cause precisely the inconvenience which it is intended to prevent, namely uncertainty as to the future obligations of the parties',[49] he notes that the hirer of the room in *Krell v Henry*[50] could not have insisted on taking the room had he wished to do so.

IV. SUBSEQUENT DEVELOPMENTS

As a decision of the Privy Council, *Hirji Mulji* was not technically binding on the English courts and this fact was noted by some of its critics.[51] This could have left the theory of automatic discharge in a vulnerable position, particularly given the criticisms levelled against it by Dr McElroy and the editor of *Anson*. But the rule that frustration operates to discharge both parties automatically became a firmly entrenched part of English law as a result of the support which Lord Sumner's reasoning received in a series of cases on frustration which reached the House of Lords in the 1940s.

The first such case was the decision of the House of Lords in *Joseph Constantine Steamship Line Ltd v Imperial Smelting Corp Ltd*.[52] The narrow issue before the House of Lords was whether the party invoking frustration had to prove that the frustrating event had arisen without negligence on its own part or whether it was for the party alleging that the contract had not been frustrated to prove that the event was caused by the negligence of the party relying upon the doctrine of frustration. The House of Lords held unanimously that the latter proposition was the correct one. Although the issue before the court was a narrow one, the judgments were expansive—albeit that their consideration of a number of issues, including the effect of frustration, was therefore obiter. In relation to the effects of frustration on a contract, their Lordships could not have been clearer. Thus Viscount Simon stated that frustration 'does not merely provide one party with a defence in an action brought by the other. It kills the contract itself and discharges both parties automatically'.[53] Viscount Maugham observed that '[f]rustration operates

[47] ibid 230.

[48] Brierly (ed), *Principles of the English Law of Contract and of Agency in Its Relation to Contract*, 19th edn (Oxford, Clarendon Press, 1945) 355. These criticisms disappear in the twenty-first edition, the first edition to be edited by Professor Guest.

[49] ibid.

[50] *Krell* (n 19) (discussed below at the text accompanying n 64).

[51] eg, Lord Porter in *Heyman* (n 38) 401, after stating that the decision was not binding, stated that he did not think it should be followed in relation to the effect of frustration on the arbitration clause in the contract.

[52] *Joseph Constantine* (n 1).

[53] ibid 163.

automatically—for the good or ill of both parties'[54] and that 'the law intervenes with the doctrine of frustration, and declares that the contract is at an end'.[55] Finally, Lord Wright stated that

> [f]rustration operates automatically. It does not depend on the choice or election of the parties to the contract … the contract is ended and dead, simply by the frustrating event. If the parties choose to go on with it, that is in truth entering into a new contract.[56]

Lord Wright also referred to Lord Sumner's judgment with approval in both *Fibrosa Spolka Akcyjna v Fairbairn Lawson Combe Barbour Ltd*[57] and in *Denny, Mott and Dickson Ltd v James B Fraser and Co Ltd*.[58] In the latter case he stated that it is 'now … well settled that where there is frustration a dissolution of a contract occurs automatically'[59] and that it 'does not depend … on the choice or election of either party'[60] so that an option to purchase a timber yard was no longer exercisable.

In the light of these and other authorities[61] the rule that frustration operates to bring a contract to an end forthwith, without more and automatically, must be considered to be a firmly established rule of English contract law.

V. EVALUATION

Although the rule that frustration operates to bring a contract to an end forthwith, without more and automatically must be considered to be a well-established rule of English contract law, what is the justification for the rule? The justification does not emerge with great clarity from the case law and so it is necessary to dig a little deeper in order to find the justification, if there is one, for the current state of English law. When doing so, it should be kept in mind that there could be said to be two components to the rule laid down in *Hirji Mulji*: (i) that frustration operates to discharge both parties and (ii) it does so automatically. It may also be necessary to distinguish between frustration by impossibility, by subsequent illegality and frustration of purpose when considering the justifications for the rule. The rule of automatic discharge may be easier to explain in the cases of discharge by impossibility or subsequent illegality than it is in the case of frustration of purpose.

A. Impossibility

Let us start with the case of impossibility. *Taylor v Caldwell* provides us with a good example. Why were the defendants discharged from their obligation to provide the

[54] ibid 171.
[55] ibid 174.
[56] ibid 187–88.
[57] *Fibrosa Spolka Akcyjna v Fairbairn Lawson Combe Barbour Ltd* [1943] AC 32 (HL) 65.
[58] *Denny, Mott and Dickson Ltd v James B Fraser and Co Ltd* [1944] AC 265 (HL).
[59] ibid 274.
[60] ibid.
[61] Such as *Davis Contractors Ltd v Fareham UDC* [1956] AC 696 (HL) 728 (Lord Radcliffe) and *J Lauritzen AS v Wijsmuller BV (The 'Super Servant Two')* [1990] 1 Lloyd's Rep 1 (CA) 8 (Bingham LJ).

Music Hall? The answer is that they were discharged from doing so because it had become impossible for them to provide the Music Hall as a result of the fire for which they were not responsible. The claimants were discharged from their obligation to pay for the Music Hall because the failure of the defendants to provide them with the Music Hall relieved them of their obligation to pay for it. The law did not require the claimants to pay for a service they would not receive. It could be said that the discharge of the obligation to pay for the hire was simply a consequence of the destruction of the Music Hall. In this sense the reasons for discharge may be said to be connected, but capable of separate explanation and justification. However, an explanation which focuses on the 'common object' of the parties would seem to be more faithful to the explanation which is to be found in the case law itself. Rather than view the obligation to provide the Music Hall and the obligation to pay for it separately, it may be preferable to view them as part of the parties' common object, which was to make use of the Music Hall for the purpose of holding concerts and, when that joint objective could no longer be performed for reasons beyond the control and the responsibility of the parties, both parties were discharged from their obligations to perform in the future.

Why not simply excuse the defendants from their liability in damages? This could have been a sufficient answer on the facts of the case but, given that the destruction of the Music Hall rendered performance of the contract according to its terms impossible, there was no prospect that contractual performance would take place in any event. Discharge was therefore the correct solution and, given that performance could not have taken place in accordance with the contract, talk of the need for an election to terminate seems pointless. The automatic discharge of both parties recognised the practical reality of the events that had taken place.

Matters become more difficult, however, when account is taken of the fact that the contract was not simply about the provision of the Music Hall. The defendants also agreed to provide the Surrey Gardens and the claimants had assumed an obligation not only to pay for the use of the Music Hall and Surrey Gardens but to provide the artistes who were to perform at the concerts. The discharge of the latter obligation is not difficult to explain given that it was no longer possible to hold the concerts in the Music Hall. But the obligation to provide the Surrey Gardens raises more difficult issues. What would have happened if the defendants had insisted that the claimants hire the Surrey Gardens or the claimants had insisted that the defendants provide them with the Surrey Gardens? This would not appear to be a case of impossibility given that the Surrey Gardens were presumably accessible notwithstanding the destruction of the Music Hall. But it is at this point that we must come back to the 'common object' of the parties. Catherine MacMillan has demonstrated, through her careful analysis of the background to the case, including the rise of the promenade concert in Victorian England, that 'without the splendid and enormous Music Hall, there was no venue suitable for staging the concerts'.[62] To require the defendants to

[62] MacMillan (n 16) 192.

supply, or the claimants to take, the Surrey Gardens without the ability to hold the promenade concerts would have been to impose on the parties a different contract from that which they had undertaken. Given that their 'common object' could no longer be achieved, both parties were rightly discharged from their obligations to perform their contractual obligations in relation to the Surrey Gardens.

B. Illegality

In the case where the contract is discharged by subsequent illegality, the public policy behind the rule which leads to the frustration of the contract, should also apply to the consequences of frustration. The concern of the law is not simply with the allocation or distribution of the loss caused by the supervening event, but with public policy considerations, particularly in ensuring that the law is observed.[63] For example, in the case of trading with the enemy in times of war the law is concerned to ensure that the contract is not performed, irrespective of the wishes of the parties to the contract. This being the case, the automatic discharge of both parties is the simplest way to ensure that performance does not take place and the policy of the law is upheld.

C. Frustration of Purpose

More difficult is the case in which the contract is frustrated because the common purpose for which the contract was entered into can no longer be carried out because of some supervening event. As is well-known, there are very few cases of this type in English law. The leading case is *Krell v Henry*,[64] where a contract to hire a flat in Pall Mall for two days (excluding the nights) for the purpose of viewing the coronation procession was held to have been frustrated when the coronation of Edward VII was postponed because he had to undergo surgery. The effect of the frustration of the contract was that both parties were discharged from their obligations under the contract. Why discharge both parties and why does discharge operate automatically? To return to the question posed by the editor of the nineteenth edition of *Anson*, why was the hirer of the room not entitled to insist upon hiring the room on payment of the agreed fee? The most convincing answer is that the hire of the room for the purpose of viewing the coronation procession was the purpose of both parties in entering into the contract, not simply the purpose of the hirer of the room. This point was explicitly acknowledged by Vaughan Williams LJ when he stated that the coronation procession was the basis of the contract 'as much for the lessor as the hirer' and that 'if the King, before the coronation day and after the contract, had died, the hirer could not have insisted on having the rooms on the days named'.[65]

[63] *Islamic Republic of Iran Shipping Lines v Steamship Mutual Underwriting Association (Bermuda) Ltd* [2010] EWHC 2661 (Comm); [2011] 1 Lloyd's Rep 195 [100].
[64] *Krell* (n 19).
[65] ibid 751.

Thus it was not open to the hirer unilaterally to insist upon taking the room in the changed circumstances in which the parties found themselves. Had he wished to do so, he would have had to enter into a fresh contract to hire the room. If the viewing of the procession was not the purpose of both parties but the purpose of the hirer only, then the hirer would have been entitled, and indeed, obliged to hire the room because, in such a case, the contract would not have been frustrated by the postponement of the procession. But in the narrow category of case in which the common purpose of the contract can no longer be achieved, the discharge of both parties appears to be the correct conclusion.

D. The Wishes of the Parties

What is to be done in the case where the parties wish to continue with performance of the contract where it is possible for them to do so and there is no illegality involved in them doing so? The law permits them to do so but requires that they enter into a fresh contract for this purpose. This new contract would have to be entered into after the frustration of the contract but there is no reason why the new contract cannot be on the same, or substantially similar, terms to those of the original contract. Given the freedom which the parties retain to enter into a fresh contract, the law does not impose on the parties a solution contrary to their will. It simply requires that that will be expressed in the form of a new contract.

Is it possible to waive the operation of the doctrine of frustration? A submission to this effect was advanced before Robert Goff J in *BP Exploration Co (Libya) Ltd v Hunt (No 2)*[66] and was rejected. Robert Goff J stated that it was 'somewhat difficult' to talk of one party 'waiving frustration of the agreement or any right to rely thereon'.[67] The essential basis for this conclusion was that frustration is not a right which is given to the parties and which they can choose to waive. Rather, 'it is legal doctrine, the effect of which is to determine the rights and obligations arising under the contract which has been frustrated'.[68] A contract which has been frustrated is 'forthwith determined as a matter of law'[69] so that it is the law itself which brings the relationship between the parties to an end. The right to determine the contract therefore does not belong to an individual party and, this being the case, an individual party cannot purport to waive that right. To the extent that the law has regard to the intention or wishes of the parties when deciding whether or not a contract has been frustrated, it has regard to the 'common object' of the parties so that, even on this basis, the wishes of one party cannot be determinative. Therefore, it should not be possible for one party to waive the frustration of a contract to which it is a party.

[66] *BP Exploration Co* (n 10).
[67] ibid 810.
[68] ibid.
[69] ibid 809.

E. Temporary Impediments

The case which is perhaps most difficult for the theory of automatic discharge is the case in which the performance of the contract is affected by some temporary impediment. *Hirji Mulji* itself is a case in this category. The parties entered into their agreement in November 1916, the vessel was requisitioned in March 1917 and it continued in government service until March 1919. If we view the case through the lens of the parties at the time of entry into the contract in November 1916 we might not expect a delay of the length that was actually occasioned and so might incline to the conclusion that the contract was not initially frustrated. To the extent that it is relevant, this conclusion could be reinforced by reference to the correspondence which passed between the parties in April and May 1917. But as the length of the delay increased and the correspondence between the parties came to an end, the inference that the contract was frustrated becomes a more likely conclusion. It is difficult to identify a precise point in time at which the contract was frustrated but it was not necessary for the Privy Council to identify such a date for the purpose of deciding the case. However, it is not clear that the difficulty in identifying the point in time at which the contract was frustrated was caused by the automatic theory of discharge. It is true that, were the law to adopt an elective theory of discharge, as suggested by Dr McElroy, the question might appear to admit of a simpler answer because the court would then have to look for an intimation by one or other party that the contract had been discharged and, in the absence of such intimation, the contract would continue to bind.

But the appearance of simplicity is misleading. At least two difficulties would remain. The first would be for the parties themselves. At what point in time should they intimate that in their view the contract has come to an end? Presumably, in *Hirji Mulji*, April 1917 would be too early but when thereafter should notice be given? And what are the consequences of giving notice prematurely? Would it amount to a renunciation of the contract, leaving the notice-giver vulnerable to a claim for damages for a repudiatory breach? The second difficulty is that experienced by the court when deciding whether the delay is sufficient to frustrate the contract. Should the judge seek to put herself in the position of the parties at the time at which the notice was given and ask whether the delay until that point and the delay projected thereafter was sufficient to frustrate the contract? Or should she take advantage of the benefit of hindsight and, with the benefit of that hindsight, decide whether the contract was frustrated? These difficulties resemble those experienced by judges under the automatic theory of discharge. An elective theory of discharge would simply replace the current difficulties with different ones, some of which have been noted above. While the automatic discharge theory is not easy to apply to cases of delay, it is not immediately obvious that an elective theory of discharge would be any easier to apply.

F. Invocation by the Wrong Party

One of the criticisms of the automatic discharge theory is that both parties are discharged from their obligations to perform and so the possibility is created that a party might be tempted to behave opportunistically by invoking frustration in order to get out of a contract which has become inconvenient for it. Cases that might fall into this category include *FA Tamplin Steamship Co Ltd v Anglo-Mexican Petroleum Co Ltd*[70] and *Blane Steamships v Minister of Transport*.[71] A court can prevent such opportunistic behaviour by concluding that the contract has not been frustrated, but, once it has decided that the contract was frustrated, its hands are tied in remedial terms because it is bound to conclude that the contract has come to an end. In an attempt to meet this difficulty Professor Treitel has suggested that the law should develop 'the rule that frustration should operate only so as to give an option to terminate the contract to a party who is prejudiced by the frustrating event'.[72] In the case where both parties are prejudiced by the frustrating event, Professor Treitel suggests that either party would have the option to terminate the contract.

It is not clear how much of a problem this is in practice. In the case of the opportunistic claimant, the court is most likely to conclude that the contract was not frustrated and so the problem will not arise. But in the case where the contract is frustrated because the 'common object' of the parties cannot be achieved, the law provides what Lord Sumner in *Hirji Mulji* called 'common relief from this common disappointment'.[73] To confine the entitlement to terminate the contract to one party only is to develop a rule which is at odds with the doctrine of frustration as it is currently conceived in English law. A court which wishes to avoid the abuse of the doctrine of frustration should conclude that the contract has not been frustrated: it should not conclude that the contract has been frustrated but then confine the entitlement to terminate the contract to the party prejudiced by the frustrating event.

G. Self-induced Frustration

The automatic discharge theory does, however, run into some difficulty in cases of 'self-induced' frustration. The most well-known example is, perhaps, the decision of the Court of Appeal in *FC Shepherd & Co Ltd v Jerrom*.[74] An employee, who had been sentenced to borstal training following his involvement in an affray, complained that he had been unfairly dismissed. The employer responded that the contract between the parties had been frustrated as a result of the custodial sentence which had been imposed on the employee so that there had in law been no dismissal of the employee to which the unfair dismissal legislation could apply. The employee sought to resist the invocation of frustration on the ground that the custodial sentence could not in law suffice to frustrate the contract because it was the consequence

[70] *FA Tamplin Steamship* (n 27).
[71] *Blane Steamships v Minister of Transport* [1951] 2 KB 965 (CA).
[72] Treitel (n 18) [15-010]. This passage was noted but not commented upon by the Supreme Court of New Zealand in *Planet Kids Ltd v Auckland Council* [2013] NZSC 147; [2014] 1 NZLR 149 [48].
[73] *Hirji Mulji* (n 15) 507.
[74] *Jerrom* (n 6).

of his own deliberate act and so could not be said to have arisen without the fault of either party. The Court of Appeal held that the contract had been frustrated so that the employee was not entitled to bring an unfair dismissal claim. While the employer was held to be entitled to invoke frustration, it is clear that the employee would not have been entitled to do so, given that he was responsible for the conduct which led to the imposition of a custodial sentence. Professor Treitel thus cites *Shepherd v Jerrom* as authority for the proposition that 'where an allegedly frustrating event is brought about by the deliberate act of one party … that party cannot rely on it as a ground of discharge, but the other may be able to do so'.[75] It would appear that it is the presence of fault on the part of one of the contracting parties which has the consequence that frustration does not have its usual effect of automatically discharging both parties from their obligations to perform in the future. That this is so is clear from the judgment of Mustill LJ in *Jerrom* who stated that 'the effect of the frustration is to discharge one promisor, or the other, or both, *depending on the existence and location of any fault giving rise to the event*'.[76] On this basis, if the frustrating event occurs without the fault of either party then both parties are discharged automatically from their obligations to perform. But if the otherwise frustrating event is attributable to the fault of one of the contracting parties then the party at fault is not entitled to invoke frustration but the other party is.

The latter proposition cannot easily be reconciled with the theory of automatic discharge. It is not difficult to explain the inability of the party at fault to rely on the doctrine of frustration. Given that a frustrating event is by definition an outside event or extraneous change of situation, it cannot encompass an event caused by the fault of one the parties to the contract. But it is more difficult to explain why the other party to the contract should be entitled to rely on the doctrine of frustration. The unilateral application of the doctrine of frustration is at odds with the emphasis placed by Lord Sumner on 'common relief' from 'common disappointment'.[77] This unilateral nature also makes it more difficult to explain why discharge should be automatic. If, as in *Jerrom*, the entitlement to invoke frustration is given only to the employer, should the decision whether or not to invoke the doctrine not lie with the employer? In other words, should it not depend upon the election of the employer? Of course, this proposition would not have suited the employer on the facts of *Jerrom* because it was seeking to avoid the application of the unfair dismissal legislation by submitting that it had not in law dismissed the employee. But it is not entirely clear, at least in policy terms, that employers should be entitled to avoid the application of the unfair dismissal legislation in this way. Further, as has been noted, this line of authority is very difficult to reconcile with the proposition that frustration operates to discharge both parties to the contract and that it does so automatically. For these reasons there is cause to believe that this line of cases should be over-ruled, at least in so far as they hold that the employer alone is entitled to rely on the doctrine of frustration. But, if they are not to be overruled, they have to be recognised

[75] Treitel (n 18) [15-016].
[76] *Jerrom* (n 6) 323 (emphasis added).
[77] *Hirji Mulji* (n 15) 507.

as an exception to the proposition that frustration operates to discharge both parties automatically.[78]

VI. INTERNATIONAL RE-STATEMENTS

How does English law compare with modern international conventions on contract law or re-statements of contract law? The short answer is that they differ in significant respects. They do not use the language of 'automatic discharge' to describe the consequences of an event which might be said to correspond to the frustration of a contract in English law. The earliest provision is Article 79 of the Vienna Convention on Contracts for the International Sale of Goods, which has proved to be a somewhat controversial provision. Article 79(1) provides that

> [a] party is not liable for a failure to perform any of his obligations if he proves that the failure was due to an impediment beyond his control and that he could not reasonably be expected to have taken the impediment into account at the time of the conclusion of the contract or to have avoided or overcome it, or its consequences.

Much ink has been spilt on what constitutes an 'impediment' for the purposes of this Article but we can leave that debate to one side for present purposes. Our focus is on the impact of an impediment on the obligations of the parties. Article 79(1) provides that a person 'is not liable for a failure to perform' but Article 79(5) states that 'nothing in this article prevents either party from exercising any right other than to claim damages under this Convention'. Thus the Article operates to shield the non-performing party from liability in damages but otherwise purports to leave all other remedies intact. Thus the entitlement of a party to terminate in respect of any such non-performance is not regulated by Article 79 but by the general provisions of Part III of the Convention dealing with avoidance for non-performance.

Article 7.1.7(1) of the Unidroit Principles of International Commercial Contracts builds on Article 79 of the Vienna Convention and provides that

> [n]on-performance by a party is excused if that party proves that the non-performance was due to an impediment beyond its control and that it could not reasonably be expected to have taken the impediment into account at the time of the conclusion of the contract or to have avoided or overcome its consequences.

Further, Article 7.1.7(4) provides that 'nothing in this Article prevents a party from exercising a right to terminate the contract or to withhold performance or request interest on money due'. Once again, the effect of the Article is to shield the non-performing party from liability in damages in respect of its non-performance but not to protect it from the exercise of the right to terminate, to withhold performance or to seek interest on money due. So, for example, the party who has not received the promised performance may be entitled to terminate the contract if it can establish

[78] Or they should be re-classified as cases of what Professor Freedland terms 'non-lateral termination' in which the termination is not attributable to either party but arises by operation of law: M Freedland *The Personal Employment Contract* (Oxford, Oxford University Press, 2003) 439–56.

that the failure to perform amounted to 'a fundamental non-performance'[79] or to withhold performance under Article 7.1.3.

Article 8:108(1) of the Principles of European Contract Law is drafted in terms very similar to Article 7.1.7(1) of the Unidroit Principles and Article 79 of the Vienna Convention. But an important difference is created by Article 9:303(4), which provides that 'if a party is excused under Article 8:108 through an impediment which is total and permanent, the contract is terminated automatically and without notice at the time the impediment arises'.

Not only is the contract terminated in the case of a 'total and permanent' impediment but that termination occurs 'automatically', that is to say, irrespective of the intention of the parties. In this respect the provision appears to resemble English law as laid down in *Hirji Mulji*, although the latter rule does not require the impediment to be 'total and permanent'.

The Draft Common Frame of Reference (DCFR) provides a further variance. Book III Article 3:104(1) opens in familiar style and resembles the Vienna Convention, the Unidroit Principles and the Principles of European Contract Law. But it introduces an innovation in Article 3.104(4). It provides:

> Where the excusing impediment is permanent the obligation is extinguished. Any reciprocal obligation is also extinguished. In the case of contractual obligations any restitutionary effects of extinction are regulated by the rules in Chapter 3, Section 5, Sub-section 4 (Restitution) with appropriate adaptations.

The first sentence of this Article resembles Article 9:303(4) of the Principles of European Contract Law. Although it does not use the word 'automatically' it is clear from the Comments that extinction is automatic and does not depend on the giving of notice to terminate for non-performance. The justification that is provided for dispensing with the rules on termination by notice for non-performance is that the requirement to give such notice is not only 'unnecessary and unrealistic' but potentially 'pernicious'.[80] The difficulty created by the notice requirement is that the right to terminate is lost in the case where the creditor fails to give notice within a reasonable time. This rule makes no sense in the case where the obligation can never be performed because it would condemn the contract to an existence in a 'ghostly state'.[81] In this situation 'the cleaner solution'[82] is to provide for automatic termination.

The second sentence of Article 3:104(4) is new in so far as it provides for the extinction of the reciprocal obligation. It may be that this is simply to make explicit what was implicit in Article 9:303(4) because, in the words of the Comments, 'if the debtor's obligation is extinguished it follows that any reciprocal obligation of the creditor must also be extinguished'.[83] Interestingly, there is no equivalent to

[79] As set out in Art 7.3.1. The failure to perform can amount to a 'fundamental non-performance' notwithstanding the fact that the non-performance is excused under Art 7.1.7.

[80] C von Bar and E Clive (eds), *Principles, Definitions and Model Rules of European Private Law: Draft Common Frame of Reference*, vol 1 (Oxford, Oxford University Press, 2010) 786.

[81] ibid.

[82] ibid.

[83] ibid 787.

Article 3:104(4) of the DCFR in Article 88 of the proposed Common European Sales Law.

A further point which should be noted about many of these international re-statements is that they contain provisions dealing with 'hardship' (in the case of the Unidroit Principles)[84] or 'change of circumstances' (in the case of the Principles of European Contract Law,[85] the DCFR[86] and the proposed Common European Sales Law).[87] The significance of these provisions is that they provide a much more liberal and flexible remedial response, which is not confined to the automatic termination of the contract in a narrow range of circumstances but enables the court, in an appropriate case, to adapt or vary the contract with a view to restoring its equilibrium. The danger in such provisions is that they may erode sanctity of contract if they provide too easy an escape route from what has turned out to be no more than an improvident contract. But, provided the jurisdiction is kept within suitable confines, it can perform a useful function, particularly in the case of long-term contracts where termination is often not a suitable remedy. These provisions demonstrate that, where courts are given a broader jurisdiction to intervene in cases where the obligation to perform has become extremely onerous or impracticable rather than impossible, it is beneficial to give to the courts a broader remedial armoury in order to enable them to do justice on the facts of the cases that come before them. A broad jurisdiction to intervene, combined with a rule of automatic termination, is not a sensible proposition for any legal system to adopt.

VII. CONCLUSION

The decision of the Privy Council in *Hirji Mulji* has been criticised on the ground that it 'highlights what a blunt weapon frustration is'[88] which operates 'without regard to the wishes and intentions of the parties'.[89] These criticisms might be said to gain support from international re-statements of contract law which are characterised by a much more flexible set of rules. But it is suggested that these criticisms are not as powerful as at first sight appears.

The drastic nature of the remedial response in *Hirji Mulji* is linked to the narrow scope of the doctrine of frustration.[90] In short, the doctrine is the nuclear option designed only to be available in a narrow range of cases. In the case where

[84] International Institute for the Unification of Private Law, *Unidroit Principles of International Commercial Contracts 2010*, 3rd edn (Rome, Unidroit, 2010) s 6.2.

[85] O Lando and H Beale (eds), *Principles of European Contract Law*, pts I and II (London, Kluwer, 2000) art 6:111.

[86] DCFR (n 80) book III, art 1:110.

[87] Commission, 'Proposal for a Regulation of the European Parliament and of the Council on a Common European Sales Law', COM(2011) 635 final, art 89.

[88] A Rogers, 'Frustration and Estoppel' in E McKendrick (ed), *Force Majeure and Frustration of Contract*, 2nd edn (London, Lloyd's of London Press, 1995) 252.

[89] ibid.

[90] See, eg, Hondius and Grigoleit (n 9) 9: 'jurisdictions that only offer termination as a remedy are more likely to apply very strict standards with regard to the requirements of entitlement to relief'.

performance has become physically impossible or illegal, a rule which prescribes automatic discharge of both parties appears appropriate, given that, in the case of physical impossibility, contractual performance can no longer take place and, in the case of illegality, the law has decreed that performance should not take place.

However, were the scope of the doctrine of frustration to be extended beyond its current narrow confines, it would be appropriate to re-consider the rule of automatic discharge of both parties. For example, the adoption of a doctrine of hardship would amount to commercial nonsense were it to be accompanied by a rule of automatic discharge of both parties. Instead, it would require the development of a more flexible remedial regime, including adjustment of the contract or the adaptation of its terms to restore the equilibrium of the contract in the light of the changed circumstances. It is another question whether English law should develop a more flexible and liberal doctrine of frustration. It is not the purpose of this chapter to explore that question. But the point which can be made is that the rule which requires the automatic discharge of both parties on the frustration of a contract can only be defended provided that frustration remains a doctrine of very narrow application. A more liberal doctrine of frustration would require a more liberal and flexible remedial regime.

9

Resisting Termination: Some Comparative Observations

SOLÈNE ROWAN*

I. INTRODUCTION

TERMINATION FOR BREACH of contract releases the parties from their contractual obligations to perform.[1] It is a powerful and definitive device that discharges all unperformed primary obligations under the contract yet to accrue and ends the contractual relationship, often instantaneously.[2] Significant commercial and financial consequences for the parties may ensue. These can be acute for the defaulting promisor. Not only is he deprived of the benefit of the contract; in many cases, he must also compensate the injured promisee in damages for losses caused by breach, possibly including the loss of the bargain.

With the aim of avoiding at least some of these consequences, the defaulting promisor might well wish to resist the promisee exercising his right to terminate. This chapter considers certain 'defences' that the promisor might invoke in order to do so.[3] 'Defences' here are defined by reference to their effect.[4] That is to say, they are the grounds the promisor may rely upon, once the right to terminate has arisen, to resist termination or avoid or reduce its consequences. The chapter does not, however, seek to address how the remedy arises or the ways that the promisor can deny that the remedy has arisen, such as that one of its essential elements is missing (except briefly to give context to and incidentally in the discussion of the

* I would like to thank Gregg Rowan and the organisers and attendees of the Oxford Workshop on Defences in Contract for their comments and suggestions on an earlier draft.

[1] Only termination for breach of contract will be considered in this chapter. Termination following frustration and force majeure is outside of its scope.

[2] *Photo Production Ltd v Securicor Transport Ltd* [1980] AC 827 (HL).

[3] For some possible grounds for resisting termination not considered in this chapter, see M Bridge, 'Freedom to Exercise Contractual Rights of Termination' in L Gullifer and S Vogenauer (eds), *English and European Perspectives on Contract and Commercial Law: Essays in Honour of Hugh Beale* (Oxford, Hart Publishing, 2014).

[4] See the different meanings that 'defences' can have: A Dyson, J Goudkamp and F Wilmot-Smith, 'Central Issues in the Law of Tort Defences' in A Dyson, J Goudkamp and F Wilmot-Smith (eds), *Defences in Tort* (Oxford, Hart Publishing, 2015).

defences to termination that are covered). These topics are dealt with thoroughly elsewhere.[5]

Since termination is a self-help device, a clarifying word is needed on how 'defences' might be invoked in this context. When faced with a repudiatory breach, the injured promisee has a choice: to terminate or affirm the contract. If he elects to terminate, all he must do is communicate to the defaulting promisor that he is treating the contract as being at an end.[6] He does not need to apply to the court for an order terminating the contract.[7]

This is not to say that the court has no role in this context. Recourse to the court may be necessary for a determination as to whether the contract was terminated effectively and, often more contentiously and importantly, by whom.[8] The court might also be required to decide the consequences of termination and, in particular, resolve competing claims to compensatory damages. In any of these contexts, the defaulting promisor might wish to challenge the purported termination or the consequences that are alleged by the injured promisee to flow from it. If he is still willing to perform, he might even seek to argue and claim (or, as the case may be, counterclaim) a declaration that the contract remains or should be treated as remaining on foot.

There is not necessarily inconsistency between the promisor having committed a breach that gives rise to a right to terminate and nonetheless being willing to perform.[9] He may wish to do so for any number of reasons. Usually only by performing will he be entitled to receive the reciprocal consideration promised under the contract. He might also want to protect his reputation or be able to honour commitments made to third parties in connection with the contract. It may be that he has incurred expenses in advance of performance that would otherwise be wasted.[10] Members of his workforce who would have had a role in performing the contract may end up being idle and unproductive to his and their own detriment. It should therefore be relatively uncontroversial that the promisor may wish to insist on performance even when in breach.

The subject of this chapter is explored through comparative analysis of French law, a particularly instructive comparator because it is notoriously protective of the contractual bond created by the parties. In France, the promisor can resist termination in a host of ways. If he has performed defectively, he can offer to cure the breach. If he has not performed on time, he can request a time extension even when

[5] See, for instance, H Beale (ed), *Chitty on Contracts*, 32nd edn (London, Sweet & Maxwell, 2015) ch 24.

[6] *Vitol SA v Norelf Ltd (the 'Santa Clara')* [1996] AC 800 (HL) (Lord Steyn).

[7] For a statutory exception, see s 90 of the Consumer Credit Act 1974 (UK).

[8] In practice, it is relatively common for one party to purport to exercise a right to terminate for repudiatory breach and the other party to allege that doing so itself amounts to a repudiation and purport to accept the repudiation, in which case, both parties come before the court claiming to have terminated and an entitlement to damages, usually for loss of the bargain.

[9] Except, obviously, in the case of a renunciation.

[10] See the other reasons given in E Peel, *Treitel on the Law of Contract*, 14th edn (London, Sweet & Maxwell, 2015) [18-004].

the breach is sufficiently serious to justify putting an end to the contract. Good faith also plays a role in restricting termination.

It will be shown that the grounds for resisting termination in France go beyond those in English law. This is notwithstanding that, in England, a promisee wishing to terminate often faces a high hurdle to establish that he is entitled to do so. The right to terminate arises only in limited circumstances, and the promisor cannot easily be ousted from the contract following a breach. Conversely, however, once the right to terminate has arisen, the grounds for resisting termination are relatively narrow; there is usually little that the promisor can do to resist.

The divergences between England and France will be attributed to different policy choices that have been made in each jurisdiction. In France, the contract is paramount; it should be saved and performed where possible, and termination is a remedy of last resort. There is no similar willingness to uphold a failed contract in England; the injured promisee can escape from the contract to reallocate his resources and obtain substitute performance elsewhere without any compunction. The promisor's predicament arouses less sympathy and he has correspondingly fewer defences to resist termination.

The purpose of the chapter is to describe and comment on the defences that are available in England and France, and explain the differences between them. It might provoke—but, due to spatial constraints, does not seek to engage in—debate as to whether English law should be more protective of the defaulting promisor and allow him to resist termination more widely in circumstances where a right to terminate has arisen. The focus is not so much on English law as comparative analysis of the two systems.

II. RESISTING TERMINATION IN ENGLISH LAW

The practical effect of the high threshold facing the injured promisee wishing to terminate is that the interests of the defaulting promisor are largely protected at this stage rather than when the right has arisen. Brief mention must therefore first be made of how the right to terminate arises.

A. The Circumstances Giving Rise to a Right of Termination in English Law

At common law, a contract can be terminated for breach only in narrow circumstances. The threshold for the injured promisee to be entitled to put an end to the contract is high. Only a serious breach will suffice. Such a breach would be made out where the promisor manifests a clear and absolute intention[11] not to perform[12]

[11] *Chilean Nitrate Sales Corp v Marine Transportation Co Ltd (The Hermosa)* [1982] 1 Lloyd's Rep 570 (CA).

[12] For a more detailed account of the law on renunciation, see *Chitty on Contracts* (n 5) [24-018] ff.

or disables himself from performing.[13] A right to terminate also arises where the term breached is so important[14] as to be a 'condition' of the contract, or an 'innominate term'[15] and the consequences of the actual breach deprive the injured promisee of substantially the whole benefit of the contract.[16]

The narrowness of the circumstances in which the right to terminate arises is illustrated by the fact that, in commercial contracts, the parties often incorporate an express term that confers a broader right to terminate.[17] They can agree, for instance, that the right should arise upon a breach of a term, even where it is not of essential importance or the breach has no serious consequences for the injured promisee. In practice, many commercial contracts are very prescriptive as to the circumstances in which the right to terminate will arise.

The high common law threshold shields the defaulting promisor from being deprived of the benefit of the contract too readily. It is satisfied only by the most severe breaches. When in breach, the promisor can still seek to argue that the right to terminate has not arisen because the term breached is not a condition but a warranty or an innominate term and the consequences of the breach are insufficiently serious. The flexibility of innominate terms reduces the likelihood of a term being classified as a condition such that the injured promisee has an inescapable right to terminate for any breach.[18] This achieves proportionality: the more serious the breach, the more serious are the consequences.

B. 'Defences' to Termination in English Law

In English law, where a common law right to terminate for breach has arisen, it is relatively unrestricted. Few defences are available to the promisor, who has little prospect of preventing the injured promisee from exercising the right, should he wish to do so. It is generally not possible to require a second chance to perform or even a period of grace where time is of the essence. There is no general right to cure or any requirement that the promisee should exercise his election between affirming and terminating in good faith.

Only in specific circumstances can the promisor resist termination. He is confined to relying on the equitable jurisdiction of the court to grant relief against forfeiture or any indirect fetter on termination that results from the doctrine of loss mitigation, which may cause the promisee to accept a new tender from the promisor.

[13] For a more detailed account of the law on impossibility, see *Chitty on Contracts* (n 5) [24-029] ff.

[14] Peel (n 10) [18-023] ff.

[15] *Bremer Handelsgesellschaft mbH v Vanden Avenne-Izegem PVBA* [1978] 2 Lloyd's Rep 109 (HL) 113 (Lord Wilberforce); *Hong Kong Fir Shipping Co Ltd v Kawasaki Kisen Kaisha Ltd* (*The 'Hongkong Fir'*) [1962] 2 QB 26 (CA).

[16] *The 'Hong Kong Fir'* (n 15) 70 (Lord Diplock).

[17] S Whittaker, 'Termination Clauses' in A Burrows and E Peel (eds), *Contract Terms* (Oxford, Oxford University Press, 2007) 253, 256.

[18] Peel (n 10) [18-050]. For a similar conclusion, see G Treitel, *Remedies for Breach of Contract: A Comparative Account* (Oxford, Clarendon Press, 1988) [259].

(i) No Second Chances

(a) No General Entitlement to a Grace Period

The court does not have a general power to grant a period of grace to a defaulting promisor in repudiatory breach.[19] Where time is of the essence and the promisor does not perform by the due date, the injured promisee's right to terminate arises immediately.[20] The promisor cannot apply to the court for or require from the promisee an extension in time.[21]

One justification for the strict enforcement of time stipulations is the desire for commercial certainty. This was made clear in *Union Eagle Ltd v Golden Achievement Ltd*.[22] A contract for the sale of a flat provided that completion should take place before a certain time and that time was of the essence. The purchaser paid the purchase price 10 minutes late. Citing the stipulation making time of the essence, the seller refused to accept payment and terminated the contract. It was held by the Privy Council to be entitled to do so. Lord Hoffmann justified the decision on the ground of commercial certainty. He said 'in many forms of transaction it is of great importance that if something happens for which the contract has made express provision, the parties should know with certainty that the terms of the contract will be enforced'.[23]

In some circumstances the promisee's right to terminate can even arise before the due date for performance. If the promisor clearly renounces the contract or disables himself from performing, this is an anticipatory breach and the promisee can exercise his right to terminate straight away. It makes no difference that the time for performance is in the future, and he need not wait until then to terminate.[24] Once he has exercised his right to terminate, the contract is definitively discharged.

(b) No General 'Right to Cure' the Breach

In the same vein, where the performance rendered by the promisee does not comply with the contract and the breach is repudiatory, the promisor cannot require the promisee to grant him an opportunity to cure the breach before exercising the right to terminate.[25] The promisor has no entitlement to a 'second chance' to perform.

[19] S Whittaker, 'A "Period of Grace" for Contractual Performance?' in M Andenas and others (eds), *Liber Amicorum Guido Alpa: Private Law Beyond the National Systems* (London, British Institute of International and Comparative Law, 2007) 1083. For examples of statutory exceptions, see the Law of Property Act 1925 (UK), s 146 and the Consumer Credit Act 1974 (UK), ss 76, 87, 98.

[20] *Chitty on Contracts* (n 5) [21-015].

[21] Whittaker, 'A "Period of Grace"' (n 19) 1100.

[22] *Union Eagle Ltd v Golden Achievement Ltd* [1997] AC 514 (PC).

[23] ibid 518.

[24] *Albert Hochster v Edgar Frederick De la Tour* (1853) 2 Ellis & Blackburn 678; 118 ER 922.

[25] *Buckland v Bournemouth University Higher Education Corp* [2010] EWCA Civ 121; [2010] 4 All ER 186 (CA), esp [40]; *Lamarra v Capital Bank Plc* [2006] CSIH 49; [2007] SC 95 [61] but see *Ampurius Nu Homes Holdings Ltd v Telford Homes (Creekside) Ltd* [2013] EWCA Civ 577; [2013] 4 All ER 377 [63]. Peel (n 10) [18-066] explains the latter decision in the following terms: 'the court was … primarily concerned with whether there had been a repudiatory breach based on the forward looking element of the

Instead, the promisee can terminate the contract and reject any further tenders that the promisor might make.[26] As is explained in *Chitty*,

> English law does not permit a contracting party unilaterally to cure a repudiatory breach once it has been committed … the choice whether to affirm or not is the choice of the injured party. It cannot be taken from him by the party in breach making an offer of amends.[27]

(ii) The Irrelevance of Good Faith and Fairness in Terminating the Contract

The defaulting promisor is also unable to challenge the decision of the injured promisee to exercise a common law right to terminate as not having been made in good faith. The right is not subject to any general requirement of good faith or fairness.[28] The promisee's motives in exercising the right are irrelevant and he can put an end to the contract without giving reasons.[29] He can therefore terminate to escape what has turned out to be an unprofitable bargain, for instance due to market fluctuations.[30] This has been justified by a desire for commercial certainty and speedy resolution of disputes.[31] Both are facilitated by the courts not investigating the promisee's motives for terminating. It is also consistent with the absence in English law of a general duty to act in good faith or concept of abuse of rights.[32]

Where the promisee has a contractual right to terminate, it is similarly unfettered. Outside the sphere of consumer contracts, for which there is specific legislation,[33] termination clauses do not have to pass a threshold test of fairness or reasonableness in order to be valid. As long as they are clearly drafted, there is little inclination on

uncertainty of future performance and here the fact that the breach had been remedied, or the prospect of a cure, was a relevant consideration'. Note that consumer-buyers can, under ss 19(3), 19(4) and 23 of the Consumer Rights Act 2015 (UK), require defaulting sellers to repair or replace non-conforming goods. However, sellers have no right to demand an opportunity to repair or replace: see *Chitty on Contracts* (n 5) [38-414]. There is also nothing to prevent the parties from stipulating that the promisee is permitted to terminate only after the promisor has had an opportunity to remedy the breach within a defined period of time: see text following n 79 below.

[26] Peel (n 10) [17-004].

[27] *Chitty on Contracts* (n 5) [24-002].

[28] On this topic, see R Hooley, 'Controlling Contractual Discretion' (2013) 72 *CLJ* 65.

[29] *James Spencer & Co Ltd v Tame Valley Padding Co Ltd* (CA, 8 April 1998); *SNCB Holding v UBS AG* [2012] EWHC 2044 (Comm); [2012] All ER (D) 259 [73] (Cooke J); on this point, see R Brownsword, 'Retrieving Reasons, Retrieving Rationality? A New Look at the Right to Withdraw for Breach of Contract' (1992) 5 *Journal of Criminal Law* 83. But see *Heisler v Anglo-Dal Ltd* [1954] 1 WLR 1273 (CA).

[30] The flexibility of the innominate terms has to a certain extent restricted termination where ulterior motives are in play: see Peel (n 10) [18-036], [18-050]–[18-053]. See also the restriction in s 15A of the Sale of Goods Act 1979 (UK) on the buyer's right to terminate for breach of a condition where the breach is so slight that it would be unreasonable for him to reject the goods, which is narrow in scope and has been described by Peel as 'an unfortunate provision': Peel (n 10) [18-057]. Benjamin describes it as a section 'of severely limited effect' in practice with no reported decisions on it since its enactement in 1994: M Bridge (ed), *Benjamin's Sale of Goods*, 9th edn (London, Sweet & Maxwell, 2015) [12-026].

[31] Hooley (n 28) 84.

[32] ibid. See *Chitty on Contracts* (n 5) [1-039]–[1-056] and Whittaker, 'Termination Clauses' (n 17).

[33] See the Consumer Rights Act 2015 (UK). For a general discussion of the Act, see *Chitty on Contracts* (n 5) ch 15.

the part of the courts to impede their operation.[34] The most that might be expected is that, when ambiguously worded, they will be construed narrowly.[35] There is no requirement that they are exercised in good faith.[36]

That no duty of good faith or standard of reasonableness arises, whether at common law or in the context of contractual rights to terminate, has been made clear in several cases. For instance, in *Lomas v JFB Firth Rixon Inc*,[37] Longmore LJ said obiter that:[38]

> The right to terminate is no more an exercise of discretion, which is not to be exercised in an arbitrary or capricious (or perhaps unreasonable) manner, than the right to accept repudiatory conduct as a repudiation of a contract ... [N]o one would suggest that there could be any impediment to accepting repudiatory conduct as a termination of the contract based on the fact that the innocent party can elect between termination and leaving the contract on foot. The same applies to elective termination.

It has, however, been suggested in a recent case that good faith could in certain circumstances constrain the promisee's election to affirm or terminate. In *MSC Mediterranean Shipping Co SA v Cottonex Anstalt*,[39] the promisee, faced with a repudiatory breach, sought to affirm the contract and claim the contract price. Leggatt J thought that the decision to affirm and obtain payment had to be exercised in good faith. In his view, there should be no difference of approach between the exercise of a contractual discretion, which cannot be done arbitrarily and capriciously, and a choice whether to affirm or terminate a contract following a repudiatory breach. He said:[40]

> In each case one party to the contract has a decision to make on a matter which affects the interests of the other party to the contract whose interests are not the same. The same reason exists in each case to imply some constraint on the decision-maker's freedom to act purely in its own self-interest.

He concluded that the tests were the same and the decision to affirm the contract had to be exercised in good faith. On the facts, the election to affirm the contract was wholly unreasonable. It had not been invoked for a proper purpose but rather to seek to generate a new revenue stream.

[34] J Cartwright, *Contract Law: An Introduction to the English Law of Contract for the Civil Lawyer* (Oxford, Hart Publishing, 2007) 272.

[35] *Rice (t/a Garden Guardian) v Great Yarmouth Borough Council* [2003] TCLR 1 (CA) criticised by Whittaker, 'Termination Clauses' (n 17) 279–81.

[36] See Whittaker, 'Termination Clauses' (n 17).

[37] *Lomas (Joint Administrators of Lehman Brothers International (Europe)) v JFB Firth Rixon Inc* [2012] EWCA 419; [2012] 2 All ER (Comm). See also *Sucden Financial Ltd v Fluxo-Cane Overseas Ltd* [2009] EWHC 3555 (QB); *TSG Building Services PLC v South Anglia Housing Ltd* [2013] EWHR 1151 (TCC); [2013] BLR 484.

[38] *Lomas* (n 37) [46]. See, however, Hooley (n 28) at 87–88 who argues that the promisee *does* have a discretion when faced with a repudiatory breach and that 'there would be much to gain, in terms of reducing opportunistic behaviour or other cases of perceived unfairness, if English law were expressly to adopt a similar approach to the exercise of a right to termination for breach as it does to the exercise of contractual discretion'.

[39] *MSC Mediterranean Shipping Co SA v Cottonex Anstalt* [2015] EWHC 283; [2015] 2 All ER (Comm) 614.

[40] ibid [97].

It remains to be seen whether Leggatt J's implication of a duty of good faith into the election between affirmation and termination will be applied more widely to all decisions between affirming or terminating. It was made in the particular context of the promisee wanting to affirm, as opposed to terminate the contract, in order to perform and obtain the contract consideration.

This type of situation has generated controversy in the past in *White and Carter (Councils) Ltd v McGregor*.[41] In that case, Lord Reid suggested two possible limitations to the right to affirm the contract and claim the agreed price: first, performance by the injured promisee cannot require the cooperation of the other party; second, the promisee must have a legitimate interest in performing the contract rather than claiming damages.[42] It was this second limitation that was the focus of Leggatt J's comments, not whether all elections between affirming and terminating for breach should be made in good faith. It also appears only to have been this limitation that he thought should be reinterpreted in the light of what he characterised as the increasing recognition of good faith principles in contractual dealings.

Another reason for doubting that Leggatt J's implication of a duty of good faith should have general application is that he made no mention of the authorities that draw a distinction between the exercise of a contractual discretion, which involves a choice from a range of options, and a binary decision as to whether to exercise a contractual right.[43] Some recent authorities have suggested that good faith obligations are only relevant in the former case, not the latter. On one view, an injured promisee who elects between terminating and affirming the contract is faced with a binary choice and therefore no duty of good faith arises.

Another feature of Leggatt J's judgment is that he dealt with the consequences of repudiation in just 10 paragraphs, of which only two were focused on good faith and its potential application to the election to terminate. To introduce a general duty of good faith into this election would potentially impose a significant fetter on the promisee. Greater exploration and justification may be necessary in future cases for the duty to achieve wide acceptance.[44]

(iii) Defences in Specific Situations

While English law confers no general right on the defaulting promisor to cure his breach and good faith is irrelevant, except possibly to the injured promisee's election to affirm, an effective termination can be challenged in limited situations.

[41] *White and Carter (Councils) Ltd v McGregor* [1962] AC 413 (HL (Sc)).

[42] ibid 443.

[43] Leggatt J's analysis does not sit easily with the approach of Sir William Blackburne in the recent High Court decision of *Myers v Kestrel Acquisitions Ltd* [2015] EWHC 916 (Ch); [2015] All ER (D) 11; *Compass Group UK and Ireland Ltd (t/a Medirest) v Mid Essex Hospital Services NHS Trust* [2013] EWCA Civ 200; [2013] BLR 265.

[44] See Peel's (n 10) view at [18-078] that 'the right to terminate is in the nature of an "absolute right" which is not subject to [an implied term that it must be exercised in good faith]'.

(a) A Second Chance to Perform

1. *Relief Against Forfeiture*

If the promisor is willing to perform, equity can intervene to grant relief against forfeiture in narrow circumstances. This arises where, upon the promisor's breach, the promisee invokes a forfeiture clause to forfeit the promisor's contractual rights. The relief generally takes the form of the promisor being allowed additional time to remedy the breach.[45] As long as the promisor remedies the breach within the time fixed by the court, the contract is preserved and the promisee's right to terminate is lost.[46]

A classic example is in the context of leases.[47] In certain circumstances the landlord's right to forfeit a lease for breach is subject to the tenant having an opportunity to cure the breach. Where, for instance, the lessee defaults on rent payments, the court may protect him against the landlord's right of re-entry or other power to terminate the lease. It does so by affording him more time to pay the outstanding rent, and any order for possession of the property is postponed in the meantime. This jurisdiction is now on a statutory footing.[48]

The restriction on freedom of contract inherent in the equitable jurisdiction is regarded as a lesser evil than unconscionable insistence on contractual terms.[49] In the example of leases, as long as the lessor obtains what is contractually due, even if belatedly, it is thought fairer to keep the relationship alive. The alternative of termination could have potentially significant negative ramifications for the promisor.[50]

The equitable jurisdiction is, however, limited and exceptional,[51] so as not to undermine contractual certainty.[52] Relief is not available as of right but rather is discretionary and is only available where the forfeiture clause serves as security for the promisee to obtain payment or another advantage, the contract concerns the transfer or creation of proprietary or possessory rights and the forfeiture would result in the promisor losing those rights. The mere loss of a personal contractual right does not trigger the jurisdiction.[53] Most contracts are therefore outside the scope of the doctrine.

45 *Chitty on Contracts* (n 5) [21-016]–[21-017].

46 ibid [21-016]–[21-017].

47 Another classic example arises in the context of mortgages: *Shiloh Spinners Ltd v Harding* [1973] AC 691 (HL) 722ff.

48 Law of Property Act 1925 (UK), s 146.

49 J McGhee (ed), *Snell's Equity*, 33rd edn (London, Sweet & Maxwell, 2014) [13-001].

50 N Andrews, M Clarke, A Tettenborn and G Virgo, *Contractual Duties: Performance, Breach, Termination and Remedies* (London, Sweet & Maxwell, 2012) [25-065].

51 *Snell's Equity* (n 49) [13-027].

52 *Union Eagle* (n 22) 519 (Lord Hoffmann).

53 *Scandiniavian Trading Tanker Co AB v Flota Petrolera Ecutoriana ('The Scaptrade')* [1983] 2 All ER 763 (HL).

2. *A Limited Right to Cure in the Sale of Goods Context*

The court also has jurisdiction to allow a second chance to a defaulting seller under a sale of goods contract, albeit in similarly limited circumstances.[54] There are some authorities, concerned mainly with the tender of documents, which support the proposition that a seller who has made a non-conforming tender before the time for performance can re-tender.[55] The scope of this right to cure is narrow, applying only to defective tenders that are not repudiatory. Where the non-conforming tender amounts to a repudiation, the injured promisee is entitled to terminate and is not bound to accept the second tender.[56] It therefore does not restrict the promisee's right to terminate as such.

(b) Restrictions Arising by Operation of the Mitigation Principle

Another 'defence' potentially available to the defaulting promisor as a means of impeding, even if not formally restricting, the right to terminate arises through the doctrine of mitigation, which serves to limit the injured promisee's recovery of compensatory damages for losses that he could reasonably have avoided.[57]

While in principle the promisee has a free choice between terminating and affirming the contract, the way that he exercises his election could draw criticism from the promisor for any unreasonable failure to mitigate loss.[58] If the criticism is justified, the court could reduce his entitlement to compensatory damages by a sum representing the amount of loss that he should have mitigated. The practical effect is to impose a fetter on his right to terminate or affirm.

In many situations, the doctrine of mitigation leaves the promisee with little alternative than to terminate and seek substitute performance from a third party. If he prefers to persist with the promisor and affirms the contract, despite the promisor's

[54] R Ahdar, 'Seller Cure in the Sale of Goods' [1990] *Lloyd's Maritime and Commercial Law Quarterly* 364; A Apps, 'The Right to Cure for Defective Performance' [1994] *Lloyd's Maritime and Commercial Law Quarterly* 525; V Mak, 'The Seller's Right to Cure Defective Performance—A Reappraisal' [2007] *Lloyd's Maritime and Commercial Law Quarterly* 409. Note that consumer buyers have a right to have defective goods repaired or replaced unless this is impossible or disproportionate: s 48A of the Sale of Goods Act 1979 (UK) and s 23 of the Consumer Rights Act 2015 (UK) but this does not *require* the buyer to give the seller an opportunity to cure.

[55] *Borrowman Phillips & Co v Free & Hollis* (1878) 4 QBD 500; *EE & Brian Smith (1928) Ltd v Wheatsheaf Mills Ltd* [1939] 2 KB 302 (QB); *Tetley v Shand* (1871) 25 LT 658; *Motor Oil Hellas (Corinth) Refineries SA v Shipping Corporation of India ('The Kanchenjunga')* [1990] 1 Lloyd's Rep 391 (HL). See Bridge, *Benjamin's Sale of Goods* (n 30) [12-032]; M Bridge, *The Sale of Goods*, 3rd edn (Oxford, Oxford University Press, 2014) [10.129] ff.

[56] However, where the first tender puts the promisor in repudiatory breach, the promisee can refuse any second tender from the promisor: Peel (n 10) [17-004].

[57] *British Westinghouse Electric and Manufacturing Co Ltd v Underground Electric Railways Co of London Ltd (No 2)* [1912] AC 673 (HL).

[58] Peel (n 10) [18-009]; S Whittaker, 'Contributory Fault and Mitigation, Rights and Reasonableness: Comparisons between English and French Law' in L Tichy (ed), *Causation in Law* (Prague, Konrad Adenauer Stiftung, 2007) 147, 160–61; Andrews, Clarke, Tettenborn and Virgo, (n 50) [10-073] ff, [24-056] ff; A Kramer, *The Law of Contract Damages* (Oxford, Hart Publishing, 2014) 399–404. For a possible restriction of the right to terminate resulting from the rule on penalties, see Bridge (n 3).

default and in circumstances where to do so is unreasonable, this could amount to a failure to mitigate. It could cost him some or all of the damages that he might otherwise have recovered.[59]

The doctrine can have the very opposite effect in other situations. The promisee could find that, in order to mitigate losses resulting from the breach, he should accept the promisor's offer of substitute performance, despite being entitled to terminate the contract. This does not mean that he is obliged to do so, and he can freely terminate and end his relationship with the promisor if he so wishes, but his damages award may be reduced commensurately. In this way, the mitigation doctrine incentivises the promisee to accept the promisor's offer to cure the harm caused by the breach and enter into a new contract with him. To this extent, both mitigation and the right to cure share similarities: they minimise the promisee's loss but also reduce the financial impact of breach on the promisor.[60]

The leading case on the interrelation between the mitigation doctrine and the right to terminate is *Payzu Ltd v Saunders*.[61] The seller had agreed to sell to the buyer a fabric called crêpe de chine. Delivery was to take place over a period of nine months in return for payment within a month of each delivery. The buyer failed to make punctual payment after the first delivery. Erroneously believing that non-payment was due to the buyer's lack of means, the seller refused to deliver more goods under the contract and instead offered to deliver the goods at the contract price only if the buyer agreed to pay in cash at the time of placing the orders. This offer was rejected by the buyer, which instead terminated the contract on the basis of the seller's repudiation. The market price of the goods having risen in the interim, the buyer sued the seller for compensatory damages based on the difference between the market price and the contract price.

The trial judge, with whom the Court of Appeal agreed, held that the buyer should have mitigated its loss by accepting the seller's offer and revised payment terms. Scrutton LJ said 'in commercial contracts it is generally reasonable to accept an offer from the party in default. However, it is always a question of fact'. As a result, the measure of damages awarded was not the difference between the market price and the contract price but instead was confined to the loss that the buyer would have suffered, if it had accepted the offer.

The rationale cited by the first instance judge was to avoid overburdening the defaulting promisor with liability. If the promisee can avoid part of his loss by accepting a reasonable offer made by the promisor, then he is expected to do so. Any remaining loss can be compensated in damages so as not to leave the promisee worse off. On the facts, the court found that the buyer was able to pay cash for the goods and the seller's offer was bona fide. The buyer would only have suffered a small

[59] *Habton Farms (an unlimited company) v Nimmo* [2003] EWCA Civ 68; [2004] QB 1 [128] (Auld LJ).

[60] M Bridge, 'Mitigation of Damages in Contract and the Meaning of Avoidable Loss' (1989) 105 *LQR* 398, 412.

[61] *Payzu Ltd v Saunders* [1919] 2 KB 581 (CA). See also *Houndsditch Warehouse Co Ltd v Waltex Ltd* [1944] KB 579 (KB); *Clegg v Andersson (t/a Nordic Marine)* [2002] EWHC 943 (QB); [2002] All ER (D) 315 [61] (HHJ Richard Seymour QC).

loss because of the less favourable payment conditions, for which damages would have been recoverable.[62] It should therefore not have permitted itself 'to sustain a large measure of loss which as prudent and reasonable people they ought to have avoided'.[63]

In *The Soholt*,[64] the Court of Appeal went further, finding that the promisee, the buyer of a ship, should actually have solicited such an offer from the defaulting seller after exercising a contractual right to terminate the sale contract for late delivery. By this stage, the value of the ship had appreciated by US$500,000, which the buyer claimed as compensatory damages. It was held that the buyer's failure to purchase the ship from the seller for the original price under a revised contract was a failure to mitigate, even though this had not been proposed by the seller. There was an onus on the buyer to take the initiative and offer to repurchase the ship at the original price after terminating the contract and the judge found that such an offer would have been accepted. It would then have been open to the buyer to seek to recover any losses resulting from the delay as damages. The implication appears to be that the promisee should consider not only any offer made by the defaulting promisor, but also making an offer to the promisor.[65]

It is not solely in relation to sale of goods contracts that the promisee has been found to have acted unreasonably in rejecting the promisor's offer to contract on new terms. An employee who has been dismissed can also in certain circumstances be expected to accept an offer of re-employment. In *Brace v Calder*,[66] for instance, the manager of a business was dismissed automatically under his employment contract as a result of a change in the ownership of the business. The Court of Appeal held that he should have accepted an offer of re-engagement by the new business owners on the same terms as previously applied. His refusal to do so was unreasonable and the resulting loss was of his own making. Similarly, in building contracts, the refusal by an employer to allow a contractor to undertake remedial works may amount to a failure to mitigate. In *Woodlands Oak Ltd v Conwell*,[67] for example, the Court of Appeal upheld the first instance judge's decision that the claimant homeowners should have allowed their builders an opportunity to rectify defects that were mere 'snagging' items.

It is important, however, not to overstate the effect of the mitigation doctrine. Whether the promisee should seek substitute performance from the promisor is a question of fact.[68] The standard of reasonableness that must be attained for the duty to mitigate to be discharged is relatively low. The courts are sensitive to the circumstances of the promisee, as epitomised by Tomlinson J's observation in *Britvic Soft*

[62] See the explanation given by MacKenna J in *Strutt v Whinell* [1975] 1 WLR 870 (CA) 875.

[63] *Payzu* (n 61) 586 (McCardie J).

[64] *Sotiros Shipping Inc v Sameiet Solholt ('The Solholt')* [1983] 1 Lloyd's Rep 605 (CA).

[65] Both *Payzu* (n 61) and *The Soholt* (n 64) were forcefully criticised by Bridge (n 60) 420 for rendering the 'buyer's right of contractual discharge for late delivery utterly illusory'.

[66] *Brace v Calder* [1895] 2 QB 253 (CA). See also *Wilding v British Telecommunications Plc* [2002] EWCA Civ 349; [2002] IRLR 524 (CA).

[67] *Woodlands Oak Ltd v Conwell* [2011] EWCA Civ 254; [2011] BLR 365.

[68] *Payzu* (n 61) 589 (Scrutton LJ).

Drinks Ltd v Messer UK Ltd[69] that there should be a 'tender approach to those who have been placed in a predicament by a breach of contract'.[70] This was echoed by HHJ Coulson QC, sitting as a Judge of the High Court, in *Iggleden v Fairview New Home (Shooters Hill) Ltd*,[71] when considering whether the purchasers of a house that had defects failed to mitigate their loss by not allowing the builders to remedy the defects. He said that

> it would take a relatively extreme set of facts to persuade me that it was appropriate to deny a homeowner financial compensation for admitted defects, and leave him with no option but to employ the self-same contractor to carry out the necessary rectification works.[72]

There are many cases in which the courts have found that the promisee has acted reasonably and not failed to mitigate loss by refusing the promisor's offer. By way of example, it has been held to be unreasonable for the promisor to require the promisee to forfeit his right to compensatory damages.[73] It has also been said to be unreasonable to require the promisee to accept an offer where the terms proposed are inferior to those originally agreed,[74] or where the relationship between the parties has been badly damaged, for instance where confidence has been lost[75] or the promisor has 'grossly injured' the promisee. This is especially true in personal service contracts.[76] Some judges have also expressed concern that the mitigation doctrine undermines the promisee's right of termination by covert means and should not be allowed to curtail his choice between alternative remedies.[77]

(c) Defences to Termination by Agreement

A more direct way of limiting or even excluding a common law right to terminate is by the agreement of the parties. It has already been shown that termination clauses prescribing when the right to terminate arises feature widely in commercial contracts. Many such provisions extend the scope for terminating the contract beyond the common law right to accept a repudiatory breach.

There is nothing, however, to prevent the parties from agreeing to narrow[78] or even exclude altogether[79] the common law right. Alternatively, they might stipulate that the promisee is permitted to terminate only after the promisor has had an

[69] *Britvic Soft Drinks Ltd v Messer UK Ltd* [2002] 1 Lloyd's Rep 20 (QB).
[70] ibid 46.
[71] *Iggleden v Fairview New Home (Shooters Hill) Ltd* [2007] EWHC 1573 (TCC).
[72] ibid [79].
[73] *Houndsditch* (n 61); *Shindler v Northern Raincoat Co Ltd* [1960] 1 WLR 1038 (MA); *Strutt* (n 62).
[74] In an employment context, see *Jackson v Hayes Candy & Co Ltd* [1938] 4 All ER 587 (QB); *Yetton v Eastwoods Froy Ltd* [1967] 1 WLR 104 (QB); in the context of sale of good, see *Heaven & Kesterton v Etablissements Francois Albiac et Cie* [1956] 2 Lloyd's Rep 316 (QB) 321.
[75] *Jackson* (n 74) (Du Parcq LJ).
[76] *Payzu* (n 61) 588 (Bankes LJ), 589 (Scrutton LJ).
[77] eg *Heaven* (n 74) 321 (Devlin J).
[78] *The 'Hong Kong Fir'* (n 15) 69 (Lord Diplock). On the relationship between a contractual right to terminate and the right to terminate at common law, see *Stocznia Gdynia SA v Gearbulk Holdings Ltd* [2009] BLR 196 (CA).
[79] Peel (n 10) [18-074].

opportunity to remedy the breach within a defined period of time. He would be able to make good his default under the terms of the contract, which in practical effect is tantamount to a contractual right to cure.

Clauses of this nature are by no means unusual in commercial contracts. Guidance on their drafting and usage can be found in standard texts on boilerplate commercial clauses. Such provisions owe their validity to the widely accepted principle of freedom of contract. By enabling the parties to tailor the remedy to their particular needs and wishes, they are an efficient means of giving the defaulting promisor a second chance and preserving his interest in performing.

C. Concluding Remarks on Defence to Termination in English Law

The common law right to terminate arises only in narrow circumstances. The defaulting promisor's interests are protected mainly in the rules as to when the right arises, and his primary defence to a purported termination will often be that no right has arisen. However, when the right does arise, the defences available to the promisor are correspondingly narrow. The right is relatively unfettered and there are few grounds on which he might hope to resist termination. This contrasts with French law, in which the grounds for opposing termination are wider.

III. RESISTING TERMINATION IN FRENCH LAW

Before analysing the approach of French law to defences to termination, it is important to point out that French contract law is in the process of being substantially reformed. By way of context, the section of the Civil Code on contract law has remained largely unchanged since its creation in 1804. It does not reflect the actual state of the law in this area, which has evolved significantly over the last two centuries.

At the time of finalising this chapter (March 2016), new articles of the Civil Code on contract law had just been published.[80] They are due to come into force in October 2016. Both the approach of French law before the reforms and the changes to the law that they will bring are considered here. It will be shown that, while the reforms introduce changes to the process of terminating a contract, they are unlikely to have a significant impact on the wide defences that the promisor can draw upon to resist termination.

The wider availability in France of defences to termination for breach can be attributed partly to the way that termination has traditionally operated, which is very different from England. A significant role in deciding the fate of the contract is (at least until the incoming reforms) reserved to the French court. Its role is to decide whether the promisee should be entitled to terminate.

[80] *Ordonnance no 2016-131 of 10 February 2016 portant réforme du droit des contrats, du régime général et de la preuve des obligations*: www.legifrance.gouv.fr/eli/ordonnance/2016/2/10/JUSC1522466R/jo/texte (accessed 17 March 2016). It follows two other reform proposals: the 'Proposals for Reform of the Law of Obligations and the Law of Prescription' prepared under the direction of P Catala, 22 September 2005 and the 'Ministry of Justice project' (*Projet de la Chancellerie*) of July 2008.

A. The Process of Termination

As in England, termination is available in France for 'serious' breaches of contract.[81] Factors that are relevant to whether a breach justifies termination include the consequences of the breach, whether the contract would still serve its intended purpose, the nature of the contract, whether the obligation that has been breached is essential, whether the failure to perform is total or partial, and the behaviour of the contracting parties.[82]

Unlike in England, termination has historically not been a self-help remedy. This will change when the reforms are implemented: the promisor will have a choice between judicial and self-help termination. Until then, the long-standing rule is that, subject to certain exceptions,[83] the injured promisee wishing to terminate for breach must apply to the court.[84] Only by an order of the court can the contract be discharged. He cannot of his own accord treat the breach as discharging him from his contractual obligations.[85] As such, he cannot be said to have a 'right' of termination, at least in the sense that the term is used in England.

First instance judges in France have considerable room for manoeuvre when deciding whether a contract should be terminated for breach. Generally they endeavour to protect the contractual relationship and the interests of the promisor.[86] An initial step in this process is to ascertain whether he really is unable or unwilling to perform or if the contract can be saved.[87] This reflects a belief that he should not be deprived of the benefit of the contract too quickly or arbitrarily;[88] termination is the last possible resort.[89] Whatever the severity of the breach, the court can still refuse termination and order another remedy[90] or an intermediate measure such as a grace period in which the promisor may attempt anew to perform. Judicial discretion in relation to termination will remain after the reforms where the promisee elects

[81] eg Civ 1, 12 March 1956, D 1956, 302; Civ 1, 15 July 1999, Bull civ I no 245. Article 1184 of the Civil Code is silent as to the circumstances in which a contract may be terminated. Case law has evolved to require the breach to be 'serious' in order to justify termination. Whether a breach crosses this threshold of seriousness is in the discretion of first instance judges: see S Rowan, *Remedies for Breach of Contract: A Comparative Analysis of the Protection of Performance* (Oxford, Oxford University Press, 2012) 80–94.

[82] See Rowan (n 81) 81.

[83] On termination in French law, see Rowan (n 81) 80–94.

[84] Article 1184, para 3 of the Civil Code.

[85] Whittaker, 'A "Period of Grace"' (n 19) 1090.

[86] F Terré, P Simler and Y Lequette, *Droit civil: Les obligations* 11th edn (Paris, Dalloz, 2013) [642]; J Rochfeld, 'Résolution et exception d'inexécution' in P Rémy-Corlay and D Fenouillet (eds), *Les concepts contractuels français à l'heure des principes du droit européen des contrats* (Paris, Dalloz, 2003) 216.

[87] R Cassin, 'Réflexions sur la résolution judiciaire des contrats pour inexécution' RTD civ 1945.12, [2].

[88] Introductory comments of J Rochfeld, 'Inexécution des obligations (art. 1157 à 1160-1)' in *Avant-Projet de Réforme du Droit des Obligations (Articles 1101 à 1386 du Code civil) et du Droit de la Prescription (Articles 2234 à 2281 du Code civil)* under the direction of P Catala, 22 September 2005 (Paris, Documentation française, 2006).

[89] ibid; Jamin, 'Les conditions de la résolution du contrat: vers un modèle unique?—Rapport français' in M Fontaine and G Viney (eds), *Les sanctions de l'inexécution des obligations contractuelles: études de droit comparé* (Bruxelles/Paris, Bruylant/Libraire Générale de Droit et de Jurisprudence, 2001) [482].

[90] A Ogus and D Tallon, 'Remedies—Summary of Discussion' in D Harris and D Tallon (eds), *Contract Law Today: Anglo-French Comparisons* (Oxford, Clarendon Press, 1989) 290, 294; Terré, Simler and Lequette (n 86) [652] ff.

judicial termination over self-help termination or where the issue comes before the court because the promisor disputes the attempted termination, as explained below.[91]

B. Defences to Termination in French Law

This judicial discretion over termination and the prevailing willingness to protect the contractual relationship and the promisor's interests together give rise to several grounds on which termination can be resisted.

(i) Offer from the Defaulting Promisor to Perform and Grace Period

If a promisor faced with termination proceedings offers to perform or requests an extension of time, this may result in the promisee being deprived of the remedy.

(a) Offer from the Defaulting Promisor to Perform

There is no general 'right to cure' breach in the French Civil Code but several provisions do nonetheless confer such a right on the promisor in the context of specific contracts. As an example, in contracts for the construction and sale of buildings, article 1646-1 of the code expressly provides that the promisor has a right to cure any defects in the building works. If the defects are remedied, the promisee cannot terminate the contract.

In other situations, and in contrast with English law, even if a breach is sufficiently serious to justify termination, it is well established and uncontroversial that the court may refuse the remedy where the promisor is still willing to perform his side of the bargain.[92] If he makes an offer to perform that is considered by the court to be satisfactory from the perspective of the promisee, the contract remains on foot.[93] The promisor can therefore generally resist termination by making a reasonable offer to perform. It is open to him to make such an offer either before termination has been ordered or even when an appeal against the remedy is pending.[94]

The willingness of courts in France to uphold the contract in this way is illustrated by a case arising out of the sale of a plot of land.[95] The parties had agreed that

[91] See the new article 1228 of the Civil Code: *Ordonnance no 2016-131 of 10 February 2016.*

[92] Terré, Simler and Lequette (n 86) [651]; J Flour, J-L Aubert and E Savaux, *Les obligations, Le rapport d'obligations*, 7th edn (Paris, A Colin, 2011) [251]; Civ 1, 17 May 1954, Gaz Pal 1954.2.83; Civ 1, 22 October 1956, Bull civ I no 362); Civ 3, 22 March 1983, Cull civ III, no 84, 67, Defrenois 1984.296, obs J-L Aubert; Civ 1, 15 April 1986, Bull civ I, no 84, p 83; RTD civ 1987, p 315 obs Mestre.

[93] Jamin (n 89) [12]; Terré, Simler and Lequette (n 86) [651]; Civ 1, 27 January 1961, Bull civ I, p 102, no 128; Civ 30, November 1949, JCP 1952.II.6802, note Rech, RTD civ 1956.183, noted by H et L Mazeaud.

[94] Terré, Simler and Lequette (n 8686) [651]; Treitel (n 18) [243]; Civ 27 March 1911, DP 1915.1.97, note Cezar-Bru; 6 January 1932, DH 1932.114. *classification*, thèse Paris I, 2000, no 569, 736 ff; ME Pancazi-Tian, *La Protection judiciaire du lien contractuel* (Aix-Marseille, PUAM, 1996) No 331, 274 ff.

[95] Civ 1, 17 May 1954, Gaz Pal 1954.2.83.

the price would be paid in three instalments. Only the first two instalments were paid. After several years, the seller applied to the court for an order terminating the contract. The buyer sought to resist termination by offering to pay the third instalment. The Montpellier Court of Appeal, with which the Cour de Cassation agreed, refused to order termination: the offer to cure was held to be satisfactory in the circumstances.

(b) Grace Periods (*Délai de Grâce*)

The Civil Code also gives the court jurisdiction to grant the promisor a period of grace (*délai de grâce*),[96] provided that performance remains possible and would still serve its intended purpose. Although the agreed timetable can no longer be met and even if the breach is sufficiently serious to justify termination, belated performance is acceptable[97] and perceived as being better than none at all.[98]

First instance courts have a very wide discretion as to whether to order a grace period, provided that the promisor acts in good faith.[99] The Cour de cassation rarely interferes.[100] There is no limit on the possible duration of the grace period,[101] except that it is not renewable. It is therefore open to the court to grant the promisor whatever time is necessary for him to perform and 'save the contract'.[102] The court must also take account of the interests of the promisee and any loss that he would suffer from more time being granted, thereby striking a balance between the interests of both parties.

(ii) The Relevance of Good Faith

It has been held in France that termination 'can only be granted if the injured promisee acts in good faith'[103] and should be rejected 'if his behaviour is tainted

[96] See art 1184, paragraph 3 of the Civil Code and the new article 1224 of the Civil Code: *Ordonnance no 2016-131 of 10 February 2016*. Aside from the *délai de grâce*, the court can order the partial termination of the contract, see Terré, Simler and Lequette (n 86) [652] ff.

[97] S Whittaker, '"Termination" for Contractual Non-Performance and its Consequences: French Law Reviewed in the Light of the Avant-Projet de réforme' in J Cartwright, S Vogenauer and S Whittaker (eds), *Reforming the French Law of Obligations, Comparative Reflections on the Avant-Projet de Réforme du Droit des Obligations et de la Prescription ('The Avant-projet Catala')* (Oxford, Hart Publishing, 2009) 187, 191.

[98] Genicon, *La résolution du contrat pour inexécution* (Paris, Libraire Générale de Droit et de Jurisprudence, 2007) [357]; Whittaker, 'A "Period of Grace"' (n 19) 1098.

[99] Y-M Laithier, 'Comparative Reflections on the French Law of Remedies for Breach of Contract' in N Cohen and E McKendrick (eds), *Comparative Remedies for Breach of Contract* (Oxford, Hart Publishing, 2005) 103, 121; contra Jamin (n 89) 470.

[100] Whittaker, 'A "Period of Grace"' (n 19) 1098.

[101] The absence of any temporal limit on the grace period that may be ordered is in contrast with article 1244-1 of the Civil Code, which gives the court a discretion to allow an extension of time of up to two years to pay a debt that is due.

[102] P Simler, *Fasc 10: Contrats et obligations—Classification des obligations—Distinction des obligations de donner, de faire et de ne pas faire* (LexisNexis Jurisclasseur, 2011) [51].

[103] Court of Appeal of Poitiers, 1st Civ Chamber, 4 July 2006, Juris-data no 2006-313835: a case in which the injured promisee had waited 19 years before taking formal steps to terminate the contract.

with bad faith'[104] or his request for termination 'can be characterised as disloyal speculation'.[105] The promisor can therefore pray in aid the principle of good faith to challenge the promisee's attempt to terminate. This enables the court to take into consideration the behaviour and motives of the promisee, in particular any evidence of good or bad faith,[106] in deciding whether to order termination. As an example from the cases, a promisee was found to have acted in bad faith by seeking to terminate where he had not complained about the breach for 19 years.[107]

Good faith is also relevant where the contract contains a termination clause. In principle, where the promisee invokes a contractual right to terminate, the court can do no more than ascertain whether the conditions for the exercise of the right have been met. However, in practice, termination clauses have been read restrictively and as being subject to a requirement that they be exercised in good faith. When invoked in bad faith, a termination clause will not be enforced.[108]

The potential impact of good faith in the context of termination clauses is neatly illustrated by a case from 1994.[109] The Limoges Court of Appeal refused to enforce a termination clause on the ground, amongst others, that the injured promisee had sought to rely on the promisor's breaches and invoke the clause as a pretext in order to be able to enter into more profitable transactions with third parties. This decision was upheld by the Cour de cassation.

(iii) The Reform of the Civil Code

A notable change relating to termination, brought about by the reforms, that shifts French law towards the position in England is that the promisee will no longer be obliged to seek a court order to terminate a contract. Instead he will be able to elect between judicial and self-help termination.[110] Judicial termination will closely resemble the current termination regime. Where the promisee chooses self-help termination, the contract will be discharged unless the promisor brings proceedings to challenge his right to do so.[111]

The promisor will not, however, be deprived of the currently available defences. If he challenges a purported self-help termination following the implementation of the reforms, the court will still be able to allow a grace period.[112] In deciding whether or not to do so, the court is likely to apply the same criteria as at present, with

[104] ibid.

[105] Court of Appeal of Paris, 22 December 1873 cited in Genicon (n 98) [505].

[106] Flour, Aubert, and Savaux (n 92) [252]; Civ 3, 29 April 1987 RTD civ 1987.536, noted by J Mestre; Civ 3, 3 June 1992, GP 1992.II.656, noted by J-P Barbier.

[107] Poitiers Court of Appeal, 1ere Ch civ, 4 July 2006, juris-data no 2006-313835.

[108] See Rowan (n 81) 85; Jamin (n 89) [34]; Com 31 March 1978, Bull Civ IV, no 102, p 84; Civ 3, 6 June 1984, Bull civ II, no 111, p 88; Civ 14 March 1956, D 1956, p 449; Y Picod, 'La Clause résolutoire et la règle morale' JCP 1990, ed G, I, 3447.

[109] Civ 3, 12 Jan 1994, no 91-17023.

[110] See the new article 1224 of the Civil Code: *Ordonnance no 2016-131 of 10 February 2016.*

[111] See the new article 1226 of the Civil Code: *Ordonnance no 2016-131 of 10 February 2016.*

[112] See the new article 1228 of the Civil Code: *Ordonnance no 2016-131 of 10 February 2016.* On the remedy for wrongful termination, see Rowan (n 81) 87–88.

particular focus on whether the promisor has made a satisfactory offer to perform. If the court finds that termination is not justified and performance remains possible, it is likely that performance will be ordered.[113] Much of the considerable protection for the promisor willing to perform therefore remains.

It will be interesting to observe the take-up of the self-help variant of termination as French legal practice acclimatises to the reforms.[114] On the face of things, it is a streamline option that should appeal to contracting parties, enabling them to end failed and failing contracts and move on swiftly. The knock-on effect may be fewer termination disputes coming before the French courts. There is, however, also a possibility that legal practitioners and disputants will proceed cautiously at least initially, and some may yet prefer the certainty and definitiveness of judicial termination.

C. Concluding Remarks on Termination in French law

French courts have wide discretion in relation to termination. It is not confined to protecting the promisee; account can also be taken of the defaulting promisor's circumstances and interests and he is allowed generous opportunity to avoid termination and perform belatedly. It is not unusual for a promisor to be granted a second chance.

IV. DEFENCES TO TERMINATION: COMPARATIVE REMARKS

The preceding survey of the defences to termination in England and France has revealed differences in approach and broader grounds for resisting termination in France than England. It will be argued in the remaining part of this chapter that these differences are largely attributable to divergent policy choices in the two jurisdictions.

A. Divergent Policy Choices

The broad availability in France of defences to termination owes much to a desire to uphold contractual relations and protect performance.[115] It is widely believed amongst French lawyers that performance is the essence of a contract. Where a breach has been committed, the parties are encouraged to persist in their relationship and find a solution. The contractual relationship should be saved, if possible.[116]

[113] ibid.

[114] Cases on the existing exception to judicial termination where breach is serious (*comportement grave*) have been relatively sporadic: see Rowan (n 81) 86.

[115] Rowan (n 81) 52, 82, 93–100.

[116] On one view, by granting a grace period or giving a second chance to the defaulting promisor, French courts are not enforcing the contract as agreed by the parties; rather, they are re-writing the contract.

It is preferable to try to rescue rather than to terminate it. Termination should be the very last resort.

This reflects the importance that French law ascribes to contractual obligations. The concept of the contract is much more subjective than in England, being seen as a consensual bond that has intrinsic value.[117] Only performance by the original contracting party is regarded as being truly satisfactory. In the words of the renowned French contract lawyer, Mestre:[118]

> the *raison d'être* [of the contract] is to unite individuals ... It is to be performed loyally ... and is ... above all a human affair ... The contract cannot be reduced, in an economic approach, to a transfer of values or a modification of estates.

The promotion of performance that is at the heart of the French law on termination is linked to a belief that it is not simply the promisee that has an interest in the performance of the contract. The promisor also has an 'interest in performing'[119] worthy of protection. This interest continues to exist where he has committed a breach and regardless even of its seriousness. Restricting the promisee's right to terminate ensures that the interest is upheld and cannot be defeated lightly.[120] Another eminent French contract lawyer, Genicon, goes as far as to say that 'the position of the promisor is of prime importance'.[121]

The commitment to the survival of the contractual relationship in France is not confined to the context of defences to termination. It pervades the whole remedial framework of French law.[122] For instance, specific remedies such as specific performance and injunctive relief are central and given primary importance. They are available as of right and subject to very few restrictions.[123] There is in this respect internal coherence and consistency in the French remedial system: the restrictions on termination interconnect with, and complement, the primacy and wide availability of specific performance.[124] As between terminating the contract and compelling its performance, French law very clearly favours the latter.

There is no similar willingness to uphold a failed contract in England, where ensuring that the promisor performs the primary obligations that he has undertaken is markedly less important.[125] It is generally considered that contracting parties should not have to remain tied together when their relationship has been unsuccessful. In many situations the promisee can put an end to the failed contract quickly so as to obtain substitute performance and reinvest his resources in another way. Upholding

[117] ibid.

[118] J Mestre, 'Préface' in B Fages, *Le comportement du contractant* (Aix-en-Provence, Presses Universitaires d'Aix-Marseille, 1997). On the concept of the contractual relationship in French law; see more generally Rowan (n 81).

[119] Whittaker, 'A "Period of Grace"' (n 19).

[120] ibid 1104.

[121] Genicon (n 98) [511].

[122] Rowan (n 81).

[123] ibid 37–52. See, however, the new restriction introduced in the new article 1221 of the Civil Code: *Ordonnance no 2016-131 of 10 February 2016.*

[124] ibid 97–99.

[125] Whittaker, 'A "Period of Grace"' (n 19) 1103.

the contractual relationship is subordinate to the overall economic outcome[126] and only encouraged if this serves to minimise loss.

The approach adopted in England has been attributed to the commercial nature of the disputes that typically come before English courts. Certainty and speed serve the interests of commercial parties.[127] The emphasis is on providing an expeditious and convenient way for the promisee to obtain the bargained-for benefit, which often means exiting the contract and using his resources elsewhere. Any additional cost that he incurs in doing so will often be recoverable as damages.

The liberality of this approach has been noted by commentators. As McKendrick has said:[128]

> English law ... places considerable emphasis on the importance of termination as a remedy in the event of breach ... At the risk of some over-statement it can be said that the philosophy of English law is that when one encounters a problem which has been caused by a breach of contract committed by the other party to the contract, the law should make it easy for the innocent party to walk away from the transaction to enter into a fresh transaction elsewhere.

The comparatively narrow circumstances in English law in which the promisee is required or incentivised to give the promisor another chance suggest that there is no particular desire to uphold contractual relationships. A more diverse set of policy considerations is in play and their collective aim appears to be to balance the competing interests of the parties. Beyond this, there does not seem to be any common thread running through the cases in which the promisor has been given a second chance to perform. Relief against forfeiture seeks to prevent unconscionable insistence on a contractual right of forfeiture. The mitigation principle, on the other hand, aims to minimise economic waste,[129] to encourage self-reliance in the promisee[130] and deter him from burdening the defaulting promisor with all conceivable losses.[131]

Unlike in France, there is also no or little emphasis on, and indeed barely any mention of, the promisor having an 'interest in performing'.[132] The focus in the case law and literature has predominantly been on the protection of the 'performance interest' or 'expectations interest' of the promisee and these terms are commonly used to describe his interest in obtaining the promised performance under the contract.[133] Comparatively little work has been done on the corresponding interest

[126] Rowan (n 81) ch 1.

[127] J Cartwright, 'Damages, Third Parties and Common Sense' (1996) 10 *Journal of Contract Law* 244, 272.

[128] E McKendrick, 'Contracts, the Common Law and the Impact of Europe' in S Mazzamuto (ed), *Il Contratto e le Tutele: Prospettive di Diritto Europeo / a cura di Salvatore Mazzamuto* (Torino, Giappichelli, 2002) 101, 110–11.

[129] *Chitty on Contracts* (n 5) [26-102]; D Campbell and D Harris, 'In Defence of Breach: A Critique of Restitution and the Performance Interest' (2002) 22 *Legal Studies* 208, 219.

[130] Bridge (n 60).

[131] A Burrows, *Remedies for Torts and Breach of Contract*, 3rd edn (Oxford, Oxford University Press, 2004).

[132] Whittaker, 'Contributory Fault and Mitigation' (n 58).

[133] Rowan (n 81) 2.

of the promisor.[134] As Treitel summarised, 'Anglo-American courts are, in the matter of termination, less concerned with the protection of the debtor than either German or French law. Their emphasis tends ... to be on speedy and convenient remedies for the creditor'.[135]

This approach to termination also fits coherently and consistently in the wider framework of contractual remedies under English law. The limited restrictions on the right to terminate dovetail with the limited availability of specific performance. There is an inverse and complementary relationship between the two mutually exclusive remedies. As between terminating the contract and compelling its performance, English law inclines towards the former, preferring to compensate any loss suffered with an award of damages.[136]

B. Approaches Taken by International Instruments

This is not to say, however, that the differing approaches in England and France are necessarily irreconcilable. Some international instruments have adopted the essential elements of each system. The key tenets of the English approach of encouraging loss mitigation and promoting contractual certainty operate in tandem with those from French law, namely preserving the contractual relationship and protecting the interests of the contracting parties.

For instance, the UNIDROIT Principles do not allow the court to grant a grace period. It is feared that this would only delay the injured promisee in exercising the right to terminate.[137] The promisor does, however, have a right to cure defective performance where the cure is prompt and the injured promisee has no legitimate reason to refuse.[138] This is available for all kinds of breach, except where time is of the essence.[139] Cure can consist of repair or replacement and can be effected before or after the due date of performance. It is not precluded by a notice of termination having been given, meaning that 'a contract that has been formally terminated' can be revived.[140] Only where the time allowed for cure has expired can the injured promisee terminate the contract if cure is unsuccessful. The rationale for allowing

[134] With the exception of Whittaker, 'Contributory Fault and Mitigation' (n 58) and Rowan (n 81) 99–102.

[135] Treitel (n 18) [259].

[136] Rowan (n 81) 97–98.

[137] H Schelhaas, Commentary on article 7.1 of the Unidroit Principles in S Vogenauer (ed), *Commentary on the Unidroit Principles of International Commercial Contracts (PICC)*, 2nd edn (Oxford, Oxford University Press, 2015) 828.

[138] See article 7.1.4 of the UNIDROIT Principles 2010. Schelhaas (n 137) 845–50.

[139] Schelhaas (n 137) 846–47.

[140] UNIDROIT Principles 2010, Official Comment 10 to art 7.1.4, p 230; Schelhaas (n 137) p 849, who criticises this as hardly conducive to legal certainty and open to criticism: the injured promisee is under the impression that he has lawfully terminated the contract, yet the defaulting promisor may subsequently exercise his right to cure with the effect that the contract turns out not to be terminated after all.

cure is to preserve the contract, minimise economic waste and achieve a solution that is in the interests of both parties.[141]

There is similarly no grace period under the UN Convention on the International Sale of Goods (CISG).[142] This is attributable to concern that the parties could be exposed to judicial discretion that is too broad and creates too much uncertainty.[143] The defaulting seller does, however, have a right to cure where he fails to perform by the due date, which principally arises where goods delivered are not in conformity with the contract.[144] Unlike under the UNIDROIT Principles, the promisee's right to terminate seems to take priority over the promisor's right to cure.[145]

The apparent priority of the right to terminate is controversial and has been criticised for depriving the promisor's right to cure of any substance.[146] In the legal literature, the prevailing view is that, even where the defect in the non-conforming goods is serious, the promisee's right to terminate should not prevent the promisor from curing the breach where this can be done without undue delay or unreasonable inconvenience to the promisee.[147] The right to terminate should only prevail where this serves to protect special interests of the buyer, for instance where time is of the essence or there has been a breach of trust between the parties.[148]

Although not without problems themselves,[149] the defences to termination found in the international instruments demonstrate that there is middle ground between the rules in England and France. In giving less ammunition to the defaulting promisor than in France but more than in England, the instruments have achieved a compromise and a balance between the termination regimes of the two jurisdictions.

V. CONCLUSION

It is fair to say that 'English law seems reluctant to give second chances to [defaulting parties] who fail to get it right the first time round'.[150] The interests of the defaulting promisor are protected mainly in the rules as to when the right to terminate arises. Once the right has arisen, it is relatively unrestricted and there are few defences that

[141] ibid. The same approach can be found in the Draft Common Frame of Reference. The right to cure is justified by the desire to uphold contractual relations where possible and appropriate: see articles III.-3:201–3:204.

[142] Articles 45(3), 61(3).

[143] P Huber, Commentary to article 45 at p 369 and G Hager, Commentary on article 61 at p 481 in P Schlechtriem and G Thomas (eds), *Commentary on the UN Convention on the International Sale of Goods (CISG)*, 2nd edn (Oxford, Clarendon Press, 1998).

[144] Article 48.

[145] See arts 48–49.

[146] Huber (n 143) 406–11.

[147] ibid.

[148] ibid.

[149] For a criticism of the approaches taken in the international instruments, see the comments made by the contributors in P Schlechtriem and G Thomas (eds), *Commentary on the UN Convention on the International Sale of Goods (CISG)*, 2nd edn (Oxford, Clarendon Press, 1998) and S Vogenauer (ed), *Commentary on the Unidroit Principles of International Commercial Contracts (PICC)*, 2nd edn (Oxford, Oxford University Press, 2015).

[150] Mak (n 54) 409 in a sale of goods context.

he can invoke to resist termination. This contrasts with French law, which has wider grounds for opposing termination, thereby giving greater protection to the defaulting promisor and more generally the contract. Underpinning this is a wider policy of protecting contractual performance.

It is beyond the scope of this chapter to consider whether English law should in the future evolve in this direction to recognise more numerous defences to termination in English law or indeed the form that any such defences might take. What the chapter has shown, however, is that there are currently few defences that enable termination to be resisted. There is therefore scope for developing new defences, if this were considered desirable.

A possible progression in the near future is a more significant role for good faith, potentially as an aspect of increasing prominence of good faith principles in English law. There have also been calls in the literature for the recognition of a general right to cure in the context of sale of goods contracts, which it is argued would better protect the interests of the parties, increase loss mitigation, and help avoid the possibility of the injured promisee escaping the contract for an ulterior motive such as to take advantage of market fluctuations.[151] However, the introduction of such a defence in England presently seems unlikely. It was firmly rejected by the Law Commission in the context of consumer and non-consumer sales.[152] In relation to consumer sales, the Law Commission's view was that it would give too much power to sellers against buyers and be too difficult to implement. For commercial contracts, it described a right to cure as 'positively inappropriate': it would be impractical in many situations and unsuited to large commercial transactions.[153] The Law Commission recommended instead that contracting parties who wish to have a right to cure following breach should make appropriate provision in their contract.[154] While this approach disappointed many,[155] it has the merit of being simple and easy to adopt: it is founded on the key principle of freedom of contract, requires no drastic change in the law and policy, and gives the parties responsibility for the level of protection that they perceive as being adequate.

[151] Ahdar (n 54); Apps (n 54); Mak (n 54).

[152] The Law Commission considered conferring on the seller in breach of contract a right to cure in order to prevent abusive termination by the buyer where the breach was slight. See now ss 15A and 30(2A) of the Sale of Goods Act 1979 (UK).

[153] See Law Commission, *Sale and Supply of Goods* (Law Com No 160, 1987) [4.13] ff and Law Commission, *Sale and Supply of Goods* (Law Com CP No 58, 1983) [4.52].

[154] ibid [4.55].

[155] See the references in n 54 above.

10

The Contract Remoteness Rule: Exclusion, Not Assumption of Responsibility

VENKATESAN NIRANJAN*

I. INTRODUCTION

SIR ROBIN COOKE (later Lord Cooke of Thorndon) once said that '[t]he law about remoteness of damage in contract and tort is in a strangely unsettled state'.[1] This remains true today. The reason for this is that two conceptual questions about remoteness remain unanswered in both contract and tort law. The first question is why remoteness rules exist. The second question is how remoteness rules relate to the obligation to pay damages: in particular, are the reasons that justify the obligation to pay damages the same reasons that justify limitations to the scope of that obligation? Ever since the (supposed) heresy in *Re Polemis*,[2] these questions have been more familiar to tort than to contract lawyers. But they are no less important in contract law and an opportunity to consider their conceptual foundations has arisen in the light of the speeches delivered in the *Achilleas*,[3] in which the House of Lords rejected[4] what may be described as the 'conventional' understanding of the contract remoteness rule: that it is an external rule of law imposed for policy[5] reasons ('the external rule theory').

To understand the implications of the *Achilleas*, it is essential to examine the underlying basis of the remoteness rule in the common law and its relationship with the obligation to pay damages.[6] That is the task of this chapter. The conclusion it

* Barrister, One Essex Court. I am grateful to Andrew Dyson, James Goudkamp and Fred Wilmot-Smith for inviting me to present this paper at a stimulating conference and to them, the participants, Adam Kramer, James Ruddell and Sam Williams for their very helpful comments and suggestions.

1 Sir R Cooke, 'Remoteness of Damage and Judicial Discretion' (1978) 37 *CLJ* 288, 288.

2 *In re an Arbitration between Polemis and Furness, Withy and Co Ltd* [1921] 3 KB 560 (CA).

3 *The Achilleas* [2008] UKHL 48, [2009] 1 AC 61.

4 Some have doubted whether the new approach forms part of the ratio of the case. Floyd LJ recently left this open: *Wellesley Partners LLP v Withers LLP* [2015] EWCA Civ 1146; [2016] PNLR 19 [71]. However, as Adam Kramer has said, this is (now) an arid debate: see A Kramer, *The Law of Contract Damages* (Oxford, Hart Publishing, 2014) 290–91.

5 The meaning of 'policy' is considered at text to n 15.

6 As Professor Burrows has also recently pointed out: A Burrows, 'Lord Hoffmann and Remoteness in Contract' in PS Davies and J Pila (eds), *The Jurisprudence of Lord Hoffmann: A Festschrift in Honour of Lord Leornard Hoffmann* (Oxford, Hart Publishing, 2015) 261.

reaches, based in part on an analysis of the origins of the remoteness rule in the nineteenth century, is that the external rule theory is incapable of explaining the law. It argues that the best interpretation of the authorities is that an implied *exclusion* rather than *assumption* of responsibility limits the obligation to pay damages that is otherwise imposed by law.

Although there is no space in this chapter to consider the implications of this claim in detail, there are many. First, it shows that there is no inconsistency between the agreement-centred approach and the fact that the obligation to pay damages is itself imposed rather than assumed. Second, it shows that the so-called 'inclusionary cases', such as *Supershield v Siemens*[7] and Lord Pearce's well-known example in the *Heron II*,[8] are clearly correct but not in fact 'inclusionary'. Third, it provides a coherent rationale for a number of doctrinal rules in the law of remoteness that have never been satisfactorily explained by the external rule theory: for example, the rule that the degree of culpability of the defendant is irrelevant under the contract remoteness rule (unlike its tort counterpart); that events subsequent to the date of conclusion of the contract are generally ignored; and that the defendant is liable to pay damages for unforeseeable loss to the extent that a loss of a different type was foreseeable, though that loss was not in the event incurred by the claimant. Fourth, it illustrates why it is erroneous to assimilate the principle in the *Achilleas* with the quite different and unrelated principle in the *SAAMCO* case.

The chapter is divided into three sections. The first considers a preliminary question: when does a remoteness question arise? The second section argues that the external rule theory does not withstand scrutiny. It is inconsistent with the circumstances in which the reasonable contemplation test was first introduced into the common law by *Hadley v Baxendale*[9] and it cannot explain a number of doctrinal rules that have emerged subsequently. The third section defends the agreement-centred approach but suggests that it has not properly distinguished between an implied *assumption* and an implied *exclusion* of responsibility. It is the latter, rather than the former, that provides the best explanation of the remoteness rule.

II. THE RELATIONSHIP BETWEEN REMOTENESS AND THE COMPENSATORY PRINCIPLE

Lord Sumption recently described the compensatory principle as the 'fundamental principle of the common law of damages'.[10] The formulation of the compensatory principle—what would have happened if the wrong had not been committed—entails a counterfactual assessment involving a comparison between the 'breach position' and the 'non-breach position'.[11] But the principle is, of course, only the 'aim' or 'object' of the award of damages: it does not reflect what the claimant actually

[7] *Supershield Ltd v Siemens Building Technologies FE Ltd* [2010] EWCA Civ 7; [2010] 1 CLC 241.
[8] *Koufos v C Czarnikow Ltd ('The Heron II')* [1969] 1 AC 350 (HL) 417.
[9] *Hadley v Baxendale* (1854) 9 Ex 341; 156 ER 145.
[10] *Bunge SA v Nidera BV* [2015] UKSC 43; [2015] 3 All ER 1082 [14].
[11] This helpful terminology is taken from A Dyson and A Kramer, 'There is No "Breach Date Rule": Mitigation, Difference in Value and Date of Assessment' (2014) 130 *LQR* 259, 261. See also Kramer (n 4) 14–16.

gets, because there are other legal rules that limit the defendant's liability. The most important of these in the law of contract are the doctrines of mitigation, intervening cause, coincidence and remoteness.

Many scholars treat these limitations to the compensatory principle as homogenous limitations imposed for reasons of policy. For example, Professor Burrows has argued that:[12]

> Remoteness, *like the law on causation of loss, and the duty to mitigate*, and the law on contributory negligence … are externally imposed rules and are based on the law seeking a fair solution in a situation not dealt with by the contract. (emphasis added)

Similarly, Roth J has recently said that '[t]he concept of remoteness is … based on considerations of policy' and that 'the concepts of legal causation (as opposed to causation in fact) and remoteness are interrelated'.[13]

In contrast, the position adopted in this chapter is that there is an important distinction between causal and non-causal rules in the law of contract. Causal rules are concerned with whether some loss is to be regarded as an outcome or consequence of the defendant's breach of contract. Non-causal rules (of which remoteness is an instance) are concerned with whether there is some reason why the defendant should not be liable for that loss even though it is a consequence of his breach of contract. As the following sub-sections explain, this distinction is central to any analysis of remoteness.

A. Causal and Non-causal Rules in Contract Law

It has often been said that causation is a matter of common sense. On one interpretation, what this means is that causal judgments are entirely discretionary and vary from case to case. This is undoubtedly how some judges have used the expression 'common sense'[14] and it has been rightly criticised in recent years for reasons that it is not necessary to develop here.[15] But this has unfortunately obscured a more important and deeper way in which causation can be said to be a matter of common sense: that causal judgments made by judges are based on principle, not policy or free-standing discretion, but those principles are not *distinctively legal*. In other words, the principles used by judges to resolve causal problems in private law are the same principles used to resolve similar causal problems in ordinary life.

It is the second claim—though it is often confused with the first—that was made by Professors HLA Hart and AM Honoré in their magisterial work on causation in 1959.[16] One of their most important insights is that there is more than one concept

[12] Burrows (n 6) 262.

[13] *Wellesley* (n 4) [145], [154].

[14] See, eg, *Galoo v Bright Grahame Murray* [1994] 1 WLR 1360 (CA) 1375A (Glidewell LJ) and *March v E & MH Stramare Pty Ltd* (1991) 171 CLR 506 (HCA) 515 (Mason CJ).

[15] See, in particular, The Rt Hon Lord Hoffmann, 'Common Sense and Causing Loss' (Lecture to the Chancery Bar Association, 15 June 1999) and The Hon James Edelman, 'Unnecessary Causation' (Lecture to the Association of Anglo-Australian Lawyers, 25 June 2014).

[16] H Hart and T Honoré, *Causation in the Law* (Oxford, Clarendon Press, 1959); H Hart and T Honoré, *Causation in the Law*, 2nd edn (Oxford, Clarendon Press, 1985). All subsequent references are to the second edition.

of causation both in ordinary life and in private law. The first, which they described as the 'central notion' of cause, is concerned with the relationship between physical events or between physical events and a single human act. In its most primitive form, it is illustrated by 'causal recipes', that is, statements about how to bring about some event by a simple bodily movement. These statements often use transitive verbs of action rather than causal language (eg 'D 'broke', 'bent' or 'moved' the teacup, wire or book'). In these cases, one tends to identify the bodily movement as the cause because it is an 'interference in the natural course of events which *makes a difference* in the way these develop'.[17] Hart and Honoré were able to show that the notion, prominent in causal recipes, that a cause is an intervention that makes a difference to the *normal* course of events, is also influential when one makes more complex causal statements, usually to explain some event or to attribute responsibility for it. For example, if the black box is recovered following a plane crash and it shows that there was a catastrophic fire that incapacitated the crew shortly before the plane went down, the fire, rather than the fact that the plane took off that night, would be identified as the cause, even though both were 'necessary' in the same sense for the outcome. This is a distinction that one would draw in ordinary life in explaining why the plane crashed: it does not depend on any legal system.[18]

Hart and Honoré thought that there are two stages in the causal enquiry in cases of this kind. The first stage is concerned with whether some condition (eg the breach of contract/the fire) is 'causally relevant' to some loss. Causal relevance may for present purposes be taken to be analogous to the 'but-for' test though this was not in fact Hart and Honoré's view. The second stage is concerned with distinguishing *between* two or more causally relevant conditions in order to identify one of them as the 'cause'. In distinguishing between condition and cause, Hart and Honoré attached great importance to the contrast between *normal and abnormal* natural events, and *voluntary* human acts and all other conditions:[19] so if a building is destroyed by fire, one would identify the act of the arsonist, rather than the presence of oxygen, as the cause, even though both were causally relevant in the same sense.[20] This is because to cite the oxygen as the cause is to explain what must accompany *every* fire, whenever it occurs, not 'why *this* fire broke out where fire usually does not'.[21] Contract or tort law, when it makes causal judgments, draws on the same concepts: it may make them more *determinate* but it does not thereby adopt some specially legal notion of cause.[22]

[17] Hart and Honoré (n 16) 29.

[18] ibid 33–44.

[19] For discussion of the rationale for the voluntary act rule generally, see S Steel, 'Causation in Tort Law and Criminal Law: Unity or Divergence?' in M Dyson (ed), *Unravelling Tort and Crime* (Cambridge, Cambridge University Press, 2014) 246–51.

[20] Hart and Honoré (n 16) 37.

[21] H Hart and A Honoré, 'Causation in the Law I—A Survey of Common-Sense Principles' (1956) 72 *LQR* 58, 75. See also A Broadbent, 'The Difference between Cause and Condition' (2008) 108 *Proceedings of the Aristotelian Society* 355. This is why Justice Edelman's suggestion that even the plain man would identify the oxygen as the cause may be respectfully doubted: Edelman (n 15) 14.

[22] 'The distinction between causes and mere conditions is not a peculiarity of the legal uses of causal notions … we make the distinction … whenever, for example, we select the bent rail as the cause of a

Hart and Honoré identified two other types of causal connection which are analogous to the central notion but distinct from it. They called these 'interpersonal transactions' and 'opportunities', respectively. Interpersonal transactions may be ignored for the purposes of this chapter.[23] But the third type, 'opportunities', is prominent in the law of contract:[24] it is concerned with cases where D provides an opportunity for a third party's voluntary act or for an abnormal event (eg leaving the house unlocked, allowing a thief to enter) or fails to provide a stipulated opportunity for gain.[25]

This rather crude summary does not, of course, do justice to Hart and Honoré's theory, which remains controversial:[26] indeed, it has probably become unfashionable today.[27] It is not possible to address these criticisms in this chapter. For present purposes, it is enough to say that their distinction between abnormal events or voluntary acts and all other conditions explains a number of doctrinal rules in the law of damages. Three examples can be given. First, many distinguished judges have said that there is a principle in the common law that a causal connection cannot normally[28] be traced through a voluntary human act even if it was reasonably foreseeable.[29] Second, the defendant's culpability is relevant to certain rules in the law of damages but not to others. For example, the doctrines of mitigation and intervening cause apply even in a deceit claim but the claimant can recover damages for unforeseeable loss. As Toulson J pointed out, this is because mitigation is a causal rule.[30] Third, it explains why a pre-existing condition is generally treated as part

railway accident and relegate the weight and speed of the train to the status of mere conditions': Hart and Honoré, 'Causation—Part I' (n 21) 69.

[23] See Hart and Honoré (n 16) 51–59.

[24] ibid (n 16) 310–12.

[25] It was, in substance, Hart and Honoré's analysis that Lord Denning MR adopted in *H Parsons (Livestock) Ltd v Uttley Ingham & Co Ltd* [1978] QB 791 (CA) 802. But the Master of the Rolls appears to have thought that Hart and Honoré were in favour of a foreseeability test for cases involving physical harm, albeit with a lower degree of probability. They were not: see Hart and Honoré (n 16) 319–21.

[26] One objection that is frequently made is that the law is interested not in causation but in responsibility, which may be based on non-causal grounds: see, eg, R Stevens, 'Causation and Contribution' (Lecture to the Tort Law Research Group, Western Law, 19 March 2014) and Edelman (n 15). However, Hart and Honoré accept that it is for the law to determine: (i) whether responsibility is based on conduct (the liability of an insurer, for instance, is not); (ii) where it is based on conduct, whether the conduct must be shown to have caused the harm or merely occasioned it or provided a reason for it; and (iii) between what facts or events a causal connection in any of these forms must be shown to exist. Their analysis of causal concepts is relevant only if the law has first made these determinations: see Hart and Honoré (n 16) xlii–li.

[27] Professor Stapleton is a prominent critic: see, eg, J Stapleton, 'Reflections on Common Sense Causation in Australia' in S Degeling, J Edelman and J Goudkamp (eds), *Torts in Commercial Law* (Pyrmont NSW, Thomson Reuters, 2011).

[28] Not always. An omission is sometimes abnormal precisely because it creates an opportunity for a third party's voluntary intervention. These are the cases that Hart and Honoré third causal notion (opportunities) is concerned with: see Hart and Honoré (n 16) 37 and, for an illustration, *Stansbie v Troman* [1948] 2 KB 48 (CA) 52 (Tucker LJ).

[29] The best example is *McKew v Holland & Hannen & Cubitts (Scotland) Ltd* [1969] 3 All ER 1621 (HL) 1623 (Lord Reid). See also *Smith v Littlewoods Organisation Ltd* [1987] AC 241 (HL) 270 (Lord Goff) and *Environment Agency v Empress Car Co (Abertillery) Ltd* [1999] 2 AC 22 (HL) 30H (Lord Hoffmann).

[30] *Standard Chartered Bank v Pakistan National Shipping Corp* [1999] CLC 761 (QB) 772–77.

of the 'background'[31] even if it was unusual or unforeseeable, while a post-breach intervention of the same kind is treated as a novus actus.[32]

Some of these examples were taken from tort law but contract law is no different.[33] Hart and Honoré's principle that a voluntary human act is ordinarily treated as a new cause is the best explanation of the doctrine of mitigation, which is concerned with whether the claimant's own act was voluntary. Robert Goff J made this point in a well-known passage in the *Elena D'Amico*[34] and it has been recently reiterated by the Court of Appeal[35] and the Supreme Court.[36] Similarly, a voluntary act of a third party is usually[37] treated as an intervening cause even if it was foreseeable. For example, in *Wiseman*, Virgin Atlantic was in breach of contract in refusing to allow Dr Wiseman to board a London-bound flight in Nigeria. He consequently remained there for an additional 12 days. Unfortunately, he was assaulted by some robbers during this period. His claim for damages for this loss failed even though the 'but-for test' was satisfied. Eady J correctly pointed out that it was 'inappropriate to analyse the matter in terms of remoteness'[38] because the act of the robber was voluntary and therefore treated on ordinary causal principles as a novus actus. The doctrine of coincidental loss can also be explained in this way.[39] In these cases the question of remoteness simply does not arise and it is, with respect, unhelpful to say[40] that the reason the defendant is not liable is that he did not 'assume responsibility' for the claimant's or some third party's voluntary conduct.

B. Why Does the Distinction Matter in the Law of Contract?

It may be asked why the distinction between causal and non-causal rules matters if both lead to a 'no-liability' result. The answer is that the justifications for the existence of these rules in the law of contract (as in the law of tort) are very different. This point, which is controversial, can only be addressed in outline in this chapter.

31 See the cases cited in Hart and Honoré (n 16) 172–76.

32 See H McGregor, *McGregor on Damages*, 19th edn (London, Sweet & Maxwell, 2014) [8–139]. This was doubted in *Total Transport Corp v Arcadia Petroleum Ltd (The Eurus)* [1998] CLC 90 (CA) 102–3, Staughton LJ noting that the arbitrators (wrongly, he thought) 'had with commendable scholarship regard to what I might call the Oxford school of jurisprudence'. But it is best regarded as a remoteness case.

33 See, further, Hart and Honoré (n 16) ch 11.

34 *Koch Marine Inc v d'Amica Societa di Navigazione arl ('The Elena D'Amico')* [1980] 1 Lloyd's Rep 75 (QB) 87–88.

35 *Hooper v Oates* [2013] EWCA Civ 91; [2014] Ch 287 [38] (Lloyd LJ).

36 *Bunge* (n 10) [17] (Lord Sumption) [80] (Lord Toulson).

37 Again, unless the purpose of the contractual obligation was to protect the claimant from such an intervention (eg the obligation of a security guard to not fall asleep). This is consistent with Hart and Honoré's analysis and the reason they distinguished between the central causal notion and opportunities.

38 *Wiseman v Virgin Atlantic Airways Ltd* [2006] EWHC 1566 (QB); [2006] All ER (D) 344 [22].

39 In the law of contract, the most well-known example is *Monarch Steamship Co v Karlshamns Oljefabriker (A/B)* [1949] AC 196 (HL) 214–16 (Lord Porter). But see *Davis v Garrett* (1830) 6 Bing 716; 130 ER 1456, 1459 (Tindal CJ) and Hart and Honoré (n 16) 321–24.

40 See, eg, A Kramer, 'An Agreement-Centred Approach to Remoteness and Contract Damages' in N Cohen and E McKendrick (eds), *Comparative Remedies for Breach of Contract* (Oxford, Hart Publishing, 2005) 264, 281, fn 148.

There is a close relationship between the justification for the common law's use of ordinary causal principles and the justification for requiring the defendant to pay damages in the first place. The latter question has spawned a vast literature.[41] One answer—by no means uncontroversial but shared by a wide range of scholars—is that it is justified by the moral obligation to do corrective justice. Corrective justice scholars differ about precisely why there is such a moral obligation, but many appeal in some form to the *reasons* why the duty (whatever it was) originally existed. Paying damages, it is said, is the 'next-best thing' to not committing the breach of contract; in the post-breach world, one can no longer conform to the obligation itself (eg deliver the sugar at Basrah by 22 November 1960) but one can conform to the reasons why one had that obligation (eg enable the charterer to sell the sugar at market price).[42] This analysis, which Professor Gardner describes as the 'continuity thesis',[43] will not be defended here.[44] But it has great plausibility and, if correct, helps explain why there is an important distinction between causation and remoteness in both contract and tort law.

Causation, understood not as 'but-for' or 'policy' but as the ordinary (ie non-legal) causal principles described above, has been said to be a 'necessary but not sufficient' condition of corrective justice.[45] In other words, the obligation to make reparation (in order to conform to one's original reasons) only exists in relation to an outcome that can be regarded as one's own, independently of the law. Though they did not develop this point in much detail, Hart and Honoré were conscious of it: in the Preface to the second edition, they argued that the common law uses their ordinary causal principles (rather than merely 'but-for' or policy) because these are the principles by which actions are *individuated* in ordinary life.

Remoteness, on the other hand, is very different. The fact that some loss was unforeseeable does not mean that it was not caused by the breach: as this chapter shows below, this was accepted in *Hadley v Baxendale* itself. Equally, the fact that a loss was unforeseeable does not mean that paying damages ceases to be the next-best thing to not committing the breach of contract. If, therefore, the defendant is not required to pay damages for such a loss, this is not because it did not cause it or because corrective justice is not called for; it is because there is some legal principle that *qualifies* the pursuit of corrective justice.

[41] For a small sample, see J Gardner, 'What is Tort Law For? Part 1: The Place of Corrective Justice' (2011) 30 *Law and Philosophy* 1; E Weinrib, 'Two Conceptions of Remedies' in C Rickett (ed), *Justifying Private Law Remedies* (Oxford, Hart Publishing, 2008); and S Smith, 'Remedies for Breach of Contract: One Principle or Two?' in G Klass, G Letsas and P Saprai (eds), *Philsophical Foundations of Contract Law* (Oxford, Oxford University Press, 2014).

[42] Gardner, 'Corrective Justice' (n 41) 29, 31 ('obligations … are individuated according to the action that they make obligatory [but] every reason for action is potentially a reason for multiple actions').

[43] Gardner, 'Corrective Justice' (n 41) 26–50. See also J Raz, 'Personal Practical Conflicts' in P Baumann and M Betzler (eds), *Practical Conflicts: New Philosophical Essays* (Cambridge, Cambridge University Press, 2004) 189–92; J Gardner, 'The Way Things Used to Be' (draft, October 2014, cited with permission) 21 and R Stevens, 'Should Contributory Fault be Analogue or Digital?' in A Dyson, J Goudkamp and F Wilmot-Smith (eds), *Defences in Tort* (Oxford, Hart Publishing, 2015) 252–53.

[44] For a contrary view, see, eg, Smith (n 41).

[45] See, eg, T Honoré, *Responsibility and Fault* (Oxford, Hart Publishing, 1999) 80.

It is for this reason that remoteness, in contrast to causation, raises special problems for theorists who seek to explain private law solely in terms of corrective justice. Remoteness rules (arguably) lack a corrective rationale.[46] In the law of tort, some corrective justice scholars have tried to address the problem by re-analysing remoteness (notably the rule in *The Wagon Mound*)[47] in terms of the scope of the primary obligation.[48] This has been largely unconvincing.[49] But in the law of contract there is, subject to a few well-known objections,[50] an obvious answer: the obligation to do the next-best thing, which is imposed by law, is qualified because the parties agreed that it would be qualified.

Critics of this (agreement-centred) approach have tended to object to it not for conceptual or normative reasons but on the ground that it is fictional to talk of what the parties intend in relation to the consequences of breach. This objection is considered below. But it has often been overlooked that two important questions arise if this objection is well-founded. First, is there any justification for limiting liability for breach of contract by rules that lack a corrective rationale if those rules cannot be derived from the intentions of the parties? Second, if there is, does it explain what the cases actually say about the common law's remoteness rule? On analysis, the external rule theory can be accepted only if it is able to answer both questions in the affirmative. To say that remoteness is an 'external rule' or that it is a 'rule of policy' or 'fairness' is not,[51] with respect, an answer, because that is a description of the nature of the rule rather than an explanation of why it exists.

The first question raises an important theoretical issue about remoteness generally. But it is not one that this chapter will pursue: it may be assumed for present purposes that it is legitimate for the courts to limit liability for breach of contract by free-standing rules of policy or fairness which lack a corrective rationale and which cannot be traced to the intentions of the parties. The problem for the external rule theory is that a remoteness rule of this kind is simply inconsistent with the law as it stands. It does not fit the authorities: one would expect the law to be different in a number of respects if the courts were concerned to limit the defendant's liability just as a matter of policy or fairness.

[46] Professor Gardner is one of the few scholars to have recognised this: see J Gardner, 'What is Tort Law For? Part 2: The Place of Distributive Justice' in J Oberdiek (ed), *Philosophical Foundations of the Law of Torts* (Oxford, Oxford University Press, 2014) 347. But his alternative analysis (see 347–49) appears to assume that the remoteness rule is concerned with causal attribution (albeit not on an 'all-or-nothing' basis) which, with respect, may be doubted.

[47] *Overseas Tankship Ltd v Morts Dock & Engineering Co Ltd ('The Wagon Mound')* [1961] AC 388 (PC).

[48] See, eg, E Weinrib, *The Idea of Private Law*, revised edn (Oxford, Oxford University Press, 2012) 157 and A Beever, *Rediscovering the Law of Negligence* (Oxford, Hart Publishing, 2007) 125.

[49] For reasons it is unnecessary to develop here.

[50] Considered below.

[51] See, eg, R Samek, 'The Relevant Time of Foreseeability of Damage in Contract' (1964) 38 *Australian Law Journal* 125, 126; Burrows (n 6) 262.

III. THE AUTHORITIES: EXTERNAL RULE OR IMPLIED EXCLUSION?

It is no mere form of words to say that any analysis of this subject must begin with *Hadley v Baxendale*. Alderson B's statement of principle in that case is the high-water mark of the theory that the remoteness rule is an external rule imposed by the law for policy reasons. Indeed, many of the more recent authorities, notably the *Heron II*,[52] have been concerned not with the principle underlying remoteness but with the correct interpretation of particular passages in *Hadley v Baxendale*, such as the expression 'great multitude of cases'. The case therefore requires close analysis.

A. Background to *Hadley v Baxendale*

The measure of damages for breach of contract was, for many years, 'an unregulated jury matter'.[53] The emergence of rules of law on this subject is closely linked to the development of procedural mechanisms by which judges were able to review or otherwise control the determinations of the jury.[54] But it is clear from early statements of principle that what was protected was the claimant's expectation interest. For example, Lord Wilmot CJ is reported to have said in 1768 that the measure of damages for the breach of a contract to buy goods is the difference between what the seller was entitled to get and what he actually got.[55]

The question that arose then, as now, is whether there were any legal rules that limited the protection of the claimant's expectation interest. The initial answer that the courts gave, with little dissent until 1854,[56] was that it was limited *only* by causal rules. This is illustrated by *Waters v Towers*[57] and *Black v Baxendale*.[58] In *Waters*, the defendant failed to install some mill-gearing equipment in the claimants' mill. The claimants sought damages for lost profits arising out of their inability to fulfil contracts while the mill was closed.[59] Counsel for the defendant, relying on Chancellor Kent's *Commentaries*,[60] argued that damages were not recoverable because this was not a loss 'which may reasonably be supposed to have entered into the contemplation of the parties'. This submission was rejected by none other than Alderson B, who said that the claimants were entitled to recover damages for any loss 'occasioned by the defendant's breach of contract'.[61]

[52] *The Heron II* (n 8).
[53] A Simpson, *Legal Theory and Legal History: Essays on the Common Law* (London, Hambledon Press, 1987) 220.
[54] D Ibbetson, *A Historical Introduction to the Law of Obligations* (Oxford, Oxford University Press, 2001); J Barton, 'Contractual Damages and the Rise of Industry' (1987) 7 *OJLS* 40, 46–49.
[55] *Smee v Huddlestone* (1768) cited from Joseph Sayer, *The Law of Damages* (Dublin, J Moore, 1792) 49–54. See also Florian Faust, 'Hadley v Baxendale—An Understandable Miscarriage of Justice' (1994) 15 *The Journal of Legal History* 41, 54–56.
[56] But see Barton (n 54) 47–50, who suggests that there was some resistance in relation to claims concerning consequential loss.
[57] *Waters v Towers* (1853) 8 Ex 401; 155 ER 1404.
[58] *Black v Baxendale* (1847) 1 Ex 410; 154 ER 174.
[59] In fact the 'buyers' were two of the claimants themselves (in their capacity as the owners of a different business in Manchester) but nothing turns on this for present purposes.
[60] J Kent, *Commentaries on American law*, 4th edn (New York, EB Clayton, 1840) 480, fn b.
[61] For a contrary view, see Faust (n 55) 53–54.

Similarly, in *Black v Baxendale*, the defendant, a carrier, agreed to deliver the claimant's goods in Bedford by a certain day. Unknown to the defendant, the claimant intended to sell the goods at a market which was to be held in Bedford that day. As a result of a delay in delivery, the claimant incurred expenses in removing the goods to another location with view to selling them there. The jury awarded damages for these wasted expenses and this award was upheld in the Court of Exchequer. Parke B said that the rule of the common law is that the defendant should pay damages for the 'reasonable consequences' of his breach of contract. This entailed asking whether claimant 'went down [to Bedford] unnecessarily, or remained there an unreasonable time'.[62] This, again, is a purely causal question, although Parke B did not use the language of causation or mitigation. What is significant is that he did not think it necessary to investigate whether the claimant's intention to sell the goods at a market in Bedford was within the reasonable contemplation of the defendant, which indeed it plainly was not.

Thus, there was, before 1854, little authority for the proposition that the quantum of damages for breach of contract depended on the reasonable contemplation of the parties.[63] As Washington observed, if this had remained the law 'we should be troubled with few questions of remoteness today'.[64] How was the Court of Exchequer able to introduce a different rule into English law in 1854?

B. *Hadley v Baxendale*: Crompton J and the Court of Exchequer

The case is so well-known that it would ordinarily be unnecessary to describe the facts but it is worth doing so in some detail because the judgment of the trial judge, Crompton J, is less well-known.

Joseph and Jonah Hadley owned the City Flour Mills near the Gloucester docks. They placed an order for a new crankshaft with a firm of engineers, W Joyce & Co, who wanted the broken crankshaft to be sent to them in Greenwich. Joseph Baxendale—the protagonist in *Black v Baxendale* and a serial litigant during this period[65]—was a common carrier who carried on business in the name of Pickford & Co. On Friday 13 May 1853, the Hadleys made enquiries of Perrett, Baxendale's clerk, about when the crankshaft would be delivered in Greenwich. They were told that it would be delivered in one day. There was some evidence about this conversation[66] that suggested that the Hadleys had also specifically mentioned to Perrett that their mill had stopped for want of a spare steam-engine. In the event, the crankshaft was given to Baxendale on 14 May but he delivered it to the engineers only on 21 May. The reason for the delay was Baxendale's decision to send the crankshaft to

[62] *Black* (n 58) 175.

[63] Save for a dictum of Pollock CB in *Black* (n 58) 175.

[64] G Washington, 'Damages in Contract at Common Law' (1932) 48 *LQR* 90, 102.

[65] He is said to have brought 34 actions against railroad companies between 1858 and 1863: see R Danzig, 'Hadley v Baxendale: A Study in the Industrialization of the Law' (1975) 4 *Journal of Legal Studies* 249, 256, fn 26.

[66] Discussed more fully at the text to n 91.

Greenwich by water rather than by rail.[67] It is likely that he did this for his own benefit,[68] just as the owner of the *Heron II* many years later chose to deviate from the voyage to Basrah for its own benefit.[69] The cost of the carriage was £2 4s and Baxendale's profit was about 10s.[70] The Hadleys claimed around £300 as damages for their lost profits.

The trial is reported in *The Times*[71] but more fully in *The Gloucester Journal*.[72] It is apparent from these reports that Crompton J's direction to the jury was entirely consistent with what the law was understood to be in August 1853: Baxendale, said the learned judge, was 'answerable for the breach of contract, and the damages *caused by the natural consequences* of that breach' (emphasis added).[73] For this purpose, the jury was simply to consider 'what under the circumstances was a reasonable time for delivering the shaft; and next, what was the damage caused to the plaintiffs by the delay in the delivery'.[74] In other words, there was not a hint of reasonable contemplation or of foreseeability: liability depended, consistently with the authorities of the day, on purely causal[75] considerations. The jury awarded £50 in damages.

Baxendale obtained a *rule nisi* for a new trial on the ground that Crompton J had misdirected the jury. The case was then argued in the Court of Exchequer on 1 and 2 February 1854 by eminent counsel, including Sir James Shaw Willes[76] for Baxendale. The resulting statement of principle in Alderson B's judgment[77] has probably been quoted more frequently in the common law world than any other authority. But there are two less frequently quoted observations that are of immediate interest. First, Alderson B did not doubt that the Hadleys' loss had been entirely caused by Baxendale's breach of contract: there was no suggestion that the Hadleys had failed to mitigate or that there was some other novus actus. As the learned judge put it, 'the only cause of the stoppage of the mill'[78] and of the Hadleys' lost profits was Baxendale's failure to deliver the broken crankshaft on time. But the Hadleys could not recover damages because this loss, although caused by the breach, would not

[67] Danzig (n 65) 251.

[68] 'It was proved that the shaft might have arrived … in the course of Monday, the 16th of May; but, instead of being forwarded by waggon immediately, it was kept for several days in London, and was at length forwarded by water on the 20th, *along with many tons of iron goods which had also been consigned to the same parties*' (emphasis added): *Hadley v Baxendale*, *The Times*, 8 August 1853, p 10, col 1, available at: www.thetimes.co.uk/tto/archive/page/1853-08-08/10.html.

[69] Whether this should make any difference to remoteness is discussed at the text to n 114.

[70] *Hadley* (n 9) 345.

[71] *Hadley*, *The Times* (n 68).

[72] *Hadley v Baxendale*, *The Gloucester Journal*, Supplement, 13 August 1853, p 1, col 3, available via: www.britishnewspaperarchive.co.uk (last visited 5 December 2015).

[73] ibid.

[74] ibid *Hadley*, *Gloucester Journal* (n 72).

[75] Which, to repeat, does not mean merely 'but-for': see text to n 45.

[76] He was called to the Bar in 1840 and is reported to have been described by no less an authority than Sir Thomas Scrutton as the 'best commercial lawyer since Lord Mansfield': Danzig (n 65) fn 38. Willes J (as he had by then become) adopted an agreement-centred approach to remoteness in *The British Columbia and Vancouver's Island Spar, Lumber, and Saw-Mill Co Ltd v Nettleship* (1867–68) LR 3 CP 499. This version of the agreement-centred approach is not supported in this chapter: see further, below.

[77] *Hadley* (n 9) 355.

[78] ibid 356.

have arisen in the 'great multitude of cases'[79] and was therefore not within the reasonable contemplation of the defendant.

Second, Alderson B did not cite any English authority[80] for the proposition that there was some legal rule apart from causation by which the defendant's liability for breach of contract could be limited. But it is fairly clear from the interventions of the judges during the argument[81] that the rule was derived from the work of Theodore Sedgwick,[82] who in turn took it from the work of the French jurist, Pothier, whose views on this point were inspired by Molineaus and perhaps indirectly by Roman law.[83] Whatever the merits of this view, it was clearly not English law at the time the Court of Exchequer heard argument in the case. Its foundations have rarely been questioned since then only because the rule seems (to some, at any rate) to be obviously right. But it is easy precisely for that reason to overlook just how radical an innovation it was in 1854. Unsurprisingly, many contemporary judges, notably Wilde B[84] and Martin B,[85] expressed dissatisfaction with the reasoning in *Hadley v Baxendale* soon after it was decided: in 1862, the editors of *Smith's Leading Cases* described it as 'a merely arbitrary rule, laid down in our courts for the first time'.[86]

As the *fons et origo* of the remoteness rule—especially of the external rule version of it—*Hadley v Baxendale* would be an unsatisfactory authority for these reasons alone. But it is not even clear that it was a contract case. The Hadleys' declaration had two counts: the first pleaded a 'special contract' by which Baxendale undertook to deliver the crankshaft in two days; and the second pleaded his duty as a common carrier to deliver it within a reasonable time.[87] During the trial, counsel for the Hadleys abandoned the first count because of a concern that Perrett did not have authority[88] to vary Baxendale's ordinary liability.[89] So the case proceeded to the Court of Exchequer on the footing that it was concerned with the common carrier's ordinary liability: as Professor Ibbetson has observed, it thus 'fell in the awkward hinterland of tort and contract'.[90]

There is also a curious anomaly about a central factual finding in the case. A law student reading Alderson B's judgment for the first time would presumably (and no doubt correctly) take the whole point of the case to be that the defendant is not liable for a loss arising out of special circumstances unless he is told of the those circumstances: in other words, that the result would have been different if the Hadleys had

[79] ibid 355.

[80] See also Washington (n 64) 102; Danzig (n 65) 254–55.

[81] See esp Parke B's observations: *Hadley* (n 9) 347. See also Faust (n 55) 42–43.

[82] T Sedgwick, *A Treatise on the Measure of Damages*, 2nd edn (New York, JS Voorhies, 1852) 58–60. The first edition was cited in *Hadley* but the relevant section was substantially the same.

[83] For detailed discussion, see G Mulligan, 'Damages for Breach: Quantum, Remoteness and Causality' (1956) 73 *South African Law Journal* 27, 30–34; Barton (n 54) 41; R Zimmermann, 'Limitation of Liability for Damages in European Contract Law' (2014) 18 *Edinburgh Law Review* 193, 201–4 and Faust (n 55) 42–44.

[84] *Gee v Lancashire and Yorkshire Railway Co* (1860) 6 H&N 211; 158 ER 87, 91.

[85] *Collard v South Eastern Railway Co* (1861) 7 H&N 79; 158 ER 400, 403.

[86] F Maude and T Chitty, *Smith's Leading Cases*, 5th edn (London, William Maxwell, 1862) 473.

[87] For a more detailed explanation, see Faust (n 55) 46–49.

[88] The law of agency was at the time unclear on this point: see Danzig (n 65) 261, fn 50.

[89] *Hadley*, *The Times* (n 68).

[90] Ibbetson (n 54) 230.

said to Baxendale that their mill had stopped for want of a machine. But there was evidence that this is precisely what they did when they spoke to Perrett (Baxendale's clerk) on 13 May 1853, although Alderson B proceeded on the assumption that they did not.[91] Indeed, the headnote states that the Hadleys expressly told Perrett that the mill had stopped. In *Victoria Laundry*, Asquith LJ said that the headnote must be wrong[92] but this may be doubted.[93] For one thing, counsel for Baxendale argued in the Court of Exchequer that 'a mere notice to him, *such as was here given*, could not make the defendants, as carriers, liable as upon a special contract' (emphasis added):[94] this argument would presumably have been unnecessary if notice in fact had not been given. Nor did judges and scholars at the time understand *Hadley v Baxendale* in the way that Asquith LJ suggests. For example, the fourth edition of *Smith's Leading Cases*—edited by Sir James Shaw Willes and Sir Henry Singer Keating, counsel for Baxendale and the Hadleys, respectively—stated that the Hadleys had specifically mentioned that the mill had stopped because of the broken shaft.[95]

David Pugsley has advanced the ingenious explanation that the Hadleys did (as the headnote suggests) give notice but that this did not count because it was given on 13 rather than 14 May (ie, the day *before* the crankshaft was delivered to Baxendale rather than on that day).[96] This seems plausible, especially because notice to Perrett may not have been treated by the law of agency at the time as notice to Baxendale.[97] But it is by no means clear that this was the point that counsel was making when he referred in argument to the relevance of notice. Indeed, in a later case, Martin B (who was a member of the Court of Exchequer that decided *Hadley*) treated the notice given to Perrett as notice to Baxendale himself.[98] Similarly, Crompton J, the trial judge in the case, is reported to have said subsequently that he simply could not understand the decision of the Court of Exchequer:[99]

> [T]he curious part of that case is that there was a most distinct notification *to the carrier* of the consequences that would follow the non-delivery of the shaft, and yet the court held that those consequences could not be taken into consideration.

It may be that Professor Faust, whose analysis of the case is illuminating, perhaps goes too far in his criticism.[100] But this much is clear: the external rule theory rests,

[91] *Hadley* (n 9) 356.
[92] *Victoria Laundry (Windsor) Ltd v Newman Industries Ltd* [1949] 2 KB 528 (CA) 537.
[93] Based on an analysis of assize procedure, Professor Stebbings argues that the headnote is likely to be correct. It would, she points out, have been based on a statement of the facts prepared by Crompton J, of which the Exchequer judges would also have had a copy: see C Stebbings, *Law Reporting in Britain: Proceedings of the Eleventh British Legal History Conference* (London, Hambledon Press, 1995) 139–40.
[94] *Hadley* (n 9) 352.
[95] J Willes and H Keating, *Smith's Leading Cases*, 4th edn (London, William Maxwell, 1856) 430.
[96] D Pugsley, 'The Facts of Hadley v Baxendale' (1976) 126 *New Law Journal* 420, 421.
[97] See, further, F Dawson, 'Reflections on Certain Aspects of the Law of Damages for Breach of Contract' (1995) 9 *Journal of Contract Law* 125, 131–32.
[98] *Wilson v Newport Dock Co* (1866) LR 1 Ex 177, 183 ('[the defendants] were told that the mill was stopped in consequence of the shaft being broken').
[99] *Simons v Patchett* (1857) 7 E&B 568, 26 LJQB 195, 197. The Jurist report is slightly different: this records Crompton J as having said that Perrett was told only that the mill had stopped, not that it had stopped for want of a spare machine: see 1 Jur NS 358. But that is at odds with Alderson B's statement that the only fact communicated was that the claimants were millers. See further Pugsley (n 96) 420.
[100] Faust (n 55) 65.

at least as a matter of authority, almost entirely on the unsatisfactory reasoning in *Hadley v Baxendale*; there was little or no support for it before 1854 and virtually every authority since has taken Alderson B's analysis as the starting-point. The House of Lords in the *Achilleas* was clearly right to think that the time had come to revisit the foundations of the remoteness rule in the law of contract.

C. The External Rule Theory: The Authorities

The previous section has highlighted the murky origins of the reasonable contemplation rule in the common law. Leaving that to one side, it is not even clear that the rule was conceptualised as an external rule of policy. Although the justification for it was not explicitly considered at the time, there are some indications in *Hadley v Baxendale* itself, and certainly in subsequent authority, that it was just thought to be a presumption about what the parties intended.

(i) Pothier and the Rule in Flureau v Thornhill

As pointed out above, the rule in *Hadley v Baxendale* was derived not from prior English authority (which was to the contrary) but from the views of Sedgwick and Pothier,[101] to which Parke B referred with approval in the argument.[102] Pothier, it is true, did say that the defendant should be liable only for 'the damages and interest which might have been contemplated at the time of the contract'[103] but this was not because he thought there should be a 'default rule' imposed by law for policy reasons. It is not possible to consider his views in detail here, but in summary, Pothier distinguished between losses relating to the subject-matter of the contract[104] and extrinsic losses. He gave the example of the sale by an individual of some pieces of defective wood. The buyer uses the wood to prop up a building, which gives way. Pothier said that the seller would be liable for the difference between the value of sound wood and the value of the wood delivered but not for the loss of the building. This was because, in general, only a loss 'in respect to the particular thing which is the object'[105] of the contract (the wood itself, rather than the buyer's use of the wood) could have been within the defendant's contemplation. On the other hand, the loss of the building could also have been contemplated if the seller had been a trader 'acting in the course of his business'.[106] The important point, however, is that in both cases reasonable contemplation was thought to matter only because it

[101] R Pothier, *A Treatise on the Law of Obligations or Contracts*, 3rd American edn (Philadelphia PA, RH Small, 1853).

[102] *Hadley* (n 9) 347.

[103] Pothier (n 101) [159]–[161].

[104] *Damnum propter ipsam rem non habitam*: ibid (n 101) [160], [161].

[105] ibid [161].

[106] ibid [163]. See also the following examples: the sale of a horse ([161]), the lease of a house ([161]), the carpenter ([163]) and sale of wine ([165]).

is 'to such [loss] alone the debtor can be considered as having *intended to submit*' (emphasis added).[107] Whatever one's views about the merits of this analysis,[108] this undermines the theory that the remoteness rule adopted in *Hadley v Baxendale* was thought to be a free-standing rule of policy: it is unlikely that the counsel who cited or the judges who adopted Pothier's view were unaware of the reason he gave for it.

Second, Alderson B's treatment of the rule in *Flureau v Thornhill*[109] also suggests that—consistently with Pothier's views—he conceived of reasonable contemplation as an agreement-centred rule. In *Flureau*, which was decided in 1776, De Grey CJ held that a vendor of land who is in breach of contract in failing to make title is, in general, liable to pay damages only for the buyer's wasted expenses and not for the loss of his bargain. This was, of course, what became the rule in *Bain v Fothergill*[110] before it was eventually abolished in 1989. It gave rise to a large body of case law in between, which it is not necessary to discuss. The point only matters here because Alderson B seems to have thought that the existence of the rule could be said to be inconsistent with the general principle of remoteness that he adopted. He sought to address the perceived inconsistency in this way:[111]

> But as, in such cases, both parties must be supposed to be cognisant of that well-known rule, these cases may, we think, be more properly classed under the rule above enunciated as to cases under known special circumstances, because there both parties may reasonably be presumed to contemplate the estimation of the amount of damages according to the conventional rule.

In this passage, Alderson B appears to be saying that a special rule about damages for a certain kind of contract can be rationalised by treating the rule itself as the basis on which the parties entered into the contract in a particular case. It would have been unnecessary for Alderson B to re-analyse *Flureau v Thornhill* in terms of the intentions of the parties if he had thought that the remoteness rule that he articulated was itself a rule of policy.

For these reasons, it is doubtful whether the statement of principle formulated in *Hadley v Baxendale* was ever thought to be an external rule of law concerned with fairness or policy: on the contrary, Alderson B seems to have treated it as a presumption about what the parties intended.[112] This is also consistent with at least three doctrinal rules that have emerged subsequently.

[107] ibid [160]. See, too, [161]–[162]: '[extrinsic loss] is a damage which … was not contemplated at the time of the contract, and to which it cannot be supposed that I had any intention to submit … [but] the debtor is liable for [extrinsic] damages and interests … when it appears that … the debtor submitted to them either expressly or tacitly'.

[108] It is worth noting that the justification given by Pothier seems to require an *assumption* rather than *exclusion* of liability, but the latter approach is preferable: see further, Section IV.

[109] *Flureau v Thornhill* (1776) 2 Blackstone W 1078; 96 ER 635.

[110] *Bain v Fothergill* (1874) LR 7 HL 158.

[111] *Hadley* (n 9) 355.

[112] See also, for contemporary academic accounts that treated it as an agreement-centred rule, *Smith's Leading Cases* (n 86) 432 and W Eggleston, *Eggleston on Damages* (Terre Haute IND, Hebb & Goodwin, 1880) 11.

(ii) The Nature of the Breach is Irrelevant

In the law of tort, it is clear law that remoteness rules, unlike causal rules, are influenced by the defendant's culpability: for instance, damages can be recovered for unforeseeable loss in a claim for deceit but not in a claim for negligent misrepresentation.[113] A question that has received little attention in the literature[114] is whether the contract remoteness rule is similarly influenced by the culpability of the defendant in a particular case. Although there is no clear authority on the point, the better view is that it is not.

The question indirectly arose in *Hadley v Baxendale* itself. As the previous section explained, the reason for the delay in delivering the broken shaft was Baxendale's decision (for his own benefit) to send it by water rather than rail. Counsel for the Hadley brothers seems to have argued in the trial that this was a factor that should be taken into account in the assessment of damages. Crompton J, however, told the jury that: 'To that they should not attend. They had not to consider whether the neglect was wilful or accidental, they should give their damages for the natural consequences of the defendant's breach of contract'.[115]

This direction was not criticised by the Court of Exchequer. Indeed, the distinction between fraudulent or culpable[116] and ordinary breaches of contract was central to Pothier's theory[117] but does not feature in Alderson B's statement of principle.[118] The third edition of *Mayne on Damages* also expressed the view the circumstances of the breach could not 'either increase or diminish the amount of the recovery'.[119] The point was left open in *Smith v Green*[120] and does not appear to have been considered in any English authority until the *Heron II*.[121] In that case, the reason for the delay in delivery was, as in *Hadley v Baxendale*, a decision by the carrier made for its own benefit, although it was the fact of the deviation rather than the reason for it that constituted the breach of contract. It has been suggested[122] that the case might have been decided differently if the breach had not been deliberate in this way. It is doubtful whether this is correct. With the exception of Salmon LJ in the Court of Appeal, none of the judges attached any importance to the reason for the breach and

[113] *Smith New Court Securities Ltd v Citibank NA* [1997] AC 254 (HL) 284–86 (Lord Steyn).

[114] See, however, Samek (n 51); Andrew Robertson, 'The Basis of the Remoteness Rule in Contract' (2008) 28 *Legal Studies* 172, 192–93 and Kramer (n 4).

[115] *Hadley*, *Gloucester Journal* (n 72).

[116] The terminology is inexact because the breach need not, and indeed usually does not, involve any deception. 'Fraudulent' or 'culpable' is used in this section only to signal that the breach was in some way out of the ordinary: this is usually because the defendant intended to cause loss or 'cynically' saw the breach as an opportunity for some gain: for further analysis, see Pothier (n 101); Danzig (n 65) and Samek (n 51) (who uses the expression 'gross fault').

[117] Pothier (n 101) [166]–[168].

[118] Although Parke B referred to it (seemingly with approval) in argument: *Hadley* (n 9) 347.

[119] J Mayne, L Smith and H Wood, *Wood's Mayne on Damages*, 3rd edn (Albany NY, JD Parsons Jr, 1880) 52–53.

[120] *Smith v Green* (1875) 1 CPD 92 (DC). See also *Nettleship* (n 76) 508 (Willes J).

[121] *The Heron II* (n 8).

[122] D McLauchlan, 'Remoteness Re-Invented?' (2009) 9 *Oxford University Commonwealth Law Journal* 109, 130, fn 146.

even Salmon LJ only thought that the fact that the breach was deliberate was added justification for requiring the defendant to pay damages for *foreseeable* loss.[123]

The law therefore appears to be that the nature of the breach makes no difference to remoteness. It is tempting to justify this on the basis that culpability is not, unlike in deceit, an element of the claimant's cause of action: as some commentators have said, since liability for breach of contract is not (generally) based on fault,[124] the amount of damages to which the claimant is entitled should not depend on it either. But this is, with respect, a non sequitur: remoteness (whether agreement-centred or external) is an answer or defence to what is in any case a complete cause of action. To put the point another way, a claimant who relies on the defendant's culpability at the remoteness stage has, ex hypothesi, shown (without taking culpability into account) that there was a loss which was caused by a breach of contract. The relevance of culpability at the remoteness stage cannot, therefore, be ruled out on conceptual grounds: it must depend on the rationale for the remoteness rule.

If remoteness is a 'rule of policy designed to ensure that the award of damages … does not impose an unreasonable burden of liability on a defendant',[125] it is difficult to explain why culpability is *always* ignored. Consider a modification of an example given by Professor Gordley.[126] D, the owner of a warehouse, agrees to store C's goods in the warehouse and to take all reasonable precautions against any damage by fire. C's goods include a rare Constable painting. This was entirely unforeseeable. Ten days later, a fire breaks out. D deliberately chooses not to call the fire service because he wants to collect insurance money once the warehouse is reduced to rubble. If remoteness is a policy rule, it is hard to see why C should not recover damages for the loss of the Constable, even though it was unforeseeable. There can, after all, be no doubt that it was caused by the breach of contract (there was no failure to mitigate or any other novus actus); and the fact that D's reason for committing the breach is not part of C's cause of action is, for this purpose, neither here nor there. As Professor Samek, who favoured the external rule theory, put it:[127]

> Any limitation of the responsibility of the party in default is a matter of policy (of what is reasonable, of what is just, of what is commercially desirable), and a party who wilfully breaks his contract … is surely less entitled to protection than a party who breaks his contract accidentally or negligently.

On the other hand, if the common law's remoteness rule is agreement-centred, it is not surprising that the nature of the breach—no matter how culpable or wrongful—is generally irrelevant: the circumstances of a future breach are unlikely, as a matter of construction, to have featured in any implied agreement that the parties made about the scope of the defendant's liability. In principle, of course, the parties can agree at the time of the contract that there is no exclusion of liability (or 'assumption of

[123] *C Czarnikow Ltd v Koufos ('The Heron II')* [1966] 2 QB 695 (CA) 739.

[124] For discussion, see G Treitel, 'Fault in the Common Law of Contract' in M Bos and I Brownlie (eds), *Liber Amicorum for Lord Wilberforce* (Oxford, Clarendon Press, 1987).

[125] Burrows (n 6) 262, fn 47.

[126] J Gordley, *Foundations of Private Law: Property, Tort, Contract, Unjust Enrichment* (Oxford, Oxford University Press, 2006) 415.

[127] Samek (n 51) 126–27.

responsibility')[128] even for a loss not within the defendant's reasonable contemplation, if the breach was fraudulent or wrongful. But the problem is that as a matter of construction it will often be impossible to define at the time of the contract precisely what makes a breach fraudulent or culpable in this way. It is the type of loss,[129] rather than the circumstances of a future breach, that is more likely to have influenced any implied agreement that the parties made about the scope of the defendant's liability.

In short, if there is a policy-based remoteness rule in the law of contract designed out of fairness to the defendant, one would expect it to take the circumstances of the breach into account. The fact that the common law does not do so suggests that it does not recognise any free-standing policy jurisdiction to limit the defendant's liability for breach of contract. It is then a matter of construction in each case whether the implied agreement that the defendant was not to be liable for a loss not within his reasonable contemplation distinguished between culpable and ordinary breaches.[130]

(iii) The Degree of Likelihood and Other Rules

Many of the classic remoteness authorities—notably *Victoria Laundry*,[131] *Parsons*[132] and the *Heron II*[133]—have largely been concerned with the correct formulation of the degree of likelihood in the remoteness test. Is the test 'not unlikely', 'probable', 'on the cards', 'serious possibility', 'liable to result' or one of the many other possibilities canvassed in the *Heron II*? The answer must depend on the rationale for the remoteness rule: one cannot decide how likely a loss should be without knowing why a loss should be likely in the first place.[134] If remoteness is an external rule of law of policy, it is difficult to see how *any* choice can be made. One can, no doubt, say that the test actually adopted by Lord Reid—'not unlikely'—is in general a fair or just solution, but there is nothing about the supposed rationale for the rule that points to this test rather than to some other test (for instance, 'on the cards' or 'liable to result').[135] On the agreement-centred approach, on the other hand, there is no bright-line rule: 'not unlikely' is merely a starting-point for ascertaining the intentions of the parties and can be displaced by a variety of factors, such as the salience

128 On the choice between these versions of the agreement-centred approach, see Section IV.

129 And other factors ascertainable at the time of the contract, such as pricing, insurance etc: see text to n 136.

130 As, perhaps, it might have done if the term could *only* have been breached in that way, eg, the implied term of honesty formulated by Leggatt J in *Yam Seng Pte Ltd v International Trade Corp Ltd* [2013] EWHC 111 (QB); [2013] 1 All ER (Comm) 1321 [135]. Another exception may be an act which constitutes a breach of contract and concurrently an intentional tort: this was the question left open in *Smith v Green* (n 120).

131 *Victoria Laundry* (n 92).

132 *Parsons* (n 25).

133 *The Heron II* (n 8).

134 J Cartwright, 'Remoteness of Damage in Contract and Tort: A Reconsideration' (1996) 55 *CLJ* 488, 493.

135 In truth, Lord Reid's test was itself derived not from an analysis of the principle underlying remoteness but from Alderson B's observation that the loss must arise in 'the great multitude of cases'. This was (rightly) taken to mean that a mere possibility of loss is not sufficient.

of the loss, the availability of insurance, the nature of the contract, pricing, any market understanding and so on.[136]

Similarly, if the remoteness rule is a free-standing rule of policy or fairness, it is difficult to see why knowledge acquired after the date of conclusion of the contract is ignored. As a matter of authority, it is clear that this is almost always ignored:[137] the necessary degree of probability is tested as at the date of contract. The conventional explanation for this is that the defendant may have chosen not to enter into the contract, or only on different terms, if these risks had been made known to him at the time. But this just seems to highlight that one is in essence concerned with (objectively) interpreting the agreement, notwithstanding the language of risk allocation or fairness.

Commentators who favour the external rule theory have tried to address some of these criticisms. The most comprehensive treatment is to be found in Professor Burrows' recent paper. He proposes two qualifications to Alderson B's test which would explain both the inclusionary (eg *Supershield*) and exclusionary (eg taxi-driver/barrister) effects of the *Achilleas*. The first qualification ('Category 1') seems correct, though it can be accommodated on the agreement-centred approach as well. The second qualification ('Category 2') would apply if, in Professor Burrows' words,[138]

> the type of loss is so exceptional in relation to the standard purpose of the duty that the only reason why it was reasonably contemplated as a serious possibility by the defendant at the time of the contract is that the claimant informed the defendant of the special risk.

In Category 2, reasonable contemplation is not sufficient and the court, it is said, should take further factors into account in 'deciding on a fair and reasonable allocation of the risk',[139] such as disproportionality and insurance.

The difficulty with this analysis is that Category 2 appears to contain a 'gateway': it sanctions a departure from Alderson B's test only if notice was the only reason the defendant could have contemplated the (otherwise exceptional) loss as a serious possibility. So it is not clear whether Professor Burrows' model can accommodate cases where the loss is *not* exceptional but the parties nevertheless contracted in the light of a market understanding (whether correct or wrong) that the defendant is not liable for it. It is true, as he points out, that the House of Lords in the *Heron II* made no reference to any market understanding derived from the *Parana*,[140] but the explanation for this may be that the shipowners did not take the point. At first instance, McNair J had found[141] that any contract in the shipping market in October 1960 would have been made on the basis that the shipowner would be liable only for interest on the value of the goods for the period of delay. In the Court of Appeal, Diplock LJ, who decided in favour of the charterers, said that this was 'the

[136] See text to 139.
[137] For discussion, see A Kramer, 'Remoteness: New Problems with the Old Test' in D Saidov and R Cunnington (eds), *Contract Damages: Domestic and International Perspectives* (Oxford, Hart Publishing, 2008) 298–302.
[138] Burrows (n 6) 262.
[139] ibid 262.
[140] *The Parana* (1877) 2 PD 118 (CA).
[141] *C Czarnikow Ltd v Koufos* [1966] 1 Lloyd's Rep 259 (QB) 274.

only consideration which [had] really given me pause'[142] and rejected it only because '[s]uch a case was not, however, sought to be made by the shipowner, nor was there any evidence to sustain it'. It seems, therefore, that he would have decided the case differently if the shipowners had adduced evidence that the *Parana* formed part of the basis on which contracts were made in the shipping market. But Category 2, since it seems to contain a gateway, cannot accommodate a case of this kind: lost profit is not exceptional and it may or may not be disproportionate.

For these reasons, it is submitted that the theory that remoteness is an external rule of policy designed out of fairness to the defendant simply cannot explain the authorities. The agreement-centred approach can do so, provided it is formulated in terms of an exclusion rather than assumption of responsibility. These points are considered below.

IV. IMPLIED EXCLUSION OR IMPLIED ASSUMPTION?

The agreement-centred approach to remoteness has been subjected to searching criticism by commentators, especially after the *Achilleas* was decided. Two themes stand out. The first is that it wrongly assumes that there is no obligation to pay damages for breach of contract in the absence of an undertaking by the defendant to do so. The second is the well-known objection that it is fictional to talk of what the parties intend in relation to the consequences of breach. This section accepts that the first objection is well-founded, but suggests that the correct analysis is not that remoteness is thereby best understood as an external rule of law, but rather that the (imposed) obligation to pay damages is impliedly *excluded* by agreement in certain circumstances. It does not deal with the second objection in detail but suggests that it is misconceived, notwithstanding the important recent decision of the Supreme Court in *Marks and Spencer*.[143]

At the outset, one must ask precisely what it means to say that the defendant did not assume responsibility for a loss of a certain kind. Three different answers have been given. The first is that there is simply no obligation to pay damages for breach of contract in the absence of an undertaking by the defendant to do so. This may be described as the '*Nettleship* thesis'. The second is that the obligation to pay damages is imposed by law but that it is 'shaped' by an 'internal allocation of responsibility' or by the 'purpose' of the contractual obligation in question. This may be described as the 'assimilation thesis'. The third is that the obligation to pay damages is imposed by law but excluded by a term implied in fact. This may be described as the 'implied exclusion' thesis.

[142] *The Heron II* (CA) (n 123) 736. See also Salmon LJ at 744.

[143] *Marks and Spencer plc v BNP Paribas Securities Trust Co (Jersey) Ltd* [2015] UKSC 72; [2015] 3 WLR 1843.

A. The *Nettleship* Thesis

There is considerable support for the *Nettleship* thesis. It was adopted, as the name suggests, by Willes J in that case,[144] consistently with Pothier's views. It was also favoured by what was perhaps the leading judicial exposition of the agreement-centred approach before the *Achilleas*: Diplock LJ's judgment in the Court of Appeal in the *Heron II*.[145] Lord Hoffmann himself appears to have endorsed it, certainly extra-judicially[146] and perhaps also in the *Achilleas*,[147] though it should be said that his Lordship was not concerned in these passages with the distinction between an implied exclusion of responsibility and an implied assumption of responsibility.

The *Nettleship* thesis is wrong. It can be tested by supposing that C and D enter into a contract which provides that D will pay no more than £1m as damages for the breach of a certain clause. Assume that this limitation clause is found to be unenforceable under some common law rule or a statutory provision (eg formality or unfair terms). It does not follow that D is now free to break his contract without consequence: his liability would instead depend upon the ordinary common law rule that damages are payable for any loss that is caused by a breach of contract. The correct analysis is, therefore, that the obligation to pay damages does not depend upon any undertaking by the defendant (which, where it exists, is sufficient but not necessary): it is imposed by law. As explained above, it is imposed by law arguably because it does no more than require the defendant to do what he already has reason to do: conform to the reasons underlying the original obligation.[148] Most scholars who favour the agreement-centred approach have now rightly conceded that this version of it is unsustainable.[149]

B. The Assimilation Thesis

This is the most popular version of the agreement-centred theory.[150] It accepts that the obligation to pay damages is imposed by law but claims that it merely gives effect to an 'internal allocation of responsibility'. Importantly, this 'internal allocation' is not said to be an implied term; rather, the primary obligation has a certain 'orientation' (largely) because of its 'purpose'. This approach relies heavily on (what is said to be) an analogous principle established in the *SAAMCO* case.[151] In *SAAMCO*[152] the House of Lords decided that a negligent valuer is not liable for

[144] *Nettleship* (n 76).

[145] *The Heron II* (CA) (n 123) 730–33.

[146] Lord Hoffmann, 'The Achilleas: Custom and Practice or Foreseeability?' (2010) 14 *Edinburgh Law Review* 47, 55.

[147] *The Achilleas* (n 3) [12].

[148] See also Gardner (n 41) 39: 'it is not thanks to the interpretation of the agreement that we are bound to do the next-best thing. Rather, it is because we are anyway bound to do the next-best thing, according to the continuity thesis, that we need to interpret the agreement to find out what that next-best thing is'.

[149] See, eg, Kramer (n 4).

[150] See, eg, ibid; A Tettenborn, 'Hadley v Baxendale Foreseeability: A Principle Beyond Its Sell-by Date?' (2007) 23 *Journal of Contract Law* 120.

[151] *South Australia Asset Management Corp v York Montague Ltd* [1997] AC 191 (HL).

[152] The valuer owed the lender concurrent duties in contract and tort.

a loss which would have been incurred by the lender even if the valuation given had been accurate. Lord Hoffmann said that this was because such a loss was beyond the scope of the valuer's duty.[153] This language of scope of duty—and the fact that Lord Hoffmann cited *SAAMCO* in his speech in the *Achilleas*[154]—has led many commentators to conclude that the two principles are in essence the same.[155] For example, Lord Hoffmann, writing extra-judicially, said that the 'causal relationship with the contractual objective'[156] can both expand and limit liability, and cited *SAAMCO* as an example of the latter. Similarly, Professor Burrows, who is critical of both *SAAMCO* and the *Achilleas*, nevertheless prefers to assimilate the two rules.[157]

The *SAAMCO* principle has given rise to a large body of case law and its proper interpretation remains a matter of dispute.[158] In particular, the assumption that it is a case about the purpose of the duty may be wrong. But it is unnecessary to analyse these cases here because it is possible to demonstrate in a simpler way that the purpose of the contractual obligation cannot explain the current law on remoteness.

First, the assimilation thesis can explain why liability is sometimes imposed for an unforeseeable loss (the so-called 'inclusionary cases') but not why liability is sometimes *not* imposed for foreseeable loss (the so-called 'exclusionary cases'). For example, in the hypothetical case discussed by Lord Pearce in the *Heron II*,[159] it is meaningful to say that the purpose of the contractor's duty (to ensure that there is a safe ceiling) is the reason why he is liable for a loss (the collapse of the ceiling on someone) even though it was unlikely or unforeseeable.[160] But the purpose of the duty (as distinguished from an implied exclusion of liability for its breach) cannot explain the authorities in which the defendant has *not* been held liable for foreseeable loss:[161] indeed, Professor Tettenborn ultimately accepts that his *SAAMCO*-based 'instrumental promises' theory of contract remoteness leads to the conclusion that *Hadley v Baxendale* is itself wrongly decided on its facts.[162]

Second, the assimilation thesis cannot accommodate a sub-rule, commonly called the '*Cory* cap', that has emerged in the contract remoteness cases.[163] In summary,

[153] That is, the claimant's loss must be a consequence of the making of the false statement *and* of the falsity of the statement.

[154] *Achilleas* (n 3) [14]–[17].

[155] See, eg, Tettenborn (n 150) 137.

[156] Lord Hoffmann (n 146) 58.

[157] A Burrows, 'Comparing Compensatory Damages in Tort and Contract: Some Problematic Issues' in S Degeling, J Edelman and J Goudkamp (eds), *Torts in Commercial Law* (Pyrmont NSW, Thomson Reuters, 2011) 374.

[158] See, recently, *Astle v CBRE Ltd* [2015] EWHC 3189 (Ch); [2016] PNLR 16 [51]–[94] (Trower QC).

[159] *The Heron II* (n 8) 417.

[160] See also *Supershield* (n 7).

[161] The purpose of a duty should be distinguished from the act or omission specified by the duty. The subject-matter of the promise is the latter, not the former. If it (ie act/omission) is not done, the defendant is under an obligation to do the next-best thing (which the purpose may help identify) without having to make any fresh promise. Assume that C and D contract in the light of a market understanding that D is not liable for some foreseeable lost profit which C would normally earn if D does not break the duty. This does not mean that allowing C to earn that profit was not one of the purposes of D's duty: it means that it is considered too remote even though it was.

[162] Tettenborn (n 150).

[163] This point was first made in M Stiggelbout, 'Contractual Remoteness, "Scope of Duty" and Intention' [2012] *Lloyd's Maritime and Commercial Law Quarterly* 97, 99–102. But his conclusion that

what *Cory* decides is that the claimant can recover damages for an unforeseeable loss to the extent to which loss of a different type was foreseeable, though that loss was not in fact incurred.[164] An example of it is the award of the 'conjectural sum' in *Victoria Laundry*: this cut out the Ministry of Supply contract because it was unforeseeably lucrative, but allowed the claimants to recover for 'loss of business in respect of [other] dyeing contracts to be reasonably expected',[165] though they had not entered into any. So it is correct to describe the *Cory* rule as a 'cap'[166] on damages but the important point is that it is a *monetary* cap: it limits damages by reference to the *value* of the non-remote loss, though the claimant never incurred it. The *nature* of the remote opportunity that was actually lost is irrelevant: all that the loss of such an opportunity proves is that there was *some* loss.

If the *SAAMCO* principle is indistinguishable from the principle in the *Achilleas*, one would expect to find a similar cap in operation in the *SAAMCO* cases. Indeed, Adam Kramer has argued that the fact that the lender was able to recover losses not exceeding the overvaluation shows that there is such a cap.[167] However, this may be doubted. As Briggs J has noted in a different context, the appearance of a cap in the *SAAMCO* cases is purely accidental.[168] What looks like a cap is actually an attempt to identify those consequences of the making of a false statement that are also consequences of the falsity of the statement. Where, as in many *SAAMCO* cases,[169] *none* of the loss is a consequence of the falsity of the statement, the claimant is awarded nothing, not a notional sum equal to the loss that, if it had occurred, *would* have been a consequence of the falsity of the statement.

In *Wellesley v Withers*[170] the Court of Appeal has recently recognised that the *Achilleas* and *SAAMCO* are distinct limitations. Wellesley was a headhunting firm that specialised in the investment banking sector. In 2008, it decided to admit a new partner, Addax, into the partnership. Addax was required to make a capital contribution. Wellesley instructed Withers to include a clause in the partnership agreement giving Addax the right to withdraw this capital only *after* 42 months but Withers, negligently and in breach of contract, drafted a clause that said that Addax could withdraw the capital at any time *during* the first 41 months following the date of the agreement. Addax exercised this option in the first 41 months. Wellesley's case was that the funds used to pay Addax had been earmarked for opening a new office in New York; and that it would have a secured a lucrative contract from Nomura to provide headhunting services if this office had been opened.

the *Achilleas* does assimilate *SAAMCO* in relation to contract remoteness seems to overlook the distinction between the extension and the limitation of liability.

164 *Cory v Thames Ironworks and Shipbuilding Co Ltd* (1868) LR 3 QB 181, 190 (Cockburn CJ) 191 (Blackburn J).

165 *Victoria Laundry* (n 92) 543 (Asquith LJ).

166 Kramer (n 4) 312.

167 ibid 312–13.

168 *Bank of Tokyo-Mitsubishi UFJ Ltd v Baskan Gida Sanayi Ve Pazarlama AS* [2009] EWHC 1276 (Ch); [2010] Bus LR D1 [1009].

169 See, eg, *Haugesund Kommune v Depfa ACS Bank (No 2)* [2011] EWCA Civ 33; [2012] Bus LR 230.

170 *Wellesley* (n 4).

The remoteness issue arose because of a factual finding by Nugee J at first instance that the loss of the Nomura mandate was reasonably foreseeable as a slight possibility (the tort test) but not as a 'not unlikely' consequence of breach (the contract test). Withers' argument in favour of the contract test consisted of three steps: (i) *SAAMCO* shows that the scope of duty of the defendant is the same in tort and contract if there are concurrent duties; (ii) the *Achilleas* shows that *SAAMCO* was a case about contract remoteness; and (iii) therefore the degree of likelihood that the claimant must meet in a concurrent duty case should depend on the contract rather than the tort remoteness test. Nugee J would have accepted this argument in its entirety if it had been open to him to do so,[171] but the Court of Appeal adopted a somewhat different approach. All three members of that Court agreed that the degree of likelihood is governed by the contract test ('not unlikely') but they did not think that *SAAMCO* and the *Achilleas* embody the same principle.[172] Indeed, Floyd LJ rightly pointed out that Wellesley's claim satisfied the *SAAMCO* principle only because the Nomura loss was a consequence of the unavailability of the money used to pay Addax,[173] and considered *separately* how 'likely' this loss had to be for the purposes of contract remoteness.

In short, the purpose of a contractual obligation does not explain why liability is not imposed for foreseeable losses that were caused by the breach of contract. The agreement-centred approach has been justifiably criticised insofar as it accepts, on the one hand, that the obligation to pay damages is imposed by law, but maintains, on the other, that the consent of the parties can exclude this imposed obligation *without becoming a term* of the contract.

C. The Implied Exclusion Thesis

For these reasons, the agreement-centred approach is coherent in principle only if the claim is that the imposed obligation to pay damages is excluded by a term implied in fact. Indeed, in 2004, Adam Kramer said that his theory was 'closely analogous to the implication *in fact* of exclusion clauses',[174] though he has subsequently adopted a seemingly different approach.[175]

The implied exclusion thesis differs in two important respects from the other versions of the agreement-centred approach. First, it only ever purports to *limit* liability. Second, it is not analogous[176] to the agreement-centred approach adopted in

[171] *Wellesley Partners LLP v Withers LLP* [2014] EWHC 556 (Ch); [2014] PNLR 22 [212]–[214].

[172] *Wellesley* (n 4) [74] (Floyd LJ, obiter).

[173] 'This is not a case like *SAAMCO* where some of the damage arose from factors which had nothing to do with the incorrectness of information'.: *Wellesley* (n 4) [81].

[174] Kramer (n 40) fn 10. See also PCK Wee, 'Contractual Interpretation and Remoteness' [2010] *Lloyd's Maritime & Commercial Law Quarterly* 150.

[175] A Kramer, 'The New Test of Remoteness in Contract' (2009) 125 *LQR* 408, 411 ('it is not argued … that there is an implied in fact … exclusion clause. Rather the new approach to remoteness is to discern, through construction, what the unspoken shape and orientation of the particular obligation was').

[176] cf Burrows (n 6) 265: '[i]t is submitted that there is no question of treating remoteness as resting on an implied term of fact … this would take us back to the rejected *Nettleship* and *Horne* approach'. See *Horne v Midland Railway Co* (1873) LR 6 CP 131.

Nettleship and *Horne* because those cases take the obligation to pay damages to *arise from* the defendant's implied undertaking. In contrast, the implied exclusion thesis accepts that the obligation is imposed by law but claims that it is excluded as a matter of (objective) construction in relation to certain kinds of loss. Foreseeability is no more than a starting point in this process of construction: the parties are not normally likely to have intended that the defendant should pay damages for a loss that was beyond his reasonable contemplation when they made the contract. It follows from these points that there are no 'inclusionary' cases at all: in Lord Pearce's example, the presumption that the defendant would objectively be taken to have excluded liability for a loss not within his reasonable contemplation is displaced by the fact that avoiding this loss was the very purpose of the contractual term in question. This does not mean that there is now an *assumption* of responsibility in relation to that loss (or at least none is necessary): it is just that there is no implied exclusion of the ordinary common law obligation to pay damages for a loss caused by a breach of contract (ie without the intervention of abnormal events or voluntary acts).

There is some support for this analysis. In *Gubbins*,[177] a consulting engineer was in breach of a term that required him to submit a plan to the local Council by March 2007. This caused a delay in the development of the claimant's project which meant that it was marketed after rather than before the financial crisis. The value of the development had declined substantially during this period. In finding that this was not too remote, Sir David Keene explained the principle adopted in the *Achilleas* in this way:[178]

> If there is no express term dealing with what types of losses a party is accepting potential liability for if he breaks the contract, then the law in effect implies a term to determine the answer. Normally, there is an implied term accepting responsibility[179] for the types of losses which can reasonably be foreseen at the time of contract to be not unlikely to result if the contract is broken.

Sir David there uses the expression '*the law* ... implies a term' but it is clear from the context that the reference is to terms implied in fact, for the next sentence points out that the term is to be implied if there is evidence *in the particular case* about the nature of the contract or the commercial background that suggests that the defendant, objectively, excluded responsibility for losses of a certain kind (emphasis added).

The principal objection to this analysis is well-known: that it is fictional to say that there is an implied agreement about the consequences of breach. It is true that intention has more explanatory work to do in relation to remoteness than, for instance, in relation to the doctrines of common mistake and frustration.[180] But the

[177] *John Grimes Partnership Ltd v Gubbins* [2013] EWCA Civ 37; [2013] PNLR 17.
[178] ibid [24].
[179] It is preferable to say 'not accepting responsibility for unforeseeable losses' rather than 'accepting responsibility for foreseeable losses'.
[180] These doctrines are also best understood as concerned with the interpretation of the agreement, but one does not need any implied term: see, in particular, R Stevens, 'Objectivity, Mistake and the Parol Evidence Rule' in A Burrows and E Peel (eds), *Contract Terms* (Oxford, Oxford University Press, 2007).

view preferred here, as others have explained at length,[181] is that this objection is nevertheless misconceived. It is not in harmony with the modern approach to the construction of contracts and (until recently) the implication of terms.

The elephant in the room—since this chapter has argued that the agreement-centred approach cannot stop short of saying that there is an implied term—is, of course, the recent decision in *Marks and Spencer*. The implied exclusion theory of remoteness normally takes as its starting-point[182] the approach to implication that was adopted by a unanimous Privy Council in *Belize*.[183] Lord Hoffmann, who gave the advice of the Board, said that the conventional tests of implication (necessity and 'officious bystander') should not be treated as independent tests which had to be satisfied before a term could be implied. However, in *Marks and Spencer*, Lord Neuberger, with whom Lord Sumption and Lord Hodge agreed, held that *Belize* has not altered the conventional tests in any way and indeed that it should no longer be treated as authoritative guidance on the subject.

It is accepted that an implied term about remoteness is unlikely to satisfy the traditional tests of necessity or officious bystander. But it is respectfully suggested that *Marks and Spencer* is not likely to be (and one hopes will not be) the last word on implication. This is not a chapter about the proper approach to construction or implication, but two points can be briefly made. First, it is notable that the Supreme Court does not question the modern approach to *construction*, which indeed it has reaffirmed more than once. The hallmark of that approach is that there is no conceptual difference between the interpretation of utterances in ordinary life and legal interpretation.[184] It is not clear from paragraph 23 of Lord Neuberger's judgment whether he would assimilate implication in the law and in ordinary life in the same way. The second proviso in that passage suggests that he would not, for it is said the reasonable man should not only have understood the proposed implied term to exist, but should have thought that 'it went without saying' or that it was 'necessary for the business efficacy' of the contract. These additional requirements can only be legal rules, for in ordinary life one either takes an utterance to bear a certain meaning, or not,[185] whether it is drawn substantially from the utterance itself or from the background. The question then arises: why in principle do these additional legal rules exist? Although Lord Neuberger says elsewhere that they represent a 'clear, consistent and principled approach' to the question of implication, it is not obvious from the judgment quite what that principle was thought to be, especially if implication (in fact) is concerned with the intentions of the parties. Second, Lord Neuberger accepts that the test, even on his approach, is not one of 'absolute necessity' and appears to favour Lord Sumption's formulation: 'a term can only be implied if, without the term, the contract would lack commercial or practical coherence'.

[181] See, in particular, A Kramer, 'Implication in Fact as an Instance of Contractual Interpretation' (2004) 63 *CLJ* 384 and Lord Hoffmann, 'The Intolerable Wrestle with Words and Meanings' (1997) 114 *South African Law Journal* 656, 662.

[182] See, eg, Wee (n 174) 164. *Marks and Spencer* (n 143).

[183] *Attorney-General of Belize v Belize Telecom Ltd* [2009] 1 WLR 1988 (PC).

[184] There are, of course, legal rules about the range of *material* that the judge can use but not about what the judge can do with that material.

[185] See Lord Hoffmann (n 181).

The language of 'commercial coherence' leaves open the possibility that clear evidence of (for instance) a long-standing market understanding can still justify the implication of a term about remoteness.

V. CONCLUSION

It is clear from the recent authorities that the principle formulated in the *Achilleas* does not normally lead to any different result.[186] As Lord Hoffmann has pointed out, this is because the reasonable contemplation rule is taken to be the starting-point of the construction exercise for the purposes of remoteness. It may therefore be wondered why the case has generated so much interest and controversy. The explanation is probably that the conceptual foundations of the common law's remoteness rules in both contract and tort are yet to be fully understood. This chapter has argued that this is partly because of the failure to distinguish between causal and non-causal rules and, consequently, to identify when a question of remoteness actually arises. That distinction also helps to illustrate that the principle that explains why there is an obligation to pay damages for breach of contract (arguably corrective justice) does not explain why there are limitations to the scope of that obligation. The remoteness rule in the law of contract is a limitation of this kind. The theory that it is a free-standing rule of policy that allows the court to limit the defendant's liability as a matter of fairness is inconsistent with the origins of the rule in the nineteenth century and with a number of doctrinal rules that have emerged subsequently. The House of Lords was therefore right to think that the reasonable contemplation rule is best understood as a presumption about the intentions of the parties, but it is important to treat this as an implied exclusion of responsibility which would otherwise exist rather than as an implied assumption of responsibility which would otherwise not exist.

[186] See McGregor (n 32) [8–177].

11

Contributory Negligence and Strict Contractual Obligations Revisited

JANET O'SULLIVAN

I. INTRODUCTION

It is now more than two decades since the Law Commission recommended in its 1993 Report *Contributory Negligence as a Defence in Contract*[1] that:[2]

> apportionment on the grounds of the plaintiff's contributory negligence should be available in actions in contract where the defendant is in breach of a contractual term which imposes a duty to take reasonable care or exercise reasonable skill or both, but not where the defendant is in breach of a contractual term which imposes a higher level of duty (... a 'strict duty').

This chapter will focus on the latter issue, the question of whether contributory negligence should be available as a partial defence[3] where the cause of action is breach of a strict contractual obligation. It should be noted that the Law Commission proposed extending contributory negligence as a defence to be available wherever the defendant has breached a contractual obligation of reasonable care or skill, not just, as the law currently stands, where there is a concurrent obligation of reasonable care in the tort of negligence; this extension was of course not implemented legislatively, but subsequent developments recognising concurrent liability in the tort of negligence[4] achieved much the same result in practice.

At the time of the Report, it was well established[5] that contributory negligence was not available as a defence in cases of breach of strict contractual obligations.

[1] Law Commission, *Contributory Negligence as a Defence in Contract* (Law Com No 219, 1993). The recommendations of the Report were never implemented.

[2] ibid [1.4].

[3] This chapter does not aim to contribute to the important debate about the theoretical status or categorisation of contributory negligence, but simply adopts the Law Commission's assumption, reflected in its language, that contributory negligence operates as a defence. Nonetheless, it must be acknowledged that, although for T Weir, *An Introduction to Tort Law*, 2nd edn (Oxford, Clarendon Press, 2006) contributory negligence was 'unquestionably a defence, if only a partial one: it is for the defendant to plead and prove it', other commentators take a different view, in particular J Goudkamp, *Tort Law Defences* (Oxford, Hart Publishing, 2013).

[4] *Henderson v Merrett Syndicates Ltd* [1995] 2 AC 145 (HL), discussed further at text to n 92.

[5] At that time, leading case law included *Forsikringsaktieselskapet Vesta v Butcher* [1986] 2 All ER 488 (QBD), affirmed [1989] AC 852 (CA), affirmed [1989] AC 852 (HL); *Tennant Radiant Heat Ltd*

The common law was entrenched in this position, given the constraints of the unambiguous language of the Law Reform (Contributory Negligence) Act 1945 (UK) (the 1945 Act), enacted to abrogate the harsh common law rule that contributory negligence was a total defence in tort. Breach of contract is not therefore within the statutory definition of 'fault',[6] which means that actions for breach of contract are not caught by section 1;[7] moreover, before 1945 contributory negligence was not a defence to an action for breach of contract and thus also falls outside the definition of 'fault' in section 4. This language left the courts with no scope for judicial development of a principle of contributory negligence in cases of breach of strict contractual obligations; in contrast, the Law Commission's precise remit is to explore broader issues of principle, policy and consistency, unencumbered by the existing statutory regime but with a view to reform.

The Law Commission's final recommendation (that contributory negligence should continue to be unavailable as a defence to actions for breach of strict contractual obligations) represented something of a *volte-face*, since precisely the opposite provisional view was expressed in the earlier Consultation Paper on the subject[8] and was backed by the majority of consultees. The Law Commission was, however, sufficiently 'impressed by the reservations expressed by the minority' to be persuaded to depart from its provisional conclusion.

The aim of this chapter is to revisit these reservations, of principle and policy, which so convinced the Law Commission, exploring whether they were justifiable and, in particular, whether they have been undermined by subsequent developments in the law of contract and of obligations more broadly.

Before doing so, it is worth noting that the non-availability of the defence of contributory negligence in actions for breach of strict contractual obligations seems, at first glance at least, to be counter-intuitive. This is because it cannot be justified by reference to the usual sense of the 'hierarchy of wrongdoing'. In general, an intentional wrongdoing is treated more harshly than a merely negligent one, and in turn a negligent wrongdoer more harshly than a strictly liable one. The common law's approach to exclusion clauses is illustrative: it is absolutely impermissible as a matter of public policy to exclude liability for one's own fraud;[9] further down the hierarchy the courts are more hostile to attempts to exclude liability for negligence

v Warrington Development Corp [1988] 1 EGLR 41 (CA); *Bank of Nova Scotia v Hellenic Mutual War Risk Association (Bermuda) Ltd (The Good Luck)* [1990] 1 QB 818 (CA), appeal allowed but reasoning on question of contributory negligence approved: [1992] 1 AC 233 (HL).

[6] 'Fault' is defined in section 4 as 'negligence, breach of statutory duty or other act or omission which gives rise to liability in tort or would, apart from this Act, give rise to the defence of contributory negligence'.

[7] Section 1 of the 1945 Act provides, 'Where any person suffers damage as a result partly of his own fault and partly of the fault of any other person or persons, a claim in respect of that damage shall not be defeated by reason of the fault of the person suffering the damage, but the damages recoverable in respect thereof shall be reduced to such extent as the court thinks just and equitable, having regard to the claimant's share in the responsibility for the damage'.

[8] Law Commission, *Contributory Negligence as a Defence in Contract* (Working Paper No 114 (1990)).

[9] *Pearson (S) & Son Ltd v Dublin Corporation* [1907] AC 351 (HL), applied in eg *Government of Zanzibar v British Aerospace (Lancaster House) Ltd* [2000] 1 WLR 2333 (QBD).

than for breach of a strict contractual obligation.[10] Of more relevance to the issue in hand, contributory negligence is no defence to trespass to the person,[11] nor is it a defence in an action for deceit or fraudulent misrepresentation: a fraudulent defendant cannot be heard to say that the claimant should have taken more care to avoid being defrauded.[12] In *Standard Chartered Bank v Pakistan National Shipping Corporation*,[13] Lord Hoffmann explained the rule in simple policy terms, '[i]t would not seem just that a fraudulent defendant's liability should be reduced on the grounds that, for whatever reason, the victim should not have made the payment which the defendant successfully induced him to make'.[14] Lord Rodger invoked the same 'hierarchy of wrongdoing' justification, quoting an early-twentieth-century American jurist that,

> [i]f the defendant's wrong be intentional, only consent, express or necessarily implied from the circumstances, will bar recovery … the unanimous current of decision is that when the defendant's wrong is something more than mere negligence—when it involves an intent to cause harm—contributory negligence is no defense.[15]

Yet this hierarchy is plainly reversed in the case of breach by the defendant of a strict contractual obligation, where the claimant has been contributorily negligent. This leads to the paradoxical outcome that, faced with a contributorily negligent claimant, the defendant will be worse off (liable to pay damages in full) if, without fault, he breached a strict contractual obligation, than if he negligently breached an obligation of reasonable care (where the damages will be reduced to reflect the claimant's share in the responsibility for the damage). Clearly, the Law Commission was influenced by very different considerations from the normal hierarchy of wrongdoing, in supporting this counter-intuitive position. So what were those considerations?

The Law Commission's reasoning was lengthy, but can be distilled into two main threads: the first is an argument of principle and the second is one of practical policy. The argument of principle invokes the allocation of risk which is said to be inherent in a strict contractual obligation:[16] 'If the defendant commits himself to a strict obligation regardless of fault, the plaintiff should be able to rely on him fulfilling his obligation and should not have to take precautions against the possibility that a breach may occur'. The argument of policy asserts that allowing a partial defence of contributory negligence in actions for breach of strict liability obligations would lead to uncertainty, turning many straightforward contractual cases into more complex

[10] The guidelines on interpretation from *Canada Steamship Lines Ltd v The King* [1952] AC 192 (PC) are no longer rigidly applied, but the sense remains that clear, unambiguous language is needed to exclude liability for negligence: see for example *HIH Casualty and General Insurance Ltd v Chase Manhattan Bank* [2003] UKHL 6; [2003] 1 All ER (Comm) 349.

[11] *Co-operative Group (CWS) Ltd v Pritchard* [2011] EWCA Civ 329; [2012] QB 320.

[12] The same justification is offered for the more draconian remoteness of damage rule for fraud: see *Smith New Court Securities Ltd v Scrimgeour Vickers (Asset Management) Ltd* [1997] AC 254 (HL).

[13] *Standard Chartered Bank v Pakistan National Shipping Corporation* [2002] UKHL 43; [2003] 1 AC 959.

[14] ibid [16].

[15] FH Bohlen, *Studies in the Law of Torts* (Indianapolis IND, Bobbs-Merrill Company, 1926) 528–29, referred to by Lord Rodger in *Standard Chartered Bank* (n 13) [44].

[16] *Contributory Negligence* (n 1) [4.2] (footnotes omitted).

disputes about comparative blameworthiness:[17] '[Apportionment would require consideration of the quality of the defendant's conduct and t]his would increase the number of issues which have to be determined, and would lead to undesirable complexity'.

This chapter will consider each broad objection in turn, arguing in each case that developments since 1993 have undermined their premise and, moreover, that the original force of these objections is also open to question.

II. OBJECTION OF PRINCIPLE: THAT ASSUMING RESPONSIBILITY FOR THE CLAIMANT'S FAULT IS INHERENT IN A STRICT CONTRACTUAL OBLIGATION

A. Argument Proves Too Much—Ought to Rule Out Claimant Novus Actus Interveniens and Mitigation Too

In Part III of its 1993 Report (dealing with the issues arising from consultations), the Law Commission explored the relationship between contributory negligence and the principles of legal causation and mitigation, and recognised there that situations of claimant contributory fault could not adequately be accommodated by utilising those other, related principles. For example, when discussing legal causation, it said:[18]

> First, the absence of apportionment leads to a manipulation of the point at which the court regards the chain of causation as having been broken. Second, the rules of causation will, save where the plaintiff's negligent act breaches a legal duty owed to the defendant, produce an 'all or nothing' result. Third, even in the limited circumstances where it is possible … apportionment on the basis of causation does not have the same flexibility to produce a fair result as apportionment under the 1945 Act, and it would not in our view be conducive to certainty. We do not, therefore, regard causation as an adequate substitute for a statutory apportionment remedy.

Similar reservations were expressed in Part III about utilising mitigation to perform the role of a contributory negligence defence. Despite these reservations, however, by the time it reached Part IV detailing its recommendations, the Law Commission accepted the objection of principle that, 'if the defendant commits himself to a strict obligation regardless of fault, the plaintiff should be able to rely on him fulfilling his obligation and should not have to take precautions against the possibility that a breach might occur',[19] content to observe that the other principles, 'although not a perfect substitute for apportionment' would go some way to ameliorating the hardship to the defendant.

It is suggested that the application of the argument of principle to contributory negligence alone is problematic, because contributory negligence is just one of the ways the law takes account of the claimant's contribution to the outcome, forming part of the value judgment the court must make about whether to attribute

[17] ibid [4.5].
[18] ibid [3.15].
[19] ibid [4.2] (footnotes omitted).

responsibility to the defendant.[20] For example, the Court of Appeal recognised in *Spencer v Wincanton Holdings Ltd*[21] that, in the tort of negligence, contributory negligence and claimant novus actus interveniens are shades of the same normative enquiry,[22] allowing the courts where appropriate to apply the nuanced contributory negligence apportionment regime, rather than the 'all or nothing' conclusion that the claimant's conduct broke the chain of causation.[23] Mitigation also involves an evaluation of the reasonableness of the claimant's conduct, and a conclusion that the claimant failed to act reasonably to keep her loss to a minimum will rule out recovery of any additional loss that would not otherwise have been incurred. Since all three principles allow the judge in a tort case to answer the normative question of whether any, and if so, how much, responsibility ought to be attributed to the defendant, in the light of the claimant's contribution to the harm, it is not surprising that it is difficult to discern clear factual boundaries between them.[24] It is suggested that Stevens'[25] criticism of contributory negligence as being unacceptably 'analogue', requiring the judge to weigh up incommensurable items, is incomplete and needs to explain why the same objections do not apply to the process of deciding whether the claimant's conduct broke the chain of causation[26] or amounted to a failure to mitigate.

For the purpose of this chapter, however, the main point is that there is no difference of principle where the cause of action is for breach of a strict contractual obligation—the question of whether the claimant's conduct was a novus actus interveniens and the requirement of mitigation are just as much part of the same normative enquiry as contributory negligence, yet are applied without reservation in

[20] eg, Lord Nicholls in *Kuwait Airways Corporation v Iraqi Airways Co (Nos 4 and 5)* [2002] UKHL 19; [2002] 2 AC 883 [70]: '[t]he law has to set a limit to the causally connected losses for which a defendant is to be held responsible. In the ordinary language of lawyers, losses outside the limit may bear one of several labels. They may be described as too remote because the wrongful conduct was not a substantial or proximate cause or because the loss was the product of an intervening cause. The Defendants' responsibility may be excluded because the plaintiff failed to mitigate his loss'.

[21] *Spencer v Wincanton Holdings Ltd* [2009] EWCA Civ 1404; [2010] PIQR P8.

[22] ibid [45] (Aikens LJ): '[t]he line between a set of facts which results in a finding of contributory negligence and a set of facts which results in a finding that the "unreasonable conduct" of the claimant constitutes a novus actus interveniens is not, in my view, capable of precise definition. The cases I have referred to have provided guidance. But, in my view, each case will depend on the facts and, in Lord Nicholls' phrase, the court will have to apply a value judgment to the facts as found'.

[23] See J Goudkamp, *Tort Law Defences* (Oxford, Hart Publishing, 2013) who rightly regards a finding of 100% contributory negligence as impermissible: 'A judge who concludes that the claimant is solely responsible for his or her damage ought to hold that the claimant has failed to establish causation and withhold liability on that basis'.

[24] Timing certainly does not seem to be critical—*Spencer* (n 21) (contributory negligence) involved claimant conduct more than three years after the tort caused the initial injury, whereas in *McKew v Holland & Hannen & Cubitts (Scotland) Ltd* [1969] 3 All ER 1621 (HL), the claimant's conduct that was held to break the chain of causation occurred 'some days after the first accident'.

[25] R Stevens, 'Should Contributory Fault be Analogue or Digital?' in A Dyson, J Goudkamp and F Wilmot-Smith (eds), *Defences in Tort* (Oxford, Hart Publishing, 2015).

[26] Here (and in cases of third-party intervention) the court is required to weigh up similarly 'incommensurable' factors including whether the intervention was deliberate or reckless, its degree of 'independence' or 'voluntariness', and how foreseeable it was, then compare that 'combined' conclusion with the defendant's responsibility. The process does not shift from analogue to digital simply because the metaphorical conclusion is that the defendant's responsibility is wholly and not just partially 'eclipsed' by the claimant's.

cases of breach of strict contractual obligations.[27] The Law Commission's argument of principle does not explain why a defendant under a strict liability obligation should not bear the risk of *all* aspects of the claimant's unreasonable behaviour that contributed to the loss.

B. Strict Liability Under the Consumer Protection Act 1987 (UK) Distinguished

In 1987, just six years before the Law Commission Report, Parliament enacted the Consumer Protection Act, to implement the regime of strict liability imposed on the producer of a defective product for harm caused by that product by the European Directive on Liability for Defective Products.[28] The statute included the following provision:[29]

> Where any damage is caused partly by a defect in a product and partly by the fault of the person suffering the damage, the Law Reform (Contributory Negligence) Act 1945 and section 5 of the Fatal Accidents Act 1976 (contributory negligence) shall have effect as if the defect were the fault of every person liable by virtue of this Part for the damage caused by the defect.

This does not sit comfortably with the Law Commission's argument of principle that strict contractual liability inevitably involves allocating the risk of the claimant's fault wholly onto the defendant. The Law Commission sought to distinguish this form of strict tortious liability as follows: '[t]he analogy with section 6 of the Consumer Protection Act was thought to be not wholly convincing because there, although liability is strict, it is, in substance, fault based'.[30] This puzzling proposition was explained by reference to the 'state of the art defence', which gives the defendant a defence where he can show:[31]

> that the state of scientific and technical knowledge at the relevant time was not such that a producer of products of the same description as the product in question might be expected to have discovered the defect if it had existed in his products while they were under his control.

[27] Many examples include *Lambert v Lewis* [1982] AC 225 (HL) (claimant *novus actus*), discussed further at the text following n 69, and *Jamal v Moolla Dawood Sons & Co* [1916] 1 AC 175 (PC) (failure to mitigate).

[28] Council Directive 85/374/EEC of 25 July 1985 on the approximation of the laws, regulations and administrative provisions of the Member States concerning liability for defective products [1985] OJ L210/29.

[29] Consumer Protection Act 1987 (UK), s 6(4).

[30] *Contributory Negligence* (n 1) [3.40], sub-para 5.

[31] Consumer Protection Act 1987 (UK), s 4(1)(e). The ECJ in C-300/95 *Commission of the European Communities v United Kingdom* [1997] ECR I-2649 held that the defence should be interpreted to match the slightly different wording of the equivalent defence in the Directive (n 28) art 7(e), which provides the producer with a defence if he can establish that 'the state of scientific and technical knowledge at the time when he put the product into circulation was not such as to enable the existence of the defect to be discovered'.

According to the Law Commission, this defence 'modifies' the statute's strict liability regime, as follows:[32]

> This could operate where there is a production flaw but all practicable quality control measures are taken. If it does, the protection under the Act will be reduced from strict liability to the level of liability for negligence, but with the reversed burden of proof.

This was indeed the contemporary view of the Consumer Protection Act, and the state of the art defence in particular,[33] at a time before the statute had been interpreted by the courts. Likewise, at the time, commentators regarded the statutory definition of 'defect' as potentially importing at least some aspects of fault reasoning.[34] Section 3(1) provides that there is a defect in a product 'if the safety of the product is not such as persons generally are entitled to expect', which entitlement is to be determined under section 3(2) by taking into account 'all the circumstances'. This was generally interpreted to mean that persons generally are not entitled to expect absolute safety.[35]

Since 1993, however, the Law Commission's interpretation of the statute has been comprehensively rejected, in favour of an extremely strict test of liability and correspondingly narrow reading of the 'state of the art defence'. The Court of Appeal in *Abouzaid v Mothercare (UK) Ltd*[36] began the process, allowing a claim under the statute even though the claim failed in negligence because, judged at the time of the accident, reasonable manufacturers would not have taken steps to guard against the tiny, barely foreseeable risk. But the really significant development was *A v National Blood Authority*,[37] where Burton J had to decide whether blood for transfusion that was contaminated with hepatitis C fell within the statutory definition of a defective product, given that at the relevant time there was no screening test for the virus in donated blood, and thus no way of avoiding the risk whilst still maintaining the life-saving programme of blood transfusion. The National Blood Authority argued that these cost/benefit issues (the impossibility of avoiding risk and the social utility of the blood transfusion service) should be included within 'all the circumstances' in section 3(2) (article 6 of the Directive)[38] to demonstrate that 'persons generally

[32] *Contributory Negligence* (n 1) [3.40(5)].

[33] The Law Commission cited WVH Rogers, *Winfield & Jolowicz on Tort*, 13th edn (London, Sweet & Maxwell, 1989) 258. See also J Stapleton, *Product Liability* (London, Butterworths, 1994), published one year after the Law Commission Report.

[34] For example, 'the time when the product is supplied' is taken into account in section 3(2) to judge the level of safety that persons generally are entitled to expect. D Howarth, *Textbook on Tort* (London, Butterworths, 1995), published just two years after the Law Commission Report, analysed this as importing fault-based reasoning, reminiscent of the tests of foreseeability and lack of hindsight that characterise negligence.

[35] See Howarth (n 34) for a detailed consideration of whether the 'cost of precautions' and the product's 'social utility' should or should not be included within 'all the circumstances' to determine what level of safety persons generally are entitled to expect.

[36] *Abouzaid v Mothercare (UK) Ltd*, Times, 20 February 2001 (CA). The Court of Appeal also refused to apply the state of the art defence to a case where the defect could have been detected by carrying out simple safety tests: it was not a case where the state of scientific and technical knowledge had not advanced sufficiently.

[37] *A v National Blood Authority* [2001] 3 All ER 289 (QBD).

[38] Burton J focused on the text of the Directive, following *European Commission v UK* (n 31).

were not entitled to expect' absolute safety from transfused blood. Burton J rejected this interpretation, preferring to read the statute in the light of the explicit purpose of the Directive to introduce a regime of strict liability and 'eliminate proof of fault or negligence', and thus construing 'all the circumstances' to mean 'all *relevant* circumstances'.[39] The defendant's reliance on the state of the art defence was likewise rejected and the defence[40] given an extremely narrow meaning: once the defendant knows of the existence of the defect, it is irrelevant that it is not scientifically possible to eliminate that defect.

With the benefit of two decades' hindsight, the Law Commission's 1993 view of the product liability regime as being 'in substance, fault based' is no longer accurate. This in turn undermines the way in which the Law Commission distinguished the operation of the contributory negligence defence in product liability cases, compared with cases of strict contractual liability. If it is acceptable in principle[41] for a genuinely strict tort liability regime to be tempered by a contributory negligence defence, the argument that strict contractual liability invariably involves the defendant assuming the risk of the claimant's contributory fault loses force.

C. Remoteness of Damage—*The Achilleas*

The Law Commission Report adopted the then-current view of remoteness of damage in contract pursuant to *Hadley v Baxendale*[42] that[43]

> [a] defendant to an action for breach of contract is liable only for such damage as was within the reasonable contemplation of the parties at the time of contracting, that is, for damage which occurred in the ordinary course of things, or damage which a reasonable man could have foreseen if he had possessed the defendant's knowledge of special circumstances in the particular case.

Unsurprisingly, the Law Commission did not regard the remoteness test, judged at the time of contracting, as useful or relevant in dealing with claimant contributory negligence.

Since then, the decision of the House of Lords in *Transfield Shipping Inc v Mercator Shipping Inc ('The Achilleas')*[44] has modified the test for remoteness of damage in contract, so that it now depends on what the defendant has assumed responsibility for, rather than just foreseeability of damage under *Hadley v Baxendale*. Although the defendant will normally be held to have assumed responsibility for foreseeable

[39] *National Blood Authority* (n 37) [57] (emphasis added).

[40] Again Burton J used the version of the defence in article 7(e) of the Directive.

[41] In fact, there appears to be no reported domestic case under the Consumer Protection Act 1987 (UK) in which contributory negligence has been pleaded or discussed. It is impossible to know whether this is because the issue never arises, or because the operation of the contributory negligence defence in this strict liability context is so trouble-free that cases can be settled without difficulty.

[42] *Hadley v Baxendale* (1854) 9 Ex 341; 156 ER 145.

[43] *Contributory Negligence* (n 1) [3.16] (footnote omitted).

[44] *Transfield Shipping Inc v Mercator Shipping Inc ('The Achilleas')* [2008] UKHL 48; [2009] 1 AC 61, assuming for present purposes that the reasoning of Lord Hoffmann represents the ratio of the case.

losses,[45] it is now clear that there may be exceptional circumstances whereby, judged objectively, the defendant did not assume responsibility for foreseeable losses (as in *The Achilleas* itself), or did assume responsibility for unforeseeable ones (as in *Siemens Building Technologies FE Ltd v Supershield Ltd*).[46] This could allow a court to take into account aspects of the claimant's behaviour when deciding whether the losses fall within the scope of liability assumed by the defendant. For example, in *The Achilleas* the behaviour of the claimant shipowner was considered significant in two ways:[47]

(i) The following fixture entered into by the claimant with Cargill was something over which the defendant had no knowledge or control. 'Such a risk would therefore be completely unquantifiable, because although the parties would regard it as likely that the owners would at some time during the currency of the charter enter into a forward fixture, they would have no idea when that would be done or what its length or other terms would be'; and
(ii) The claimant shipowner could have refused to allow the defendant's final voyage if it had been clear that it would overrun and endanger the following fixture.

This approach to remoteness challenges the foundation of the Law Commission's objection of principle. A defendant who is subject to a strict contractual duty is not necessarily required to compensate the claimant fully, even in respect of foreseeable losses. The claimant's ability to recover damages depends on what the defendant has assumed responsibility for, and the law does not regard the defendant as having assumed responsibility for all losses suffered by the claimant merely because the claimant is relying on the defendant fulfilling a strict obligation.[48] In particular, if the claimant's actions increase the extent of the foreseeable losses, in circumstances beyond the defendant's control, this may be outside the scope of the defendant's contractual responsibility, even where (as in *The Achilleas*) the claimant's conduct could not be described as 'negligent' or even particularly unreasonable.

This in turn raises the question of whether remoteness be used to *apportion* damages, as a substitute for an overt contributory negligence defence. The Law Commission in 1993 answered this question in the negative, for two reasons. The first was that remoteness tends to produce an 'all or nothing' result in cases other than those involving recovery for loss of profits.[49] It is not clear that the new approach from

[45] *John Grimes Partnership Ltd v Gubbins* [2013] EWCA Civ 37; [2013] PNLR 17.

[46] *Siemens Building Technologies FE Ltd v Supershield Ltd* [2010] 2 All ER (Comm) 1185; [2010] 2 All ER (Comm) 1185.

[47] *The Achilleas* (n 44) [23], [34] and [86].

[48] A related point could be made about Lord Reid's qualification in *White and Carter (Councils) Ltd v McGregor* [1962] AC 413 (HL) that, where the claimant has no 'legitimate interest' in performing the contract, he must accept the defendant's repudiation and terminate the contract. This prevents the claimant from relying on the defendant's performance of the contract, even where its obligations are strict. So the law does not always regard the claimant's reliance on the defendant's performance of a strict contractual obligation as unconditionally justified.

[49] Presumably a reference to the result in *Victoria Laundry (Windsor) Ltd v Newman Industries Ltd* [1949] 2 KB 528 (CA), in which the loss of exceptionally lucrative profits from government dyeing contracts was held to be too remote, but where the Court of Appeal suggested that a 'general (and perhaps conjectural) sum for loss of business in respect of dyeing contracts to be reasonably expected' might nonetheless be recovered.

The Achilleas overcomes this problem. Consider, for example, the facts of *The Good Luck*.[50] The defendant P & I club (the insurer) insured a number of ships owned by Greek shipowners, which were mortgaged to the plaintiff bank. The insurer was notified of the bank's interest and gave a binding contractual promise in a letter of undertaking to advise the bank 'promptly' if it ceased to insure any vessel. One of the ships was struck by a missile when it sailed into a war zone. The shipowners made an insurance claim, on the pretence that they were unaware that the ship was entering into a prohibited zone, when in fact they were fully aware and indeed were actively permitting their charterers to enter Gulf war zones. The bank was aware of the claim but did no more than cursorily investigate the position of war risk cover; thereafter it advanced a further loan to the shipowners. Meanwhile the insurer took time to investigate the claim, and eventually the insurer gave notice to the bank that it had ceased to insure the vessel and that it would not pay any claims arising out of its loss. The bank's loan was irrecoverable, so it therefore claimed damages from the insurer for breach of its strict obligation to notify the bank promptly that the ship was uninsured. The issue of the bank's own responsibility for its loss arose. Lord Goff explained the findings of the judge at first instance as follows:[51]

> The judge held that the bank's loss was not too remote, whether the cause of action arose in contract or in tort. He considered that the loss was contributed to by the bank's own want of care, but did not go so far as to accept the [P & I] club's submission that its negligence was the sole cause of its loss. He apportioned blameworthiness in the proportions two-thirds to be borne by the club and one-third to be borne by the bank but, since the claim under the letter of undertaking was a claim under a contract, under which the club's liability did not depend upon negligence on its part, he held that the bank's claim did not fall to be reduced on the ground of contributory negligence. On the approach of the Court of Appeal, who held that there was no liability on the club, none of these points arose for decision. However they expressed agreement with the conclusion of the judge that, if the club was in breach of the letter of undertaking, such breach would have been at least a cause of the bank's loss; and they further stated that it would be clearly wrong in all the circumstances to hold that the bank's action amounted to a *novus actus interveniens* breaking the chain of causation between the club's breach and the bank's loss. They would also have agreed with him on the issue of contributory negligence.

Lord Goff, with whom the other members of the House agreed, took the same view that the bank's conduct was not a novus actus interveniens and that contributory negligence was not available in an action for breach of a strict contractual promise. Moreover the bank's loss was not too remote, falling within the first limb of *Hadley v Baxendale* as traditionally understood:[52]

> [I]f the bank suffered loss by reason of failure in the course of refinancing arrangements to take advantage of an opportunity to reduce or restrict its lending to the shipowners to take account of the cesser of a particular vessel's insurance cover of which the club, in breach of its letter of undertaking, failed to inform the bank, such loss would be within the

[50] *Bank of Nova Scotia v Hellenic Mutual War Risks Association (Bermuda) Ltd ('The Good Luck')* [1990] 1 QB 818 (CA); appeal allowed on other grounds [1992] 1 AC 233 (HL).
[51] ibid (HL) 266.
[52] ibid 267.

> contemplation of the parties at the time when the letter of undertaking was given as a serious possibility or real danger. No special knowledge was needed by the club to bring this possible loss within the contemplation of the parties; the possibility of such a loss was, in my opinion, well within the contemplation of the club as a result of its general knowledge, derived from the ordinary experience of its directors and managers, of the nature of ship financing.

Accordingly, the bank recovered damages in full, despite all three courts accepting that it had been one-third to blame for its loss. Unfortunately, it is difficult to see how the more sophisticated *Achilleas* explanation of contractual remoteness could have been used to reduce the bank's damages by one-third to reflect this unanimously accepted finding. If the bank had taken steps to verify the validity of the owners' insurance claim, the bank would not have suffered any loss. The defendant insurer either assumed responsibility for the bank's failure to discover the truth (in which case the claimant's losses were not too remote) or they did not (in which case the claimant's losses were too remote), thus leaving no room for a finding that the defendant assumed responsibility for two-thirds of the losses suffered.

The Law Commission's second reason was that remoteness does not 'reflect the fault of the plaintiff but the contemplation of the parties at the time they entered into the contract'.[53] *The Achilleas* expands the range of factors to which the court is to have regard, but this exercise is still to be carried out by reference to 'the contemplation of the parties at the time when the contract was entered into'.[54] The difficulty is whether remoteness can take into account the *relative* blameworthiness of the parties' behaviour post-contracting. As has been seen, modern remoteness reasoning under *The Achilleas* can take into account the blameworthiness of the claimant's conduct, on the basis that, at the time of contracting, the defendant did not assume responsibility for losses caused by the claimant's failure to protect his own interests. It is more difficult to see how remoteness can take into account the blameworthiness of the defendant's conduct, against which the claimant's conduct falls to be assessed.

Some commentators, such as Burrows,[55] prefer to explain contractual remoteness principles, not (as Lord Hoffmann does in *The Achilleas*) as part of the contextual interpretation of the parties' objective intentions when making the contract, but instead as an externally imposed rule of fairness, like the general principles on quantification of damages. Robertson[56] adopts this view and argues that the defendant's culpability could be taken into account when deciding whether particular loss should be regarded as too remote. However, this seems at present to be an isolated suggestion, not adopted (overtly at least) by any judicial decisions and rejected by Burrows as seeming 'alien to the English approach to contract law'.[57]

If so, it is suggested that this provides another reason why the defence of contributory negligence should be made available to all breaches of contract. The law is

[53] *Contributory Negligence* (n 1) [3.17].

[54] *The Achilleas* (n 44) [30] (Lord Hope).

[55] A Burrows, 'Lord Hoffmann and Remoteness in Contract' in PS Davies and J Pila (eds), *The Jurisprudence of Lord Hoffmann* (Oxford, Hart Publishing, 2015).

[56] A Robertson, 'The Basis of the Remoteness Rule in Contract' (2008) 28 *Legal Studies* 172.

[57] Burrows (n 55) 264, fn 48.

currently able to deny the claimant's damages in response to the claimant's behaviour by finding either that the claimant's behaviour broke the chain of causation or possibly, post *The Achilleas*, that the claimant's behaviour takes his losses outside the scope of liability assumed by the defendant. Since neither approach takes account of the blameworthiness of the defendant's conduct, it seems unlikely that a 'fair and equitable' outcome will be reached.

A similar tension is seen in negligence cases on the border with contract, involving *Hedley Byrne* liability for pure economic loss, in circumstances 'akin to contract', but where contributory negligence is available as a defence. Here the familiar *Achilleas* concept finds its place in the notion of the *scope* of the duty of care, as explained in *South Australia Asset Management Corp v York Montague*,[58] so a court must delineate the scope of the duty of care before there can be any question of defendant liability or of contributory negligence. This is seen in *Calvert v William Hill Credit Ltd*,[59] a tort case involving a compulsive gambler alleging negligence on the part of a bookmaker who agreed to exclude him from telephone gambling but then negligently failed to do so. The Court of Appeal discussed both the scope of the defendant's duty of care and contributory negligence. It was held that the claimant's loss did not fall within the scope of the duty of care assumed by defendant (the defendant only agreed not to accept telephone bets, not to protect the claimant from gambling more generally), but that, if it had, a reduction of 30 per cent would have been a proper reflection of the claimant's share in the responsibility for his financial losses. This decision shows how the two doctrines, which respond to different concerns, do not produce the same results.

D. 'Justifiable Reliance' Should Not Be Defined as Fault

As has been seen, the gist of the Law Commission's objection of principle is that if the defendant commits himself to a strict contractual obligation, the claimant should be able to rely on him fulfilling his obligation and should not have to take precautions against the possibility that a breach might occur. It is noteworthy that the hypothetical examples given in Part IV of the Law Commission Report all involve this pattern—what might be described as 'justifiable reliance' on the defendant's compliance with a strict warranty, such as:[60]

> Another example is that of the proprietor of a restaurant who purchases an electrical deep fat fryer. The fryer has a defect which means that it overheats dangerously. If the chef employed by the proprietor had been alert he might have realised that the fryer was overheating. However, he did not notice and a fire ensued. In those circumstances we believe it is right in principle for the proprietor to recover in full for the damage caused by the fire. It should not be open to the defendant to argue that the chef was contributorily negligent in failing to keep an eye on the fryer to ensure that it was functioning correctly. The defendant

[58] *South Australia Asset Management Corp v York Montague* [1997] AC 191 (HL).
[59] *Calvert v William Hill Credit Ltd* [2008] EWCA Civ 1427; [2009] Ch 330.
[60] *Contributory Negligence* (n 1) [4.4] (footnotes omitted).

had contracted to supply a fryer of merchantable quality, and the proprietor was entitled to rely on his so doing.

It is hard to disagree with the conclusion that the defendant should not be able to rely on a defence of contributory negligence in such circumstances, but this is because, looked at in the contractual context, this particular example of claimant's conduct did not amount to *fault*.[61] It is not an argument against the availability of the defence more generally, whenever the defendant is under a strict contractual obligation. Indeed, in its Working Paper No 114 the Law Commission stressed that normally a claimant should not be regarded as being at fault in relying on the defendant to perform his contractual obligation and by not checking up that he has done so, yet by the time of its Final Report, this had become an argument of principle against contributory negligence ever being available in strict contractual claims.

There are many instances where a claimant—particularly a consumer—will not be at fault in relying on a commercial or professional defendant to comply with a strict contractual obligation, without monitoring or checking up on his performance. The claimant's entitlement to rely on the defendant having performed his contract was emphasised recently in *Stacey v Autosleeper Group Ltd*[62] in the context of whether the claimant's conduct broke the chain of causation. Floyd LJ explained:[63]

> [I]n a case such as this where a warranty has been given, it is not sufficient for the defendant merely to show negligence of the claimant in failing to uncover the breach of warranty in the absence of anything even to alert him to the possibility of a breach. The claimant was entitled to rely on the defendant having performed his contract. Whilst he might have discovered the breach of contract had he run his business more carefully, he did not do so.

In fact the position is the same where the defendant's liability is not strict: in *UBS Corporate Services v Clyde & Co*[64] Beldam LJ said that a claimant is generally entitled to rely on a professional defendant performing a contractual obligation of reasonable care: 'the client is entitled to rely on solicitors to exercise the highest degree of care and skill which a competent professional would exercise in work of that kind'.[65] Herring and Foster point out that, in the UK, a finding of contributory negligence against a patient in a medical negligence action is almost unheard of,[66] reflecting a paternalistic/passive model of the doctor/patient relationship that leaves 'little room for contributory negligence': the defence is available in theory, it is just that in practice the patient is rarely regarded as at fault. For Herring and Foster, in the more contemporary cooperative model stressing patient autonomy, partnership and individual responsibility, more frequent recourse to contributory negligence might be appropriate, in fact patterns other than justified reliance on professional expertise.[67]

[61] This point was made in A Burrows, *Remedies for Torts and Breach of Contract*, 3rd edn (Oxford, Oxford University Press, 2004) 143.

[62] *Stacey v Autosleeper Group Ltd* [2014] EWCA Civ 1551.

[63] ibid [23].

[64] *UBS Corporate Services v Clyde & Co* [2000] PNLR 841 (CA).

[65] ibid 854.

[66] J Herring and C Foster, 'Blaming the Patient: contributory negligence in medical malpractice litigation' (2009) 25 *Professional Negligence* 76, citing just one reported example of a successful plea.

[67] Examples cited include the patient who gives false information or fails to disclose relevant information, leading to a misdiagnosis, or the patient who, not having been warned of a relevant risk from

Similarly, in our strict contractual liability context, there are many other fact patterns of claimant fault, going beyond what might be termed 'justified reliance and mere failure to make enquiries'. The Law Commission's Working Paper No 114 contained an example:[68]

> A customer (P), buys an iron from retailer (D). When taking it out of the package, he notices that the heat dial has fallen off and that it is defective in several other ways. Nevertheless he uses it and ruins a shirt. Assuming that there was no negligence on D's part, P sues D for breach of his undertaking that the iron will be of merchantable [now satisfactory] quality and reasonably fit for its purpose.

As the Working Paper acknowledged, this sort of knowing risk-taking is a good example of claimant conduct that should count as 'fault' and thus attract apportionment for contributory negligence, whereas under the current law, and the regime eventually endorsed by the Law Commission, a judge's only option would be the 'all or nothing' decision as to whether the claimant's conduct amounted to a novus actus interveniens.[69]

A small modification to the facts of *Lambert v Lewis* provides another example. There a farmer continued to use a defective coupling to join a trailer to a Land-rover 'over a period of many months in a state in which it was plainly damaged without taking steps to have it repaired or even to ascertain whether or not it was safe to use it in such a condition'. Imagine instead if a claimant noticed such a defect just once, but did not think to stop using the coupling, or ought reasonably to have noticed it but did not do so, before an accident occurred. It is suggested that apportionment for contributory negligence would capture the relative responsibility for the accident, rather than the *Lewis v Lambert* 'all or nothing' options.

Another example, modifying a well-known tort authority, might involve a strict contractual warranty given by a defendant, perhaps a private bodyguard, to a sane but eccentric claimant that, for a suitably high fee, the defendant will ensure the claimant's safety: the claimant subsequently commits suicide or a lesser act of self-harm. The example is perhaps commercially implausible, but the legal issues it throws up are closely analogous to those considered by the House of Lords in *Reeves v Commissioner of Police for the Metropolis.*[70] In *Reeves*, all members of the House of Lords declined to hold that the claimant prisoner's suicide amounted to a novus actus interveniens (or the defence of volenti) because it was the very sort of harm the duty of care was imposed to guard against—reasoning that must apply a fortiori in the case of a strict contractual warranty. The majority of the House of Lords went on to apply a 50 per cent reduction for the claimant's contributory negligence, yet that outcome would be unavailable in our contractual example. That is not to say that it would be the right outcome—only that it should not be ruled out because of its

particular medication, continues to take the medication having obtained it not from the defendant physician but over the internet.

[68] Working Paper (n 8) [2.9] (footnote omitted) and [5.2].

[69] *Lambert v Lewis* [1982] AC 225 (HL)—not itself a case of claimant fault, but a failed attempt by a negligent defendant to seek an indemnity against a strictly liable supplier for breach of the implied fitness for purpose obligation under the Sale of Goods Act.

[70] *Reeves v Commissioner of Police for the Metropolis* [2000] 1 AC 360 (HL).

unsuitability in completely different factual circumstances. In other words, it is a pity that the Law Commission reasoned from one specific sort of claimant conduct ('justified reliance and mere failure to make enquiries') to the conclusion that no other form of claimant conduct could ever, on principle, amount to contributory negligence.[71]

E. Contrast with the Contribution Regime

Since the Law Commission's 1993 report, it is now well established that a defendant who is strictly liable for breach of contract can seek a contribution from a negligent *third party* under the Civil Liability (Contribution) Act 1978 (UK), as long as the third party's negligence contributed to the same damage.[72] The analogy is not perfect: apportionment in these circumstances is expressly allowed by a deliberately balanced statutory regime, one which does not challenge the defendant's full responsibility vis-à-vis the claimant. Nonetheless it should give us pause—if a strictly liable defendant's responsibility can be apportioned as against that of a negligent but unconnected third party (who owes no duties to the defendant and can incur no liability to him outside of the statute itself), we should be wary of assertions that apportionment is unacceptable in principle as against a negligent contractual counterparty.

The contribution cases involving defendants who are strictly liable for breach of contract and negligent third parties are more pertinent in addressing the Law Commission's other major objection—that contributory negligence is undesirable as a matter of practical policy, because it would introduce uncertainty and complexity into otherwise simple disputes, a bare assertion to which we must now turn.

III. OBJECTION OF POLICY—UNCERTAINTY AND COMPLEXITY

This policy objection can be challenged in two main ways. The first is to analyse whether the current position—contributory negligence being unavailable in cases of strict contractual liability but available in most cases of contractual obligations of reasonable care—is any better from the perspective of uncertainty and complexity. The second is to tackle the premise that introducing apportionment for contributory negligence in cases of strict contractual obligations will necessarily lead to the

[71] J Goudkamp, 'Rethinking Contributory Negligence' in SGA Pitel, JW Neyers and E Chamberlain, *Tort Law: Challenging Orthodoxy* (Oxford, Hart Publishing, 2013) 314–23 points out that the courts frequently disapply the defence of contributory negligence for reasons of public policy, such as where the defendant's duty is protective of the claimant, so that allowing the partial defence would undermine the defendant's duty. Unlike the Law Commission's inflexible view of risk allocation in strict contractual cases, Goudkamp's insight would allow a nuanced decision about the purpose and scope of the particular contractual term breached and whether it would be appropriate as a matter of policy to apportion any responsibility to the claimant.

[72] Examples include *Prekookeanska Plovidba v Felstar Shipping Corp* [1994] CLC 277 (CA); *Eastgate Group Ltd v Lindsey Modern Group Inc* [2001] EWCA Civ 1446; [2002] 1 WLR 642; *National Museums and Galleries on Merseyside v AEW Architects and Designers Ltd* [2013] EWHC 2403 (TCC).

practical problems the Law Commission feared, or whether those potential problems were exaggerated.

A. Uncertainty and Complexity in Construction of Contractual Obligations—Strict or Reasonable Care?

The availability or non-availability of contributory negligence is one of the important subsidiary reasons why it matters whether the obligation breached by the defendant is one of strict liability or reasonable care. Outside the clear-cut statutory regimes of implied terms as to, for example, the quality of goods, this can be a surprisingly complex and uncertain process of construction.

This issue arises regularly in the context of professional retainers—when will a contractual obligation in a professional contract be construed as strict, in contrast with the usual term that the professional will use reasonable care and skill? In *Zwebner v Mortgage Corporation Ltd*,[73] the claimant's husband borrowed money from the defendant with the debt being secured by a charge on the jointly owned matrimonial home. The solicitor, acting for all parties, gave undertakings to the defendant to apply all money received solely for the purpose of securing a first mortgage over the property, and to ensure that all the appropriate documents had been properly executed before completion. Unfortunately, the husband had forged the claimant's signature on the mortgage deed and she consequently had no knowledge of the transaction. In third-party proceedings brought by the defendant against the solicitor, the judge held that the solicitor's undertakings had contractual force as strict liability obligations. The Court of Appeal agreed and held that the solicitor was in breach of warranty that all appropriate documents had been properly executed: a mortgage deed was not properly completed unless executed by or with the authority of all the proposed mortgagors. The argument turned on contractual construction. As Walker LJ said:[74]

> One of Mr Norris' [counsel for the solicitor] biggest difficulties was in formulating just how the second undertaking should be read in order to avoid the unfairness which arose, on his submission, from placing weight on 'properly' in the expression 'will be properly executed'. He said that 'properly' should be limited to matters of form (and the mechanics of completion) rather than legal efficacy: the real purpose of the second undertaking, he said, was to make clear that a 'Hong Kong completion' (see *Edward Wong Finance Ltd v. Johnson Stokes & Master* [1984] A.C. 296) was unacceptable. That was no doubt part of the purpose, but I am not persuaded that the distinction between form and efficacy can be sustained, or that the consequences of giving weight to the word 'properly' are so unreasonable as to justify a construction which largely disregards it.

Zwebner has been regularly pleaded since, requiring courts to address whether the basic tasks undertaken in professional retainers should be construed as strict obligations or merely requiring reasonable care.[75] It was, for example, distinguished in

[73] *Zwebner v Mortgage Corporation Ltd* [1998] PNLR 769 (CA).

[74] ibid 777.

[75] *Zwebner* (n 73) was recently applied in *LSC Finance Ltd v Abensons Law Ltd* [2015] EWHC 1163 (Ch), but it is more commonly distinguished, as in for example *Barclays Bank plc v Weeks Legg & Dean* [1999] QB 309 (CA).

Midland Bank plc v Cox McQueen[76] where a wife's signature was once again forged by the husband on a mortgage document. The bank argued, relying on *Zwebner*, that the solicitor's retainer imposed a strict obligation to obtain the signatures of the husband and the wife; they did not obtain the wife's signature, therefore they did not carry out their strict obligation. The Court of Appeal rejected this argument, holding that the retainer should not be construed in this way, noting that the language in the *Zwebner* retainer of 'properly execute' did not appear here. As Lord Woolf MR explained:[77]

> The question is, did the bank intend to ask for and did the solicitors intend to give a promise to answer for the fraud of the customer even if that fraud could not be detected by exercising all proper care? In my view the answer to the question should be no, unless the language used compellingly indicates otherwise.

He went on to support this conclusion with reasons of policy for keeping *Zwebner* within limited bounds:[78]

> In my judgment the decision in *Zwebner* should not be given a wide application. To do so would ignore the wider consequences of our decision. If commercial institutions such as banks wish to impose an absolute liability on members of a profession they should do so in clear terms so that the solicitors can appreciate the extent of their obligation which they are accepting ... It is not in the interests of banks as they will have to pay higher fees which they may or may not seek to recover from their customers. It is not in the interest of the public because it is important that legal services are readily available and this will not be the case if small firms are unable to survive. Unless the language used in a retainer clearly has this consequence, the courts should not be ready to impose obligations on solicitors which even the most careful solicitor may not be able to meet.

In practice, it can be hard for courts to draw the line between the normal construction of a professional obligation as requiring reasonable care and an exceptional '*Zwebner*' case. A telling example is *Platform Funding Ltd v Bank of Scotland plc*,[79] in which a valuer employed by Colleys surveyors was misled, without fault on his part, by the borrower into inspecting and valuing the wrong property (one of several new building plots, for which the numbering was unclear), which meant that the claimant lent more than the value of the actual secured property, and subsequently suffered a shortfall on sale. The valuer was initially instructed by telephone, subsequently followed up with written instructions which did not contain an express warranty on the matter, but the valuation report contained a declaration, 'I certify that the property offered as security has been inspected by me'. All three members of the Court of Appeal agreed that their task was to construe the valuer's retainer, but that is where unanimity ended. The majority held that the valuer was under a strict contractual obligation to value the right property. For Rix LJ this was a straightforward exercise:[80]

> I do not think that there can be much plainer expression than the words 'the property ... has been inspected by me'. Even against a background where otherwise the obligation to

[76] *Midland Bank plc v Cox McQueen* [1999] PNLR 593 (CA).
[77] ibid 598.
[78] ibid 602–3.
[79] *Platform Funding Ltd v Bank of Scotland plc* [2009] QB 426 (CA).
[80] ibid [55].

> inspect would only have been one of the taking of reasonable care to inspect, I do not accept that those words can properly be interpreted as meaning: 'I have taken reasonable care to inspect the property'.

In contrast, Sir Anthony Clarke MR, in dissent, thought the opposite interpretation was equally plain, adopting Lord Woolf MR's cautious policy approach from *Midland Bank v Cox McQueen*:[81]

> In my opinion, it is improbable that, if the parties had been asked after the telephone conversation in which Colleys accepted instructions whether Colleys had assumed an unqualified obligation as to the identity of the property but not as to the valuation, they would have said no. They would surely have contemplated that the same duty would apply to the execution of all their instructions, namely to inspect 1 Bakers Yard and value it. That is I think especially so here, where it was clear that the valuer was expected to be given access to the property by Mr Hewes. As I see it, part of the obligation to inspect and value the property was to locate it. It seems to me to make no sense, in the absence (as Lord Woolf MR put it) of a clear term, to hold that it was agreed that Colleys assumed an absolute obligation to locate it but only a qualified obligation to exercise skill and care in the inspection and valuation of it. The valuer was throughout acting in a professional capacity.

To return to our broader theme, the resolution of this issue on liability will in turn determine whether or not the claimant's contributory negligence operates as a defence. In *UBS Corporate Services v Clyde & Co*[82] solicitors omitted the name of the borrower from a guarantee document which made it unenforceable by the bank. The solicitors wished to rely on contributory negligence on the part of the bank, in that the bank had released other security given by the borrower, though at a time when the unenforceability of the guarantee had not come to light. In fact, the bank's conduct was held not to amount to contributory negligence, which rendered the question of whether the solicitors' obligation was strict or one of reasonable care irrelevant on the facts, but is nonetheless illustrative of the problem. The retainer obliged the solicitors to ensure that 'any steps required to make [the charge] fully enforceable are taken'. Otton LJ (as a matter of authority) and Beldam LJ (as a matter of interpretation) suggested (obiter) that this was not an absolute obligation, while Judge LJ wished to reserve his opinion on this.

Outside the professional negligence context, the courts frequently experience similar difficulties determining whether a particular obligation should be construed as strict or requiring only reasonable care, in turn determining the availability of contributory negligence. In *Trebor Bassett Holdings Ltd v ADT Fire & Security plc*[83] the defendant contracted with the claimant to design and installation of a 'fire suppression system' in the claimant's confectionary factory, which was supposed to discharge CO_2 whenever a fire broke out. A fire broke out in a popcorn hopper, but the system did not work. Members of the claimant's staff ejected a burning ball of popcorn, together with the hopper's entire load, and tried to stamp out the fire. The fire consequently spread and destroyed the whole factory. At first instance, the judge held that the defendant was

[81] ibid [64].
[82] *UBS Corporate Services v Clyde & Co* (n 64).
[83] *Trebor Bassett Holdings Ltd v ADT Fire & Security Plc* [2012] EWCA Civ 1158; [2012] BLR 441.

liable for breach of obligations of reasonable care, but that the claimant's damages should be reduced by 75 per cent for contributory negligence (principally in its failure to segregate the oil pop production area from the rest of the building and to install sprinklers). On appeal, the claimant sought to argue that the defendant was in breach of strict contractual obligations (analogous to the strict statutory implied terms in sale of goods contracts), which would therefore rule out any deduction for contributory negligence. The Court of Appeal dismissed the appeal, holding that it was inappropriate to construe the contract as including a guarantee of the system's success or as importing the result that a system failure would automatically amount to a breach of contractual obligation as to suitability. After detailed analysis and construction of the contractual language and context, Tomlinson LJ concluded:[84]

> In my judgment the judge was right to regard as implausible a construction of the Specification which imposed an absolute obligation. One must stand back and remember that the context is fire suppression, not even fire prevention. Very clear words indeed would be required to bring about the result that a designer and supplier of fire suppression systems had contracted to extinguish all fires occurring in either the hopper or the elevator.

The Court of Appeal also agreed with the judge that the actions of the claimant's staff, responding to the fire in the heat of the moment, should not be regarded as breaking the chain of causation from the defendant's breach. There was no appeal against the 75 per cent reduction for contributory negligence in relation to the claimant's other failures.

These authorities demonstrate that the Law Commission's policy objective to avoid uncertainty and complexity is not achieved by the current position on contributory negligence, because the analysis shifts to, and the outcome depends on, another equally uncertain and complex issue: whether the defendant's obligation was one of reasonable care or a strict contractual warranty. A similar shifting effect is seen in the next issue.

B. Distorting Contributory Negligence Facts

As has been seen, the Law Commission recognised that the 'all or nothing' response of novus actus interveniens and mitigation reasoning cannot provide the nuanced apportionment, based on relative fault, of a contributory negligence regime, but nonetheless treated these other legal categories as a satisfactory substitute to avoid the uncertainty and complexity of permitting contributory negligence as a defence where strict contractual obligations are concerned. But this means that the courts have no choice but to use an imperfect tool to respond to claimant fault in such cases, which perhaps unsurprisingly gives rise to its own uncertainty and complexity.

The best example is *Schering Agrochemicals Ltd v Resibel NV SA*,[85] described by Burrows as 'a classic illustration of the injustice that can result'[86] from the unavailability

[84] ibid [54].
[85] *Schering Agrochemicals Ltd v Resibel NV SA* (CA, 26 November 1992).
[86] A Burrows, 'Contributory Negligence in Contract: Ammunition for the Law Commission' (1993) 109 *LQR* 175.

of contributory negligence in cases involving strict contractual obligations. The defendant contracted to supply equipment to seal the caps onto bottles of inflammable chemicals manufactured by the plaintiffs. A month after the system was installed, there was a minor explosion caused by a defect in the equipment's safety system; this was reported to the plaintiffs' supervisor but he took no action. Three weeks later, the safety system failed again and this time a serious fire resulted. The defendant accepted that it was in breach of its strict contractual obligation under section 14(3) of the Sale of Goods Act 1979 (UK), but argued that the plaintiffs' failure to investigate the earlier incident absolved it from all responsibility. The Court of Appeal agreed, but all three members of the court adopted different reasoning, with Nolan LJ holding that the plaintiffs had failed to mitigate their loss, Scott LJ holding that the plaintiffs' inaction broke the chain of causation, and Purchas LJ espousing both principles. Each seems artificial: as Burrows points out,[87] novus actus reasoning is not comfortably applied to omissions, whereas the 'duty' to mitigate is not usually said to arise until the claimant is actually aware[88] of the defendant's breach, not merely where he was careless in failing to discover it. The reasoning in the case is both complex and confusing, because a straightforward allegation of contributory negligence could not be straightforwardly analysed as such.

Schering is also an example of the perverse outcome of the Law Commission's reasoning: the denial of contributory negligence in cases of strict contractual liability is meant to protect the claimant from having his damages reduced. In practice, the impact is the opposite—where a court does not think the claimant should receive full damages, its only remaining options (applying novus actus or failure to mitigate reasoning) perversely result in the claimant being given nothing.

It is striking that in tort claims for personal injury, for which contributory negligence is straightforwardly available, the courts now favour the nuanced option of apportionment for contributory negligence over the 'all or nothing' option of a finding that the claimant's conduct was a novus actus interveniens, which tends to be applied only in extreme cases, such as the well-known House of Lords authority of *McKew v Holland & Hannen & Cubitts (Scotland) Ltd*.[89] Courts today generally distinguish *McKew*, as the Court of Appeal did in *Spencer v Wincanton Holdings Ltd*,[90] where Sedley LJ expressly approved the following passage from Clerk and Lindsell:

> [i]t is submitted that for the claimant's subsequent conduct to be regarded as a *novus actus interveniens* it should be such as can be characterised as reckless or deliberate. Unreasonable conduct can be dealt with by a finding of contributory negligence.[91]

This sort of normative enquiry—whether responsibility should or should not be attributed to the defendant for harm which would not have occurred but for his

[87] ibid 176.

[88] *Youell v Bland Welch Co Ltd (No 2)* [1990] 2 Lloyd's Rep 431 (QBD) 461.

[89] *McKew v Holland & Hannen & Cubitts (Scotland) Ltd* [1969] 3 All ER 1621 (HL), in which contributory negligence was not pleaded.

[90] *Spencer* (n 21).

[91] ibid [18], quoting AM Dugdale and MA Jones (eds), *Clerk & Lindsell on Torts*, 19th edn (London, Sweet & Maxwell, 2006) [2-97].

breach but which was also caused by fault on the part of the claimant—is a complex and difficult one, which the nuanced tool of contributory negligence apportionment is designed to achieve. Precisely the same value judgment is needed where the underlying cause of action is breach of a strict contractual obligation, and thus precisely the same nuanced tool. It is not conducive to certainty or clarity to tackle this value judgment without the most suitable tool for the job.

C. No Insurmountable Problems of Uncertainty and Complexity in Analogous Instances of Apportionment

Since the Law Commission's 1993 Report, there has been a huge increase in the cases covered by the defence of contributory negligence, not through the implementation of any statutory reform but as an indirect consequence of the recognition of concurrent liability in the tort of negligence in contractual obligations of reasonable care under *Henderson v Merrett Syndicates Ltd*.[92] To use the *Forsikringsaktieselskapet Vesta v Butcher* classification, category (2) has now mostly[93] emptied into category (3). Many of these are professional negligence actions founded on professional advice in commercial transactions, where contributory negligence apportionment involves exploring complex factual issues. Further complexity comes from the need to apply *SAAMCO*[94] principles to determine the scope of the defendant's liability. In the valuer's negligence case of *Platform Home Loans Ltd v Oyston Shipways Ltd*[95] the majority of the House of Lords held that a deduction for the lender's contributory negligence (in lending without proper investigation of the borrower's creditworthiness) should be made from the lender's basic loss *before* applying *SAAMCO* (which is generally, if misleadingly, expressed as a cap on the defendant's liability of the amount of the overvaluation).

Space does not permit a detailed examination of this decision. Suffice it to say, it is hard to imagine a more complex example of contributory negligence apportionment, reasoning which was subjected to rigorous and sustained criticism by Stapleton.[96] Nonetheless, the courts have managed to apply the approach in *Platform Home Loans* without obvious uncertainty[97] and it has certainly not generated the wave of cases seeking to clarify its meaning and scope seen with other recent common law developments.[98] The conclusion must be that, contrary to the view of the Law Commission, a descent into chaos is not inevitable just because the claimant's conduct falls to be assessed and compared with the defendant's in a commercial setting,

[92] *Henderson v Merrett Syndicates Ltd* [1995] 2 AC 145 (QBD), cf *Tai Hing Cotton Mill Ltd v Liu Chong Hing Bank Ltd* [1986] AC 80 (PC).

[93] For an exception remaining in category (2), see *Raflatac Ltd v Eade* [1999] 1 Lloyd's Rep 506 (QBD).

[94] *South Australia Asset Management Corp v York Montague Ltd* [1997] AC 191 (HL).

[95] *Platform Home Loans Ltd v Oyston Shipways Ltd* [2000] 2 AC 190 (HL).

[96] J Stapleton, 'Risk-Taking by Commercial Lenders' (1999) 115 *LQR* 527.

[97] See eg *Nationwide Building Society v Dunlop Haywards* [2009] EWHC 254 (Comm); [2010] 1 WLR 258; *Bank of Ireland v Faithful & Gould* [2014] EWHC 2217 (TCC); [2014] PNLR 28.

[98] Such as *Fairchild v Glenhaven Funeral Services Ltd* [2002] UKHL 22, [2003] 1 AC 32.

so that damages can be reduced if necessary having regard to the claimant's share in the responsibility for the damage.

Similarly, there is no obvious problem of uncertainty where a defendant who is strictly liable for breach of contract seeks a contribution under the Civil Liability (Contribution) Act 1978 (UK) from a negligent third party, or vice versa, as long as both are liable for some element of 'same damage'.[99]

The 1978 Act was first applied in such circumstances just one year after the Law Commission Report, in *Prekooanska Plovidba v Felstar Shipping Corp.*[100] Here, the plaintiffs' vessel '*Danilovgrad*' was damaged when another vessel ('*Carnival*') was negligently moored alongside and collided with it. The plaintiffs sued D1 (owners of the '*Carnival*') for damages in negligence, and D2 (charterers of the '*Danilovrgad*') for damages for breach of the 'safe berth warranty' in the charterparty, which amounted to a strict promise that the berth or berths nominated would be prospectively safe for the vessel. D1 were found liable in negligence. The berth was found unsafe, and this placed D2 in strict breach of contract even though D2 'were not the owners of the berth and had no reason to know that the berth was protected by fenders of design which was unsafe'.

After a detailed analysis of the disputed facts, the judge at first instance disposed of the question of apportionment under the 1978 Act without undue difficulty. He found it 'impossible to distinguish the causative potency of one from the other', and went on to hold, 'having regard to the substantially greater blameworthiness of the conduct of the first defendants it seems to me to be just and equitable' to apportion liability two-thirds to D1, one-third to D2. The Court of Appeal upheld this apportionment, giving short shrift to D2's argument

> that the judge did not take into account properly the fact that his client's liability was in tort for negligence, whereas the second defendants were held liable for breach of an absolute warranty. In our judgment it is manifest that the judge took that aspect fully into account, since he was fully aware of the basis of the respective claims.[101]

It is true that slightly different considerations apply when apportioning liability between a strictly liable defendant and a negligent co-defendant, as opposed to a negligent claimant. But experience in contribution claims shows that the courts are comfortable with comparing relative blameworthiness and 'causative potency'[102] according to relatively settled, predictable principles. As Lord Reed said in *Jackson v Murray*,[103] 'the apportionment of responsibility is inevitably a somewhat rough and

[99] Civil Liability (Contribution) Act 1978 (UK), s 1(1).

[100] *Prekooanska Plovidba v Felstar Shipping Corp* [1994] CLC 277 (CA). *Prekooanska Plovidba* was later expressly applied by the Court of Appeal in *Eastgate Group Ltd v Lindsey Modern Group Ltd* [2001] EWCA Civ 1446; [2002] 1 WLR 642, where the purchaser of a company sued D1 (the vendor) for breach of contractual warranty; D1 made a Part 20 claim for contribution against D2 (the purchaser's accountants), alleging that D2 had negligently prepared inaccurate and misleading accounts. The court held that D1's claim was 'capable of being a claim to which the 1978 Act applied' and it was permitted to proceed. See also *National Museums and Galleries on Merseyside v AEW Architects and Designers Ltd* [2013] EWHC 2403 (TCC).

[101] *Prekooanska Plovidba v Felstar Shipping Corp* [1994] CLC 277 (CA) 298.

[102] Whatever that means.

[103] *Jackson v Murray* [2015] UKSC 5; [2015] 2 All ER 805.

ready exercise (a feature reflected in the judicial preference for round figures)',[104] an observation which chimes with Burrows' suggestion[105] that apportionment for contributory negligence in strict contractual cases could be restricted by statute to a few fixed percentages to avoid the risk 'of turning many straightforward claims for contractual damages into heavy disputes about comparative blameworthiness and causative potency'.[106] But evidence from analogous apportionment regimes suggests this fear is, in any event, unfounded.

IV. CONCLUSION

The modest aim of this chapter was not to reach a comprehensive answer to the question of whether contributory negligence should be available in cases of breach of strict contractual obligations, but merely to explore the two main arguments, one of principle, the other of policy, which persuaded the Law Commission not to recommend allowing the defence in such a case. The law has not stood still since 1993. In particular, the recognition of concurrent liability in tort[107] for most contractual obligations of reasonable care, for which contributory negligence is available, means that as Stevens rightly points out, 'It brings the law into disrepute if defendants are left to argue that they were negligent, whilst claimants deny this'.[108] In the light of this and other common law developments in the past two decades, it is suggested that the Law Commission's provisional conclusion in its Consultation Paper, to permit contributory negligence in case of breach of strict contractual obligations, is to be preferred.

[104] ibid [28].

[105] Burrows (n 86); Burrows (n 61) 143.

[106] Burrows (n 86) 177.

[107] And the increasing recognition that the basis of such liability is essentially contractual, so that for example the contractual test for remoteness of damage should apply even if the claim is pleaded in tort: *Wellesley Partners LLP v Withers LLP* [2015] EWCA Civ 1146; [2016] PNLR 19.

[108] Stevens (n 25).

12

The Impact of Exemption Clauses and Disclaimers: Construction, Contractual Estoppel and Public Policy

GERARD MCMEEL

> So now the Emperor walked under his high canopy in the midst of the procession, through the streets of the capital; and all the people standing by, and those at the windows, cried out, 'Oh! How beautiful are our Emperor's new clothes! What a magnificent train there is to the mantle; and how gracefully the scarf hangs!' In short, no one would allow that he could not see these much-admired clothes; because, in doing so, he would have declared himself either a simpleton or unfit for his office. Certainly, none of the Emperor's various suits, had ever made so great an impression, as these invisible ones. 'But the Emperor has nothing at all on!' said a little child.[1]

IN THE GLORIOUS television re-boot of Conan Doyle's classic detective tales the sinister Charles Augustus Magnussen goads Dr John Watson that he should have a t-shirt with the words 'I don't understand' on the front, and later 'I still don't understand' on the back.[2] The recent discovery of a new 'contractual defence'—or 'get-out-of-jail-free card'—of contractual estoppel prompts a similar observation.[3] Its adherents, judicial, and now academic, come sporting t-shirts with 'Freedom of contract rules!' on the front, and 'Sanctity of contract rules too!' on the back. This is because, as a matter of final analysis the supposed contractual estoppel doctrine has no substantive content, and adds nothing to the elementary proposition: 'properly construed this contract means…'. So why the need for the rhetorical flourish: 'and

[1] H Andersen, 'The Emperor's New Clothes' in H Andersen, *Hans Anderson's Fairy Tales* (London, Folio Society, 1995) 235.

[2] *Sherlock*, '*His Last Vow*', series 3, episode 3 (2014), by Steven Moffatt.

[3] There have been a number of papers on contractual estoppel over the last half a dozen years. The following abbreviations are used for the principal works addressed: J Braithwaite, 'The Origins and Implications of Contractual Estoppel' (2016) 132 *LQR* 120 (Braithwaite); A Dyson, 'Contractual Estoppel and the Scope of Party Autonomy', a paper for the conference *Contracts in Commercial Law* hosted by the University of New South Wales in December 2015 (Dyson) and N Goh, 'Non-Reliance Clauses and Contractual Estoppel: Commercially Sensible or Anomalous?' [2015] *Journal of Business Law* 511 (Goh). The background to the arguments developed here appears more fully in two treatises and one journal article: G McMeel, *The Construction of Contracts: Interpretation, Implication, and Rectification*, 2nd edn (Oxford, Oxford University Press, 2011) (McMeel, *Construction*); G McMeel and J Virgo, *McMeel and Virgo on Financial Advice and Financial Products*, 3rd edn (Oxford, Oxford University Press, 2014) (McMeel and Virgo, *Financial Advice*) and G McMeel, 'Documentary Fundamentalism in the Senior Courts: the Myth of Contractual Estoppel' [2011] *Lloyd's Maritime and Commercial Law Quarterly* 185 (McMeel, 'Documentary Fundamentalism').

the parties are precluded from saying otherwise.'? It is conceptually superfluous. The supposed doctrine had its gestation, and most typical deployment, where banks and financial institutions have advised, recommended and persuaded their commercial customers to enter into complex financial instruments which have proved disastrous for those counterparties. Yet the banks' extensive boilerplate insisted that no such advice took place. Their highly-trained and well-remunerated employees uttered no such words, and if they did—heaven forfend—the customer did not rely on those honeyed words of encouragement. For adherents of the twin shibboleths of freedom and sanctity of contract the virtual world of the contractual documentation trumps the actual reality of complex negotiations and deal-making. But they must feel at least slightly queasy with this unworldly literalism, so something more is required to lend some intellectual dignity to their gut instinct that printed words trump real world events; hence the reaching for that most legalistic of words, estoppel. Fair enough, if we lived in a Lockean—or Nozickian—state of nature. However, such faith in pure party autonomy requires the proponents of contractual estoppel to overlook two, not insignificant, matters.

First, the long-standing common law hostility to attempts by one party proffering goods or services to contract out of the minimum decencies of contractual performance for that type of transaction. Second, the will of Parliament. Parliamentary intervention, reflecting national public policy comes in two main forms. In the general law of contract, even outside consumer contracts, statutory standards police the reasonableness of attempts to derogate from minimum standards to be reasonably expected of the supplier of goods or services. More particularly in the financial sector, European and UK regulatory policy insists on very high standards for those who purvey securities and derivatives.

The running battle between businesses, seeking to rely on exemption clauses and analogous provisions, and their customers, who expected at least a minimum standard of contractual performance, has raged for at least a couple of centuries. In the nineteenth century the principal arena was the carriage of goods of sea, where receivers of cargo were met with elaborate lists of exempting circumstances tucked away on the back of bills of lading which they had no opportunity to negotiate. In that context the courts, and eventually international transport conventions, ensured that usually the minimum decencies were met.[4] In the last 10 years the principal battleground has been the marketing and supply of derivative financial instruments by banks to their retail customers. Two Court of Appeal cases in the second half of the last decade shut the door on claims brought by ultra-high net worth investors who had invested in derivatives based on emerging economy sovereign debt, and whose fingers were badly burned in the wake of the Russian and other sovereign

[4] F Rose, 'Carriage of Goods by Sea' in A Burrows (ed), *Principles of English Commercial Law* (Oxford, Oxford University Press, 2015) [3.26] and [3.28], citing as an example of express provisions narrowly construed in the light of common law implied terms, *Tattersall v National Steamship Co Ltd* (1884) 12 QBD 297 (QB). However, judicial efforts were not sufficient in the face of increasingly tightly-drawn terms, necessitating the introduction of the Hague Rules, implemented by the Carriage of Goods by Sea Act 1924, now superseded by the Carriage of Goods by Sea Act 1971, giving the Hague-Visby Rules the force of law.

defaults: *Peekay*[5] and *Springwell*.[6] In contrast to their nineteenth-century forbears, today's judges proved amenable to arguments which greatly circumscribed the banks' duties, and gave literal effect all manner of exemption clauses, risk disclosure statements and disclaimers. Clauses denying that advice took place were re-branded 'basis clauses' so as to fall outside statutory restrictions on exempting provisions.

To top it off, the judiciary claimed to have identified this new species of estoppel—estoppel by contract—to reinforce their strict application of the banks' boilerplate. I doubt whether the judges deciding those cases were aware that over the last decade the British and Irish banks had not merely been engaged in trades with wholesale counterparties and wealthy foreign investors—for whom there may have been limited sympathy—but had been systematically mis-selling derivatives alongside mainstream commercial lending to tens of thousands of small and medium-sized UK businesses.[7] Often entry into swaps was a pre-condition of commercial lending, and the practice was widespread amongst nearly all the commercial lenders in the marketplace.[8] The impact of these mis-sales on the recovering economy in the wake of Global Financial Crisis would be hard to estimate. Where those small and medium-sized businesses find themselves in the courts, all the unholy weapons of defence deployed on *Peekay* and *Springwell*—the transmutation of exemption clauses into basis clauses, literal application of disclaimers and contractual estoppel—are marshalled by the banks. This episode in the common law of contract has been the most disturbing of my academic and professional career. Normally, if criticism is offered of judicial developments in contract and commercial law, one is uttering counsels of perfection. But what has been unleashed here entails rank injustice. I hope to demonstrate in this chapter that the current approach to contractual defences based on exemption clauses and the like, is not merely out of step with the traditions of the common law of contract, but flies in the face of both European and UK legislative and regulatory policy. Much work is needed to redress the position, but the opportunities are there for the Supreme Court and Senior Courts, together with the Treasury, English and Scottish Law Commissions and the Financial Conduct Authority, to turn things around.

[5] *Peekay Intermark Ltd v Australia and New Zealand Banking Group Ltd* [2006] EWCA Civ 386; [2006] 2 Lloyd's Rep 511; revsg [2005] EWHC 830 (Comm).

[6] *Springwell Navigation Corporation v JP Morgan Chase Bank* [2010] EWCA Civ 1221; [2010] 2 CLC 705; affg [2008] EWHC 1186 (Comm) and [2008] EWHC 1793 (Comm), [2008] Lloyd's Rep Plus 63. It is remarkable that despite its significance, the Court of Appeal's judgment was not reported in any ICLR reports (including the Business Law Reports) or the Lloyd's Reports. For detailed accounts of *Peekay* (n 5) and *Springwell* (ibid) see McMeel and Virgo, *Financial Advice* (n 3) [6.20], [7.112]–[7.151] and [8.11]–[8.12], and McMeel, 'Documentary Fundamentalism' (n 3), 185, 192–205.

[7] Financial Conduct Authority, *Progress of sales through stages of the review as at 30 September 2015* identifies a 'review population' of 30,804 SMEs of which 14,936 firms had been found by September 2015 to have been mis-sold swaps by the nine banks participating in the review.

[8] The nine banks participating in the Financial Conduct Authority (FCA) review are RBS (including National Westminster), Lloyds (including Bank of Scotland), HSBC, Barclays, Santander UK, Clydesdale Bank/Yorkshire Bank (part of National Australia Group (Europe)), Co-operative Bank, Allied Irish Bank plc and Bank of Ireland.

I. PUBLIC POLICY INTERVENTIONS IN GENERAL CONTRACT LAW

Public policy in the response to the problems posed by one-sided exemption clauses is not confined to statutory intervention, but has a distinguished history at common law. Nineteenth-century judges developed what would now be labelled 'terms implied in law' to spell out minimum performance standards as standard incidents of routine transactions. I have borrowed the phrase 'minimum decencies' from the brilliant American Professor Karl Llewellyn, the genius behind the Uniform Commercial Code. He stated that the court is engaged in ascertaining 'what the *minimum decencies* are which a court will insist upon as essential to an enforceable bargain of a given type, or as being inherent in a bargain of that type'.[9] So in an area in which nineteenth-century judges did not lack intellectual self-confidence, Professor Francis Reynolds identified implied (and difficult to displace) minimum obligations of seaworthiness, cargo-worthiness, due care of cargo, reasonable dispatch and a duty not to deviate.[10] Express terms seeking to limit or negate these implied standards were restrictively construed.[11]

It is only possible to understand the role of exemption clauses in the context of the common law's working out of the standard incidents of the various species of common transactions: initially in respect of sales and the various species of bailments, and then contracts for the carriage of goods by sea, and then subsequently in the other supply of goods transactions, employment contracts, and most recently contracts for the provision of software. Many of these standard terms are now statutory implied terms, such as in sections 12 to 15 of the Sale of Goods Act 1979 and sections 13 to 15 of the Supply of Goods and Services Act 1982. The importance of judicially developed standard incidents of the contract and statutory implied terms, and the resulting sceptical approach to exemption clauses, can be seen in Lord Diplock's seminal account in *Photo Productions Ltd v Securicor Transport Ltd*:[12]

> My Lords, an exclusion clause is one which excludes or modifies an obligation … that would otherwise arise under the contract by implication of law. Parties are free to agree to whatever exclusion or modification of all types of obligations as they please within the limits that the agreement must retain the legal characteristics of a contract; and must not offend against the equitable rule against penalties … Since the presumption is that the parties by entering into the contract intended to accept the implied obligations exclusion clauses are to be construed strictly and the degree of strictness appropriate to be applied to their construction may properly depend upon the extent to which they involve departure from the implied obligations. Since the obligations implied by law in a commercial contract are those which, by judicial consensus over the years or by Parliament in passing a statute, have been regarded as obligations which a reasonable businessman would realise that he

[9] K Llewellyn, '*The Standardization of Commercial Contracts in English and Continental Law* by O. Prausnitz' (1939) 52 *Harvard Law Review* 700, 703 (book review). See McMeel, *Construction* (n 3) [1.17]–[1.21], [6.10]–[6.15] and [10.36]–[10.37].

[10] Rose, 'Carriage of Goods by Sea' (n 4) [3.26].

[11] For examples: *Glynn v Margetson & Co* [1893] AC 351 (HL); *London and North Western Railway Co v Neilson* [1922] 2 AC 263 (HL); *Cunard Steamship Co Ltd v Buerger* [1927] AC 1 (HL). See McMeel, *Construction* (n 3) [21.09]–[21.29].

[12] *Photo Productions Ltd v Securicor Transport Ltd* [1980] AC 827 (HL). See too Lord Diplock in *A Schroeder Music Publishing Co Ltd v Macaulay (formerly Instone)* [1974] 1 WLR 1308 (HL) 1316.

> was accepting when he entered into a contract of a particular kind, the court's view of the reasonableness of any departure from the implied obligations which would be involved in construing the express words of an exclusion clause in one sense that they are capable of bearing rather than another, is a relevant consideration in deciding what meaning the words were intended by the parties to bear. But this does not entitle the court to reject the exclusion clause, however unreasonable the court itself may think it is, if the words are clear and fairly susceptible of one meaning only.[13]

Several varieties of exemption clause were identified by Donaldson J in *Kenyon, Son & Craven Ltd v Baxter Hoare & Co Ltd*:[14]

> Protective conditions are of three distinct types, namely, first, those which limit or reduce what would otherwise be the defendants' duty; second, those which exclude the defendants' liability for breach of specified aspects of that duty and third, those which limit the extent to which the defendant is bound to indemnify the plaintiff in respect of the consequences of breaches of that duty.

Again the emphasis is what would otherwise have been the expected performance, ignoring the exemption clause. Accordingly exemption clauses have been traditionally analysed in the common law in a manner which is difficult to reconcile with the long-standing requirement that a contract should be construed as a whole. Rather the approach has been initially to construe the contract as though the exemption clause did not appear within it. As Scrutton LJ stated in *Rutter v Palmer*, 'the liability of the defendant apart from the exempting words must be ascertained'.[15]

In stark contrast, in his 1964 book on exemption clauses[16] Professor Brian Coote essayed a rival approach whereby such clauses were analysed as defining the obligations of the parties, rather than delimiting them. On this approach the usual ambition of the common law, to construe the contract as a whole, is taken seriously. As the editors of *Chitty* have suggested, 'There is considerable logical force in this contention and recent dicta have tended to support it'.[17] But as the other Holmes—Oliver Wendell—famously opined: 'The life of the law has not been logic but experience'.[18] The pragmatic experience of nineteenth-century English judges was that a more sceptical approach should be taken to exempting provisions, however they were dressed up.

Despite the Coote heresy the traditional approach continued to generally hold sway until recent years and is adopted in the Unfair Contract Terms Act 1977 (UCTA).[19] For sound public policy reasons, exemption clauses are approached with circumspection because of their tendency to cut down common law or contractual rights which would otherwise obtain. The rationale is that it is improbable that

[13] *Photo Productions* (n 12) 850–51.
[14] *Kenyon, Son & Craven Ltd v Baxter Hoare & Co Ltd* [1971] 1 WLR 519 (QBD) 522.
[15] *Rutter v Palmer* [1922] 2 KB 87 (CA) 92.
[16] B Coote, *Exception Clauses: Some Aspects of the Law Relating to Exception Clauses in Contracts for the Carriage, Bailment and Sale of Goods* (London, Sweet and Maxwell, 1964) ch 1.
[17] H Beale (ed), *Chitty on Contracts*, 32nd edn (London, Sweet and Maxwell, 2015) (*Chitty*) [15-003].
[18] O Holmes, *The Common Law* (Boston MA, Little, Brown & Co, 1881).
[19] *Chitty* (n 17) [15-003], [15-069]–[15-070].

the other party is deemed to be unlikely to have readily consented to foregoing the entitlements he would ordinarily and reasonably expect.[20]

In the statutory context, the Law Commissions and Parliament, anticipating the Coote heresy, deployed numerous 'anti-avoidance' provisions in the Unfair Contract Terms Act 1977 to prevent this rival approach from frustrating the aims of the legislation.[21] The legislation is equally concerned with clauses which are 'expressed not as excluding or restricting liability for the breach of subsisting obligations but as preventing the obligations to which they relate from arising or as providing that such obligations are to arise only in restricted or qualified form' or 'which have the same substantive effect'.[22] The Law Commissions identified the disagreement in *Anglo-Continental Holidays Ltd v Typaldos Lines (London) Ltd*[23] between Lord Denning MR and Davies LJ on the one hand and Russell LJ on the other. Travel agents' standard terms provided in respect of holiday cruises that 'Steamers, Sailing Dates, Rates and Itineraries are subject to change without prior notice'. The majority treated this as an exemption clause,[24] whereas Russell LJ considered it a duty-defining clause.[25] Rather than trust to incorporation or construction arguments the Law Commissions intended to embrace such clauses in the statutory scheme because of[26]

> the essential danger, namely that the relatively unsophisticated or unwary party will not realise what or how little he has been promised, although the legal scope and effect of the contract may be perfectly clear to a lawyer ... We propose that a term should be subject to control if it has the effect of enabling the promisor to offer in purported fulfilment of the contract a performance which is substantially different from that which the promisee reasonably expected when he entered into the contract, or if it has the effect of enabling the promisor to refuse to render any performance.

This is the root of section 3. Accordingly, the 1977 Act does not provide a comprehensive definition of an 'exemption clause'.[27] Sections 2 and 3 employ the phrase 'exclude or restrict liability' in the context of various statutory, common law, and contractual duties. Critically section 3 provides:[28]

> (1) This section applies as between contracting parties where one of them deals ... on the other's written standard terms of business.

[20] Compare *Photo Productions* (n 12) 850–51 (Lord Diplock) and *Ailsa Craig Fishing Co Ltd v Malvern Fishing Co Ltd* [1983] 1 WLR 964 (HL) 970 (Sc) (Lord Fraser).

[21] See Law Commission and Scottish Law Commission, *Exemption Clauses (Second Report)* (Law Com No 69, Scot Law Com No 39) (1975) [143]–[146].

[22] ibid [143].

[23] *Anglo-Continental Holidays Ltd v Typaldos Lines (London) Ltd* [1967] 2 Lloyd's Rep 61.

[24] ibid 63, 66.

[25] ibid 67. But even Russell LJ would not permit the clause to 'alter the substance of the arrangement'.

[26] Law Com No 69, Scot Law Com No 39 [145]–[146]. This is the ultimate source of s 3. See cl 1 of the draft Exemption Clauses (England and Wales) Bill, and Explanatory notes (pp 118–19).

[27] The phrase is not defined in the 'interpretation' section: s 14. See Law Com No 69, Scot Law Com No 39 [143].

[28] Unfair Contract Terms Act 1977, s 3. As amended by the Consumer Rights Act 2015, Sch, [5(2)]. The 2015 Act also adds in a new s 3(3) of the 1977 Act: 'This section does not apply to a term in a consumer contract (but see the provision made about such contracts in section 62 of the Consumer Rights Act 2015)'.

(2) As against that party, the other cannot by reference to any contract term—
    (a) when himself in breach of contract, exclude or restrict any liability of his in respect of the breach; or
    (b) claim to be entitled–
        (i) to render a contractual performance substantially different from that which was reasonably expected of him, or
        (ii) in respect of the whole or any part of his contractual obligation, to render no performance at all,

except in so far as (in any of the cases mentioned above in this subsection) the contract term satisfies the requirement of reasonableness.

Professor Elizabeth Macdonald has bemoaned the 'unused potential' of section 3(2)(b)(i).[29] Some leading appellate cases—conspicuous by their absence in *Peekay*, and *Springwell*—adopt the same approach as the common law in this context of the 1977 Act: that is, to consider what the position would be, setting the contractual provisions to one side.[30] Chitty suggests that this section can only be given sensible content by, in effect, disregarding the Coote heresy, and identifying the contractual obligation apart from the exemption (or allegedly duty-defining) term.[31] Case law makes clear that the 'reasonable expectations' in section 3(2)(b)(i) can be derived from pre-contractual representations, and cannot be confined to the four corners of any document.[32]

In addition, section 13 of the 1977 Act provides:[33]

To the extent that this Part of this Act[34] prevents the exclusion or restriction of any liability it also prevents—

(a) making the liability or its enforcement subject to restrictive or onerous conditions;
(b) excluding or restricting any right or remedy in respect of the liability, or subjecting a person to any prejudice in consequence of his pursuing any such right or remedy;

[29] E Macdonald, 'Unfair Contract Terms Act—Thirty Years On' in A Burrows and E Peel (eds), *Contract Terms* (Oxford, Oxford University Press, 2007) 153, 158–64.

[30] The important House of Lords authority of *Smith v Eric S Bush (a firm)* [1990] 1 AC 831 (HL) 848–49 on negligence (Lord Templeman), 856–57 (Lord Griffiths, expressly citing the Law Commissions' Report) and 873–74 (Lord Jauncey), and the decision of the Court of Appeal in a breach of contract case, *Phillips Products Ltd v Hyland* [1987] 1 WLR 659 (CA) (referred to with approval by Lord Griffiths in *Smith v Bush* (ibid) 857). The suggestion in *Titan Steel Wheels Ltd v Royal Bank of Scotland* [2010] EWHC 211 (Comm); [2010] 2 Lloyd's Rep 92 [104] (David Steel J) that *Smith v Bush* (ibid) 'may have been somewhat overtaken by later decisions in regard to the assumption of responsibility' must be wrong. Compare *Robinson v PE Jones (Contractors) Ltd* [2011] EWCA Civ 9; [2012] QB 44 [64] (Jackson LJ) and *Avrora Fine Arts Investment Ltd v Christie, Manson & Woods Ltd* [2012] EWHC 2198 (Ch); [2012] PNLR 35 [136]–[146] (Newey J).

[31] *Chitty* (n 17) [15-069]–[15-070].

[32] *SAM Business Systems Ltd v Hedley & Co* [2002] EWHC 2733 (TCC), [2003] 1 All ER (Comm) 465 [62], where HHJ Peter Bowsher QC observed, despite the presence of an 'entire agreement' clause: 'What was reasonably expected was what was represented in the pre-contractual representations'. Approved by the Court of Appeal in *AXA Sun Life Services plc v Campbell Martin Ltd* [2011] EWCA Civ 133, [2011] 2 Lloyd's Rep 1 [50].

[33] As amended by the Consumer Rights Act 2015, Sch 4, [12]. Note s 13 does not qualify ss 3 (liability arising under contract, other than for 'contractual negligence' which is comprised in s 2(2)). Law Com No 69, Scot Law Com No 39 [162].

[34] Sections 1 to 14 (now excluding ss 4 and 5 which have been removed by the Consumer Rights Act 2015, Sch 4 [6], [7]).

(c) excluding or restricting rules of evidence or procedure;

and (to that extent) sections 2, [6 and] 7 also prevent excluding or restricting liability by reference to terms and notices which exclude or restrict the relevant obligation or duty.

Together with sections 3(2), and 11(3), section 13 constitutes the 'anti-avoidance' provisions of the 1977 Act.[35] One would imagine that they would be in the forefront of the cases in this context. However, save for the consideration of section 3(2)(b) in *AXA Sun Life Services plc v Campbell Martin Ltd*[36] there has been little detailed consideration of their impact in recent case law. Of equal concern is that the last reference in appellate authority to the Law Commissions' second report on exemption clauses as the *travaux preparatoires* of the 1977 Act appears to have been in *Watford Electronics Ltd v Sanderson CFL Ltd* in 2001, before the invention of contractual estoppel.[37]

A. Differentiating Counterparties

At the highest level of generality both UK and EU institutions now resort to 'text-speak' to make the elementary differentiation between 'B2B'—business-to-business contracts—and 'B2C' or business-to-consumer contracts. That simple dichotomy is insufficient to explain even the principal interventions by UK statute in freedom of contract. Further differentiation is possible based on the size and wealth of business entities. Both EU and UK law now make provision for identifying with precision the small and medium-sized enterprises (SME) community, comprising two sub-categories:[38]

- an SME is an entity of any economic form that employs fewer than 250 persons, with an annual turnover not exceeding €50 million and/or a balance-sheet total not exceeding €43 million;
  - a small enterprise employs fewer than 50 persons, with an annual turnover not exceeding €10 million and/or a balance-sheet total not exceeding €10 million;
  - a micro-enterprise employs fewer than 10 persons, with an annual turnover not exceeding €2 million and/or a balance-sheet total not exceeding €2 million.

In some areas less differentiation is required: as we shall see in relation to the supply of securities and derivatives, the distinction is generally between wholesale deals

[35] Section 11(3) provides: 'In relation to a notice (not being a notice having contractual effect), the requirement of reasonableness under this Act is that it should be fair and reasonable to allow reliance on it, having regard to all the circumstances obtaining when the liability arose or (but for the notice) would have arisen'.

[36] *AXA Sun Life Services* (n 32) [50].

[37] *Watford Electronics Ltd v Sanderson CFL Ltd* [2001] EWCA Civ 317; [2001] 1 All ER (Comm) 696, [16]–[17] (Chadwick LJ). See also *Smith v Bush* (n 30) 856–57 (Lord Griffiths).

[38] European Commission Recommendation 2003/361/EC; and now Small Business, Enterprise and Employment Act 2015 ss 33 and 34. See also Financial Conduct Authority, *Our approach to SMEs as users of financial services* (DP 15/7), November 2015 (FCA, *Our approach to SMEs*) [3.1]–[3.4].

(generally between two financial firms) and all other deals. Nearly all customers are 'retail' in that context.[39]

Under existing UK law, first there are bespoke commercial arrangements between two business entities which do not engage a standard form drafted or put forward by one party. This could also embrace a situation where two parties are both members of the same trade association and use the standard forms of that entity. For example, two banks in a wholesale derivative trade agreeing on the use of the ISDA terms.[40] Let us call these 'B2B1'. Secondly, there are deals between two business parties where one party deals on the other's standard terms. Let us call that 'B2B2'. Even here there is a potential issue as to what is meant by the other's standard terms. An easy example is where the business uses its own-badged standard terms: eg 'Barclays Bank's Terms for Business Customers'. Then there is the instance of one party putting forward the standard terms of a trade association, such as a bank incorporating the ISDA terms in a swap where the counterparty is not another financial institution. Differentiate also where the counterparty is not an SME. Let us call that 'B2B2(a)'. Contrast the business dealing on standard terms with an SME. Let us call that 'B2B2(b)'. Then, of course there is B2C. Everyone agrees that such transactions require the greatest restraints on unbridled freedom of contract, and these are now contained in Part 2 of the Consumer Rights Act 2015.

So just looking at the general UK statutory interventions in business deals, in reverse order, B2B(2)(b) deals obviously merit the greatest scrutiny. First, they fall within the sections 3 and 6 of UCTA, requiring the minimum decencies to apply unless the exempting party can satisfy the statutory requirement of reasonableness.[41] In addition section 3 of the Misrepresentation Act 1967 will be engaged. The same powers exist over B2B(2)(a), where the counterparty is not an SME, but may be less likely to be deployed. Lastly, whilst 'B2B(1)' cases fall outside of section 3 of UCTA, section 3 of the 1967 Act is still engaged. Whatever the type of B2B contract,[42] attempts to exclude liability for misrepresentation fall to be assessed against the statutory requirement of reasonableness in section 11 of UCTA. This is at the very least suggestive that as a matter of national public policy, Parliament has taken seriously since 1967 attempts to contract out of liability for misrepresentation.[43]

[39] See further below at text to nn 84 to 86.

[40] The International Swaps and Derivatives Association. Also a widespread phenomenon in the mercantile contexts of international trade for sales (eg GAFTA and FOSFA), insurance and carriage. See *Pioneer Shipping Ltd v BTP Tioxide Ltd ('The Nema') (No 2)* [1982] AC 724 (HL) (Lord Diplock) and McMeel, *Construction* (n 3) [1.52]–[1.53] and [6.06]–[6.09]. For a domestic commercial example pushed to an extreme—but clearly right—conclusion, consider *British Crane Hire Co Ltd v Ipswich Plant Hire* [1975] QB 303 (CA) (both parties were members of same trade association, but neither explicitly adverted to governing terms); McMeel, *Construction* (n 3) [15.82].

[41] Under s 11. Sections 3 and 6 as amended by the Consumer Rights Act 2015, Sch 4, [5], [8].

[42] B2C are now regulated by Part 2 of the Consumer Rights Act 2015. See s 3(2) of the 1967 Act as inserted by Schedule 4, [1(3)] of the 2015 Act.

[43] See s 3 of the 1967 Act as originally enacted. For full discussion see J Cartwright, 'Excluding Liability for Misrepresentation' in A Burrows and E Peel (eds), *Contract Terms* (Oxford, Oxford University Press, 2007) 213, especially at 218–20, discussing the Law Reform Committee's Tenth Report (Cmnd 1782, 1962) which lay behind the 1967 Act. The Committee favoured a non-excludable remedy for misrepresentation.

Furthermore so far as the supply of goods is concerned the minimum decencies can only be contracted out of if the exempting party can satisfy the statutory requirement of reasonableness.[44]

B. The Rise of the 'Basis Clause'

Despite this comprehensive policy background, which permits and encourages a sensitive approach to dealings between big business and SMEs, there is still a tendency to treat all businesses as though they were on a level playing-field. So whilst the courts should be alive to the distinction between B2B(1) and B2B(2), and between B2B(2)(a) and (b),[45] in a case like *AXA Sun Life Services plc v Campbell Martin Ltd* the Court of Appeal treated all parties as commercial entities, even though on one side there was one of the world's largest insurance companies, and on the other side a handful of small mortgage and insurance brokerages, presumably micro-enterprises, with fewer than 10 employees. Worse still is the rise of the so-called 'basis clause' which is said to side-step statutory review of exemption clauses. Modern difficulties stem from the judgment of Toulson J (as he then was) in *IFE Fund SA v Goldman Sachs International*.[46] That was clearly a wholesale deal between a financial institution and an arranging bank in relation to a syndicated loan agreement. Toulson J upheld the provisions in the Information Memorandum stating that its content had not been independently verified and that the arranger accepted no responsibility, and held that they were not exemption clauses within the meaning of UCTA. They defined the duties of the parties and there could be no question of a general duty to advise.[47] This was embraced by Gloster J in *Springwell* and further refined by Christopher Clarke J in *Raiffeisen Zentralbank Osterreich AG v Royal Bank of Scotland plc*,[48] who confirmed the existence of duty-defining or 'basis clauses'. In the Court of Appeal in *Springwell* this analysis was adopted[49] but there was some differentiation made between those of the 'Relevant Provisions', which were said to merely define the parties' relationship—and therefore immune from review under section 3 of UCTA—and those which were on their face exclusions of liability, such as those restricting liability save for gross negligence or willful misconduct.[50] Sometimes overlooked, the Court of Appeal in *Springwell* did, on balance, find that the

[44] Unfair Contract Terms Act 1977, s 6.

[45] Compare Law Commission and Scottish Law Commission, Unfair Terms in Contracts (Law Com No 292, Scot Law Com No 199; 2005); discussed in H Beale, 'Exclusion and Limitation Clauses in Business Contracts: Transparency' in A Burrows and E Peel (eds), *Contract Terms* (Oxford, Oxford University Press, 2007) 191.

[46] *IFE Fund SA v Goldman Sachs International* [2006] EWHC 2887 (Comm); [2007] 1 Lloyd's Rep 264; affd [2007] EWCA Civ 811; [2007] 2 Lloyd's Rep 449.

[47] [2006] EWHC 2887 (Comm), [2007] 1 Lloyd's Rep 264 [71] affd [2007] EWCA Civ 811, [2007] 2 Lloyd's Rep 449 [28] (Waller LJ).

[48] *Raiffeisen Zentralbank Osterreich AG v Royal Bank of Scotland plc* (*Raiffeisen*) [2010] EWHC 1392 (Comm); [2011] 1 Lloyd's Rep 123 [230]–[315].

[49] *Springwell* (n 6) [180]–[181] (Aikens LJ).

[50] ibid [181] (Aikens LJ).

'no representation' and 'no warranty' clauses were exemption clauses and subject to statutory review.[51] The same principle was extended to 'entire agreement' clauses by the Court of Appeal in *AXA Sun Life Services plc v Campbell Martin*.[52] However, the discovery of a new species of 'basis clauses', allegedly immune from statutory review, is of significant concern. The analysis has proceeded without appropriate consideration of the statutory rules and the background to it. The Law Commissions sensibly and practically directed the courts to approach the issue of whether a term was an exemption clause as a question of substance, informed by all the background circumstances and reasonable expectations of the parties. The inquiry was not confined to the four corners of the document. In contrast, modern courts appear to approach this as a pure question of construction. The test for whether a so-called basis clause constitutes an exemption clause is now said to be, in the words of Christopher Clarke J's in *Raïffeisen*,[53] whether it 'attempts to re-write history or parts company with reality'. That may or may not be more stringent than the Law Commission's simpler test, but has certainly been applied as erecting a high threshold for claimants to overcome. We shall revert to the issue of the basis clause below.

II. PUBLIC POLICY INTERVENTIONS IN THE FINANCIAL SERVICES CONTEXT

As we have said the modern arena where contractual defences have developed is the sale of derivative products by banks to SMEs, bundled with credit financing—usually interest rate swaps (swaps), also dubbed by the regulator 'interest rate hedging products' (IRHPs). It should not be overlooked that swaps are a comparatively novel financial instrument.[54] The Financial Conduct Authority (FCA) in November 2015 published a Discussion Paper tackling the many concerns expressed in the wake of the Global Financial Crisis of the treatment of SMEs by financial institutions.[55] The importance of SMEs to the UK economy cannot be under-estimated, with the nation's 5.4 million SMEs accounting for 47 per cent of private sector turnover, 60 per cent of employment and 70 per cent of net job creation.[56] The FCA acknowledged that concerns about the treatment of SMEs by financial institutions (and implicitly the regulator's failure to deal with the problem) had been raised in many quarters, including by the Treasury Select Committee and the Parliamentary Commission on Banking Standards.[57] The principal example of detriment was its predecessor's own review of IRHPs or swaps in 2012.[58]

[51] ibid [181]–[182] (Aikens LJ).
[52] *AXA Sun Life Services* (n 32) [51].
[53] *Raiffeisen* (n 48) [314]; adopted by the Court of Appeal in *Springwell* (n 6) [180]–[182] (Aikens LJ).
[54] The date of 1982 is suggested in D Kynaston, *The City of London Volume IV: A Club No More 1945–2000* (London, Chatto and Windus, 2001) 614.
[55] FCA, *Our approach to SMEs* (n 38).
[56] ibid [2.1].
[57] ibid [2.4].
[58] ibid [4.1].

In the critical case of *Springwell*, Gloster J, as she then was, was persuaded that the investment bank's representative purveying derivatives was ultimately a 'salesman' rather than a 'financial adviser' or 'broker'. The most her Ladyship was prepared to accept was that there might be a 'low level duty of care' on the part of the bank's representative not to make negligent misstatements and to use reasonable care not to recommend a high-risk investment without pointing out that it was such.[59]

Stepping back for a moment, the analogy with the car salesman, which appears to have appealed to the judge, is wholly inapt for complex financial products, delivered in a highly regulated environment, by highly-trained and -remunerated individuals in whom customers repose trust. The complexity of the modern vehicle lies beneath the bonnet, and its recondite details need only trouble enthusiasts. Most drivers are only concerned with the resulting performance and handling. In contrast, the complexity of financial instruments is integral to their structure, risks and monetary consequences for counterparties. This mis-characterisation of the relationship by Gloster J, and those following her,[60] involves a fundamental misunderstanding of the history of the legal regulation of banks and financial institutions in the UK. It takes a little scene-setting to explain why this widespread misperception is false.

A. The Impact of 'Big Bang'

The City of London in its pre-'Big Bang' days generally operated on the basis that those wishing to engage in major financial transactions should be protected by having to engage a broker or agent on their side of the transaction who would represent their interests and owe their clients fiduciary duties. The broker on the Lloyd's of London insurance market provides an obvious example. Turning to dealings in listed company shares or securities, investors—big or small—had to engage a stockbroker. Prior to the London Stock Exchange's so-called 'Big Bang' of 1986 the traditional regime had been one of 'single capacity' dealings.[61] A dealer in securities was either buying or selling as principal—a 'stockjobber', or in the modern idiom a 'market maker'—or was dealing as an agent or broker. This had required an investor initially to seek advice from, or at least the services of, a stockbroker, who acted as intermediary between the investor and a stockjobber, or retailer of shares. In theory the broker would approach numerous jobbers to get the best price available on the market. Investors were not allowed to deal with a jobber directly. This provided some protection for the investor through the ordinary principles of the law of agency, and in particular the fiduciary duties owed by agents to their principals. After Big Bang, 'dual capacity' dealing became the norm; that is, a single firm could purchase and sell securities either as principal or agent. The changes introduced by the Big Bang necessitated a major revision of the investor protection regime. Step forward the

[59] *Springwell* [2008] EWHC 1186 (Comm) (n 6) [108]; *Springwell* (CA) (n 6) [123] (Aikens LJ).

[60] Most recently by the Manchester Mercantile Court in *Thornbridge Ltd v Barclays Bank plc* [2015] EWHC 3430 (QB).

[61] For the background to the Big Bang see Kynaston, *The City of London* (n 54) 581–724.

legendary Professor Jim Gower of the London School of Economics, then the leading academic company lawyer.[62] He recognised that the introduction of dual capacity dealings made conflicts of interest inevitable. A firm would often have an interest in off-loading a portion of shares to a customer at a price to suit it. Accordingly in the wake of the Big Bang, the original regulatory statute, the Financial Services Act 1986 (the 1986 Act) instituted a new set of conduct of business rules to govern all dealings in investments.[63] As Professor Gower observed,[64]

> in the coming era of financial supermarkets and the ending of single-capacity it will no longer be practicable to maintain a rigid distinction between those acting as agents, and thereby owing fiduciary duties to their clients, and those acting as principals on their own account, and thereby owing no such duties. The solution proposed is that whether acting as principal or agent the investment business must comply with a principle of fair dealing and observe a duty of care, skill and diligence and a duty of disclosure. In agency business the principle of fair dealing will entail, in addition, observance of principles of 'best execution' on behalf of the client and of 'subordination of interest' so that the clients' interests are paramount.

Clearly what was envisaged was a relationship at least akin to a fiduciary or advisory standard. Professor Gower's approach was echoed more than 20 years later by another LSE academic, Professor John Kay, in the Coalition Government-commissioned Review in 2012, aimed at improving 'long-termism' in investment markets. Kay, an economist, identified the fiduciary standard as the benchmark for financial markets where a firm provided advice or exercised discretion, all the way down chains of intermediation. Kay also considered that the fiduciary standard should apply irrespective of client classification, and should not be capable of being contracted out of.[65] The UK Government accepted the findings of Kay and has asked the FCA to examine the extent to which the current regulatory regime conformed to these high standards.[66] It fell to the Law Commission in its 2014 paper on investment intermediaries to point out how far the common law (regulation aside) falls short, with the courts 'reluctant to override the contractual arrangements of sophisticated parties'.[67] It is ironic that economists and politicians wrongly assume that the courts

[62] Kynaston, *The City of London* (n 54) 595, 624, 640, 650 and 682–84.

[63] For the background, see: L Gower, *Review of Investor Protection: A Discussion Document* (London, Her Majesty's Stationery Office, 1982); L Gower, *Review of Investor Protection, Part I* (Cmnd 9125, 1984); a Government White Paper followed: Department for Trade and Industry, *Financial Services in the United Kingdom—A New Framework for Investor Protection* (Cmnd 9432, 1985) which to a large extent adopted Professor Gower's recommendations in Part I of his Report. Subsequently the second part of Professor Gower's Report was published: L Gower, *Review of Investor Protection—Part II* (Cmnd 9125, 1985). For his account of the resulting system, see L Gower, '"Big Bang" and City Regulation' (1988) 51 *MLR* 1.

[64] Gower, *Review of Investor Protection—Part II* (n 63) [4.14]. Professor Gower was commenting on DTI, *Financial Services in the United Kingdom* (n 63) [7.1]–[7.7].

[65] J Kay, *The Kay Review of UK Equity Markets and Long-Term Decision Making: Final Report* (July 2012) [9.9] and recommendation 7.

[66] Department for Business, Innovation and Skills, *Ensuring equity markets support long-term growth: The Government response to the Kay Review* (November 2012) [2.8].

[67] Law Commission, *Fiduciary Duties of Investment Intermediaries* (Law Com No 350; HC 368; 30 June 2014) [10.11]. See ch 11 of the Law Commission paper for fuller discussion.

will assume the role of imposing certain minimum decencies on the parties and will police such bargains in the name of the fiduciary standard expected of trusted advisers.

Professor Gower's brilliant reports were the backdrop to the Financial Services Act 1986 and the introduction of 'conduct of business' rules for banks and investment houses engaged in investment business largely modelled on American standards of appropriate risk disclosure and suitability of investment recommendations.[68] It was originally implemented by the detailed rules introduced under the 1986 Act. With hindsight the complexity of the institutions and legislative techniques of the 1986 Act undermined its effectiveness. First, there was the over-elaborate institutional structure with two tiers of regulatory bodies, modelled on US securities law—with the Securities and Investments Board (apeing the US Securities and Exchange Commission) as the head regulator, and myriad bodies such as the Securities and Futures Authority (and the acronymous LAUTRO and FIMBRA) as front-line regulators. Secondly, and perhaps more significantly, it was probably an error of judgment that the relationship between front-line regulators and their regulated communities was notionally 'contractual' under the 1986 Act, in the name of supposed 'self-regulation'.[69] Reading recent judgments I detect an underlying assumption that modern financial regulatory standards are akin to default rules which can be ousted or contracted around. However, even under the 1986 Act, breach of each individual conduct of business requirement was actionable by a counterparty which suffered loss as a result under section 62. That is, each rule was a mini-tort.[70] Originally such breaches would have been actionable by any counterparty, including wholesale players, but that was retreated from with the express statutory right of action confined to 'private investors'[71] and subsequently 'private persons'.[72] This reflected a concern that regulatory rules might be routinely relied on in litigation between market counterparties who in fact could look after themselves.

B. The Financial Regulatory Framework

To the cognoscenti of financial regulation it is well-known that despite the New Labour Government's rhetoric in 1997 of a 'single financial regulator'—in the

[68] On these new standards see R Cranston, *Principles of Banking Law* 2nd edn (Oxford, Oxford University Press, 2002) 198–200.

[69] DTI, *Financial Services in the United Kingdom* (n 63) [5.1]: 'self-regulation within a statutory framework'. See Professor Gower's concerns about the proposed private law nature of the relationship between SROs and regulated community: L Gower, *Review of Investor Protection—Part II* (n 63) [2.10].

[70] L Gower, *Review of Investor Protection—Part II* (n 63) [7.09]. See the first edition of G McMeel and J Virgo, *Financial Advice and Financial Products: Law and Liability* (Oxford, Oxford University Press, 2001) [7.15]–[7.20].

[71] Section 62A of the 1986 Act as inserted by section 193 of the Companies Act 1989; Financial Services Act 1986 (Restriction of Right of Action) Regulations 1991 (SI 1991/489).

[72] Section 150 of FSMA (from 1 December 2001), replaced by s 138D (from 1 April 2013); and Financial Services and Markets Act 2000 (Rights of Action) Regulations 2001 (SI 2001/2256), regs 3 and 5(1).

shape of the Financial Services Authority (FSA)[73] covering the three traditional sectors of investment, banking (in the sense of deposit taking) and insurance—what was in fact introduced under the original FSA *Handbook of rules and guidance* was less ambitious. The new Financial Services and Markets Act 2000 (FSMA) did decisively sweep away any pretence of 'self-regulation' and the façade of a 'contractual' basis for regulatory rules. The rules were made by the regulator in pursuit of statutory objectives and principles.

After the Coalition Government's reforms the principal enactment remains FSMA, albeit heavily amended over the succeeding dozen years, especially in the wake of the global financial crisis, by the Financial Services Act 2012, with the latter initiating the new 'twin peaks' regime. On 1 April 2013 the FSA was split into the Financial Conduct Authority (FCA) and the Prudential Regulation Authority (PRA). FSMA still provides only the framework, with a large part of the substance of the reforms left to secondary legislation. A large volume of statutory instruments, mostly emanating from the Treasury, flesh out the detail of the primary legislation. These encompass many topics, including such crucial matters as what count as regulated activities under FSMA. In addition, the fruits of the FCA's and the PRA's own rule-making powers contained in their respective *Handbooks* provide in practice much of the essential detail of financial services regulation, such as the investment conduct of business rules (COBS).

I have elsewhere described the resulting picture of financial legislation and regulation as resembling a wedding cake,[74] with the first or top tier comprising FSMA, as amended, and other related primary legislation (including what remains of the Consumer Credit Act 1974, now that the FCA is the credit regulator). The second or middle tier comprises hundreds of separate pieces of secondary legislation—including such significant measures as the Regulated Activities Order[75] and the Payment Services Regulations.[76] The bottom and largest tier comprises the *Handbooks* consisting of the rules made under delegated powers in FSMA by the statutory regulators, originally the FSA, and subsequently the FCA and PRA.

Financial regulation distinguishes prudential measures from conduct of business rules. The former are concerned with the financial health of providers, their soundness and resilience: classically the capital and liquidity requirements that banks and insurers must meet. The latter are explicit interventions in freedom of contract, designed to redress the expertise imbalance between financial institutions and professionals on the one hand and their customers on the other, arising from

[73] In fact the same corporate body as the Securities and Investments Board established under the 1986 Act, but launched—in advance of a legislative reform—with a change of name. Financial Services (Change of Name of Designated Agency) Rules 1997, made under the 1986 Act. The FCA is the same corporate body as the FSA, following another name-change.

[74] McMeel and Virgo, *Financial Advice* (n 3) [1.23].

[75] Financial Services and Markets Act 2000 (Regulated Activities) Order 2001 (SI 2001/544) as amended (RAO), made by HM Treasury under s 22 of FSMA. The scope of the regulated activities depends on the language of the RAO and the ordinary processes of statutory construction, as illustrated by the decision of the Supreme Court in *Re Digital Satellite Warranty Cover Ltd* [2013] UKSC 7; [2013] 1 WLR 605.

[76] Payment Services Regulations 2009 (SI 2009/209).

information asymmetry and other market failures: these embrace disclosure requirements, requirements to be clear, fair and not misleading in communications, 'know your customer' (KYC) obligations, and rules requiring advice and discretionary decisions to be suitable or appropriate. Our concern is with the latter.

In 2001 the FSA became a single prudential regulator (albeit—as we now know—not a very successful one), but only carried on the previous regime of conduct of business regulation for the investment sector alone. Conduct of business rules would eventually be rolled out for the general insurance sector in 2005, and for banking business as late as 2009. The point is that since 1986 investment business—corporate securities and derivatives—has been regarded as sufficiently complex to require detailed curtailing of freedom of contract by regulatory rules. Furthermore, the UK was under an EU law obligation under the Investment Services Directive to have in place investment conduct of business rules, although with an uncharacteristic lack of prescription as to what they should be.[77]

So the original FSA *Conduct of Business Sourcebook* for investment business (COB) was most definitely not self-regulation, nor contractually based, nor merely industry standards: it was statutory regulation made under FSMA, forming part of the FSA *Handbook*, based on an EU law obligation. The hard-edged statutory nature of modern financial regulation was reinforced when the Investment Services Directive was superseded at EU level by the Markets in Financial Instruments Directive (MiFID),[78] a maximum harmonisation measure, which was implemented on 1 November 2007 by the deletion of COB and the insertion of the MiFID-based, heavily revised *Conduct of Business Sourcebook* (now COBS). To emphasise the point the Interpretation Act 1978 is expressly applied to the construction of provisions of the Handbook.[79]

Section 150 (subsequently replaced by section 138D) of FSMA carried on the statutory right of action for breaches of the FSA's rules, confined to private persons. What counts as a private person entitled to the statutory right of action has proved controversial in the context of IRHP sales to SMEs, with judges perhaps too readily holding that non-financial services firms fall outside the test.[80] The Court of Appeal was due to hear a challenge to the current restrictive construction of the Rights of Action Regulations[81] in July 2016.[82] If a wider construction is not adopted by the courts it is strongly arguable that the UK Government has not properly implemented the relevant EU law (described below) by leaving the mis-match between

[77] Investment Services Directive (EEC) 93/22, [1993] OJ L141/27, art 11. See J Welch and P Parker, 'European Financial Services' in G Walker, R Purves and M Blair (eds), *Financial Services Law*, 3rd edn (Oxford, Oxford University Press, 2014) [3.106]–[3.110].

[78] Markets in Financial Instruments Directive 2004/39/EC. See Welch and Parker (n 77) [3.111]–[3.118].

[79] That the meaning of rules in the FSA/FCA *Handbook* is a question of statutory construction is acknowledged in the 'General Provisions' (GEN) of the *Handbook*, and in particular GEN 2.2.1R, GEN 2.2.2G, GEN 2.2.11R and GEN 2.2.12G.

[80] *Titan Steel Wheels* (n 30) [44]–[76] (David Steel J); *Camerata Property Inc v Credit Suisse Securities (Europe) Ltd* [2011] EWHC 479 (Comm); [2011] 2 BCLC 54 [89]–[98] (Flaux J); and the Scottish case of *Grant Estates Ltd v Royal Bank of Scotland Plc* [2012] CSOH 133 [41]–[62] (Lord Hodge).

[81] Financial Services and Markets Act 2000 (Rights of Action) Regulations 2001 (SI 2001/2256).

[82] *MTR Bailey Trading Ltd v Barclays Bank plc* [2015] EWCA Civ 667 (Kitchin LJ, granting permission to appeal from the judgment of HHJ Keyser QC in the Cardiff Mercantile Court: [2013] EWHC 2882 (QB)). See also FCA, *Our approach to SMEs* (n 38) [1.13] and fn 5.

'retail clients' in COBS/MiFID (which would embrace all non-authorised SMEs) and 'private persons' in the Right of Action Regulations.[83] What would then be needed is an amendment to those Regulations by the Treasury to bring the rights of action into line with MiFID obligations.

MiFID is not principally concerned with wholesale transactions, where a bank or investment firm deals purely as a contractual counterparty, or on its own account. Dealing on its own account is an investment activity within MiFID and not an investment service. However, investment advice is clearly an investment service.[84] For the purposes of providing investment services COBS 3 (Client categorisation) contains the MiFID-based regime for classification of clients. The two principal categories of client under MiFID are retail client and professional client. A 'retail client' is defined negatively as one who is neither a professional client nor an eligible counterparty.[85] The definition of 'professional client' is elaborate, but includes entities required to be authorised in the financial market and other large undertakings.[86] Most non-financial firms, and all non-financial SMEs, are entitled to the maximum protection of the rules for retail clients.

The critical point about MiFID is that it virtually eliminated the scope for financial firms to deal on an 'execution only' (or freedom of contract) basis with counterparties other than other financial institutions or very large corporates. First, MiFID article 19(1) requires Member States to ensure that each investment firm acts 'honestly, fairly and professionally and in accordance with the best interests of its clients', which forms the basis for COBS 2.1.1R for retail clients.[87] This is clearly analogous to a fiduciary standard, requiring the subordination of the financial firm's own interest. For most counterparties a suitability, or at least an appropriateness, standard applies to the provision of securities and derivatives.[88] The important rules on the suitability of advice form COBS 9 (Suitability, including basic advice).[89] The 'know your

[83] Note also the disastrous decision of the Court of Appeal in *Green v Royal Bank of Scotland plc* [2003] EWCA Civ 1197, [2014] Bus LR 168, which perversely treats the restrictive approach to statutory claims under FSMA as a reason to curtail common law rights in negligence rather than expand them. It is difficult to see how this can be reconciled with existing common law authority on the standard of care (eg *Seymour v Caroline Ockwell & Co* [2005] EWHC 1137 (QB); [2005] PNLR 39 [77] and *Shore v Sedgwick Financial Services Ltd* [2007] EWHC 2509 (QB); [2008] PNLR 10 [161]), let alone MiFID and the EU principle of effectiveness. This ruling is also reminiscent of the unsatisfactory reasoning of the Court of Appeal in the concurrent liability case of *Robinson* (n 30) in the construction industry context, albeit that the case is not cited. For discussion of *Robinson* see *Chitty* (n 17) [1-170]. Contrast *Gorham v British Telecommunications plc* [2000] 1 WLR 2129 (CA).

[84] MiFID, Annex I. See D Busch, 'Agency and Principal Dealing under the Markets in Financial Instruments Directive' in D Busch, L Macgregor and P Watts (eds), *Agency Law in Commercial Practice* (Oxford, Oxford University Press, 2016) 141 (Busch) [9.04]–[9.09]; [9.25]–[9.33].

[85] COBS 3.4.1R.

[86] COBS 3.5.1R, 3.5.2R and 3.5.3R. MiFID, Annex II.

[87] The client's best interests rule. Busch (n 84) [9.34]–[9.36].

[88] McMeel and Virgo, *Financial Advice* (n 3) [12.57]–[12.72]; Busch (n 84) [9.42]–[9.45].

[89] See also MiFID Implementing Directive (2006/73/EC), arts 35, 37 and 52. See also recital 58. For the background see: FSA Consultation Paper 06/19, *Reforming Conduct of Business Regulation (including proposals for implementing relevant provisions of the Markets in Financial Instruments Directive, and related changes in SYSC, DISP, TC, SUP and other Handbook modules)* (October 2006) (FSA CP 06/19), ch 14 and FSA Policy Statement 07/6, *Reforming Conduct of Business Regulation—Feedback on CP06/19—Reforming Conduct of Business Regulation (October 2006) and Financial promotion and other communications (October 2006)* (May 2007) (FSA PS 07/6), ch 12.

customer' and suitability requirement were spelt out economically in article 19(4) of MiFID:

> When providing investment advice or portfolio management the investment firm shall obtain the necessary information regarding the client's or the potential client's knowledge and experience in the investment field relevant to the specific type of product or service, his financial situation and his investment objectives so as to enable the firm to recommend to the client or potential client the investment services or financial instruments that are suitable for him.

These are implemented in COBS 9. The MiFID inspired 'suitability' rule provides:[90]

> (1) A *firm* must take reasonable steps to ensure that a *personal recommendation*, or a decision to trade, is suitable for its *client*.
> (2) When making the *personal recommendation* or *managing* his *investments*, the *firm* must obtain the necessary information regarding the *client's*:
> (a) knowledge and experience in the investment field relevant to the specific type of *designated investment* or service;
> (b) financial situation; and
> (c) investment objectives;
>
> so as to enable the *firm* to make the recommendation, or take the decision, which is suitable for him.

In addition, MiFID introduced a new standard of 'appropriateness' for non-advisory services. The rules are contained in COBS 10.[91] This new standard does not appear to have been explicitly referred to in recent cases on swaps. Whereas previously UK regulation drew a line between those transactions (advisory and discretionary portfolio management) where a suitability regime applied and 'execution only' transactions, MiFID recognises a distinct 'appropriateness' standard. For those transactions, which fall within article 19(5), the firm must carry out a form of KYC. It must ask:

> the client or potential client to provide information regarding his knowledge and experience in the investment field relevant to the specific type of product or service offered or demanded so as to enable the investment firm to assess whether the investment service or product envisaged is appropriate for the client.

If the firm concludes that the investment is not appropriate it must warn the (potential) client. Where the (potential) client elects to provide no information or inadequate information the firm must warn the client that they are unable to judge the appropriateness of the service or product for him the (potential) client.

The vestiges of 'execution only' business derive from MiFID, article 19(6), which permits services that 'only consist of execution and/or the reception and transmission of client orders' where all of four conditions are met:[92]

> (1) The services relate to 'non-complex financial instruments', which include shares traded on regulated markets, bonds and UCITS;[93]

[90] COBS 9.2.1R.
[91] For the background see: FSA CP 06/19, ch 15 and FSA PS 07/6, ch 13.
[92] MiFID, art 19(6).
[93] The definition is further developed in MiFID Implementing Directive (2006/73/EC), art 38.

(2) The service is provided at the initiative of the (potential) client;
(3) The (potential) client is warned (in a standardised format if preferred) that the suitability regime does not apply and the protection of the conduct of business rules is inapplicable;
(4) The firm complies with the conflict of interest rules in MiFID, article 18.

These provisions are implemented by COBS 10.4.[94] Given the novelty of the regime the FSA/FCA provided further guidance on the appropriateness regime in COBS 10.5 and 10.6. I have seen no reference to the 'appropriateness' standard, nor to the stringent conditions under which a financial firm may claim to be dealing on an 'execution only' basis in recent authorities on swaps. Quite the contrary. The banks' legal representatives instead insist that their freedom to deal on an 'execution only' basis in derivatives is extensive. That is simply not correct. What MiFID preserved was my ability to ring up my stockbroker and order listed company shares (on the FTSE or AIM) or email a fund supermarket to purchase authorised unit trusts or equivalents. That is, it preserved 'execution only' dealings in 'vanilla', readily realisable, financial instruments, where the customer genuinely acted on his or her own initiative. This limited pocket of 'execution only' business was the result of the careful efforts of UK MEPs to preserve some own-initiative transactions. What it does not license is banks advising on and selling 'over the counter' complex derivatives to retail customers, by-passing the suitability and appropriateness standards.

The original COB 2.5 (Exclusion of liability) prevented an authorised person from excluding or limiting any duty or liability it has to customers which it had under the regulatory system.[95] In relation to private customers, firms were required not to attempt to exclude any other duty or liability 'unless it is reasonable to do so'.[96] Like its predecessor COBS adopts a similar clumsily-worded rule to preventing regulated firms contracting out of their obligations. So COBS 2.1.2R provides:

> A *firm* must not, in any communication relating to *designated investment business* seek to:
>
> (1) exclude or restrict; or
> (2) rely on any exclusion or restriction of;
>
> any duty or liability it may have to a *client* under the *regulatory system.*

So it would appear that every time a bank purports to deny it has provided advice on securities or derivatives, when it has in fact done so, or pleads a contractual estoppel, it is in breach of its regulatory obligations in COBS, ultimately based on the EU measure, MiFID. Section 138D of FSMA (replacing section 150 with effect from 1 April 2013)[97] continues the statutory right of action for breaches of the FCA's rules. A breach of COBS 2.1.2R is itself actionable by any person (not just private persons) who suffers a loss under the Rights of Action Regulations.[98]

[94] COBS 10.4.1R.
[95] COB 2.5.3R.
[96] COB 2.5.4R, in effect applying a regime akin to the Unfair Contract Terms Act 1977.
[97] Under the Coalition Government's changes to FSMA: Financial Services Act 2012, s 24.
[98] COBS Sch 5; Financial Services and Markets Act 2000 (Rights of Action) Regulations 2001 (SI 2001/2256), reg 6(3)(a).

Against this backdrop it is difficult to read recent English judgments without a sense that the nature and effect of modern financial regulation has not really been taken on board. These measures are policy-driven, targeted interventions in freedom of contract in a field where regulated providers of financial services are seen as having all the aces and the technical expertise, and are required to play fair with their retail customers. With a little historical perspective it can be seen that each time a bank's boilerplate disclaims any advisory relationship with their retail clients, or purports to oust regulatory standards, or negatives a fiduciary relationship, they are attempting to tear up the compromise embodied in the Big Bang reforms of the 1980s. Those reforms permitted them to provide securities and derivatives as either principal or agent, but to do so under the constraints of the investor protection rules recommended by Professor Gower. Furthermore the banks are attempting to circumvent EU rules, and thumbing their nose at Professor Kay's initiatives, and UK Government policy.

III. THE RISE AND RISE OF CONTRACTUAL ESTOPPEL

A. Four Now-notorious Paragraphs

The t-shirt philosophy underlying *Peekay* and *Springwell* is to be found in four now notorious paragraphs. First, Moore-Bick LJ in *Peekay*:[99]

> There is no reason in principle why parties to a contract should not agree that a certain state of affairs should form the basis for the transaction, whether it be the case or not. For example, it may be desirable to settle a disagreement as to an existing state of affairs in order to establish a clear basis for the contract itself and its subsequent performance. Where parties express an agreement of that kind in a contractual document neither can subsequently deny the existence of the facts and matters upon which they have agreed, at least so far as concerns those aspects of their relationship to which the agreement was directed. The contract itself gives rise to an estoppel: see *Colchester Borough Council v Smith* [1991] Ch 448, affirmed on appeal [1992] Ch 421.
>
> It is common to include in certain kinds of contracts an express acknowledgment by each of the parties that they have not been induced to enter the contract by any representations other than those contained in the contract itself. The effectiveness of a clause of that kind may be challenged on the grounds that the contract as a whole, including the clause in question, can be avoided if in fact one or other party was induced to enter into it by misrepresentation. However, I can see no reason in principle why it should not be possible for parties to an agreement to give up any right to assert that they were induced to enter into it by misrepresentation, provided that they make their intention clear, or why a clause of that kind, if properly drafted, should not give rise to a contractual estoppel of the kind recognised in *Colchester Borough Council v Smith*. However, that particular question does not arise in this case.

[99] *Peekay* (n 5) [56]–[57]. See for discussion A Trukhnatov, 'Misrepresentation: Acknowledgement of Non-reliance as Defence' (2009) 125 *LQR* 648.

Secondly, Aikens LJ in *Springwell*:[100]

> Before I examine *Lowe v Lombank* and subsequent cases on this issue, I will try and analyse the matter from principle. If A and B enter into a contract then, unless there is some principle of law or statute to the contrary, they are entitled to agree what they like. Unless *Lowe v Lombank* is authority to the contrary, there is no legal principle that states that parties cannot agree to assume that a certain state of affairs is the case at the time the contract is concluded or has been so in the past, even if that is not the case, so that the contract is made upon the basis that the present or past facts are as stated and agreed by the parties … A 'conclusive evidence' clause in a sale contract, viz. that a report on eg. the amount or condition of a commodity sold under a contract between A and B shall be 'conclusive evidence' of the matters stated in the report is to the same effect. The parties are agreeing that the statements in the report shall be the case for the purposes of the contract of sale and the parties cannot go behind that agreement.
>
> So, in principle and always depending on the precise construction of the contractual wording, I would say that A and B can agree that A has made no pre-contract representations to B about the quality or nature of a financial instrument that A is selling to B. Should it make any difference that both A and B know at and before making the contract, that A did, in fact, make representations, so that the statement that A had not is contrary to what each side knows is the case? Apart from the remarks of Diplock J in *Lowe v Lombank*, Mr Brindle [Counsel for the investor] did not show us any case that might support the proposition that parties cannot agree that X is the case even if both know that is not so. I am unaware of any legal principle to that effect. The only possible exception might be if the particular agreement between A and B on the certain state of affairs concerned contradicts some other specific or more general rule of English public policy. Like Moore-Bick LJ in *Peekay* I see commercial utility in such clauses being enforceable, so that parties know precisely the basis on which they are entering into their contractual relationship.

It is difficult not to observe how rudimentary the reasoning is in both these passages. Little more is in practice said than my variant on Dr Watson's t-shirt encapsulates in nine (or six) words. Again the point is that if we were living in an environment of freedom of contract—with parties of relatively equal bargaining power and no legislative intervention—such simplistic reasoning may be defensible. Even then there may be issues about the reality of consent. Fortunately, in the light of the heavily regulated environment described above, we must conclude that such reasoning is not only backward-looking, but impermissible.

B. Application of Contractual Estoppel in the Swaps Context

(i) Crestsign

The central case on swaps is *Crestsign Ltd v National Westminster Bank plc.*[101] If its reasoning stands it will determine the shape and direction of our contract law.

[100] *Springwell* (n 6) [143]–[144] (footnotes omitted).

[101] *Crestsign Ltd v National Westminster Bank plc* [2014] EWHC 3043 (Ch) [2015] 2 All ER (Comm) 133; permission to appeal granted: [2015] EWCA Civ 986. An appeal to the Court of Appeal was scheduled to take place in the first half of 2016 but settled. All subsequent references are to the High Court decision.

What kind of jurisdiction do we want to be in commercial and financial disputes? Are we determined to retreat to an island of literalism in some attempt to attract cross-border business from New York or nascent Middle Eastern dispute resolution centres? Or do we want to be true to our common law heritage? Should the business with the printing press always triumph? Or do we adopt a healthy scepticism toward contractual boilerplate which parts company with reality? Perhaps most pressingly, will the Senior Courts abandon a path which may put them on a collision course with our European partners by permitting banks and financial institutions to cock a snook at their European regulatory obligations? Will the judiciary embrace the zeitgeist and recognise that sales of complex investment products (other than to wholesale counterparties) are both fiduciary and advisory transactions by their very nature, or at least as a matter of fundamental, national public policy?

For the reasons already described,[102] the claims in *Crestsign* were brought at common law for negligence, and for damages under section 2(1) of the Misrepresentation Act 1967. Crestsign was clearly a micro-enterprise, indeed a family commercial property company with three commercial properties let to tenants run by mum, dad, son and daughter (the Parkers). The defendant banks were both NatWest and its parent, Royal Bank of Scotland (RBS). The ordinary commercial banking role was managed by a NatWest relationship manager, Mr Flack. The problematic products were proffered by Mr Gillard, an RBS 'interest rate risk manager responsible for introducing the banks' derivative products to customers'.[103] The Judge, Tim Kerr QC, sitting as a Deputy Judge of the High Court, Chancery Division, introduced the first-tier FSMA, and the second-tier rules establishing the regulated activities of dealing in investments as principal (under article 14 of the RAO)—which the banks could not gainsay—and advising on investments, including derivatives (under article 53 of the RAO), which they denied. He also introduced the third-tier rules of COB (up to 31 October 2007), and the MiFID-based COBS (from 1 November 2007).

The Judge noted that it was common ground that the COBS rules were not actionable under the relevant first- and second-tier rules, although he made the surprisingly common error of assuming the relevant first-tier rule was section 138D of FSMA, rather than section 150 in force at the relevant times when any relevant cause of action would have accrued (up to 1 April 2013).[104] As we have said the restrictive

[102] It was common ground that on the current approach to section 150 (138D) and the Rights of Action Regulations the claim only lay at common law: [13].

[103] *Crestsign* (n 101) [3].

[104] Section 150 of FSMA (itself replacing Financial Services Act 1986 ss 62 and 62A, in force from 29 April 1988 to 30 November 2001) was in force from 1 December 2001 to 30 March 2013 when it was replaced or 'substituted' by s 138D as a result of s 24 of the Financial Services Act 2012, *albeit not with any retrospective effect*: Financial Services Act 2012 (Commencement No 2) Order 2013 (SI 2013/423) (C 17). Whilst similar in effect, s 150 made the rules of the then Financial *Services* Authority presumptively actionable by (generally) private persons. In contrast, s 138D is the equivalent provision for the new 'twin peaks' regime, making the rules of the successor Financial *Conduct* Authority presumptively actionable by (generally) private persons, but the rules of the new Prudential Regulatory Authority presumptively not actionable. Compare *Plevin v Paragon Personal Finance Ltd* [2014] UKSC 61; [2015] 1 All ER 625, [12] (Lord Sumption: 'actionable under what was then s 150 of the Act').

interpretation of the second-tier rules was to be challenged in the Court of Appeal in 2016.[105]

Mr Parker Senior wished to re-finance Crestsign's commercial lending of about £3.3 million on an interest-only basis at the best possible floating rate, and intended to continue the business for about 10 years when he would be in his mid-sixties. He was also willing to dispose of individual properties during that period if a favourable opportunity presented itself. The Judge noted that at the relevant time, March 2008, RBS was itself predicting that interest rates would fall from 5.25 to 4.75 per cent and then 4.5 per cent, where they would remain for the remainder of 2009.[106] In May 2008 NatWest's credit committee sanctioned a five-year loan facility to Crestsign but expressly conditional on 'Interest Rate Management to be taken on via' RBS's 'Global Banking and Markets Division'.[107] Step forward Mr Gillard of RBS who introduced himself as the banks' specialist in interest rate protection and met with Mr and Mrs Parker at their home. Mr Parker had not understood the reference to interest rate management and professed himself 'particularly stupid' about 'these hedging products'.[108] The Judge concluded that meeting lasted less than an hour. He observed: 'Mr Gillard is a salesman to his bones ... His performance at the meeting was, I am satisfied, polished'.[109] Critically, at the meeting Mr Parker was clear he wanted a variable, not a fixed, rate loan and believed that Crestsign could weather changes because he believed interest rates would fall as the country was entering a recession. In an ironic (reverse) encapsulation of the case he was willing to bet £50 with Mr Gillard as to the future direction of interest rates. Conversely Mr Gillard said that interest rates would rise, somehow failing to mention RBS's published forecast to the contrary. The Judge rejected evidence that Mr Gillard would have said he was not able to give advice or recommend particular products, and also rejected his evidence that he introduced a range of swap products, including 'a "five year swap", a "vanilla cap" (in the jargon mixing culinary and sartorial metaphors), a "collar" and a "10 year forward swap"'.[110]

The Judge found that as a result of the meeting Mr Gillard had failed to make Mr Parker—there is no mention of Mrs Parker—understand two fundamental points. First, the swap was a separate and independent contract from the variable rate loan agreement. Secondly, the swap was a 10-year deal, twice the length of the proposed loan, which might not be renewed.[111] Whilst Mr Parker understood that there may be a penalty for early termination (such as a number of months' interest payments, in the low tens of thousands of pounds), there was only brief mention in the meeting of 'break costs' and no attempt to explain or quantify what these were likely to be. Subsequently Mr Gillard emailed Mr Parker on 30 May 2008 with four proposed structures, two of which he knew would not be acceptable to Mr Parker.

105 See note 83 above.
106 *Crestsign* (n 101) [21].
107 ibid [24].
108 ibid [27].
109 ibid [31]. He was also an evasive witness, happily trimming evidence to the banks' advantage: [32].
110 ibid [34].
111 ibid [38]–[40].

An email attachment did warn in 'notes' at the end that break costs for what was now described as an 'over-the-counter derivative transaction' could be 'substantial'. Then came the inevitable:[112]

> You should consult with such advisers as you deem necessary to assist you in making these determinations. [RBS] will not act and has not acted as your legal, tax, accounting or investment adviser or owe any fiduciary duties to you in connection with this, or any related transaction, and no reliance may be placed on RBS for advice or recommendations of any sort. RBS makes no representations or warranties with respect to the information, and disclaims all liability for the use you or your advisers make of the contents of this document.

On 4 June RBS sent RBS's terms for 'Retail Clients' and its 'Standalone Derivatives Terms', two days before the deadline when Crestsign would have to complete refinancing. These contained another suite of similar boilerplate terms, and also insisted the deal was 'principal to principal', that no 'personal recommendations (as defined by the FSA)' had been made in the absence of specific agreement to do so, and that the FSA rules on 'best execution' (COBS 11.2.1R) did not apply.[113] Revised structures for the deal were then proposed, with Crestsign agreeing to a fixed rate swap of 5.65 per cent, albeit with a discount in the first two years. The deal was done by a tape-recorded 'trade call' on 6 June 2008, followed by a written confirmation encapsulating all RBS's terms. The bank immediately earned some £70,000 from this trade.[114]

The run on Northern Rock of September 2007, the collapse of Lehmann Brothers in September 2008 and the reduction of Bank of England base rates to 0.5 per cent in March 2009 then ensued. At the second anniversary of the transaction, following the discount period, reality hit, and Crestsign's low variable rate was more than cancelled out by having to pay RBS the difference between 0.5 per cent base rate and 5.65 per cent fixed rate swap. Mr Parker tried to refinance but that was precluded by the eye-watering break costs of £600,000 for the swap. Crestsign formally complained of mis-selling in June 2012 and issued its claim in May 2013. Crestsign relied on both an advisory duty of care and an information duty of care.

On the first key issue as to whether the banks owed an advisory duty, Crestsign relied on both regulatory[115] and common law[116] authority. The test is clearly an objective one. One of the best common law accounts of what constitutes investment advice, albeit not cited in *Crestsign*, is the analysis of Henderson J in *Walker v Inter-Alliance Group plc*,[117] where he observed that 'any element of comparison or

[112] ibid [50].

[113] ibid [54]–[59].

[114] ibid [70]. Given EU and UK (dating back to Professor Gower's time) view of the necessity for rules on 'best execution' for securities and derivatives providers it is of concern that the bank only called expert evidence 'under protest', given its contention that 'the pricing of this transaction was entirely a matter for the banks' ([77]).

[115] FSA/FCA *Perimeter Guidance Manual*: PERG 8.28.4G(3).

[116] *Zaki v Credit Suisse (UK) Ltd* [2011] EWHC 2422 (Comm); [2011] 2 CLC 523 [83]–[85] (Teare J); *Rubenstein v HSBC Bank plc* [2011] EWHC 2304 (QB); [2011] 2 CLC 459 [81]–[85] (HHJ Havelock-Allan QC); [2012] EWCA Civ 1184; [2013] 1 All ER (Comm) 915 [52] (Rix LJ).

[117] *Walker v Inter-Alliance Group plc* [2007] EWHC 1858 (Ch); [2007] Pens LR 347 [30]. See also *Martin v Brittania Life Ltd* [2000] 1 Lloyd's Rep PN 412.

evaluation or persuasion is likely to cross the dividing line'. Henderson J concluded that:[118]

> [T]he concept of investment advice is broad enough to include any communication with the client which, in the particular context in which it is given, goes beyond the mere provision of information and is objectively likely to influence the client's decision whether or not to undertake the transaction in question.

Of most concern is the submission on behalf of the banks that 'there is and remains no regulatory prohibition against selling swaps and other derivative products to retail customers on a non-advised basis'.[119] It is unclear what materials the Judge was shown in support of this submission, which is difficult to reconcile with an holistic reading of COBS Chapters 9 and 10, and the underlying requirements of MiFID. First, if the customer is properly categorised as retail, we are not in own account dealing territory. Second, once advice is given in the real world the COBS rules must be engaged.[120] Despite the robust submissions of the banks, leaving aside the contractual provisions, the Judge concluded that advice was an ordinary English word, and that Mr Gillard had in fact proffered advice, and not merely information. Furthermore, Mr Parker relied on Mr Gillard for his expertise in this area. Mr Gillard did make recommendations as to suitable interest rate products.

Then in the critical switch in reasoning mandated by *Peekay* and *Springwell* the Judge abandoned his 'real world' conclusion in favour of the 'virtual world' mandated by the boilerplate entailing that:[121]

> [T]he banks successfully disclaimed responsibility for any advice that Mr Gillard might give and (as I have found) did give … Although Crestsign was a retail client and not a large and sophisticated commercial party, it was not in a position akin to the buyer of a second hand car.

The banks' terms did not re-write history or part company with reality.

If it needed to do so the bank could rely on contractual estoppel to prevent any duty of are from arising. All the terms were 'basis clauses' and not exemption clauses so the '1977 Act does not apply'. However the Judge found that if the Act had applied, the banks had not satisfied the requirement of reasonableness. There had been a 'hard sell', and the banks had access to expertise not readily available to Crestsign.[122] The Judge concluded that this was a case typical of the regulatory failings found by the FSA in 2012 in its pilot findings on swaps:[123]

> [P]oor disclosure of exit costs …; failure to ascertain the customer's understanding of risk; non-advised sales straying into advice; a mismatch between the duration of the hedge product and the underlying loan; and rewards and incentives being a driver of such practices.

[118] *Walker* (n 117) [97].
[119] *Crestsign* (n 101) [93] (submission of Andrew Mitchell QC).
[120] Furthermore, 'investment advice' as defined in article 2 of MiFID and governed by article 19 must be given an autonomous EU interpretation, which makes it consistent with the principle of *effet utile*. See the penetrating criticism of the similarly troubling Scottish case of *Grant Estates* (n 80) by Busch (n 84) [9.69]–[9.82].
[121] *Crestsign* (n 101) [114].
[122] ibid [106]–[111].
[123] ibid [121].

Whilst it did not arise, the Judge concluded the bank was negligent in recommending the swaps.[124] In contrast, the banks were acquitted of their duty to provide information about the products, having been found—mainly in the documents—to have provided 'just enough information to avoid a breach'.[125] In any event the banks' terms were immune from challenge under section 3 of the 1967 Act because of the characterisation of its terms as 'basis clauses'.[126] The Judge concluded it is 'not the role of the common law and this court to act as a regulator'.[127]

That must be wrong. Would the Judge's nineteenth-century forebears have held back from imposing minimum standards on shipowners? More pertinently, can a Judge in an EU Member State permit financial institutions to 'contract out' of regulatory standards? Whilst characteristically Delphic, the guidance we have from the European Court in the *Genil* case strongly suggests that Member States are required to give effect to the obligations in MiFID through private law measures consistently with the EU principles of effectiveness and equivalence.[128] Overall the Judge's conclusions in *Crestsign* are a curate's egg par excellence. He was clearly right to find that an advisory relationship existed in the real world, that the bank was negligent and correctly held that the bank—by denying any responsibility at all for advice—would not have been able to satisfy the 1977 Act's requirement of reasonableness. In contrast, the conclusions—probably all mandated by recent precedent—about terms preventing advisory relationships from arising, contractual estoppel and the apparent shield for 'basis clauses' from the 1977 Act are deeply unsatisfactory in the light of the arguments marshalled above. The defects in the reasoning in *Crestsign* were at least capable of being reversed on appeal,[129] either by a Court of Appeal brave enough to repudiate *Peekay*, *Springwell* and 'basis clauses', or by the Supreme Court, perhaps following a reference to the European Court of Justice. However there will be no appeal in *Crestsign*.[130]

(ii) Thornbridge

It is not as easy to see how the problems thrown up by the subsequent swaps case of *Thornbridge v Barclays Bank plc*,[131] a decision of the Manchester Mercantile Court, can be as easily remedied. Thornbridge was a husband and wife commercial property company. The swap's break costs were an eye-watering £565,000.[132] The Judge

[124] ibid [130].
[125] ibid [165].
[126] ibid [168].
[127] ibid [177].
[128] Case C-604/11, *Genil 48 SL v Bankinter SA* (30 May 2013) EU:C:2013:344, [2013] Bus LR 1132; [2013] 3 CMLR 43 [57]; Busch (n 84) [9.81]–[9.82].
[129] Compare the unsatisfactory approach to financial regulation of the Court of Appeal in *Harrison v Black Horse Ltd* [2011] EWCA Civ 1128; [2012] Lloyd's Rep IR 521—a payment protection insurance case where the undisclosed commission was an eye-watering 87% of the premium—which had to be remedied by the Supreme Court in a subsequent case: *Plevin* (n 104).
[130] Permission to appeal granted: [2015] EWCA Civ 986, but, perhaps unsurprisingly, settled. It now joins the long list of unsatisfactory cases in banking law where the banks settle an appeal having achieved a result they can live with.
[131] *Thornbridge Ltd v Barclays Bank plc* [2015] EWHC 3430 (QB).
[132] ibid [17].

refused to accept that the bank's 'Corporate Risk Adviser' had provided advice, and in any event even if advice was in fact given, the Bank had not assumed an advisory duty. This, in effect, extends analogous reasoning from the duty-defining clause approach to the scope of the assumption of responsibility in the tort of negligence.[133] Somewhat uncommercially, HHJ Moulder noted that Barclays had not charged a fee for investment advice (overlooking the other financial benefits of the transaction) and indicated that this told against an advisory relationship.[134] Predictably the Judge then reinforced this 'no advice' conclusion by reference to boilerplate terms, which she held did not re-write history.[135] The perfunctory finding that (if relevant) the terms were reasonable was premised on the supposed equality of bargaining power of a two-person company and a leading international bank, and on the false basis that this was an 'arm's-length, "execution only"' transaction.[136] The claimant also failed on breach and causation. HHJ Moulder robustly concluded:[137]

> This is in my view a case based on hindsight and a loan agreement which did not operate as the parties intended. As I have found on the evidence before me, it was not a case of claimant being advised to enter, or being misled into entering a swap which in the circumstances was unsuitable.

On those factual findings the small business in *Thornbridge* was a remarkably sophisticated SME, and the Bank's conduct was commendably out of step with the more routine mis-selling of swaps found by the FSA in its review. It is understood the case is to be appealed, but it is difficult to see how anything short of a re-trial will undo the damage done at first instance. The FCA must appear at any appeal in this context and assist the court with the provenance and policies behind its rulebook.[138]

C. The Myth of 'Basis Clauses'

This is relatively easily demonstrated. We are concerned principally with banks' and financial institutions' standard terms insisting that no advice has been given, no representations made, no fiduciary obligations assumed and that no reliance should be placed on the institution as adviser or fiduciary. Contrast the following 'basis clauses' which could be imagined in sectors other than the financial services one:

[133] ibid [30], [38] and [96]. This is based on Hamblen J's dictum that 'there is a clear distinction between giving advice and assuming legal responsibility for that advice': *Standard Chartered Bank v Ceylon Petroleum Corporation* [2011] EWHC 1785 (Comm) [508]. That distinction cannot stand in the EU law context.

[134] *Thornbridge* (n 131) [96(i)]. HHJ Moulder's conclusions at [96(ii)] on 'execution only' business cannot stand in the light of the correct interpretation of MiFID/COBS, and appear to misunderstand the scope of Barclays' authorisation under FSMA, which clearly embraces advising on investments.

[135] ibid [97]–[112]; relying on *Barclays Bank plc v Svizera Holdings BV* [2014] EWHC 1020 (Comm); [2015] 1 All ER (Comm) 788 [58]–[61] (Flaux J).

[136] *Thornbridge* (n 131) [117].

[137] ibid [226].

[138] Ideally it should not scuttle away as it did in the Court of Appeal in *Green* (n 83), when faced with a Court determined not to find an advisory relationship between a bank and an SME in relation to a swap. It will need to be braced for submissions of the type run by Barclays at *Thornbridge* (n 131) [154], unless the Bank recollects it duty under FSMA and PRIN 2.1.1R to co-operate with its regulators.

(1) The parties agree that the provision of services by B to A is a contract for services, and not one of employment, and B hereby agrees, acknowledges, represents and warrants that he is not hereby constituted an employee for any purpose.
(2) The parties agree that the provision of the premises by B to A is a contractual licence, and not a lease, and B hereby agrees, acknowledges, represents and warrants that he is not hereby constituted a tenant or lessee for any purpose.
(3) The parties agree that the provision of goods and/or services and/or digital content by B to A is a business transaction, and B hereby agrees, acknowledges, represents and warrants that he, she or it enters this transaction in the course of carrying on a business for the purposes of that business, and is not hereby constituted a consumer for any purpose. B further irrevocably acknowledges, represents and warrants that he, she or it does not fall within the category of a small or medium-sized business.

The so-called 'basis clauses' recently discerned in the financial sector are no different to the above three attempts to denude particular classes of transactions of their common law, statutory or regulatory attributes and protections. We all know that the modern regimes for employment contracts,[139] leaseholds and tenant protection,[140] and consumer contracts[141] would not weather such naked attempts to evade those protections. Even in the context of commercial agency, EU law as implemented in the UK is emphatic that contracting out of core provisions is not tolerated.[142] It is not a question of the 'sham' doctrine, but of the proper characterisation of the transaction. The point was neatly put by Lord Walker in the commercial context of the proper classification of company charges as fixed or floating:[143]

> Whether or not it is appropriate to describe this by some disparaging term such as camouflage, it is the court's duty to characterise the document according to the true legal effect of its terms ... In each case there is a public interest which overrides unrestrained freedom of contract.

It is puzzling that the financial sector is different, but it must be attributed to unfamiliarity with MiFID, COBS and financial regulation in general outlined above.

IV. THE CRITIQUE

I will not repeat my detailed critical account of *Peekay* and *Springwell*, written immediately after the Court of Appeal's judgment was handed down in the latter case.[144] The main issues and difficulties which have troubled subsequent commentators were all present and correct. The subsequent papers have addressed basically the same concerns.[145] In a nutshell the criticisms embraced, first, the weakness of the

[139] *Autoclenz Ltd v Belcher* [2011] UKSC 41; [2011] 4 All ER 745.
[140] *Street v Mountford* [1985] AC 809 (HL); see McMeel, *Construction* (n 3) [1.24]–[1.26].
[141] Part 2 of the Consumer Rights Act 2015 and the Unfair Contract Terms Act 1977 (for SMEs).
[142] Commercial Agents (Council Directive) Regulations 1993 (SI 1993/3053), regs 5 and 19.
[143] *Re Spectrum Plus Ltd* [2005] UKHL 41; [2005] 2 AC 680 [141].
[144] McMeel, 'Documentary Fundamentalism' (n 3).
[145] See n 3 above.

alleged precedential basis of the doctrine. Was it really open to the courts in *Peekay* and *Springwell* to do what they did: was the reasoning impermissible, contrary to precedent, indeed *per incuriam*? Secondly, whatever the doctrine purported to be, it was not by any stretch of the imagination, a traditional estoppel. Accordingly the question arose: what was the juridical basis for the doctrine? I suggested the nearest analogy, although not cited in *Peekay* or *Springwell*, was estoppel by deed. Thirdly, what were the common law exceptions to contractual estoppel? Lastly, what was the likely impact of statutory controls?

A. Precedential Basis

Bluntly *Colchester Borough Council v Smith*[146] was a pretty thin basis for such a radical change in the common law.[147] Goh agrees that the cases relied on were 'weak bases' for the doctrine.[148] In contrast Braithwaite insists the cases provide valid foundations for subsequent developments in this area of law.[149] Her LSE colleague, Andrew Dyson goes further, and marshals additional case law in support of contractual estoppel reasoning. I imagine the late Jim Gower is ruefully shaking his head at his successors. Despite what he accepts were thin beginnings, Dyson describes the doctrine of contractual estoppel as 'now firmly entrenched'.[150] However, nobody suggests that the doctrine was established before 2005. This is the common law at work, in the sense of judges making it up, and it has not proved very edifying. It bears little family resemblance to the efforts of Lord Mansfield or Lord Atkin.

B. The Juridical Basis of Contractual Estoppel

I have been taken to task for not defining an estoppel, whilst castigating contractual estoppel as an 'illegitimate species of estoppel'.[151] However I would regard it as reasonably uncontroversial that the indicia or ingredients of estoppels typically embrace unconscionability, reliance, and, on occasion, representation and detriment. Accordingly contractual estoppel bears 'little or no family resemblance' to evidential estoppel, promissory estoppel or estoppel by convention. This is based on the holdings in *Springwell* that neither reliance nor unconscionability[152] are necessary ingredients of contractual estoppel. As Goh suggests, 'by ditching the requirements of reliance, detriment and unconscionability, *Peekay* and *Springwell* appear to have effectively created an anomaly which undercuts the common basis of the other estoppels'.[153]

[146] *Colchester Borough Council v Smith* [1991] Ch 448 (Ch D); [1992] Ch 421 (CA).
[147] McMeel, 'Documentary Fundamentalism' (n 3) 185, 199–200.
[148] Goh (n 3) 519.
[149] Braithwaite (n 3) 123–30.
[150] Dyson (n 3) 2.
[151] McMeel, 'Documentary Fundamentalism' (n 3) 185, 207.
[152] *Springwell* [2008] EWHC 1186 (Comm) (n 6), [551]–[560]; *Springwell* (CA) (n 6) [177]–[178].
[153] Goh (n 3) 520.

Andrew Smith J has similarly spoken about the 'so-called principle of contractual estoppel' which he regards as no more than a 'convenient label'.[154] In contrast, Dyson looks to the legal effect rather than the ingredients as the touchstone of an estoppel, whilst conceding 'it may be best to steer clear of the taxonomical debate altogether'.[155] Ultimately Dyson characterises what he terms 'agreed basis clauses' as directions to the court, rather than promissory undertakings. This, as he acknowledges, puts them in same category as agreed specific performance clauses which the courts are free to ignore.

My suggested analogy with estoppel by deed[156] has been taken up by other commentators, who have obviously noted the congruence with the 2013 decision of the Privy Council in *Prime Sight v Lavarello*.[157] Dyson, whilst noticing the complete absence of reference in that case to *Peekay* or *Springwell*, considers that 'Lord Toulson's reasoning strongly supports the argument that estoppel by deed has now been subsumed within contractual estoppel to form a single unified doctrine'.[158] This approach now has the support of Lewison LJ, describing estoppel by deed as 'part of a sub-species of estoppel known as contractual estoppel'.[159]

Sean Wilken has always considered that estoppel by deed was anomalous,[160] and extends the same analysis to contractual estoppel.[161] Estoppel by deed reasoning based on faulty recitals in contracts made some sense in the conveyancing context in which it developed, where the parties may need to agree about the root of title, or the existence or otherwise of leases,[162] although it contradicted the original law stated in *Coke upon Littleton*.[163] The old treatises and cases treat estoppel by deed as a doctrine to be kept within strict bounds, readily undermined by one party's mistake. Indeed *Norton on Deeds* cites the distinguished authority of Sir George Jessel MR in *General Finance, Mortgage and Discount Co v Liberator Permanent Benefit Building Society*[164] for the proposition that the doctrine of estoppel by deed was not one to be extended. Proponents of contractual estoppel should spend time reading the nineteenth-century case law on estoppel by deed, imbibe the conveyancing

[154] *Credit Suisse International v Stichting Vestia Groep* [2014] EWHC 3103 (Comm); [2015] Bus LR D5 [302], [309].

[155] Dyson (n 3) 8–9.

[156] McMeel, 'Documentary Fundamentalism' (n 3) 185, 206.

[157] *Prime Sight Ltd v Lavarello* [2013] UKPC 22; [2014] AC 436; A Trukhnatov, 'Receipt Clauses: From Estoppel by Deed to Contractual Estoppel' (2014) 130 *LQR* 3, a note on *Prime Sight v Lavarello*. See Goh (n 3) 521–23.

[158] Dyson (n 3) 6. See also A Trukhnatov, 'The Limits of Contractual Estoppel' [2012] *Lloyd's Maritime and Commercial Law Quarterly* 358.

[159] *Richards v Wood* [2014] EWCA Civ 327 [15].

[160] S Wilken, *Wilken & Villiers: The Law of Waiver, Variation and Estoppel*, 2nd edn (Oxford, Oxford University Press, 2002) ch 12.

[161] S Wilken and K Ghaly, *The Law of Waiver, Variation and Estoppel*, 3rd edn (Oxford, Oxford University Press, 2012) 90–91.

[162] R Norton, R Morrison and H Goolden (eds), *Norton: A Treatise on Deeds*, 2nd edn (London, Sweet and Maxwell, 1928) 211–15, 226, 228, 260, 626–27; G Dworkin, *Odgers' Construction of Deeds and Statutes*, 5th edn (London, Sweet and Maxwell, 1967) 154–60, 167–68, 275.

[163] Co Litt 352b.

[164] *General Finance, Mortgage and Discount Co v Liberator Permanent Benefit Building Society* (1878) 10 Ch D 15 (Ch D) 24–25: *Norton on Deeds* (n 162) 215.

context in which it had operation, and note how our forebears still thought it should only be available sparingly.

Similar restraint is not shown in the modern species of contractual estoppel. The requirements for the doctrine to operate appear to be minimal or exiguous. Braithwaite accepts they are 'light' and that the doctrine applies whenever a binding contract contains an 'acknowledgment of a state of affairs'.[165] Not even the signature on a document, which appeared to be jumping off point in *Peekay*, is required in subsequent authorities. Certainly not the formality of the execution of a deed. As long as the relatively low threshold of the common law tests of incorporation of terms are met, boilerplate provisions will apply. In *Crestsign*, an email attachment containing terms sufficed. The legally and philosophically challenging proposition is rather the sophisticated analysis of Diplock J in *Lowe v Lombank*[166] with its persuasive reasoning that there was a limit to what could constitute an actionable promise.

Having reviewed the supposed indicia and ingredients of contractual estoppel we are led to an ineluctable conclusion. It must be accepted there is nothing conceptually impossible about contractual estoppel. Rather contractual estoppel is conceptually redundant. It simply adds nothing to the elementary proposition that—once properly construed and subject to rules of public policy—the contract means what it says on its true interpretation. Once the rules of construction (and where applicable statutory controls and over-rides) have been applied, sanctity of contract prevails. One could parrot contractual estoppel in every case about the meaning of a contract: 'that is what the contract says and neither party can deny that is what it says'. The redundancy of the last 10 words is manifest. The emperor has no clothes. That may explain how the common law lived for centuries before the supposed discernment of contractual estoppel. Despite the ink spilt, contractual estoppel has no juridical basis, save for freedom, and sanctity, of contract.

C. Common Law Exceptions

I discussed this in some detail in 2011, as I was obviously concerned that *Peekay* and *Springwell* appeared to circumscribe the previous availability of the usual vitiating factors to the signature rule.[167] The modern cases appeared to require misrepresentation as to the whole effect of the agreement, and perhaps the necessity of rescinding the whole contract.[168] That is still the state of the English modern authorities, which has not troubled other commentators to the same extent as it concerns me. It remains arguable that the reasoning in *Peekay* and *Springwell* is just dicta or *per incuriam* because of earlier binding authority.[169] Some relief lies over

[165] Braithwaite (n 3) 120, 122.

[166] *Lowe v Lombank* [1960] 1 WLR 196 (CA).

[167] McMeel, 'Documentary Fundamentalism' (n 3) 185, 201–2.

[168] Braithwaite (n 3) accepts misrepresentation as to the effect of the contract, and arguably(!), fraud: 123.

[169] *Lloyds Bank plc v Waterhouse* [1993] 2 FLR 97 (CA).

the horizon from Gibraltar where the Privy Council's Lord Toulson in *Prime Sight v Lavarello*,[170] whilst reciting freedom of contract as a starting-point was nevertheless emphatic that 'fraud, illegality, mistake and misrepresentation' and public policy[171] were all limits on estoppel-based reasoning. If that is accepted, and the narrower 'misrepresentation as to the nature of the entire contract' test rejected, much will have been done to rectify English common law.

D. Statutory Controls

First, the non-existence of basis clauses needs to be established. The current approach of the English courts is premised on Christopher Clarke J's suggested test in *Raiffeisen*,[172] adopted by the Court of Appeal in *Springwell*.[173] Whilst there was some acceptance in the appellate authorities that certain provisions must be characterised as exemption clauses, it is clear that first instance judges are likely to be much more reluctant to say a commercial contract re-writes history. In both *Crestsign* and *Thornbridge* claimants did not overcome this critical hurdle. Surely the banks' terms were re-writing history in those cases? As Goh suggests, the test should be abandoned not least because it is difficult to apply in practice.[174] The 'substance' test now appears to commend itself to the Singapore Court of Appeal.[175] Goh, despite sharing many of my concerns, is sanguine about the recognition of contractual estoppel in Singapore because he has faith in the operation of the statutory controls once the proper test is recognised; so too Dyson. Similarly, Braithwaite appears to rest her faith in the relevant statutory controls, although she appears relaxed about the case law on 'basis clauses' in contracts.[176] My sense is that there is too little differentiation in her paper between wholesale financial deals and the treatment of SMEs, which are the concern of this chapter. Oddly the red-in-tooth-and-claw world of wholesale deals is being allowed to set the agenda for the remainder of transactions. The courts need to revisit the actual language of the 1967 and 1977 Acts, the background materials and underlying policies. The brief and rudimentary consideration of the requirement of reasonableness in the majority of cases needs to be addressed.[177] Also of concern is that it has been suggested that the 'aspiration of certainty'[178] in dealings between commercial parties of equal bargaining power is 'itself a facet of reasonableness'. This heretical suggestion has the potential to

[170] *Prime Sight* (n 157).
[171] ibid [47].
[172] *Raiffeisen* (n 48) [314].
[173] *Springwell* (n 6) [180]–[182].
[174] Goh (n 3) 525.
[175] *Deutsche Bank AG v Chang Tse Wen* [2013] SGCA 49, [2013] 4 SLR 886 [60]–[68]; Goh (n 3) 527.
[176] Braithwaite (n 3) 135–43.
[177] For example, just two paragraphs (out of 222) of the Court of Appeal's judgment in *Springwell*, where it is treated as a question of fact: *Springwell* (n 6) [183]–[184].
[178] Echoing Lewison J in *Food Co UK LLP (t/a Muffin Break) v Henry Boot Developments Ltd* [2010] EWHC 358 (Ch) [177].

re-write the statutory test in a manner which could never have been envisaged by Parliament.[179] As I understand the test, a contractual term which purports to take away a minimum performance standard—suitable advice—and puts nothing in its place must always fail the statutory test, as in *Crestsign* (if the Acts had been held to apply). Furthermore, the financial services regulatory rules need to be properly applied in that context.

E. Other Common Law Jurisdictions

There is little time for a review of other jurisdictions. The legendary Australian equity text of Meagher, Gummow and Lehane[180] in its chapter on estoppel laments that 'in England allowance must for now be made for a doctrine of "contractual estoppel"', which (ignoring or over-looking *Peekay*) it ascribes as 'an invention of Gloster J'. Its merit is said to be 'uncertain'. It contradicts high authorities[181] including that of Dixon J in *Thompson v Palmer*,[182] recognising the role of mistake and misrepresentation as vitiating factors, which is, in their view, to be preferred.[183]

In Singapore there was a brief flirtation with treating non-reliance clauses as giving rise to a contractual estoppel, but more recently a considered retreat. Initially in *Orient Centre Investments Ltd v Société Générale*[184] the Singapore Court of Appeal rejected an investment claim against a bank, holding that the contractual provisions erected an 'insuperable obstacle' to a suite of claims for breach of contract, negligence and breach of fiduciary duty.[185] That was followed in obiter dicta by the High Court of Singapore in an injunction case.[186] However, more caution was expressed in *Als Memesa v UBS AG*[187] where a wealthy, 95-year-old, retired businessman and his daughter, who were both unfamiliar with the English language, had their claim for misrepresentation and the mis-selling of US$4 million of Russian bonds by a trusted representative of the defendant bank struck out in the High Court on the basis of the bank's non-reliance clauses. There were allegations that the nature and risks of the bonds were misrepresented. Obviously concerned about the reputation

[179] *Crestsign* (n 101) [104] (submission of the banks).

[180] J Heydon, M Leeming and P Turner, *Meagher, Gummow and Lehane's Equity: Doctrines and Remedies*, 5th edn (Chatswood NSW, LexisNexis Butterworths, 2015), ch 17.

[181] Citing K Handley, 'Reinventing Estoppel in the Privy Council' (2014) 130 *LQR* 370, a note on *Prime Sight* (n 157).

[182] *Thompson v Palmer* (1933) 49 CLR 507 (HCA) 547 (mistake and misrepresentation preclude estoppel *in pais* or by deed).

[183] *Meagher, Gummow and Lehane's Equity* (n 180) [17-015] ('Further species') and [17-035] (citing *Thompson v Palmer*).

[184] *Orient Centre Investments Ltd v Société Générale* [2007] SGCA 24, [2007] 3 SLR (R) 566.

[185] ibid [50]–[51], citing *Peekay* (n 5).

[186] *Jurong Shipyard Pte Ltd v BNP Paribas* [2008] 4 SLR (R) 33.

[187] *Als Memesa v UBS AG* [2012] 4 SLR (R) 992. See K Low, 'Misrepresentation and Contractual Estoppel: The Raiffeisen Clarifications' (2011) 23 *Singapore Academy of Law Journal* 390 and K Loi and K Low, 'Non-Reliance Clauses and the Unfair Contract Terms Act: Welcome Clarity from Singapore' [2014] *Journal of Business Law* 156.

of Singapore as the regional banking hub, the Singapore Court of Appeal, led by Chief Justice Chan, reversed that decision and sent out a very clear message to the local banking and legal community:[188]

> [I]n the light of the many allegations made against many financial institutions for 'mis-selling' complex financial products to linguistically and financially illiterate and unwary customers during the financial crisis in 2008, it may be desirable for the courts to reconsider whether financial institutions should be accorded full immunity for such 'misconduct' by relying on non-reliance clauses which unsophisticated customers might have been induced or persuaded to sign without truly understanding their potential legal effect on any form of misconduct or negligence on the part of the relevant officers in relation to the investment recommended by them.

Needless to say I would support a similar signalling of intent by the English courts. I note that since that decision was handed down in August 2012 Singapore's banking community has shied away from providing the courts with an opportunity to reject decisively contractual estoppel in that jurisdiction. Singapore's judiciary is more attuned in this decision to the true common law. As I stated in the Preface to my book on contractual interpretation it is difficult to see how the English approach, in the wake of the Global Financial Crisis, of applying the strict letter of the contract to defeat all claims for misrepresentation 'will enhance the reputation of the jurisdiction as a place to conduct commercial and financial litigation'.[189] It may be that that warning is only heeded in other common law jurisdictions, but I fail to see how the extreme literalism of recent developments is intended to promote our legal system. Sophisticated investors may choose other fora. The unsophisticated and SMEs have no such bargaining power. Public policy and the national mood clearly favour holding the UK banks to account for their misconduct, where it can be established. It will not do simply to assert that the banks' boilerplate terms rule all such claims out of court. It is of concern that many judges of the Senior Courts appear instinctively to think the opposite. The beacon here is the late Lord Denning, who as counsel mercilessly enforced the strict terms of big businesses' contracts, but took no prisoners when elevated to the Bench on the proliferation of unfair exemption clauses in the pre-legislative era.[190]

V. CONCLUSION AND LESSONS

The English courts have been beguiled by an allegedly new contractual defence which on closer analysis turns out to have no substantive content. It is no more and no less than a retreat to literalism in the enforcement of express contractual terms. Retreat

[188] *Als Memesa* (n 187) [29]. Note also the difference in view between the High Court and the Court of Appeal in *Deutsche Bank AG v Chang Tse Wen* [2013] 1 SLR (R) 1310; revsd [2013] SGCA 49, [2013] 4 SLR 886 [79], leaving the issue of contractual estoppel to be revisited on a future occasion.

[189] McMeel, *Construction* (n 3) ix.

[190] Contrast the success of AT Denning KC as Counsel in *L'Estrange v F Graucob Ltd* [1934] 2 KB 394 (KB) with his swansong judgment in *George Mitchell (Chesterhall) Ltd v Finney Lock Seeds Ltd* [1983] QB 284 (CA) 286–89.

may not be entirely appropriate, as the cul de sac into which the Senior Courts have backed themselves is not one which would have attracted their nineteenth-century predecessors who were careful to ensure that the rules on deeds did not become a vehicle for abusing the court's process. The 'discovery' and nurturing of contractual estoppel is even more surprising in the light of the public policy choices clearly articulated by Parliament to prevent contracting parties from shirking the minimum decencies, and in the financial sector making banks and investment houses generally subject to a fiduciary standard. The default position at common law should be that retail sale of securities and derivatives (other than to wholesale counterparties) are both fiduciary and advisory transactions by their very nature, or at least as a matter of policy, just as ships under charter should be seaworthy. Basis clauses should be exposed for what they are: exemption clauses.

It can now be seen that Lord Diplock wisely foresaw in *Lowe v Lombank*[191] that there were sensible limits to the nature of propositions which could be comprehended in a binding contract. A legal system which routinely permitted contracting parties (usually the economically stronger party) to insert provisions asserting a factual basis for the deal which both parties knew to be false, would be one where the valuable social institutions of promising and contracting would be brought into disrepute. Indeed that is what has happened in England and Wales over the last decade. Tens of thousands of business people have had to listen incredulously as their solicitors and counsel have regretfully explained that as the authorities currently stand their otherwise valid causes of action will be defeated by boilerplate terms which had never previously been a visible factor in their relationship. There is cause for optimism. This chapter provides an agenda for the Treasury, the Financial Conduct Authority and the Supreme Court (with, it is to be hoped, the cooperation of the Senior Courts) to remedy the situation. If the status quo persists I for one will be asking the modern incarnation of Dr Watson if I can borrow his t-shirt.

[191] *Lowe* (n 166).

13

Illegality: Where Are We Now?

ROGER TOULSON

I. INTRODUCTION

IF CASES IN tort may be regarded as scenes in a drama, illegality had a dramatic opening scene in the celebrated *Highwaymen's case*. On 30 October 1725 lawyers acting for John Everet presented a bill in equity against Joseph Williams in the Court of Exchequer. The plaintiff asked the court for an account of an oral partnership between himself and the defendant. According to the recital he was 'skilled in dealing in several sorts of commodities' and the pair had 'proceeded jointly in the said dealings with good success on Hounslow Heath, where they dealt with a gentleman for a gold watch'. Later the defendant had allegedly recommended Finchley as a commodious business location because 'the said commodities were very plenty' and to deal there would 'be almost all gain to them'. The bill was dismissed as 'scandalous and impertinent' and a warrant was issued for the arrest of the solicitors who presented it. The court was evidently unimpressed by the pleader's not very artful attempt to draw a veil over the true nature of the partnership. It not only declined to divvy up the partners' ill-gotten gains, but the solicitors were fined, and within five years both the plaintiff and defendant were tried, convicted and hanged for the highway robberies they had committed.[1]

A court which presided over the distribution of criminals' ill-gotten gains among themselves would be awarding redress for liability arising out of an illegality which it might later punish in its criminal capacity. For the courts so to take with one hand and give with another would 'create an intolerable fissure in the law's conceptually seamless web'.[2] Yet as the Law Commission observed in 2010, the English courts' attempts to avoid such a fissure by the development of the illegality defence has itself led to 'an intricate web of tangled rules that are difficult to ascertain and distinguish'.[3]

[1] *Highwaymen's case* (1893) 9 *LQR* 197.

[2] *Hall v Herbert* [1993] 2 SCR 159 (SCC) (McLachlin J), referring to E Weinrib, 'Illegality as a Tort Defence' (1976) 26 *University of Toronto Law Journal* 28, 42. McLachlin J considered that the critical question was whether denial of the claim was required in order to uphold the consistency and integrity of the legal system, but that evaluation is capable of including a variety of considerations.

[3] Law Commission, *The Illegality Defence* (Law Com No 320, 2010) [3.5].

It is unsurprising that the rules are tangled and have produced an unsatisfactory weave. The cases concerned cover a vast variety of circumstances, and are normatively fragile in that a slight alteration of their facts can lead the defence to seem callous where formerly it was condign. If the test for applying an illegality defence is to exist as more than a courtly abstention from involvement, then the underlying policy rationales need to play a clearer part in court's navigation of the area.

To give some examples of the sets of factual variations that arise, there are contracts which on their face contain an implied or explicit obligation to commit an illegal act. There are contracts which though legal on their face, are intended to be performed illegally. In the latter case this illegal performance may be by one party or both. Where only one party intends illegal performance, the other may be ignorant, passively aware, or aware and actively assisting in some way. Where both parties perform illegally, their culpability may vary. In short both within and outside contractual illegality the parties' respective relationship with the illegality will fluctuate wildly. Across these variations cuts another dimension of difference: the gravity of the illegality. This may range from strict liability statutory offences to the most serious crimes, from crimes to breaches of the law giving rise to administrative penalties, 'quasi-crimes' and deceitful behaviour which may be tortious but not necessarily criminal. Yet another set of variations is generated by the relationship of the illegality to the claim: Is the taxi driver who executes an illegal U-turn en route entitled to his fare? Is a shipowner who overloads his vessel eligible to the charterhire? Does an accountant who allows his licence to lapse for the last week of a four-week audit forfeit his fee? Does a foreign national who enters the country on a false passport to commence illegal employment deserve the statutory protection against an employer's racial abuse? Peter Oborne's biography of the cricketer Basil D'Oliveira told how he falsely represented his age in order to obtain a contract to play in league cricket. He performed the contract, but would his lie have entitled his employers to refuse to pay him, on the ground that enforcement of the contract would have permitted him to profit from his wrongdoing? They could have repudiated the contract, if they had known the facts in time, but could they have refused to pay him when it was performed?

Already three aspects of variation can be identified: (1) the degree of illegality, (2) the relationship of the illegality to the claim being brought (3) the relationship of the parties to the illegality (including perpetrator, victim, innocent bystander and enabler). It is also important to recognise that public policy is not a one-way street. Not infrequently, there are serious grounds for saying that to allow the illegality defence would run counter to public policy in a significant respect. Because this area covers a vast factual and normative range and carries a propensity for intricacy, my thesis is this: if a court is to do justice it should be able to evaluate the conflicting considerations and do so transparently. I agree with the Law Commission that:[4]

> Ultimately a balancing exercise is called for which weighs up the application of the various policies at stake. An illegality defence should only succeed when depriving the

[4] Law Commission, *The Illegality Defence in Tort* (Law Com CP No 189, 2009) [1.14].

claimant of his or her rights is a proportionate response based on the relevant illegality policies. In giving judgment, the court should explain the balancing exercise it has undertaken.

II. ORIGINS

The doctrinal origins of the illegality defence are generally attributed to Lord Mansfield CJ's frequently quoted statement in *Holman v Johnson*:[5]

> The objection, that a contract is immoral or illegal as between plaintiff and defendant, sounds at all times very ill in the mouth of the defendant. It is not for his sake, however, that the objection is ever allowed; but it is founded in general principles of policy, which the defendant has the advantage of, contrary to the real justice, as between him and the plaintiff, by accident, if I may so say. The principle of public policy is this; ex dolo malo non oritur actio. No Court will lend its aid to a man who founds his cause of action upon an immoral or an illegal act … for where both are equally in fault, potior est conditio defendentis.

It is important to keep in mind that from the outset that the doctrine was located in 'general principles of policy', and we would therefore expect considerations of public policy to be central to its development and application. As with the locus classicus of any doctrine we should also note its limitations. First, it contains no definition of 'an immoral or illegal act'. Second, it is unclear how the illegality needs to relate to the claim. The words 'founded on' might be interpreted as including any factual connection or might be interpreted more narrowly. Third its conclusion indicates that its concern is with 'where both were equally at fault'. As such it does not explicitly address situations where one party is more involved in the illegality than the other.

III. POLICY

Over time the underlying policy reasons for the defence have been fleshed out. In some cases this has been done explicitly, and in others they may be gleaned. The Law Commission's 2009 Consultation Paper, after a careful and extensive consideration of the case law, detected the following policies at work:[6]

> The purpose of the rule infringed ought to be protected. Where the claimant's illegal behaviour has broken a rule against the sale of weaponry, say, that claimant should not expect the courts to require the sale price to be paid over.

The law ought to be internally consistent. As expressed in the Canadian case of *Hall v Herbert*, 'the law must aspire to be a unified institution, the parts of which—contract, tort, the criminal law—must be in essential harmony'.[7]

[5] *Holman v Johnson* (1775) 1 Cowp 341, 343; 98 ER 1120, 343.
[6] Law Commission (n 4) [2.5]–[2.31].
[7] *Hall v Herbert* [1993] 2 SCR 159 (SCC) 169.

The claimant ought not to be able to profit from his wrong (as expressed in *Beresford v Royal Insurance Co Ltd*)[8], although it is salutary to remember Lord Goff's observations in the *Spycatcher* case that '[t]he statement that a man shall not be allowed to profit from his own wrong is in very general terms, and does not of itself provide any sure guidance to the solution of a problem in any particular case'[9] and that '[i]t is not to be forgotten that wrongful acts can be inadvertent, as well as deliberate'.[10]

The law ought to deter wrongdoing: as expressed in Millett LJ's admonition in *Taylor v Bhaill*:

> it is time that a clear message was sent to the commercial community. Let it be clearly understood if a builder or a garage or other supplier agrees to provide a false estimate for work in order to enable its customer to obtain payment from his insurers to which he is not entitled, then it will be unable to recover payment from its customer.[11]

However, precisely because illegality covers such a plethora of circumstances, these policy factors may not all be present to the same degree in every case. As the Law Commission identified in relation to deterrence, this may be because some are not aware of the law or, even if they are, a rule deterring one party may induce the other, as he or she anticipates an unmerited windfall.[12]

IV. TANGLE

The problems of trying to draw hard and fast lines go back a long way. They are illustrated by cases involving the supply of goods, not of a prohibited nature, but which the supplier knows that the other party intends to use in an illegal manner. In *Langton v Hughes*[13] the plaintiffs were suppliers of spirits and spices. The defendants were brewers in Chester. There was a statutory prohibition on the use of anything but malt and hops in the brewing of beer. The plaintiffs' salesman took orders for goods which he knew were to be used in the brewery. An action for the price of the goods was met with the defence of illegality. The defence succeeded.

A few months later a similar question arose in *Hodgson v Temple*.[14] The plaintiff sued for the price of spirits sold and delivered to a distillery run by the defendant. The defendant also had a retail shop for the sale of spirits. It was an offence to carry on the dual trades of distilling and retailing spirits. The claim was met with the defence of illegality but on this occasion it failed. Lord Mansfield CJ said that mere

8 *Beresford v Royal Insurance Co Ltd* [1938] AC 586 (HL) 599.
9 *Attorney-General v Guardian Newspapers Ltd* (No 2) [1990] 1 AC 109 (HL) 286.
10 ibid 287.
11 *Taylor v Bhaill* [1996] CLC 377 (CA) 383–84.
12 Law Commission (n 4) [2.21]. See [1.12] for the example that whilst denying redress to an employee who accepts cash in hand will disincentive the employee, it may well incentivise the employer. See also Lord Lowry in *Tinsley v Milligan* [1994] 1 340 (HL) 368.
13 *Langton v Hughes* (1813) 1 M & S 593; 105 ER 222.
14 *Hodgson v Temple* (1813) 5 Taunt 181; 128 ER 656.

knowledge that the goods were to be used for an illegal purpose was not sufficient to deprive the seller of his right to payment. For the claim to be barred for illegality, it was necessary that the vendor should be a 'sharer in the illegal transaction'.[15]

In *Pearce v Brooks*[16] the contract was for the sale of an 'ornamental' brougham carriage, particularly appropriate for the purchaser's trade as a prostitute. It was held that the seller was not entitled to recover the price. The questions put to the jury were whether the defendant acquired the coach for the purpose of prostitution and, if so, whether the plaintiff knew of that purpose. The jury answered both questions in the affirmative and the judge, Bramwell B, directed a verdict for the defendant. The verdict was upheld by the Court of Exchequer Chamber.

Lord Denning MR reviewed the case law in *JM Allan (Merchandising) Ltd v Cloke*,[17] a case about the supply of a roulette table and book of rules, one of which contravened a provision in the Betting and Gaming Act 1960 (UK). The supplier's claim failed. Lord Denning MR held that 'active participation [in an illegal purpose] debars, but knowledge by itself does not'.[18]

What amounts to 'participation' from which a common design may be inferred? The Law Commission discussed this vexed question in its consultation paper,[19] and observed that the law lacks guidance. In plain language, the authorities are a mess.

Various judicial attempts have been made to develop an approach which combines fairness, transparency and coherence. The history of the 'public conscience' test is too well known to require repetition. It was considered in detail by the Law Commission and more recently summarised by Lord Wilson in *Hounga v Allen*.[20] The test was rejected by the House of Lords in *Tinsley v Milligan*.[21] As Lord Wilson observed in *Hounga*, the majority of the House in *Tinsley* considered that, once that test was stripped out of the law, a reliance test was laid bare, namely that, in the words of Lord Browne-Wilkinson, a claimant 'is entitled to recover if he is not forced to plead or rely on the illegality, even if it emerges that the title on which he relied was acquired in the course of carrying through an illegal transaction'.[22]

As many have commented, it is unsatisfactory that the outcome in such a case should depend on a point of pleading rather than the facts. It raises the possibility of a good lawyer being able to outmanoeuvre the test by skilful pleading, so as to allow a claimant involved in illegality to bring a claim, whilst a claimant who is more sinned against than sinning may be barred.

Tinsley was a dispute about title to property and it does not follow that the reliance test should necessarily apply in the same way in all other types of case.

[15] ibid 182; 656.
[16] *Pearce v Brooks* (1866) LR 1 Exch 213.
[17] *JM Allan (Merchandising) Ltd v Cloke* [1963] 2 QB 340 (CA).
[18] ibid 348.
[19] Law Commission, *Illegal Transactions: The Effect of Illegality on Contracts and Trusts* (Law Com CP No 154, 1999).
[20] *Hounga v Allen* [2014] UKSC 47; [2014] ICR 847.
[21] *Tinsley v Milligan* [1994] 1 AC 340 (HL).
[22] ibid 376.

The failings did not go undetected. Lord Phillips in *Stone & Rolls Ltd v Moore Stephens* observed:

> I do not believe ... that it is right to proceed on the basis that the reliance test can automatically be applied as a rule of thumb. It is necessary to give consideration to the policy underlying *ex turpi causa* in order to decide whether this defence is bound to defeat [the company's] claim.[23]

At the same time in tort another overlapping but not identical test was being developed: the inextricable link test. In *Cross v Kirkby*,[24] a case concerning a claim for assault and battery, Beldam LJ expressed the test as whether the claimant's claim is so closely connected or inextricably bound up in his own illegal contact that the court could not permit him to recover without appearing to condone that conduct.[25] This test was deployed in the employment context in *Hall v Woolston Hall Leisure Ltd*,[26] where the question arose whether an employee could claim for sex discrimination when that employee had known of a tax fraud perpetrated by misrepresentations on her wage slips. Mance LJ added that while the underlying test remains one of public policy it evolved for application in a tortious context and requires an inextricable link.[27] Subsequently Lord Hoffmann in *Gray v Thames Trains Ltd*[28] questioned this expression of the test and suggested a test which drew on concepts of causation.

Throughout the history of attempts to find a unifying principle, public policy continues to exert a pull but it is not a monolithic concept. Lord Wright observed in *Vita Food Products Inc v Unus Shipping Co Ltd*,

> Each case has to be considered on its merits. Nor must it be forgotten that the rule by which contracts not expressly forbidden by statute or declared to be void are in proper cases nullified for disobedience to a statute is a rule of public policy only, and public policy understood in a wider sense may at times be better served by refusing to nullify a bargain save on serious and sufficient grounds.[29]

Seventy years later, Lord Hoffmann observed in *Gray* that: 'The maxim ex turpi causa expresses not so much a principle as a policy. Furthermore, that policy is not based upon a single justification but on a group of reasons, which vary in different situations'.[30]

The Law Commission wrestled with the problems for many years. After lengthy consultation it concluded that the law was capable of judicial reform and that there were signs that this was happening. It considered that judicial reform of this part of the common law was the best way forward, and it made recommendations with that end in view. The role of the Law Commission as a promoter of judicial reform

[23] *Stone & Rolls Ltd v Moore Stephens* [2009] UKHL 39; [2009] AC 1391 [25].
[24] *Cross v Kirkby*, *The Times*, 5 April 2000 (CA).
[25] ibid [76].
[26] *Hall v Woolston Hall Leisure Ltd* [2001] 1 WLR 225 (CA).
[27] ibid [79].
[28] *Gray v Thames Trains Ltd* [2009] UKHL 33; [2009] AC 1339 [54].
[29] *Vita Food Products Inc v Unus Shipping Co Ltd* [1939] AC 277 (PC) 293.
[30] *Gray* [2009] UKHL 33; [2009] AC 1339 [30].

has not been as fully developed as it might. Its combination of depth of analysis, comparative research and detailed consultation may properly assist the courts to be bolder in re-shaping the law than they might otherwise feel able to be.

The Law Commission's report was considered by the Court of Appeal in *ParkingEye Ltd v Somerfield Stores Ltd*.[31] The claimant agreed to provide the defendant supermarket with automated control systems for its carparks. The claimant received no fee from the defendant but had the right to collect fines from those motorists overstaying their slots. The letters the claimant sent to such motorists contained falsities, stating for example that it could initiate proceedings when it could not. The contract had not spelt out the terms but the defendant approved the draft letters. When the defendant terminated the contract the claimant claimed for repudiatory breach and was faced with the illegality defence. The defence was rejected. The leading judgment was given by Sir Robin Jacob. Encouraged by the Law Commission's report he adopted a 'disproportionality' test, which he stressed was not the same as exercising a general discretion. In a concurring judgment, I considered the gravity of the illegality, its centrality to the claim and whether it was intentional.[32] I did so in the context of the underlying public policy considerations, policies which provided the essential guiding lights for my judgment. I concluded:[33]

A. The contract was not a 'one off' deal but created a relationship. Had it not been terminated early it could have been lawfully performed over the rest of the term.
B. The illegality was not essential or central to the performance of the contract. The primary work done by the claimant was in installing the carpark system which was done lawfully.
C. The defendant's position was not entirely innocent, having read the draft letters, yet it would get a windfall here since it now had a working carpark system.

In summary, the court decided that disallowance of the claim was not compelled by the authorities, and it would not be a just and proportionate response to the illegality.

The Supreme Court has not so far been asked to consider the Law Commission's report in any depth, nor has it been asked to revisit *Tinsley*. Those are important limitations to bear in mind when considering its latest decisions.

V. RECENT SUPREME COURT CASES

The three most recent Supreme Court cases are *Hounga*, *Les Laboratoires Servier v Apotex*[34] and *Jetivia v Bilta*.[35] Unsurprisingly commentators have found the net result confusing.

[31] *ParkingEye Ltd v Somerfield Stores Ltd* [2012] EWCA Civ 1338; [2013] QB 840.
[32] ibid [66]–[74].
[33] ibid [74]–[78].
[34] *Les Laboratoires Servier v Apotex* [2014] UKSC 55; [2015] AC 430.
[35] *Jetivia v Bilta* [2015] UKSC 23; [2016] AC 1.

A. *Hounga v Allen*

In *Hounga* the claimant was a Nigerian national of around 14 years old. The defendants arranged for her to arrive illegally in the UK where they employed her as a maid and child carer in exchange for promised board, lodging, an education and £50 per month. During this time the claimant had no right to work in the UK. The defendants did not keep to their side of the bargain and subsequently dismissed her. The question arose in the Supreme Court whether the claimant was entitled to compensation for racial discrimination despite the illegality of the contract of employment.

Lord Wilson considered that if the 'inextricable link' test was applicable it was not met so as to allow the illegality defence to succeed. However, he asked whether the test was applicable.[36] Identifying that the defence rests on public policy, Lord Wilson noted that it was necessary to ask, first, what aspect of public policy founds the defence and, second, whether there is another aspect of public policy to which the defence would run counter.[37] In answer to the first question Lord Wilson posed and answered these sub-questions:[38]

(a) Did the tribunal's award of compensation to Miss Hounga allow her to profit from her wrongful conduct in entering into the contract? No, it was an award of compensation for injury to feelings consequent on her dismissal, in particular the abusive nature of it.
(b) Did the award permit evasion of a penalty prescribed by the criminal law? No, Miss Hounga has not been prosecuted for her entry into the contract and, even had a penalty been thus imposed on her, it would not represent evasion of it.
(c) Did the award compromise the integrity of the legal system by appearing to encourage those in the situation of Miss Hounga to enter into illegal contracts of employment? No, the idea is fanciful.
(d) Conversely, would application of the defence of illegality so as to defeat the award compromise the integrity of the legal system by appearing to encourage those in the situation of Mrs Allen to enter into illegal contracts of employment? Yes, possibly: it might engender a belief that they could even discriminate against such employees with impunity.

In answer to whether there was another public policy at work, Lord Wilson cited the UN Protocol to Prevent, Suppress and Punish Trafficking in Persons, signed in 2000 and ratified by the UK on 9 February 2006. He found that the decision of the Court of Appeal to uphold Mrs Allen's defence of illegality to her complaint 'runs strikingly counter to the prominent strain of current public policy against trafficking and in favour of the protection of its victims'. He added that 'The public policy in support of the application of that defence, to the extent that it exists at all, should give way to the public policy to which its application is an affront'.[39] The claimant's claim was allowed.

[36] *Hounga v Allen* [2014] UKSC 47; [2014] ICR 847 [40]–[41].
[37] ibid [42].
[38] ibid [44].
[39] ibid [52].

As I noted at the end of my judgment in *Bilta*,[40] Lord Wilson's statement was part of the ratio in *Hounga*. It formed the foundation for the conclusion in the final paragraph of the judgment. Although *Hounga* was a case in tort, Lord Wilson's approach was followed by the majority of the Court of Appeal in the case of *R (Best) v Chief Land Registrar*,[41] which concerned the acquisition of a registrable title to land by the equitable doctrine of prescription.[42]

B. *Les Laboratoires Servier v Apotex Inc*

Apotex concerned two pharmaceutical companies and the patent of a new product. The defendant acquired an injunction in Canada preventing the claimant from selling the product in that jurisdiction. An interim injunction was obtained in the UK but it was discharged and a claim was asserted in respect of the cross-undertaking in damages. The question was whether this claim could succeed when the manufacture of the product in Canada would have been illegal.

In delivering his judgment, Lord Sumption reasoned from the premise that 'we are concerned with a principle based on the application of general rules of law and not on fact-based evaluations of the effect of applying them in each individual case'.[43] He further observed that the content of the rules must recognise that within the vast and disparate category of cases where a party in some sense founds his claim on an immoral or illegal act there are important differences of principle.[44] However, he described his approach as firmly rooted in 'established rules of law' (Lord Goff in *Tinsley*)[45] and noted that Lord Goff's main concern in that case was that the defence was indiscriminate rather than unprincipled.[46] He disapproved[47] of the reliance that Etherton LJ (in the Court of Appeal below) placed on Lord Hoffmann's policy-focused comment in *Gray* quoted above, and distanced himself from Etherton LJ's statement of the Court of Appeal judgment that

> the court is able to take into account a wide range of considerations in order to ensure that the defence only applies where it is a just and proportionate response to the illegality involved in the light of the policy considerations underlying it.[48]

He preferred to ask three questions which would often arise in the application of the illegality defence: (1) What acts constitute turpitude for the purpose of the defence? (2) What relationship must the turpitude have to the claim? (3) On what principles should the turpitude of an agent be attributed to his principal?[49] After recognising

[40] *Bilta* [2015] UKSC 23; [2016] AC 1 [173].
[41] *R (on the application of Best) v Chief Land Registrar* [2015] EWCA Civ 17; [2016] QB 23.
[42] See Section VI.
[43] *Les Laboratoires Servier v Apotex Inc* [2014] UKSC 55; [2015] AC 430 [22].
[44] ibid.
[45] *Tinsley v Milligan* [1994] 1 AC 340 (HL) 364F.
[46] *Apotex* [2014] UKSC 55; [2015] AC 430 [16].
[47] ibid [19].
[48] *Les Laboratoires Servier v Apotex Inc* [2012] EWCA Civ 593; [2013] Bus LR 80 [73].
[49] *Apotex* [2014] UKSC 55; [2015] AC 430 [22].

that the first question was relevant to this case, and analysing the sorts of turpitude which would give rise to the defence,[50] he concluded[51] that the breach of a patent was not a sufficiently significant turpitude because the public interest was not engaged by a breach of a patentee's rights, only private interests.

My judgment differed in approach. Whilst I agreed that the illegality defence should fail, I did not share Lord Sumption's criticism of the Court of Appeal.[52] Etherton LJ had approached the matter by considering whether public policy considerations merited the application of the doctrine of illegality to the facts. In doing so he adopted an approach similar to that which was later applied by the court in *Hounga*.

C. *Jetivia v Bilta*

A company under the stewardship of its directors perpetrated a fraud. It became insolvent. Under the fresh stewardship of its liquidators, the company brought a claim for the benefit of the creditors against the erstwhile directors for losses caused by their breach in committing the fraud. The question arose whether this was barred by the illegality of the company's own fraud committed through those former directors.

Lord Sumption asked the three questions which he posed in *Apotex*: (1) What were the illegal or immoral acts giving rise to the defence? (2) What was the relationship between those acts and to the claim? And (3) whether the illegal or immoral acts of the directors could be attributed to the principal.[53] Considering the critical question to be the third, he held that the fraud of the directors could not be so attributed. The claim was therefore not barred for illegality.

Reaching the same result, Lord Hodge and I preferred to take a simpler and more direct route. When a company reaches the verge of insolvency, the duties owed by the directors undergo an important conceptual shift. Whilst still being owed to the company, the company's interests embrace the creditors, whereas before they were synonymous with the shareholders. This rule is enshrined in case law and in statute. The public policy served by the rule would be undermined if the directors were able to defeat the claim by reliance on the doctrine of illegality. Noting that the doctrine of illegality is founded on public policy,[54] we considered that it would be perverse to allow it to be raised so as to defeat the very object of this fundamental rule of company law, designed for the protection of the creditors for whose benefit the claim was brought. We also agreed that applying principles of attribution would lead to the same result. The majority concluded that the case should be decided on that ground, on which there was unanimity, rather than by considering any wider question about the law of illegality.

[50] ibid [23]–[29].
[51] ibid [30].
[52] ibid [61]–[62].
[53] *Bilta* [2015] UKSC 23; [2016] AC 1 [63].
[54] ibid [129].

Lord Neuberger noted that 'the proper approach to the defence of illegality needs to be addressed by this court (certainly with a panel of seven and conceivably with a panel of nine Justices) as soon as appropriately possible'.[55] There the matter rests in the Supreme Court for the time being.

VI. THE COURT OF APPEAL

In *Best* the claimant had been squatting in a manner recently criminalised by section 144 of the Legal Aid, Sentencing and Punishment of Offenders Act 2012 (UK) (LASPOA). The question arose whether in light of this criminalisation the claimant could still take advantage of the statutory adverse possession mechanism and apply to the Land Registry to be entered on the register as the registered proprietor under paragraph 1 of Schedule 6 to the Land Registration Act 2002 (UK) (LRA).

The Court of Appeal held that he could. Its judgment was delivered after the decisions of the Supreme Court in *Hounga* and *Apotex*, but before *Bilta*. Arden LJ approached the problem as one of statutory interpretation (whether Parliament had intended to alter the effect of the Schedule 6 of the LRA by enacting section 144 of LASPOA), but Sales LJ (with whom McCombe LJ agreed) asked whether the public interest in active use of land should continue to have priority over the concern that a person should not be able to benefit from their own wrong, even where the adverse possession now involved newly criminalised activity. He considered that the best guidance on the analytical framework was currently that provided by Lord Wilson in *Hounga*. He added that there is not one single rule with blanket effect across all areas of the law. Instead, there are a number of rules which may be identified, each tailored to the particular context in which the illegality principle is said to apply.

In a commentary on the case, Mark West suggested that

> [i]t is not easy … to see how questions of degrees of turpitude can readily be resolved by a process of legislative interpretation, when the subject was unlikely to have been in the mind of the draftsman, as surely what needs to be assessed is the correct balance to be struck between competing public policies.[56]

This is an astute observation, particularly bearing in mind that the illegality may take many forms, which may have fascinating implications for public law on which I do not pass any comment.

VII. WHERE NOW?

There is almost universal agreement not only that the present state of the law is unsatisfactory because of its uncertainty, but also that the law as stated in *Tinsley*

[55] ibid [15].

[56] M West, 'Adverse possession, illegality and land registration: the balancing of conflicting public policies' [2015] *Conveyancer* 432, 444.

was unsatisfactory. Lord Goff said so in that case. He referred to the rules as 'indiscriminate in their effect and capable of producing injustice'. In *Nelson v Nelson*, the High Court of Australia unanimously declined to follow it.[57] Lord Goff in *Tinsley* expressed the hope that the subject would be investigated by the Law Commission and said that he would be more than happy if a new system could be evolved which was both satisfactory in its effect and capable of avoiding the kind of result which flowed from the established rules in cases such as *Tinsley*. But he thought that any reform should only be instituted by the legislature after a full inquiry by the Law Commission.

The Law Commission has now carried out that full inquiry. Initially its thoughts were towards legislative reform, possibly on the lines of the New Zealand model. But after much consultation and thought, it came round to the view that judicial reform is both possible and preferable.

The two linked questions are how and by whom the law should now be reformed. Things have moved on since *Tinsley* in a number of ways. First, there is the obvious fact that we now have the benefit of the Law Commission's work. Secondly, the common law has become much more familiar with an approach based on proportionality. It has recently been applied by the Supreme Court in relation to the doctrine of penalty clauses. Thirdly, the courts in *ParkingEye* and *Hounga* have developed and applied such an approach. I have yet to read any convincing argument that such an approach is unfair, insufficiently clear or otherwise undesirable. Why then should the courts now wait for Parliament to clear up an area of the common law in which the problems are of the courts' creation? What merit would a statutory discretionary scheme have over the *Hounga* approach? Moreover, we know that finding parliamentary time for reform of the common law is as rare as finding hens' teeth. For that reason the need is all the more urgent for the courts to work in partnership with the Law Commission in the clarification, modernisation and simplification of the common law where it has become confused and unsatisfactory. In *Clayton v The Queen*[58] Kirby J used another metaphor. He said that waiting for a modern parliament to grapple with issues of law reform is like 'waiting for the Greek Kalends. It will not happen'; and that 'Eventually courts must accept this reality and shoulder their own responsibility for the state of the common law'.

The Law Commission's report and the decisions in *ParkingEye* and *Hounga* provide a principled approach, which is not the same as an unfettered discretion. It involves examining the relationship between the illegality and the particular relief claimed, and reaching a judgment whether it would be disproportionate to allow the illegality defence, having regard to the particular facts and to the different public policy factors which favour or disfavour its application. The Law Commission observed that there are signs that the courts sometimes do so covertly, in an attempt to avoid counter-intuitive results, but it is better that the process should be open. It is hard to suppose that Lord Mansfield of all judges would have stood against such an approach.

[57] *Nelson v Nelson* (1995) 184 CLR 538 (HCA). See in particular the criticisms of *Tinsley v Milligan* by Toohey J at 595–97 and McHugh J at 612–13.

[58] *Clayton v The Queen* [2006] HCA 58; (2006) 231 ALR 500 [119].

Author Index

Index

www.ingramcontent.com/pod-product-compliance
Ingram Content Group UK Ltd.
Pitfield, Milton Keynes, MK11 3LW, UK
UKHW051449290926
15471UKWH00008B/1108

9 781509 930081